TRANSFORMING GRADUATE BIBLICAL EDUCATION

Society of Biblical Literature

Global Perspectives on Biblical Scholarship

Number 10

TRANSFORMING GRADUATE BIBLICAL EDUCATION
ETHOS AND DISCIPLINE

TRANSFORMING GRADUATE BIBLICAL EDUCATION
ETHOS AND DISCIPLINE

Edited by

Elisabeth Schüssler Fiorenza and Kent Harold Richards

Society of Biblical Literature
Atlanta

TRANSFORMING GRADUATE BIBLICAL EDUCATION

Copyright © 2010 by the Society of Biblical Literature

All rights reserved. No part of this work may be reproduced or transmitted in any form or by any means, electronic or mechanical, including photocopying and recording, or by means of any information storage or retrieval system, except as may be expressly permitted by the 1976 Copyright Act or in writing from the publisher. Requests for permission should be addressed in writing to the Rights and Permissions Office, Society of Biblical Literature, 825 Houston Mill Road, Atlanta, GA 30329 USA.

Library of Congress Cataloging-in-Publication Data

Transforming graduate biblical education : ethos and discipline / edited by Elisabeth Schüssler Fiorenza and Kent Harold Richards.
    p. cm. — (Society of Biblical Literature global perspectives on biblical scholarship ; no. 10)
    Includes bibliographical references.
    ISBN 978-1-58983-504-7 (paper binding : alk. paper) -- ISBN 978-1-58983-505-4 (electronic library copy)
    1. Theology—Study and teaching. I. Schüssler Fiorenza, Elisabeth, 1938–. II. Richards, Kent Harold, 1939–.
    BV4020.T73 2010
    220.071'1—dc22   2010020798

18 17 16 15 14 13 12 11 10   5 4 3 2 1
Printed in the United States of America on acid-free, recycled paper
conforming to ANSI/NISO Z39.48-1992 (R1997) and ISO 9706:1994
standards for paper permanence.

Contents

Abbreviations   vii
Introduction: Transforming Graduate Biblical Studies: Ethos and Discipline
   Elisabeth Schüssler Fiorenza   1

Part 1: Changing the Ethos of Graduate Biblical Studies

From "Mono"- to "Multi"-Culture: Reflections on a Journey
   Elaine M. Wainwright   19

Cross-Textual Biblical Studies in Multiscriptural Contexts
   Archie C. C. Lee   35

Social Location: Dis-ease and/or Dis-cover(y)
   Yak-hwee Tan   47

Taking *Spaces* Seriously: The Politics of Space and the Future of Western Biblical Studies
   Abraham Smith   59

Biblical Studies and Public Relevance: Hermeneutical and Pedagogical Consideration in Light of the Ethos of the Greater China Region (GCR)
   Philip Chia   93

Part 2: Cultural-National Locations of Graduate Biblical Studies

Graduate Studies Now: Some Reflections from Experience
   Athalya Brenner   111

Graduate Biblical Studies in India
   Monica Jyotsna Melanchthon   119

Biblical Study in Korea in the Twenty-First Century
   Kyung Sook Lee   137

The Practice and Ethos of Postgraduate Biblical Education: A Glance at Europe and in Particular Switzerland
   Gabriella Gelardini   153

Contents

Part 3: New Voices from the Margins

Biblical Studies: A View from the Feminist Margins and the Jewish Fringes
    Cynthia M. Baker   173

On the Fringes of the "Big Tent" of Graduate New Testament Studies
    Thomas Fabisiak   183

Giving an Account of a Desirable Subject: Critically Queering Graduate Biblical Education
    Joseph A. Marchal   199

To a Black Student in First-Year Hebrew
    Nyasha Junior   221

Intoxicating Teaching as Transformational Pedagogy
    Wil Gafney   231

Beyond Socialization and Attrition: Border Pedagogy in Biblical Studies
    Roberto Mata   247

Part 4: Transforming the Curriculum

Redesigning the Biblical Studies Curriculum: Toward a "Radical-Democratic" Teaching Model
    Susanne Scholz   269

Biblical Studies for Ministry: Critical and Faithful Interpretation of Scripture in an Either/Or World
    Cynthia Briggs Kittredge   293

Placing Meaning-Making at the Center of New Testament Studies
    Hal Taussig with Brigitte Kahl   307

Mapping the Field, Shaping the Discipline: Doctoral Education as Rhetorical Formation
    Melanie Johnson-DeBaufre   319

The Work We Make Scriptures Do for Us: An Argument for Signifying (on) Scriptures as Intellectual Project
    Vincent L. Wimbush   355

Breadth and Depth: A Hope for Biblical Studies
    Kent Harold Richards   367

Appendix

Rethinking the Educational Practices of Biblical Doctoral Studies
    Elisabeth Schüssler Fiorenza   373

Contributors   395

Abbreviations

AB	Anchor Bible
AJT	*Asia Journal of Theology*
BibInt	*Biblical Interpretation*
BibInt	Biblical Interpretation Series
BTF	*Bangalore Theological Forum*
BiSh	*Bible Bhashyam*
CSSR Bulletin	Council of Societies for the Study of Religion Bulletin
CurBS	Currents in Biblical Research
Did	Didache
ExpTim	*Expository Times*
HTS	Harvard Theological Studies
IDB	*The Interpreter's Dictionary of the Bible.* Edited by George E. Butterick et al. 4 vols. Nashville: Abingdon, 1962.
IJT	*Indian Journal of Theology*
JAAR	*Journal of the American Academy of Religion*
JAOS	*Journal of the American Oriental Society*
JBL	*Journal of Biblical Literature*
JBLE	*Journal of Biblical Literature and Exegesis*
JFSR	*Journal of Feminist Studies in Religion*
JSOTSup	Journal for the Study of the Old Testament Supplement Series
PMLA	*Proceedings of the Modern Language Association*
SBLAcBib	Society of Biblical Literature Academia Biblica
SBLBAC	Society of Biblical Literature Bible in American Culture
SBLBSNA	Society of Biblical Literature Biblical Scholarship in North America
SBLGPBS	Society of Biblical Literature Global Perspectives on Biblical Scholarship
SBLSymS	Society of Biblical Literature Resources for Biblical Study
SBLRBS	Society of Biblical Literature Symposium Series
SemeiaSt	Semeia Studies
TThRel	*Teaching Theology and Religion*

USQR *Union Seminary Quarterly Review*
ZNT   *Zeitschrift für Neues Testament*

Transforming Graduate Biblical Studies: Ethos and Discipline

Elisabeth Schüssler Fiorenza

After the publication of my book *Democratizing Biblical Studies: Toward an Emancipatory Educational Space*,[1] I received a note from a former student thanking me for "being a radical democratic dreamer." This reminded me of the first seminar session on "Graduate Biblical Studies: Ethos and Discipline" at the Society of Biblical Literature (SBL) International Meeting in Cambridge, England, in 2003, which ended on a similar note. At this first meeting, we discussed my "Rethinking the Educational Practices of Biblical Doctoral Studies" (see appendix).[2] A Wabash Center Grant had made it possible for me to investigate the question of doctoral education, which I thought was crucial for changing biblical studies so that those who were excluded from the discipline until the twentieth century could fully participate as equal members in its discourses.

My argument built on the swelling critical feminist work on pedagogy in general. In particular, it continued a long-standing discussion spearheaded by Fernando Segovia and Mary Ann Tolbert with their three volumes of collected essays on *Reading from This Place*[3] and *Teaching the Bible: The Discourses and Politics of Biblical Pedagogy*.[4] However, while their work focused on the biblical reader and pedagogy in general, as well as on the significance of international contextualization and social-religious location, I became more and more convinced that the ethos of the discipline and the standards of doctoral education in biblical studies were at the heart of the problem. Hence, I approached the executive director of the SBL, Kent Richards, to co-organize

---

1. Louisville: Westminster John Knox, 2009.
2. Elisabeth Schüssler Fiorenza, "Rethinking the Educational Practices of Biblical Doctoral Studies," *TThRel* 6 (April 2003): 65–75.
3. Minneapolis: Augsburg Fortress, 1995.
4. Maryknoll, N.Y.: Orbis, 1998.

a seminar on this topic in the hope that the seminar would engender a broad discussion in the center of the discipline.

We began this discussion in 2003 with the two sessions at the SBL International Meeting in Cambridge, England. One discussed my "Rethinking the Educational Practices of Biblical Studies"; the other focused on a paper of Professor Dr. Oda Wishmeyer entitled "Das gegenwärtige Selbstverständnis der neutestamentlichen Wissenschaft in Deutschland."[5] After the session that discussed my paper, one of the participants told me, "Elisabeth, you are an idealistic dreamer; such change will never happen." Yet, not only I but also the contributors to this volume are convinced that such change must happen if biblical studies should have a future in an emerging cosmopolitan world. It will happen if all who are concerned about the future of biblical studies work together for such a change of the discipline. We therefore hope that this volume will engender further broad discussions of the ethos and pedagogy of biblical studies.

1. SBL Seminars on Graduate Biblical Studies

The essays in this volume have been selected for their critical exploration and constructive articulation of the possibilities of such change. As the title of this collection indicates, the volume has a twofold goal, to critically explore both how to transform graduate biblical studies and how to envision graduate biblical studies as a catalyst for transformation and change. This volume gathers the critical deliberations on change that occurred in a series of seminaries that took place at SBL national and international meetings between 2003 and 2007.

After the opening sessions of the International Meeting in Cambridge, we organized seven sessions of the Seminar at Annual Meetings and four additional sessions at International Meetings: two sessions in Singapore (2005) on biblical studies in Asia, two sessions in Edinburgh (2006) on biblical studies in Europe. Because of the geographical locations of these international meetings, the volume does not contain African or Latin American voices and hence is not representative of all global locations. Further research needs to be done to get an overview of the status of graduate biblical studies in all parts of the

---

5. See Oda Wischmeyer, "Das Selbstverständnis der neutestamentlichen Wissenschaft in Deutschland," *ZNT* 10/5 (2002): 13–36; and "Die neutestamentliche Wissenschaft am Anfang des 21. Jahrhunderts: Überlegungen zu Ihrem Selbstverständnis, ihren Beziehungsfeldern und ihren Aufgaben," in *Herkunft und Zukunft der neutestamentlichen Wissenschaft* (ed. Oda Wischmeyer; Neutestamentliche Entwürfe zur Theologie 6; Tübingen: Francke, 2003). See also Eva Maria Becker, ed., *Neutestamentliche Wissenschaft: Autobiographische Essays aus der Evangelischen Theologie* (UTB Taschenbuch; Tübingen: Francke, 2003).

globe. We also do not have critical reports or explorations of the work of other biblical societies either nationally or internationally. It would be important to learn how they address the issue of diversity in particular and marginality and the ethos of the discipline in general.

The first seminar at the 2004 Annual Meeting opened with a session that explored the *status questionis* by surveying different conferences and consultations on Ph.D./Th.D. programs. This initial exploration was followed up in 2005 with two sessions, one on "Graduate Biblical Education: Faculty Present and Future," which discussed the Auburn Center for the Study of Theological Education Report, "Biblical Faculty in Theological Schools: Present State and Future Prospects." The second session brought together young scholars to discuss their "experiences and visions" for change.

The next two sessions discussed the curricula and programs of doctoral studies in North America at the 2006 Annual Meeting. Reports from Catholic University of America, Dallas Theological Seminary, Duke University, Emory University, Fuller Theological Seminary, Princeton Theological Seminary, Vanderbilt, and Yale University documented the rootedness of the discipline and of doctoral education in the U.S. in the philological-historical paradigm of biblical studies. The most change-oriented programs were those of Union Theological Seminary in New York and Drew University. As our colleagues' contributions to this volume indicate, they have begun to institutionalize such programmatic change. We had planned to have an additional seminar on biblical studies in departments of religion and the humanities. Unfortunately, this last session never materialized because of the need to end the work of the seminar. This is a significant lacuna, and we hope that the question of religious and biblical studies will receive more attention in a future seminar of SBL.

We concluded the seminar in 2007 with two sessions on the future of graduate biblical studies that considered its ethos in terms of social location and standards of excellence. The panels discussed the institutional and intellectual changes necessary to prepare graduate biblical education for the future from the perspective of the "minoritized," to use an expression of Fernando Segovia. This is also the perspective of this volume, which moves from reflections on "Changing the Ethos of Graduate Biblical Studies" (section 1) to the discussion of "Cultural-National Formation of Graduate Biblical Studies" (section 2). Section 3 explores the "Experience and Vision of Graduate Biblical Studies" of emerging scholars. The volume ends with "Proposals for Transforming the Discipline" (section 4).

All sessions of the Seminar were held under the umbrella title "Graduate Biblical Studies: Ethos and Discipline." Before moving to a short introduction of the individual contributions to this conversation, it is important to explore the key terms that compelled our investigations, *ethos* and *discipline*, and the need for their change and transformation. Both discipline and ethos are best understood as areas of inquiry and rhetorical spaces that can be changed and transformed.

2. Changing the Ethos of Biblical Studies

Etymologically, the meaning of *ethos* can be derived either from the Greek word *ethos*, meaning custom, habit, usage, folkways, or from the Greek expression *ēthos*, meaning character formation as the totality of all characteristic traits rather than mere custom or morally approved habits. Ethos understood either as habit or as character formation is open to change and transformation.

A third etymological root, suggested by Susan Jarratt and Nedra Reynolds, is *ēthea*, a plural noun that is the original root of both terms and means "haunts" or "hang-outs." This etymology understands *ethos* as a space where customs and character are formed, "where one is accustomed to being."[6] Ethos as a disciplinary space determines the professional character of individuals and expresses the way one lives. All the contributions seek to redefine the still dominant Euro-American scientist ethos of biblical studies from the perspective of different social and geographical locations and in light of different experiences of the ethos of biblical studies.

Ethos in this spatial sense allows us to theorize the often unacknowledged "positionality" inherent in scientific studies. Such a notion of ethos is, for instance, typical for Hannah Arendt's political philosophy, as John McGowan has pointed out:

> By extension, ethics can thus be understood not simply to encompass the formation and judgment of character, but also to include the production of a place that character can inhabit. To put it in even more strongly Arendtian terms, ethics must build on the intimate connection between character and place. Only where we create a certain kind of place can a certain kind of person emerge.[7]

---

6. Susan C. Jarratt and Nedra Reynolds, "The Splitting Image: Contemporary Feminisms and the Ethics of êthos," in *Ethos: New Essays in Rhetorical and Critical Theory* (ed. James S. Baumlin and Tita French Baumlin: Dallas: Southern Methodist University Press, 1994), 37–64, 48; see also Tobin Siebers, *Morals and Stories* (New York: Columbia University Press, 1992), 63.

7. John McGowan, *Hannah Arendt: An Introduction* (Minneapolis: University of Minnesota Press, 1998), 167.

Professional habits always are formed in a social space and locate the speaker in the practices and experiences of the group to which she or he belongs or speaks. *Ethos*, like experience, then, can be understood in terms of "positionality" as the "place from which values are interpreted and constructed rather than as a locus of an already determined set of values."[8] *Ethos* understood as positioning is "the awareness that one always speaks from a particular place in a social structure."[9] The willingness of the audience to step into the space occupied (temporarily) by the speaker is crucial in establishing the ethics of ethos while acknowledging the differences rather than the similarities between biblical scholars and their audiences.

Read through a feminist lens, *ethos* can be understood "as an ethical and political exploration, as a way of claiming and taking responsibility for our positions in the world, for the ways we see, the places from where we speak."[10] To understand *ethos* in terms of "rhetorical space" elucidates why voice and position are central to rhetorical inquiry and scholarly authority. According to Lorraine Code, rhetorical spaces

> are fictive but not fanciful or fixed locations whose tacit (rarely spoken) territorial imperatives structure and limit the kind of utterances that can be voiced within them with a reasonable expectation of uptake and choral support, an expectation of being heard, understood, taken seriously. They are the sites where the very possibility of an utterance counting as "true-or-false" or of a discussion yielding insight is made manifest.[11]

To understand the ethos of biblical studies as an epistemological[12] rhetorical space would mean, first of all, to examine the conditions for the possibility

---

8. Linda Alcoff, "Cultural Feminism Versus Post-Structuralism: The Identity Crisis in Feminist Theory," *Signs* 13 (1988): 405–36, 434; see also my *Rhetoric and Ethic: The Politics of Biblical Studies* (Minneapolis: Fortress, 1999).

9. Jarratt and Reynolds, "The Splitting Image," 47ff.

10. Ibid., 52.

11. Lorraine Code, *Rhetorical Spaces : Essays on Gendered Locations* (New York: Routledge, 1995), ix–x. For the discussion of feminist epistemology see also Nancy Tuana and Sandra Morgan, eds., *Engendering Rationalities* (Albany: State University of New York Press, 2001); and Liz Stanley, ed., *Knowing Feminisms: On Academic Borders, Territories and Tribes* (Thousand Oaks, Calif.: Sage, 1997).

12. See the essays in part 2, "Rhetoric and Epistemology," in John Lois Lucaites, Celeste Michelle Condit, and Sally Caudill, eds., *Contemporary Rhetorical Theory: A Reader* (New York: Guilford, 1999), 137–247; Richard A. Cherwitz and James W. Hikins, *Communication and Knowledge: An Investigation in Rhetorical Epistemology* (Columbia: University of South Carolina Press, 1986); see also Richard Harvey Brown, *Society as Text: Essays on Rhetoric, Reason and Reality* (Chicago: University of Chicago Press, 1987).

of constructing and using biblical knowledge that does not reinforce the structural violence of the status quo in society, church, and academy. It would mean to investigate the kyriarchal (gendered, raced, classed, and colonized) structures and circumstances in which wo/men and subaltern men "occupy positions of minimal epistemic authority and where questions of differential power and privilege figure centrally."[13]

Such a reconceptualization and change of the disciplinary *ethos* of biblical studies is necessary for overcoming the false dichotomy between engaged, socially located scholarship (e.g., feminist, postcolonial, African American, queer, and other subdisciplines) and value-neutral "scientific" (white malestream) biblical interpretation. Whereas the former allegedly utilizes ethical criteria, the latter is said to live up to a scientific *ethos* by making use of cognitive criteria. Instead, I would argue that a scientific ethos demands both ethical and cognitive criteria, which must be reasoned out in terms of intersubjectively understandable and communicable knowledge.

In short, if *ethos* is a habit or a pattern of social practices that are inseparable from social location and are always shaped by relations of power, it becomes important to explore the concept not just in terms of the *ethos* of the individual biblical scholar but also in terms of the professional *ethos* of the discipline that determines the social self-identity, positioning, and socialization of the emerging biblical scholar.

3. Changing the Discipline of Biblical Studies

Traditionally, ethos has therefore been linked to the goal of education as a means of transforming society. For instance, while Plato constructs a perfect *polis* in order to educate its citizens in accordance with it, Isocrates wants to educate citizens to eliminate strife and enmity by teaching them how to achieve *homonoia* (like-mindedness). For Cicero, in turn, the point of education is its application to the practical ends of daily lives, and in the pan-Hellenic program of Alexander the Great, the goal is *enkyklios paidaia*, the "rounded" education" that consists in instruction in the *trivium* grammar, rhetoric, and logic and in the *quadrivium* arithmetic, geometry, music, and astronomy. Thus, explorations of the role of ethos have been crucial not only for the rhetoric of the discipline but also for its pedagogy.[14]

---

13. Lorraine Code, *Rhetorical Spaces*, viii.

14. For this section, see not only Conley and Baumlin but especially also Nan Johnson, "Ethos and the Aims of Rhetoric," in *Essays on Classical Rhetoric and Modern Discourse* (ed. Robert J. Connors, Lisa S. Ede, and Andrea A. Lunsford; Carbondale: Southern Illinois University Press, 1984), 98–114.

In the nineteenth and early twentieth centuries, the scientific ethos of value-free scholarship that was presumed to be untainted by social relations and political interest was/became institutionalized in disciplines that assure the continuation of the dominant professional ethos. Among others, Nancy Leys Stepan and Sander Gilman have pointed out that the professional institutionalization of scholarship as a value-neutral, apolitical, universal, empirical, and methodologically objective science and an "unbiased arena of knowledge" was not a "natural" outcome of unbiased study. Instead, such institutionalization was the social outcome of a process whereby science was historically and materially constituted to have certain meanings, functions, and interests. In a complex series of innovations, science's epistemological claims were given definition and institutional representation in the form of new scientific societies and organizations sharply delimited from other institutions. These innovations were tied not only to industrialization but to the politics of class and the closing of ranks of bourgeois society. Race and gender were also crucial in the construction of modern science, in that science was defined as "masculine" in its abstraction, detachment, and objectivity.[15]

This professionalization of the academic disciplines engendered theoretical dualisms such as "pure" or impure, theoretical or applied science. Opposites such as rational and irrational, objective and subjective, hard and soft, male and female, Europeans and colonials, secular and religious were given material form, not only in professional disciplines but also in their discursive practices. For instance, the methodologically dense, scientific, depersonalized, empirical-factual text of the research paper emerged as a new standardized academic genre. This genre replaced the more metaphorically porous, literary varied, understandable forms of writing that were accessible also to the nonscientific "popular" reader.

As my article on graduate biblical education shows, the development of biblical studies as a scientific discipline adopted a similar scientific professional elite male ethos.[16] Like its brother-profession the American Historical Society, the SBL was founded by Protestant "gentlemen"[17] who were for the most part "European trained in such universities as Berlin, Heidelberg Halle,

---

15. Nancy Leys Stepan and Sander L. Gilman, "Appropriating the Idioms of Science: The Rejection of Scientific Racism," in *The "Racial" Economy of Science: Toward a Democratic Future* (ed. Sandra Harding; Bloomington: Indiana University Press, 1993), 170–93, esp. 173. See also Londa Schiebinger, *The Mind Has No Sex? Wo/men in the Origins of Modern Science* (Oxford: Oxford University Press, 1981).

16. For the medical profession, see Anne Witz, *Professions and Patriarchy* (New York: Routledge, 1992). For the notion of professional authority, see the sociological study by Terrence J. Johnson, *Professions and Power* (London: MacMillan, 1972).

17. Charles Rufus Brown, "Proceedings for December 1889," *JBL* 9.2 (1890): vi.

and Tübingen."[18] Even though the overall theoretical position of the SBL was apparently "impartial," seeking to make available "a forum for the expression and critique of diverse positions on the study of the scriptures," the position of the so-called higher criticism won increasing influence.[19] The professional scientific stance was complicated in biblical studies by the struggle of the discipline not only to prove its scientific "value-neutral" character within the Enlightenment university, which had only very recently more or less successfully thrown off the shackles of religion. It also was marked by the struggle to free itself from the dogmatic fetters of the Protestant and Roman Catholic[20] churches. Such a conflict emerged between the advocates of scientific "higher criticism" and those interested in safeguarding the theological "purity" of the Bible in the "heresy trials" at the turn of the twentieth century, and it still determines biblical studies as a professional discipline today.

Hector Avalos's *The End of Biblical Studies* has documented anew that this conflict is still emblazoned in the professional ethos of biblical criticism.[21] Questions such as the following illustrate this conflict: Should the Bible be viewed either as a collection of ancient texts or as a normative document of biblical religions? Is the critical study of the theological meaning and normativity of traditions and scriptures part of the research program of biblical studies, or must it be left to confessional theology? Is it part of the professional program of "higher criticism" to study the communities of discourse that have produced and sustained scriptural texts and readings in the past and still do so in the present? Finally, does competence in biblical studies entail the ability to engage in a critical theoretical interdisciplinary meta-reflection on the work of biblical criticism? Would this require that students of the Bible be trained not only in philological-historical-literary analysis but also in interdisciplinary, cultural, and ideology-critical analysis?

The scientist academic ethos of the discipline that shapes biblical studies in both the university and seminary also governs its pedagogical and credentializing practices. If professionalization seeks to "discipline" its practitioners,

---

18. See Jerry W. Brown, *The Rise of Biblical Criticism in America 1850–1870: The New England Scholars* (Middleton, Conn.: Wesleyan University Press, 1988); and Ernest W. Saunders, *Searching the Scriptures: A History of the Society of Biblical Literature 1880–1980* (Chico, Calif.: Scholars Press, 1982), 6.

19. Saunders, *Searching the Scriptures*, 11.

20. For the history of Roman Catholic scholarship, see Gerald P. Fogarty, S.J., *American Catholic Biblical Scholarship: A History from the Early Republic to Vatican II* (San Francisco: Harper & Row, 1989); for Jewish scholarship, see S. David Sperling, ed., *Students of the Covenant: A History of Jewish Biblical Scholarship in North America* (Atlanta: Scholars Press, 1992).

21. Amherst, N.Y.: Prometheus, 2007.

since it has the "making of professionals" as its goal, doctoral education becomes central to maintaining such a positivist elite masculine ethos. Hence, one must change the discipline both in theoretical terms and with respect to its educational practices.[22] Not only doctoral but also ministerial students need to be educated in a new interdisciplinary emancipatory paradigm of biblical studies. Programs need to require research habits that study the pervasive and often only partly conscious set of value-laden dispositions, inclinations, attitudes, and habits of biblical studies as an academic discipline. Rather than reproducing, in dissertation after dissertation, a scientist-positivist approach that restricts biblical studies to ascertaining the single past meaning of the text, research could focus both on the constructive ideological functions of biblical and other ancient texts in their past and present historical and literary contexts, as well as on the ideological justifications presented by their ever more technically refined interpretations. The contributions to this volume begin to address these questions of how to change the professional and educational practices of the discipline.

4. Changing the Ethos and Pedagogy of the Discipline

The volume is divided into four areas of investigation. The first section discusses the ethos of biblical studies and social location; the second explores different cultural-national formations of the discipline. Contributors to the third section discuss the experiences and visions of graduate biblical studies, whereas those of the last section explore how to transform the discipline of biblical studies.

In the opening section, entitled "Changing the Ethos of Graduate Biblical Studies," Elaine M. Wainwright points to the extraordinary shifts in biblical studies that have taken place in recent decades. Such shifts have engendered a great diversity of ethnic, religious, and ethical perspectives of biblical scholars themselves. They raise significant issues for graduate biblical education. Wainwright reflects concretely on changes in her own pedagogical context of Oceania to engage some of the significant issues for biblical studies of location and diversity in its uniqueness and in its participation in a global context.

Archie C. C. Lee goes on to reflect on changes in hermeneutics engendered by Asian scholars of the Bible. Asian scholars bring with them their own religio-cultural traditions and sociopolitical texts to the study of the Bible.

---

22. For a feminist educational introduction to biblical studies, see my *Wisdom Ways: Introducing Feminist Biblical Interpretation* (Maryknoll, N.Y.: Orbis, 2001). For a critical discussion of pedagogy, see chapter 6 of my *But She Said* (Boston: Beacon, 1992) and my books *The Power of the Word* and *Democratizing Biblical Studies*.

Hence, it is important to develop a cross-textual reading strategy in Asian biblical pedagogy. By "textual," Lee does not only mean written texts—such as religious classics, literary traditions, and historical documents—but also nonwritten "texts," such as orally transmitted scriptural traditions as well as social contexts, economic and political experiences, and life experiences. This multidimensional understanding of "text," which reflects the religiosity and spirituality of Asian people, provides the basic point of departure for a cross-textual reading.

In her essay, Yak-hwee Tan explores the relationship between social location and change in graduate biblical education. Globalization, she argues, has created inroads whereby borders between nations are becoming more accessible. Graduate students who are conditioned by their local social locations are now further challenged by their association with the global. The collusion between the local and the global calls for a change in biblical studies that can do justice to the demands of both the local and the global.

Exploring the future of biblical studies in the West, Abraham Smith seeks to adumbrate several dimensions of the interconnections between social location and power that must be addressed if Western biblical studies is to move forward in a viable way in the future. Utilizing the insights of cultural geographers and feminists, Smith first offers brief theoretical reflections on space as an analytical category for understanding the dynamics of power. Then he interrogates relations of power visible in some of the key spaces that bear on the profession of biblical studies in the West. These spaces include the public, the professional, and the pedagogical (largely Eurocentric) spaces that often go unacknowledged in the deployment of the basic tools of biblical studies: the canons we endorse, the cartographical frames we deploy, and the critical theories we embrace.

In the last contribution to this section, Philip Chia reflects on biblical studies and public relevance in the context of the Greater China Region (GCR; i.e., Mainland China, Hong Kong, Macau, and Taiwan) and focuses on biblical education in the GCR and Southeast Asia. He is especially interested in exploring the possibility of a public-based critical biblical theology that takes the current general ethos of the GCR as a public domain as its social location.

In this second section, scholars from Israel, India, Korea, the U.S., and Europe consider the "Cultural-National Locations of Graduate Biblical Studies." Athalya Brenner opens the discussion with a look at the discipline from the vantage point of someone who teaches graduate biblical studies in various parts of the world. She reflects upon her experience of being involved in teaching graduate students in Israel, The Netherlands, Hong Kong, and Texas and sketches the organizational and structural changes she has witnessed in those places. She argues that, as a result of those changes and the *Zeitgeist* in general, it would be best to further the process of divorcing biblical studies from its confessionally determined base and to relocate the discipline in cultural-religious studies.

From her social-geographical location in India, Monica Jyotsna Melanchthon also argues that biblical scholars must engage the rich store of cultural and religious resources available within their traditions and communities. She recounts the many challenges facing the pursuit of critical biblical studies in India that are posed by the complex cultural context of India, the history and reception of the Bible, confessional and denominational diversity, and especially the economic situation. If Indian biblical studies are to be relevant and authentic, as well as to bring about change and transformation in church and society, Melanchthon argues, they need to maintain contextual sensitivity and integrity, as well as remain committed to the poorest of the poor, to faith, liberation, life, and community.

Kyung Sook Lee in turn points out that in Korea, the Bible has been a tool of oppression and exploitation by imperialistic colonial powers of state and church. Her central question is, therefore: How we can read the Bible in the twenty-first century as God's word for hope and liberation for all? After a short survey of Korean church history and the history of Bible interpretation in Korea, she reflects on how to teach the Bible in Korea in order to deconstruct the absoluteness of the Bible as well as to build an alternative to the present academic system.

Finally, Gabriella Gelardini investigates the practice and ethos of postgraduate biblical education in Europe, and she does so from her professional location in Switzerland. She first considers the relation between state and religion in nineteenth-century Europe, the time when the present canon of religious education and its institutional configurations were shaped. Both the European canon and framework that developed in the nineteenth century, Gelardini points out, persist still today. She then characterizes the ethos of New Testament studies as she has experienced it, agonized over it, and applied it in her own doctoral studies and teaching. In light of her professional experience, she formulates proposals for a new and inspiring as well as a transformative practice and ethos of future biblical studies in Europe. Insofar as she reflects as an emerging scholar on the discipline and its ethos, her contribution functions also as a lead-in to the next section, which continues the discussion from the perspective of emerging critical scholars in the U.S.

The third section, on "New Voices from the Margins," continues the argument for change in light of variegated experiences, religious-social locations, and theoretical perspectives. Cynthia M. Baker opens the discussion by locating herself as doubly marginalized, speaking from the feminist margins and the Jewish fringes. She reflects on her training in feminist hermeneutical and rabbinic midrashic approaches to reading the Bible in order to outline a series of practical insights that arise at key intersections of modern feminist and ancient rabbinic theory and practice. They pertain to the nature of biblical texts, claims to interpretive authority, the powerful potentialities of written words, models of teaching and learning, and the relationships of individuals to communities. These intersections can serve to imagine a desirable future of graduate biblical education.

Thomas Fabisiak cogitates the difficulties of situating his research on the history of interpretation of apocalyptic literature either in the field of New Testament studies or in the related fields of early Christianity or ancient Mediterranean religions. He seeks to understand what it is, exactly, that keeps his research and the discipline at odds. His exploration concludes that the prevalent unwillingness of the discipline to account for the stakes and condition of any modern production, scholarly or otherwise, of the ancient world and its texts serves the function of neutralizing or obscuring history's role as a critical mediation in the status quo that works to keep the demands of any methodologically rigorous, self-reflective historiography at bay. He concludes that certain gestures in the direction of inclusiveness and theoretical sophistication in doctoral education mask the continued and coercive dominance of these prevailing attitudes and the interests that they serve.

Joseph A. Marchal enlists queer studies to assess the function of argumentation in and outside of the discipline, particularly where arguments activate and manage various conceptions and practices of desire, health, and legitimacy. Utilizing insights from Judith Butler's *Giving an Account of Oneself*, he argues that we can begin giving an account of what might make biblical studies a desirable subject in light of the dominating and destructive ends of far too many biblical arguments. He concludes that scholars must become accustomed to read both widely and eclectically, while developing a set of simultaneous skills, able to contest and disrupt norms even as we are being educated in them.

In her practical contribution, Nyasha Junior provides frank advice to a hypothetical black student who is considering entering the field of biblical studies. She suggests seven action items that the student should complete as part of her or his discernment process. Her reflections and recommendations are based on her personal experiences as a recent graduate of a biblical studies doctoral program.

Wil Gafney discusses a series of pedagogical practices and identifies her approach as "black feminist." She illustrates it with a practical example derived from her teaching in a theological school. The teaching practice that she delineates includes addressing the literary, geographical, cultural, and ethnic context of the biblical texts, their production, transmission, reception, and translation. She pays special attention to the problematic consequences of one strand in malestream Christian pedagogy, anti-Semitic and anti-Judaistic interpretive practices. In addition, she explores how disciplinary and guild-based tools such as archaeology and philology may be deployed in a feminist classroom. Lastly, she gives concrete examples of how a variety of interpretive ideologies and matrices—black liberationist, womanist, feminist, postcolonial, queer, and popular culture readings—can be brought to bear on the biblical text and its interpretation in a feminist biblical/theological classroom.

In his essay Roberto Mata addresses two fundamental questions: What is the impact of traditional educational models on racial and ethnic minority students, and what alternative pedagogies can enable racial and ethnic minority students and others to enter, remain, and transform biblical studies into a democratic space of equals? He argues that "banking models" of education promote forms of academic socialization that pressure racial and ethnic minority students to embrace the hegemonic ideal of the biblical scholar, while potentially making those who resist susceptible to academic attrition. He therefore advocates a border pedagogy that can enable racial and ethnic minority students to transcend the threats of hegemonic socialization and attrition. Such a border-pedagogy encourages racial and ethnic minority students and others to undertake a social, cultural, and political border-crossing journey that entails critical awakening, journeying, crossing, negotiating, and transforming. His programmatic essay builds the bridge to the last, fourth, section of our deliberations on how to transform biblical studies.

Susanne Scholz opens the discussion of the final section, on "Transforming the Curriculum," by arguing for a comprehensive curricular redesign of biblical studies. She shows that many undergraduate Bible courses and textbooks mimic the graduate curriculum, which defines biblical studies as a historical-literalist enterprise. To make her point, she first notes that the origins of the curricular status quo in biblical studies are rooted in the nineteenth-century curricular model and its critical appropriations in the twentieth-century pedagogical literature. Second, she points out further that examples from undergraduate Bible course descriptions and textbooks demonstrate the ongoing popularity of this curricular model both in U.S.-American undergraduate and graduate programs. Hence, an alternative biblical studies curriculum needs to outline curricular goals, strategies, and techniques for bringing both graduate and undergraduate teaching in alignment with a pedagogical-epistemological model that develops in students of the Bible intellectual-religious maturity, historical-cultural understanding, and literary-ethical engagement.

Whereas Scholz looks at doctoral education in light of undergraduate studies, Cynthia Briggs Kittredge reflects on the particular challenges of teaching biblical studies for ministry in an Episcopal seminary. She compares the way the Bible was taught in her graduate programs with the requirements she encountered later in seminary teaching. Briggs Kittredge describes the design and rationale of the biblical studies curriculum that is taught collaboratively by the biblical studies faculty of her institution. This changed curriculum emphasizes the ministerial arts of preaching and teaching, a broad hermeneutical process, integration of the imagination, and critical pedagogy. She ends her essay by suggesting areas for greater attention in programs of graduate biblical studies.

With his colleague Brigitte Kahl, Hal Taussig elaborates the transformation of graduate biblical studies that is well underway in the New Testament doctoral studies program of Union Theological Seminary in New York. The design of this program presupposes that North Americans use early Christian texts in one way or another to make sense of their lives and with this hermeneutical presupposition overcomes the antiquarian ethos of the nineteenth-century curriculum. If "meaning-making" is the central task of interpretation, graduate programs in biblical studies need to focus on the New Testament and meaning-making. Such a focus cannot abandon any of the critical tools of the field, since recognizing the complexity of interpreting within specific contexts requires a rigorously critical perspective. In such a New Testament doctoral program, making contemporary meaning with biblical texts must be done consciously with appreciation for the values of justice, the efficacy of materiality, empire-critical perspectives, and collectivity.

Drawing on metaphors of language and location, Melanie Johnson-DeBaufre of Drew University envisions doctoral education as rhetorical formation. Given that the practices of graduate biblical education are bound up with larger debates in the field, the academy, and society concerning diversity, knowledge production, and authority, she proposes that doctoral programs foreground a kind of cosmopolitan multilingualism based on disciplinary literacy, rhetorical contextualization, and creative cross-border inquiry. She advocates critical pedagogies that authorize students to shape the future of the discipline and socialize them in such a way that they are able to transform biblical studies in its various places in the academy and society.

We end this section and the argument of the book with a contribution by Vincent L. Wimbush, whose work provides a very important institutional example of how transformation of the discipline can be engendered. He elaborates a research agenda that is based in and institutionalized by the recently established Institute for Signifying Scriptures. This research agenda has as its focus the critical and comparative exploration of the invention, representations, and uses of "scriptures," as well as the consequences of such explorations in societies and cultures. Hence, he proposes a focus on the experiences of historically dominated peoples as an analytical wedge. Wimbush's arguments for such an agenda are rooted in the history of his own intellectual journeying as a type of transformation.

Speaking from the perspective of the "we" of majoritized scholarship, the concluding reflections of Kent Harold Richards read the contributions to this volume as a "beacon of hope" for biblical scholarship. He argues that the "boundaries between the old and the new" should be understood as "windows" rather than as "barricades." To keep these "windows" open, he suggests that the occupants of the space of graduate biblical studies need to ask ourselves four questions. These questions pertain to the wider context of the humanities, where we do our academic work, call for cultivating appreciation for innovation, remind us to keep in mind the constituents with whom we work, and urge us to become mindful of the wider cultural contexts not only of the past but also of the present in which texts acquire meaning.

To sum up the argument of this book, the essays collected in this volume circle around the ethos and ethics of biblical studies. They count on the willingness of the readers to step into the rhetorical space occupied by the speakers rather than engaging in oppositional "othering." They require the recognition that the scholarship and work of the minoritized others is constitutive of the "we" of biblical studies and may no longer be marginalized or excluded if the discipline should not become antiquated.

Written by senior and junior scholars, these contributions seek to transform the ethos and ethics of biblical studies in such a way that it can move creatively and responsibly into the twenty-first century. Such change is already underway in the discipline and not just a dream of some far-outsiders. What is necessary now is to recognize such a different disciplinary ethos and ethics, one that is not positivist, exclusivist, and antiquarian, but aware that texts always mean in a wider cultural-political context not only of the past but also of the present.

Thus this collection of essays seeks to continue the work of the SBL seminar in different ways. The seminar discussions will continue, whenever diverse sections, units, and seminars of SBL discuss the questions and suggestions articulated in this volume in terms of their own work. What, for example, is the ethos and ethics motivating work on the Pauline letters, on Q, or on the Pentateuch? They hopefully will be carried on in graduate schools and professional associations all across the country so that future doctoral students do not have the experiences of trauma they still often experience. The analyses and suggestions of the book hopefully might also be picked up internationally and continued in biblical societies and organizations around the globe. These discussions will lead to a transformation of the discipline, which still in many places is being practiced as a colonialist discipline so that its ethos will change from a Euro-American to a critical global one. The creative insights, innovative suggestions, and intellectual commitment to transform graduate biblical studies and its curricula that have been articulated by the contributors to this volume deserve nothing less.

Last but not least we want to thank, not only the contributors and each other, whose work forms the substance of this volume, but also several individuals who helped bring it into print: Bob Buller, editorial director of the SBL, whose tireless work brought this volume to fruition; Michal Beth Dinkler, who carefully and professionally proofread every essay; and Lindsay A. Lingo, who coordinated its production with the editors and the contributors. We are very grateful to all of them.

1. Changing the Ethos of Graduate Biblical Studies

From "Mono"- to "Multi"-Culture: Reflections on a Journey

Elaine M. Wainwright

Finding an appropriate title for a paper is often quite a vexing undertaking; in this instance, it was no different. I recognize the anomalies in this title, one of them being the very terminology "monoculture" and "multiculture," neither of which adequately captures the two termini of the journey I wish to reflect on in this paper. Rather than seeing these terms as a hindrance, however, I will use them as the starting point for this essay, as I challenge their easy definition and description. The proposed journey from mono- to multiculture enables me to explore a change in my own social location that I will use as the lens for analyzing the current ethos of biblical studies and its import for graduate education.

At the beginning of 2003, I began a physical journey that has enabled me to focus and reflect on a journey that many biblical scholars have been undertaking over recent decades. For twenty years I had worked in biblical and theological education in Australia and in a part of Australia adjacent to my birthplace and the locations of my family, religious, faith, and theological communities. Southeast Queensland was a context whose sociopolitical, economic, and cultural challenges were familiar even if in need of contestation.[1] Those involved in theological education represented the dominant white Anglo-European culture, especially of the north.[2]

---

1. See Noel Preston, *Beyond the Boundaries: A Memoir Exploring Ethics, Politics and Spirituality* (Burleigh: Zeus, 2006); his documentation of his own journey through the protests on behalf of justice against the conservative governments of Queensland through the 1970s and 1980s down to the present represents a journey shared with many Christian activists, including myself. It was this engagement that turned my attention to biblical hermeneutics in the early 1980s, and it is the nexus between biblical studies and praxis that has continued to shape my work down to the present.

2. During my teaching in the Brisbane College of Theology and the School of Theology of Griffith University in Brisbane from 1984 to 2001, the student body and teaching

The shift I made in 2003 was seemingly simple: across the Tasman to Aotearoa New Zealand, where one might expect to find a similar sociocultural context. The discovery was anything but that. I found myself in a situation in which biculturalism[3] and Maori-Pakeha relationships are significant in almost every avenue of life. The School of Theology that was being established in the University of Auckland at that time was no exception, having a mission statement reflective of the university's commitment to the Treaty of Waitangi.[4] Auckland, the city in which I am now located, has the largest Polynesian population in the world and is a melting pot for peoples not only from Oceania but also from Asia and other parts of the globe.[5] It is a profoundly multicultural context ethnically that is reflected in the student body of the University

---

staff were almost exclusively monocultural, namely, Anglo-Australian of predominantly European origins. Brisbane and Queensland generally were much more multicultural than a focus on theological education would suggest, while the southern states of New South Wales and Victoria and especially centers such as Sydney and Melbourne were exceedingly multicultural, Australia being one of the first nations to develop policy statements on multiculturalism, beginning with the Whitlam Labor government in 1973. The ethnic profile within theological education is not, therefore, representative of the population generally.

3. Biculturalism is a term that appeared in New Zealand parlance in the 1980s, when the Maori or indigenous people began to claim sovereignty in the hope that Maori traditions and values, language, and ways of life would flourish and co-exist with those of the Pakeha. Pakeha is a term used to designate non-Maori and generally used of those with British or European ancestry who represent the other party to the Treaty of Waitangi of 1840. Biculturalism as a political theory or ideology is constantly being challenged in the New Zealand context, as represented by the work of Dominic O'Sullivan, *Beyond Biculturalism: The Politics of an Indigenous Minority* (Wellington: Huia, 2007), 2, who claims that "[w]hile biculturalism has helped create a philosophical climate in which greater levels of self-determination are feasible, it also makes assumptions about power relationships which limit greater degrees of Maori autonomy—one step towards self-determination is permitted, but the next is prevented."

4. The key statement of commitment in the Memorandum of Agreement between the University of Auckland and its constituent theological colleges reads: "to provide theological education at university level in accordance with high international academic standards consistent with the University's mission and recognizing a special relationship with Maori arising from the Treaty of Waitangi."

5. The 2006 census figures reveal that 56–57 percent (the difference being in figures for male and female) are designated European, 11 percent Maori, 14.3 percent Pacific peoples, 18.6–19.0 percent Asian, 1.6–1.4 percent Middle Eastern/Latin American/African and 8.7–7.5 percent as "other ethnicity." It is of note that the percent of Pacific people in Auckland is double that in New Zealand as a whole. See http://www.stats.govt.nz/Census/2006CensusHomePage/QuickStats/AboutAPlace/SnapShot.aspx?type=region&ParentID=1000002&tab=Culturaldiversity&id=1000002.

of Auckland, including the School of Theology.⁶ This change of location has provided me with an opportunity to think anew about location and diversity and their import for biblical studies, which is the approach that I will take in this paper, using the lens provided by my own journey across the Tasman.

1. Naming Diversity

In thinking back to my previous location, it did seem monocultural. Reflecting on my work with postgraduate students, and especially doctoral students in my previous Australian context, I realized that the student body was anything but monocultural. I supervised doctoral theses for students working from a feminist perspective, generally second-career women whose hermeneutics were in tension with their different denominational contexts and cultures. They engaged with a range of critical theorists—Julia Kristeva, Rosi Braidotti, Michel Foucault, and others—in developing their feminist paradigms of analysis. As a result of the cross disciplinary nature of their topics, I co-supervised with feminist philosophers and sociologists from Griffith University, participating in some of the paradigm shifts which were emerging in the disciplines of biblical and theological studies.⁷ I supervised men who were challenged by

---

6. The School of Theology has a student body that reflects the diversity of Auckland: 8.5 percent Maori, 28.5 percent Pacific Islands, 37.5 percent European/Pakeha, 11.5 percent Asian, and 14 percent other. At the level of graduate studies (or what is termed postgraduate studies in the New Zealand context; I will use the terms interchangeably in this essay), the figures are: 11 percent Maori, 26 percent Pacific Island, 37 percent European/Pakeha, 15 percent Asian, and 11 percent other. The student population of the school and its postgraduate studies sector is, therefore, multicultural, with those other than European/Pakeha being the majority. This is not, however, reflected in the teaching staff, which is currently 5 percent Maori, 20 percent Pacific Islands, and 75 percent European/Pakeha.

7. See Fernando F. Segovia, "Introduction: Pedagogical Discourse and Practices in Contemporary Biblical Criticism," in *Teaching the Bible: The Discourses and Politics of Biblical Pedagogy* (ed. Fernando F. Segovia and Mary Ann Tolbert; Maryknoll, N.Y.: Orbis, 1998), 1–28, in which he outlines the major paradigm shifts that have occurred in biblical studies over the latter decades of the last century and their pedagogical implications in a way that is relatively new and challenging for biblical studies. In a second essay, he develops more fully the implications of such shifts for what he calls the emerging intercultural studies approach; see "Pedagogical Discourse and Practices in Cultural Studies: Toward a Contextual Biblical Pedagogy" (137–67). It should be noted here that, while the doctoral theses that students were undertaking in Brisbane crossed disciplinary bounds in the academic arena and were engaging with the wealth of literature emerging from the "ever-growing presence of outsiders" whom Segovia identifies ("Introduction," 1), students generally did not address the challenge of the voices of indigenous women and women of cultures other than the Anglo-Saxon dominant in Australia in their own contexts. In other words, they

the burgeoning feminist paradigm to develop alternative or new paradigms of interpretation for their interpretive work as white western males who sought to take account of location and patterns of domination and injustice.

"What then is culture (mono- or multi-)?" is the question that arises out of this experience. Is culture defined only by ethnicity? Certainly, the context of Aotearoa New Zealand has highlighted for me the diversity of ethnicities and some of the power differentials inherent in such ethnic and racial differences.[8] Closer examination of the students undertaking theological education in this context and engagement with them in their project of learning to theologize, especially in light of my prior reflection on the postgraduate students I worked with in Brisbane, alerts me to the diversity in each classroom. Some students are preparing for ordination, others for lay ministries across a number of churches, and others will use their theological education in diverse ways. The theological perspectives in each classroom are complex and different, ranging from the evangelical to the postmodern. Gender and sexuality are sites of difference as are many other perspectives, ways of being, and epistemologies, including age as students in theology range from immediate school-leavers (around 19 years of age) to those retired from the work-force (perhaps in their sixties). Indeed, the culture of the contemporary theological classroom or lecture theatre is characterized by diversity and at the level of graduate studies, courses are designed so that students develop skills in recognizing and developing their own multivalent hermeneutical perspectives.

Attention to diversity has, therefore, brought to light the experience of hybridity. Like the term multiculturism, hybridity was used initially in terms

---

did not undertake a "self-reflexive feminism and accompanying critical questioning of feminisms" that Angie Pears ("Feminist Exclusions and Re-vision," *Feminist Theology* 11 [2003]: 281–91) says is "appropriate and in fact essential."

8. At the time this essay was being prepared for publication in July–August 2008, the University of Auckland used its Winter Lecture series to focus on research. Dr. Tracey McIntosh's address (Senior Lecturer, Department of Sociology and Co-director, Nga Pae o te Maramatanga, University of Auckland) was entitled "Cross Cultural Research Dynamics" and was summarized thus: Cross-cultural research dynamics are dominated by questions of power (and often powerlessness). Power relations and power differentials are articulated from the point of setting research agendas right through to research design, research implementation and dissemination. Culture, among other things, provides a set of rules and values that guide the way the world is interpreted and experienced. The conundrum of interpreting difference across a cultural divide is one example of the challenges and opportunities that researchers and research participants may encounter. Ethical and cultural considerations, the quality of relationships, the political environment, status management, decision making, research motivation, and engagement are some of the issues that face this type of research. See http://www.maidment.auckland.ac.nz/uoa/maidment/archives/2008/07/maidment/winter-lectures-2008.cfm.

of race and ethnicity but more recently has emerged in postcolonial theories in relation to the complexity of identity formation in contexts of political and cultural diversities.[9] This finds expression among theological students in Aotearoa New Zealand who are "in-between": they may have both Maori and Pakeha ancestors,[10] or now in increasing numbers, they are New Zealand-born Samoans, Tongans, or other Pacific nationalities.[11] The term is also being used to describe the multiple perspectives that many graduate students are seeking to hold together and bring into play in their research projects: an ethnic and a gender perspective; an indigenous cultural and postcolonial perspective; an ethical and a Pakeha lens. It is this hybridity which is providing significant challenges for us in our broadly defined multicultural context.

THE CHALLENGES

CONTEXTUAL THEOLOGICAL EDUCATION

Having crossed the Tasman, I have found myself in a school of theology that is established on a foundational commitment to "quality bicultural theological education" in the context of a multicultural community. A major curriculum revision completed in 2004 and which came into effect in 2006, reflects the school's commitment to contextual theological education, especially in Aote-

---

9. See Nikos Papastergiadis, "Tracing Hybridity in Theory," in *Debating Cultural Hybridity: Multi-cultural Identities and the Politics of Anti-Racism* (ed. Pnina Werbner and Tariq Modood; London: Zed, 1997), 257–81.

10. See Melinda Webber, *Walking the Space Between: Identity and Maori/Pakeha* (Wellington, N.Z.: Nzcer, 2008), 23, who notes that "the hybrid person is often forced to occupy an 'in-between' position, or to negotiate many 'border crossings.'" At the recent Society of Biblical Literature International Meeting held in Auckland, New Zealand, Beverley Moana Hall-Smith delivered a paper entitled "A Covenant of Risk: Claiming Her Turanga (Place to Stand) in Matthew 15:21–28," in which she brought her own experience of hybridity shaped by her Maori and Pakeha genealogies into dialogue with the "border crossings" negotiated in the story of the Canaanite woman of Matt 15:21–28. Leticia A. Guadiola-Sáenz undertook a similar border-crossing reading of this same story earlier in "Borderless Women and Borderless Texts: A Cultural Reading of Matthew 15:21–28," *Semeia* 78 (1997): 69–81.

11. The number of such students who feel themselves "caught between cultures" is growing within the School of Theology. See Cluny Macpherson, Paul Spoonley, and Melani Anae, eds., *Tangata O Te Moana Nui: The Evolving Identities of Pacific Peoples in Aotearoa/New Zealand* (Palmerston North, N.Z.: Dunmore, 2001), as an example of the literature exploring this theme.

aroa New Zealand within Oceania and Southeast Asia.[12] One of the areas explored in the curriculum revision process was that of "replacing the traditional departments" that Elisabeth Schüssler Fiorenza canvases in her paper "Rethinking the Educational Practices of Biblical Doctoral Studies."[13] We were not able to achieve this because of a fear among some faculty that we would not adequately prepare our students for postgraduate study internationally. We did, however, succeed at both the undergraduate and postgraduate level in introducing what we have called integrative subjects that cross the traditional disciplines, which are co-taught, and which, by way of their location at the beginning and end of the undergraduate degree and at the beginning of postgraduate degrees, develop skills at theologizing in context among students in ways that cross what have tended to be disciplinary divides and that, we hope, will inform the students' progress through their entire degree.[14]

At the postgraduate level, two such integrative subjects, Hermeneutics and Doing Theology in Context, are foundational to the school's postgraduate program. These are also available to doctoral students who may be advised to undertake a subject during their provisional year in order to help focus and underpin their research topic. They are, therefore, a significant feature in the first year of a doctoral candidate in biblical studies who may be undertaking contextual readings or contextual interpretive projects.[15]

Given the diverse student population which I have drawn attention to earlier, these subjects are very significant, especially the course Hermeneutics, which for most students is undertaken in their first semester of postgraduate study. The first half of the course provides a traditional overview of hermeneutical theory and the major shifts from author to text- and reader-centred

---

12. It would have seemed like a dream in my previous context to be able to develop a curriculum in theological education that took context in its multiplicity seriously. For a range of definitions of and approaches to contextual theology, see Stephen B. Bevans, *Models of Contextual Theology* (rev. and enl. ed.; Faith and Culture; Maryknoll, N.Y.: Orbis, 2004).

13. Elisabeth Schüssler Fiorenza, "Rethinking the Educational Practices of Biblical Doctoral Studies," *TThRel* 6 (2003): 65–75, especially 68.

14. We have not yet articulated clearly the cultural competencies we seek to develop among students and faculty, as has Sheryl Kujawa-Holbrook, "Beyond Diversity: Cultural Competence, White Racism Awareness, and European-American Theology Students," *TThRel* 5 (2002): 141–48. This is a challenge we are currently seeking to address within the School of Theology.

15. In Aotearoa New Zealand, as in Australia, doctoral study is undertaken by way of supervised research only. Students are not required to undertake coursework, and if they do so, it is to develop or enhance skills in their research and would generally be limited to one course.

perspectives. In the second part of the course, directed to some of the varieties of current hermeneutics operative in biblical studies, students begin to find a place to stand and from which they can develop hermeneutical perspectives that take into account their different cultural contexts. The literature on postcolonialism provides a tool for analyzing the particularity of experience in the Solomon Islands, in Tonga, Samoa, Fiji, or Aotearoa New Zealand, each of which has had a different colonial history that has left varying legacies. Dialogue with the indigenous hermeneutics that are being developed in other parts of the globe provides students with confidence in developing new reading perspectives that are unique to their contexts.[16] Students also engage with a range of liberation perspectives which for many overlap with their postcolonial and indigenous hermeneutics. These include feminist, gender, sexual, and ecological perspectives.

Building on the learnings from the Hermeneutics course, students bring their developing understandings of their own perspectives, and the tools that their cultural and ethical positionings provide, to their study of a contextual issue in their second semester in Doing Theology in Context. Ideally, these two subjects provide students with the necessary grounding for the development of a cultural, intercultural or multicultural approach to undertaking biblical studies. For some students, however, the hermeneutics course is an extraordinary challenge because it brings into question objective neutral perspectives on truth and knowledge and hence on the construction and interpretation of the biblical tradition. It also uncovers some of the perspectives that Elisabeth Schüssler Fiorenza names "malestream," which she says "does not mean just male but it means elite, mostly white Western, propertied, educated, generally heterosexual male."[17] The complexity of a multicultural classroom represents the complexity of multicultural biblical studies.[18]

---

16. One doctoral student who participated in this course in his provisional year has gone on to develop a Tongan reading perspective, drawing on Tongan cultural and rhetorical features that guided his interpretation of Ezra 9–10. Another is analyzing features of his Samoan culture that provide a reading paradigm that is informing his reading of the Jesus of John's Gospel. In a recent masters thesis, a Maori woman used the *kākahu korowai*, or Maori cloak, as the image informing her interpretive frame for engaging with the strange woman of Prov 1–9. These are exciting projects that value and validate the specific contexts that have shaped each of these students. They advance biblical knowledge and interpretation and raise questions about biblical interpretations that claim value neutrality and truth as their sole prerogative.

17. Elisabeth Schüssler Fiorenza, "Pedagogy and Practice: Using *Wisdom Ways* in the Classroom," *TThRel* 6 (2003): 208.

18. While this essay is focused on graduate education in biblical studies, my own engagement with this discipline over the past thirty years has meant that I have encoun-

One of the major challenges that faces biblical scholars as pedagogues in the construction of the integrative contextual courses is the tension that some students themselves may embody between traditional and contextual knowledge. The first type of knowledge is characterized by being European/Pakeha rather than indigenous, from the north rather than the south, founded on Western rather than Pacific or Asian epistemologies and it is written rather than oral. In the face of this, the question arises in relation to the hermeneutics course, does one trace the history of hermeneutics from the shaping of the biblical text itself through the European modes of interpretation especially of the last two centuries, and then, into this context, place the burgeoning of contextual perspectives in recent decades? The literature is readily available and even geared to serving this approach. It provides the paradigms that one needs for both understanding and undertaking the task of biblical interpretation. And it has many other advantages that we could posit. It does, however, continue to privilege one form of knowing, one tradition of knowledge. Would the course be equally or even more successful as a learning experience if we began with students exploring the ways in which they and their communities interpret the Bible, bringing them to a knowledge of the biblical hermeneutic in which they stand and expanding knowledge and understanding through interaction with the hermeneutical stances of other participants in the course and of others down through history, not only of the West but in the various regions that constitute our context?

A second challenge to the development of competencies in contextual theologizing at the postgraduate level can be the structures and processes of large universities and theological colleges. I recently taught a biblical studies course in our postgraduate program called Biblical Healing. Not knowing the student composition, I prepared my course outline as required, having all the readings available to students on the electronic course management system. I shaped a course that would develop student competencies in biblical methodologies through engagement with biblical healing stories, taking account of the hermeneutical stances of the scholars that the students would encounter throughout the course. Toward the end of the course, students would engage the topic of healing in the context of Oceania. When the course began, I discovered that six of the students were Maori and Pacific Islander and only one was European/Pakeha. Had I known this, I would have turned the course

---

tered and been in dialogue with the multivalent voices of scholars in feminist, postcolonial, indigenous, and liberationalist biblical studies and have introduced these to students. Examples of these are vast and too numerous to begin to list here. What is significant for this essay is the pedagogical challenge that shifts when the multivalent voices and cultures are in the classroom, not only in the texts in the classroom.

around, beginning with and giving much more attention to the cultural and cross-cultural contexts of participants[19] and weaving this through the course. The structures of academia and our own academic competencies can work against the type of adjustment needed in relation to the student composition of classes. This challenges us as educators to be flexible within the structures. It also calls for a recognition that the students' cultural knowledge is a valuable source in the classroom together with written texts.[20]

Contextual theologizing is an important process that is preparing biblical scholars of the future in the region of Oceania. The diversities of hermeneutics already present in contemporary biblical studies and biblical interpretation will be enriched as new indigenous reading paradigms emerge. Such theologizing does, however, have its critical challenges as sources of learning and modes of instruction co-exist and compete both within students and teachers and in academic institutions.

ETHICAL CHALLENGES

Doctoral programs in the University of Auckland are overseen and administered by the Graduate Centre through the School of Theology; in this context, as in Australia, as noted earlier, doctoral degrees are by research only not by coursework and research. The doctoral student works, therefore, with two supervisors whose percentage of commitment is determined from the outset and may vary between 60/40 percent to 80/20 percent in rarer instances, enabling a crossing of disciplines and of cultures where the research project requires this. The model is that of the traditional "master-disciple," but within that, students work collaboratively in reading and seminar groups and hence are exposed to the different contextual approaches of other students from Oceania, Africa, Asia as well as Aotearoa New Zealand. This does not automatically challenge students undertaking research in biblical studies to critically evaluate their own reading context and practices from an ethical perspective.[21] I believe that attention to the hermeneutical and ethical remains

---

19. Two of the students were New Zealand–born Tongan and Samoan, and they, like many other Pacific Islanders both in New Zealand and in the islands, move between cultures of healing.

20. For a more extensive exploration of *diversity* within texts and contexts in biblical education, see Segovia, "Pedagogical Discourses and Practices," 137–67.

21. For an exploration of ethics in relation to biblical interpretation, see Elisabeth Schüssler Fiorenza, *Rhetoric and Ethic: The Politics of Biblical Studies* (Minneapolis: Fortress, 1999); Daniel Patte, *Ethics of Biblical Interpretation: A Reevaluation* (Louisville: Westminster John Knox, 1995); and Elna Mouton, *Reading a New Testament Document Ethically* (SBLAcBib 1; Atlanta: Society of Biblical Literature, 2002).

one of the most widespread challenges to standards of excellence in not only doctoral but all postgraduate and undergraduate biblical education—a challenge to faculty as well as students.

Elizabeth Schüssler Fiorenza challenged biblical scholars to a consideration of the ethics of the profession in a prophetic Society of Biblical Literature presidential address in 1987.[22] Recognizing that "[w]hat we see depends on where we stand" and that "[o]ne's social location or rhetorical context is decisive of how one sees the world, constructs reality, or interprets biblical texts,"[23] she challenges biblical scholars to take careful account of the rhetorical effect of biblical texts and traditions in ancient and contemporary contexts. Students need to develop the traditional skills for the analysis of biblical texts in their ancient contexts. They also need to develop ethical and cultural skills in analyzing the effects of traditional and contemporary biblical interpretation in terms of the politics that it constructs around power, gender, ethnicity, the more than human and other ethical issues facing today's world.

The development of an ethical perspective is a challenge to both staff and students. There is a context for this challenge in that the charter of the University of Auckland has as one of its goals to be a "critic and conscience of society."[24] This commitment critiques us as theologians asking whether our theologizing is such that we are participating in the role of the University as critic and conscience or does our theology support the political and cultural ethos of the dominant power in the society of Aotearoa New Zealand. In order to develop its ethical engagement, the School of Theology has set up a Research Unit in Public Theology and is a member of the Global Network for Public Theology.[25] Through lectures and a recently introduced undergraduate course, Issues in Public Theology, staff and students engage in the ethical challenges of the contemporary public domain and how one can best do theology in such a context. Attempts to ensure that the school allows space for

---

22. This has been published as Elisabeth Schüssler Fiorenza, "The Ethics of Interpretation: De-centering Biblical Scholarship," *JBL* 107 (1988): 3–17.

23. Schüssler Fiorenza, "The Ethics of Interpretation," 5.

24. The University of Auckland's Strategic Plan 2005–2012 states that, "[t]hrough the delivery of education and training of the highest quality, the creation and dissemination of knowledge and expertise, and through its role as a critic and conscience of society, the University makes an important contribution to the cultural, social, political and economic development of the nation" (online: http://www.auckland.ac.nz/uoa/strategic-plan-2005-2012).

25. The Global Network website is at: http://www.csu.edu.au/special/accc/about/gnpt/about.htm.

the diversity of voices—cultural, theological, gendered, sexual, economic and political—remains a constant challenge.[26]

LANGUAGE OF INSTRUCTION/PRODUCTION AND CRITICAL EVALUATION

Two related challenges in relation to standards of excellence in postgraduate theological education lie in the area of the language of instruction/production of theology and the skill of critical evaluation inherent in and necessary to theological education in a culturally and religiously diverse world. Except for students from one of the participating theological colleges in the School of Theology, the theological education provided by the school is not explicitly preparing students for ordained ministry in churches. It is envisaged, however, that it is preparing theologically competent leaders who will go into a variety of fields of work in the public arena in locations across Oceania, some of which will be within church-related contexts and others public or civic contexts. Critical evaluation is, therefore, an important skill in the theological education of students and yet not always one developed in all the diverse contexts from which students come. If the challenge of developing critically evaluative skills when this is not at the heart of one's own epistemological framework is combined with the developing of research and discursive skills in a language other than one's native tongue, the challenge is great for students and for faculty in the face of established standards developed in 'the West'. One of the challenges that we have not yet faced is how to facilitate bi- and multilingual possibilities for students learning to theologize in a bicultural and multicultural context. This is even more challenging for those majoring in biblical studies who also need to develop competencies in biblical languages. The challenges therefore of different epistemologies and different languages are great and are beginning to be explored in the discipline of theological education in ways which will inform our context.[27]

---

26. Mary Caygill and Elaine M. Wainwright, "The Gendering of Public Theology: A Contribution," *International Journal of Public Theology*, forthcoming, address the challenge that gender blindness can pose to public theology. Similar ethical challenges can come from a range of different cultural perspectives.

27. Robert K. Martin, "Theological Education in Epistemological Perspective: The Significance of Michael Polanyi's 'Personal Knowledge' for a Theological Orientation of Theological Education," *TThRel* 1 (1998): 139–53, provides another lens for an investigation of the epistemological perspectives that have governed and continue to govern theological education. Lucretia B. Yaghijnian, "Writing Cultures, Enculturating Writing at Two Theological Schools: Mapping Rhetorics of Correlation and Liberation," *TThRel* 5 (2002): 128–40, provides some challenging insights into the move, within two theological schools (Episcopal Divinity School and Weston Jesuit School of Theology, both in Cambridge,

The bicultural and multicultural context is also challenging for faculty trained in paradigms of biblical scholarship that did not have to take account of context and even for those of us for whom it has been an area of focus and teaching. Having taught and continually developed courses in biblical hermeneutics since the early 1980s, I have integrated emerging methodological and hermeneutical approaches as they have been developed and become available in print. I have been continually challenged since my move to Aotearoa New Zealand, as noted earlier, as to how to teach such a course best in this multi-cultural context. The first time I taught this subject in Auckland in 2004, the composition of the class was very different from any I had taught before. It had seven men and three women of whom three were Maori, four Polynesian (two Tongan and two Samoan); one Nigerian; one English immigrant Pakeha and one Pakeha New Zealander, and I am white Anglo-Irish Australian. Over the intervening five years the composition of the class has become more diverse. There is a challenge to provide resources that are representative of the students' multidimensional contexts,[28] conscious that in some instances such resources are not yet in print.[29] Pedagogically, we are challenged to explore ways of ensuring that the voices and the perspectives from

---

Massachusetts) from a remedial program in theological writing for international students to a pedagogical program as "rhetorical process and theological practice."

28. The *Journal of Pacific Theology* represents emerging Pacific contextual theology coming from scholars across Oceania. New hermeneutical paradigms are being explored there. In biblical studies, leadership in the field of the development of an explicitly Pacific hermeneutic and mode of interpretation is coming from Jione Havea, see *Elusions of Control: Biblical Law on the Words of Women* (SemeiaSt 41; Atlanta: Society of Biblical Literature, 2003). A gathering of Pacific Island biblical scholars at the recent Society of Biblical Literature International Meeting in Auckland, July 2008, represents the emergence of a body of scholars who will collaborate in the development of Pacific biblical scholarship. At that same meeting, the Society of Asian Biblical Scholars hosted a session and from 14–17 July they conducted their first conference in Seoul, Korea. Graduate students are now beginning to see role models in and approaches to biblical interpretation that represent the places and the perspectives from which they come and from which they can undertake their advanced studies.

29. While, for instance, there is a long history of Maori biblical interpretation that students can draw upon orally, there is little in print. A Maori woman undertaking advanced postgraduate biblical studies commented recently that biblical studies has not been a field that has attracted Maori scholars. We are participating, as are many other scholars around the world, in the emergence of new local, indigenous, contextual biblical hermeneutics. Neil Darragh in an unpublished paper, "Systematic Theology Here and Now: The Task," distinguishes between implicit and explicit theology in the New Zealand context and notes that most of the explicit theology discussed in New Zealand has come from elsewhere: Europe and North America. See Mark Lewis Taylor, "Reading from an Indigenous Place," in Segovia and Tolbert, *Teaching the Bible*, 117–36.

the variety of contexts can be heard and that the variety of ways of learning and knowing among diverse students become part of the "rhetorical processes and theological practices" of the school's contextual theologizing. Storytelling and the interrogating and analyzing of the stories may need to characterize our pedagogical and evaluative strategies more explicitly.[30] We are, however, not yet at that point but the languages of instruction/production in theology and the skills of critical evaluation further develop the framework in which to locate the challenges posed by a journey into multicultural biblical interpretation and its standards of excellence.

Supervising and Examining

One of the key functions of masters and doctoral research, both of which are research-only degrees, is the role of supervision. In a multicultural context, students in their diversity challenge participating supervisors to an awareness of and an openness to the emerging paradigms of contextual, even multicontextual hermeneutics as students bring together feminist or masculinist perspectives with lesbian or ecological or other perspectives such as the multiple identity locations already discussed above.[31] Supervisors need, therefore, to be very carefully chosen and to work collaboratively with the student to support, encourage and guide the emergence of new frameworks of interpretation that will shape our disciplines anew. Working together as co-supervisors from different disciplines for the purpose of guiding a student's work is an important step toward the contextual and cross-disciplinary approaches which location is demanding.[32]

Closely related to this, and even more importantly for the student's future, is the selection of examiners. How does one most prudently and successfully choose examiners when students working contextually are often opening up new disciplinary dialogues? My experience both in Australia and now in Aotearoa New Zealand is that it is difficult to find examiners who cross the disciplines in the same way that the research students are doing. Are we

---

30. See in this regard the rhetorical styles of Episcopal Divinity School as analyzed by Yaghjian, "Writing Cultures," 135–37. Yaghjian says in the conclusion of her article that "there is a rhetorical connection between what we write, what we ask our students to write, and the cultures in which, from which, and for which we write" because "theologians and religious scholars write and teach others to write within a particular culture" ("Writing Cultures," 139).

31. In relation to this question of multiple contexts, see the collection edited by Clive Pearson with a sub-version by Jione Havea, *Faith in a Hyphen: Cross-Cultural Theologies Down Under* (Adelaide: Openbook, 2004).

32. Schüssler Fiorenza, "Rethinking the Educational Practices," 68–69.

moving to a situation where there is only a small pool of possible examiners who would be in any way sympathetic to the new paradigms students' theses are helping to forge? If it is known that a possible examiner is opposed to a particular hermeneutical approach, is it valid in terms of our 'standards of excellence' to avoid that examiner? Similarly, what is the import in the discipline of the diversity of approaches to biblical studies? Are we developing small enclaves of scholars who are not able or willing to cross hermeneutical or methodological lines and how will this impact on an envisioned future of transdisciplinary or cross-disciplinary doctoral education? These are questions that both cross-cultural and cross-disciplinary theses are raising for me and, I believe, for standards of excellence in doctoral education.

By what standards does one evaluate emerging hermeneutics among students whose context has not yet developed or who are in the process of developing such frameworks of reading, especially when the key concepts of those cultures are not one's own as instructor/teacher/supervisor? And when such explorations emerge in theses either at Masters or Doctoral level, where does one find those competent to evaluate the thesis when the students are emerging as some of the first experts in the field? I have raised these questions as they represent some of the implications of the changes that have taken place in biblical studies in recent decades.

Hyphenation and Globalization

Teaching and studying biblical studies in a bicultural and multicultural context draws specific attention to social location. In many teaching institutions across the world today, many of the students are from elsewhere, from contexts other than those in which they are undertaking their study. They are already hyphenated in terms of location.[33] Within each student and lecturer, there are hyphenated identities also. Many come from elsewhere and others are New Zealand born (Maori or Pakeha). The biblical paradigms which both lecturers and students bring to biblical studies differ along with indigenous and ethnic origins and many other aspects of interpretive paradigms. There is in this a rich source of exploration in terms of understandings of both text and reader.[34] Students developing contextual paradigms of reading will, therefore, be challenged by the multiplicity in their very midst. They may, however, lack the critical mass of similar students who share some of their hyphenated identities. There is therefore, in the world of globalized education, a question of the community or communities of interpreters. At a very simple level, how

---

33. See Pearson and Havea, *Faith in a Hyphen*.
34. See again Segovia, "Pedagogical Discourse and Practices," 137–67.

does one construct every aspect of the teaching environment so that students from multiple ethnic and religious social locations feel 'at home' and can act as full participants in the shaping of the theological education that will take place in that space?[35] Do our standards of excellence refer to the whole pedagogical process or only its measurable outcomes?[36]

CONCLUSION

Reflecting on a journey and bringing this into dialogue with just a small portion of the emerging literature in biblical and theological pedagogy in racially and culturally diverse contexts has raised a number of questions in relation to social location and standards of excellence. I have presented them as questions from the uniqueness of the context of Aotearoa New Zealand, but they can be brought into dialogue with the diversity of issues that face biblical scholars concerned with standards of excellence in the shifting sands of biblical pedagogy in context, one aspect of that context being theological education into the new millennium.

---

35. The Teaching and Learning Plan of the School of Theology at the University of Auckland seeks to address this issue. See also Jane McAvoy, "Hospitality: A Feminist Theology of Education," *TThRel* 1 (1998): 20–26, whose questions and challenges can be extended beyond the presence of women in theological classrooms to the presence of students from many different contexts, ethnicities, genders, and religious paradigms.

36. Florence Morgan Gillman, "Ask and You Shall Find Out: Some Multicultural Dynamics in Catholic Theological Education," *TThRel* 3 (2000), 152–56, explores ways of assessing aspects of the different cultural experiences of the teaching and learning process.

Cross-Textual Biblical Studies in Multiscriptural Contexts

Archie C. C. Lee

1. The Problem of the Text-Context Paradigm

I presented a joint paper with Gale Yee on biblical pedagogy in Asia at the Society of Biblical Literature Annual Meeting in San Antonio (2004) in which I discussed the basic issues of teaching biblical studies to different groups of students in different programs at the Chinese University of Hong Kong over the past twenty-some years.[1] I spoke about the impact of the social location of Hong Kong, which is facing challenges in light of the return of the Colony's sovereignty to China in 1997. The focus on contextual interpretation and the framework of postcolonial critique have shaped biblical studies in the wake of the return of Hong Kong to China as a Special Administrative Region of China.[2] I am pleased to have this opportunity to explore further one particular concern of mine with respect to the discipline of biblical studies: namely, social location. My main focus in this paper is on the paired notions of "text" and "context".[3] In Hong Kong, students welcome the strict dichotomy between what the text meant and what it means for today in our own context, since they are inspired by the search for the theological meanings and social implications of a text. They would like to engage the Bible contextually, but only as a second stage of enquiry, since the social location of the reader only matters to these students after independent and objective exegetical work is complete.

---

1. Archie C. C. Lee and Gale Yee, "Teaching the Hebrew Bible in an Asian Context." This unpublished paper has two parts that were written separately by the two presenters with a common framework and then revised to bring the two parts together, whereupon the conclusion was written by both authors.

2. See Archie C. C. Lee, "Biblical Interpretation of the Return in the Postcolonial Hong Kong," *BibInt* 9 (1999): 164–73.

3. The notion of the "text-context" interpretive mode is briefly discussed in Archie C. C. Lee, "Biblical Interpretation in Asian Perspective," *AJT* 7 (1993): 35–39.

Even to many scholars working in Asian theology, the reader's context only affects the critical stage in which one applies a text to our own social location; there is an assumption that the meaning of a biblical text can be ascertained by an objective exegetical study without reference to the location of the reader in terms of gender, ethnicity, class, color, and power relationship. Only when one is concerned with applying and communicating will the contextual elements of language barriers, social boundaries and cultural peculiarities come into play.[4]

My dissatisfaction with the text-context interpretive mode and the current concern with social location go beyond the simple dichotomy described above. In engaging biblical studies, my pedagogical and hermeneutical issue is primarily whether the reader's context or social location has anything to contribute to the configuration of the world of the Bible. Within the multi-scriptural Asian setting, the text-context paradigm has its apparent limitations as it does not take into serious consideration the reality of the plurality of scriptures and the co-existence of diverse religious communities in Asia. In most cases, contextual biblical interpretation still tends to privilege the monotextual status of the Bible when seeking for meaning in a new context. In so doing these interpreters generally suppress all other texts, denying them scriptural significance or even condemning them as pagan, hence evil and idolatrous.[5]

D. Preman Niles, a Sri Lankan scholar, formulates this concern of mine—seeing Asia only as "the context" and the West as possessing "the text"—in the form of rhetorical questions: "Is theology always a matter of relating text to context? Is it not also a matter of relating context to text so that the context may speak to the text? Is Asia there to receive? Has it nothing to contribute?"[6]

The hermeneutical issue of probing the relations between "The Scripture and Scriptures"[7] has been one of utmost significance in Asian biblical interpre-

---

4. The paragraphs on pages 36–40 have been reworked and partially incorporated in a lecture delivered at the Jubilee Year Conference of the Korean Society of Old Testament Studies. The lecture will be included in the conference publication as "Con/textual Biblical Interpretation in Multi-Religious World of Asia."

5. I have recently published an article spelling out this problem of contextualization in biblical studies; see Archie C. C. Lee, "Cross-Textual Hermeneutics in Multi-Scriptural Asia," in *Christian Theology in Asia* (ed. Sebastian C. H. Kim; Cambridge: Cambridge University Press, 2009), 190.

6. D. Preman Niles, "The Word of God and the People of Asia," in *Understanding the Word: Essays in Honor of Bernhard W. Anderson* (ed. James T. Butler et al.; Sheffield: Sheffield Academic Press, 1985), 282.

7. "Scripture and Scriptures" is the title of S. J. Samartha's chapter in his *One Christ, Many Religions* (Maryknoll, N.Y.: Orbis, 1991).

tation. Asians have been nurtured and their lives sustained by Asian scriptural traditions that provide ethical guidance, religious ideals and spiritual strength not only to individual adherents of the religions concerned but also to the wider society. Fundamentally, the very social fabric and political order of Asian societies are shaped by scriptural insights. It is to no one's surprise that even drastic political measures aiming at eradicating the power of traditional Confucian, Buddhist and Daoist claims on the mindset and practices of the Chinese people during the Communist Cultural Revolution (1968–1978) have not succeeded in diminishing the age-old grip of these traditions and the syncretistic form in popular religion.[8] In spite of many challenges, the scriptures of these religio-cultural traditions still exert authority, guiding the social practices and the life orientations of most Chinese people. The fact of the matter is that a deep-rooted Chinese mentality has been formed by the syncretistic Chinese religious world.[9]

Hendrik Kraemer, who wrote the position document entitled *The Christian Message in the Non-Christian World* for the International Missionary Council Meeting at Tambaram in 1938,[10] provides the basis for an evangelical missionary approach to other religions. He gives legitimacy to the incarnation of Christianity, claiming that European Christianities are all adaptations. However, he also calls for a radical conversion as a break with one's religious past and an opposition to syncretism that would compromise the criterion of revelation in Jesus Christ. Kraemer opposes syncretism and assumes that converted Christians in the mission field must sever links with any pagan culture from which they come.

In reality, my experience as pastor in a local congregation is that most Christians still retain the basic tenets of their former religious world even many years after their conversion to Christianity. In Christian funerals, burials, wedding ceremonies and the celebration of the New Year and other festivals, one witnesses the vitality of the native religion in its syncretic form, mingling with the Christian practices. I firmly believe that the religious world of the reader, considered as a text, contributes to the interpretation of the world of the Bible's text. In the reading process, comparable syncretic elements in the reader's experience may shed light on the otherwise unnoticed

---

8. Richard P. Madsen, "Beyond Orthodoxy: Catholicism as Chinese Folk Religion," in *China and Christianity: Burdened Past, Hopeful Future* (ed. Stephen Uhalley Jr. and Xiaoxin Wu; Armonk, N.Y.: Sharp, 2001), 233–56.

9. Archie C. C. Lee, "Syncretism from the Perspectives of Chinese Religion and Biblical Tradition," *Ching Feng* 39 (1996): 1–24.

10. Hendrix Kraemaer, *The Christian Message in a Non-Christian World* (3rd ed.; Grand Rapids: Kregel, 1956).

syncretistic element embedded in the religious world of the text. Cross-textual reading allows the eyes of the reader to focus on commonalities and differences embedded in both religious worlds. Thus, the reader is compelled to critically re-evaluate the religious world of the Bible and re-appropriate it in the process.

There are certain basic cultural-religious elements of Asian communities that should have a great impact on our reading of the Bible. Here I want to highlight two. Firstly, the conception of the divine in terms of a divine-human continuum is a basic factor common to most Asian religions. In the case of the Chinese, deities are understood as only quantitatively different from the human; thus the subsequent possibility of crossing the boundary between divinity and humanity has given rise to the category of "immortals" in China as well as the operative power of the notion of incarnation in Chinese folk religions.[11] One observes that the veneration of ancestors and belief in ghosts and spirits are widespread features in the religious world of Asians. They have persisted even after centuries of fierce and, at times, violent attacks by Christianity.

The practice of shamanism is an indispensable arena through which one comes to a certain comprehension of the religious world of Asians in general. Korean *minjung* hermeneutics serves as a good example, as it illustrates the grasp of shamanistic beliefs and practices on the mindset and daily life of the *minjung*. Korean feminism has made efforts to recover this piece of Asian religiosity for the empowerment of women.[12]

The second influential factor from the religious world of Asia is the belief in fate of some sort. Pre-determinism is a widespread concept in Asian religions; it is more prevalent than merely determinism in terms of *karma* or deeds of one's previous existence in the various traditions of Mahayana and Theravada Buddhism. Many of the Asian articulations of fate do not fit in with the conventional conception of fatalism. There is the dialectic relationship between a strong belief in the will of heaven (*ming*, 命) as well as an equally firm position in the faith of human conduct in effecting changes in one's fate.

---

11. It is interesting to engage understanding of Jesus with the conception of incarnation in Daoism. See Archie C. C. Lee, "Asian Encountering Jesus Christ—A Chinese Reading of Jesus in the Wisdom Matrix," *Quest, An Interdisciplinary Journal for Asian Christian Scholars* 4 (2005): 41–62.

12. David Kwang-sun Suh, "Liberating Spirituality in the Korean Minjung Tradition: Shamanism and Minjung Liberation," and Lee Chung Hee, "Liberation Spirituality in Daedong Gut," in *Asian Christian Spirituality: Reclaiming Traditions* (ed. Virginia Fabella, Peter K. H. Lee, and David Kwang-sun Suh; Maryknoll, N.Y.: Orbis, 1992), 31–43; Theresa Ki-ja Kim, *The Relationship between Shamanic Ritual and the Korean Masked Dance-Drama: The Journey Motif to Chaos/Darkness/Void* (Ann Arbor, Mich.: UMI, 1988).

In the face of the seemingly unchanging fate, each Chinese person finds it a challenge to seek the best means to discern the various chances and possibilities to effect change with respect to cosmic time (*ji-yuan,* 機緣) and to determine the opportunities for change occurring at specific moments for an individual (*yun,* 運).[13] "In matching individual and cosmic time, one encounters harmonious moments, which are considered to be propitious (*ji,* 吉) and bring good fortune, and discordant moments, which are considered inauspicious (*xiong,* 凶) and bring calamities."[14] This religious element is instructive, for example, to our re-reading of the book of Ecclesiastes in the discernment of the appointed time, one's allotment and opportunity.[15]

There are other aspects of Asian religions that may also exert some influences on biblical studies. Naturalistic perception of reality vis-à-vis the biblical framework of history and historical consciousness is one of them. No wonder creation theology gets more attention in Asia! This, among other things, will engage our reading of the Bible in a way that is different than readings in a non-Asian cultural context.

2. Religiosity and Social Reality of Asia as Text in Postgraduate Biblical Pedagogy

Stanley Samartha, an Indian biblical scholar, remarks on the Bible and Asian multiscripturality I have just underlined above:

> To enter this multi-scriptural situation with the claim that the Bible "is the only written witness to God's deeds in history" is to cut off all conversation with neighbors of other faiths in the world. This attitude makes it impossible for Christians to develop "their own hermeneutics." In a continent like Asia a claim for the supreme authority of *one* scripture can be met by a counter claim for similar authority for *another* scripture.[16]

In order to avoid negative encounters to the detriment of both Asian scriptures and the Christian Bible, Samartha's warning must be taken seriously. The multi-scriptural reality of Asia resists any claim of absolute authority and

---

13. Yih-yüan Li, "Notions of Time, Space and Harmony in Chinese Popular Culture," in *Time and Space in Chinese Culture* (ed. Chun-Chich Huang and Erik Zürcher; Leiden: Brill, 1995), 387.
14. Ibid., 388.
15. See C. L. Seow's discussion on destiny in *Ecclesiastes: A New Translation with Introduction and Commentary* (AB 18C; New York: Doubleday, 1997), 24, 166–67, 230–31.
16. Samartha, *One Christ*, 76.

challenges the principles and practice of hermeneutics based on such a claim.[17] Most of the Asian scriptures, be it Hindu, Buddhist, Confucian, or Daoist, understand the notion of scripture and scriptural authority differently from that of Christianity.[18]

The complexity of Asian religiosity exhibits both the impacts of modernization and globalization as well as traces of the traditional conceptions of the supernatural, human fate, social destiny and *feng shui* (literary "wind and water") or geomancy. They are profoundly articulated in religious classics handed down from the past and still widely practiced in the daily rituals and rites today. These religious conceptions still constitute the belief system and religious mentality of the common people in Asia. For example, the water fountain in the Suntec City, Singapore, is considered a contemporary expression of *feng shui*. This notion is even publicized in tourist literature handed out to visitors to the country:

> Today, Suntec City is Singapore's largest shopping, business and entertainment centre—and according to the experts, its success is all to do with *Feng Shui*. According to *Feng Shui*, Suntec City is located in the region of Singapore's left hand. The right hand is located at the financial district of Raffles Place, and together the hands cradle City Hall. At the crucial site of the left hand's palm therefore, the developers of Suntec City built the Fountain of Wealth—a structure designed to ensure the prosperity of Suntec City. All this talk of wealth and prosperity for Suntec City however doesn't mean you can't get your piece of *Feng Shui* good fortune here. During the day, visitors to Suntec City walk around the central base of the Fountain three times, touching the water at all the times to gain some good luck of their own.[19]

It is clear from this tourist literature that *feng shui* is promoted in the setting of modern architecture, advance technology and contemporary tourist industry. The twenty-first-century urban ritual attracted my attention and I went to the Suntec City site one afternoon during a Society of Biblical Literature International Meeting to see it myself. Lined up at the fountain were a large group of

---

17. See the discussion in S. J. Samartha, *The Search for New Hermeneutics in Asian Christian Theology* (Serampore: Board of Theological Education of the Senate of Serampore College, 1987).

18. The practice of a strictly closed canon with the final revelatory authority ascribed to a christological understanding of the life and death of Jesus of Nazareth is basically foreign, if not totally strange, to the other Asian scriptural family members. See Paul A. Rule, "Does Heaven Speak? Revelation in the Confucian and Christian Traditions," in Uhalley and Wu, *China and Christianity*, 63–79.

19. "Suntec City: Feng Shui Heaven," *The Real Destination Singapore* (April–June 2005).

Chinese visitors and some local Singaporeans in order to participate in the interesting act of circling the fountain of wealth. I joined them to walk around it three times, touching the water each time as instructed by the tourist literature I quoted above. During this ritual, people seemed to be satisfied that they participated in sharing the success and wealth of Suntec City.

Context is not just a setting in the intersection of time and space; it comprises a conglomeration of texts. "Text" not only in the conventional sense of a written document, but also in the more elusive socioscientific notion of historical events, people movements, daily experiences and human actions in community as constituting "social texts."[20] In a word, the Asian context contains multiple texts and is itself a text, contributing to the reading and enriching the meaning of the biblical text.

After the Cultural Revolution in 1978, there have been tremendous changes in the ideological and social structures of China. The "cultural heat" in China, which inspires a massive interest and quest for foreign cultures, especially western culture and its alleged Christian foundation, has motivated a whole generation of non-Christian scholars attracted to the fast-growing academic subject of Christian Studies at public universities and government run research institutes. Some of these scholars are being designated as "cultural Christians" who sympathize with Christian religious ideas and ethical values.[21] A few of them can even identify themselves with a Christian worldview. For ideological and practical considerations, however, baptism and institutional affiliation are not viable options in the Chinese socio-political context. One remarkable feature of Christian studies now developing in China is the absence of input from the biblical field. Scholars could not just shift over to the biblical discipline as many of them did when Christian Studies started to emerge as a recognized discipline in the university in the Eighties of the last century. There were scholars who switched from the field of western philosophy to classical Christian philosophical and doctrinal studies and from the area of historical discipline to history of Christianity. We have now an undesirable situation, in that Christian studies in China is currently without contributions from the discipline of biblical studies. If Christian studies is to develop in a healthy manner, we have to rectify the situation and give the text a proper role in informing and shaping the whole discipline. One cannot

---

20. See William A. Graham, *Beyond the Written Word: Oral Aspects of Scripture in the History of Religion* (Cambridge: Cambridge University Press, 1987); Archie C. C. Lee, "Engaging the Bible and Asian Resources: Hermeneutics of the Globalized in the Global-Local Entanglement," *Journal of Theologies and Cultures in Asia* 2 (2003): 5–30.

21. See the essays in Joseph Leung, ed., *Cultural Christian: Phenomenon and Argument* [Chinese] (Hong Kong: Institute of Sino-Christian Studies, 1997).

imagine doing Buddhist and Daoist studies without reading the scriptures of the religious traditions concerned; the same should apply to Christian studies and the biblical text.

In 2003, I launched a postgraduate program of biblical studies in The Chinese University of Hong Kong's Department of Religion[22] and started to admit a new group of graduate students who were brought up in the communist context. The program was initiated for the purpose of developing future faculty of the Hebrew Bible for Chinese universities in China. Ten postgraduate students admitted to the program are not professing Christians or Jews. Without the constraints of the Christian concept of the authority of the Bible that may act as a limit on scholarly hermeneutical maneuverings, these students find the practice of contextual reading pertinent to the biblical studies, especially when the Bible is set against the multi-textual background of Asia. They are quite ready to undertake the academic study of the Bible, taking great interest in it as a religio-cultural text and engaging in an intellectual quest for the meaning of the Bible in light of cross-cultural encounters.

The different sociopolitical and religio-cultural experiences in the PRC have molded their perception and perspective. To take an example; the material-atheistic mindset raises a totally different set of issues when it comes to the study of Hebrew Wisdom Literature. Chinese students see themselves in possession of literature of a similar sort. Thus, they raise questions with a comparative point of view from the Chinese intellectual tradition. They immediately identify the secular nature and universal dimension of the literature. They call into question the role of the divine in articulating human experiences in the formation of wisdom literature. For example, for Christian scholars within the world of Western biblical studies, and even Christians in general, the question of theodicy dominates the horizon of discussion concerning the Book of Job. These non-Christian Chinese students, however, do not need to struggle with theodicy and human suffering. For them, the discussion of innocent suffering inevitably points to the reality of human pains and the social dimension of oppression and exploitation. The long history of economic hardship and political suppression in Chinese society contributes to their focused deliberation. It constitutes the perspective through which their reading of the meaning of the biblical text is engendered. Similarly, the Book of Lamentations and lament psalms are understood through suffering experienced under autocratic regimes and oppressive governments. For many, the Tiananmen Square Massacre in 1989 forms the context of the reading of

---

22. The department was subsequently renamed the Department of Cultural and Religious Studies with the addition of a major program of cultural studies in 2004.

Lamentations. In this reading, the lamenting female voices of the personified Mother Zion in Lamentations echo the ongoing cries of the mothers who lost their children at Tiananmen.²³

The official position of the Chinese church is usually one of harmonious concordance with the communist party line, affirming that the post-liberation era of Chinese society obviates the need to fight against injustice and corruption. Some Christian scholars and theologians in China therefore deny any legitimate place for liberation hermeneutics and praxis. In contrast, most of my mainland Chinese students, after having been educated in Hong Kong for a short while, find the biblical traditions of justice and righteousness in the Pentateuch, Prophets, and Wisdom corpus not only relevant but also essential in shaping their critical view of Chinese society. They appreciate and aspire to realize the vision of peace and justice embodied in the Old Testament. Obviously, for them, the Cultural Revolution failed to deliver and fulfill the promises it made.

When these Chinese students read the Bible they bring with them their own Chinese religio-cultural and sociopolitical texts into understanding the Bible. In facing the challenges from these Chinese students, there is a need to search for and come up with principles and methods of biblical interpretation that are relevant to non-Christian Asian reality.²⁴ In my biblical pedagogy, I try to implement a cross-textual reading strategy by bringing the Asian complexity of social texts and multiplicity of religious scriptures (text A) and the Bible (text B) together, reading them in parallel and in constant interaction.²⁵

---

23. Archie C. C. Lee, "Mothers Bewailing: Reading Lamentations," in *Her Master's Tools? Feminist and Postcolonial Engagements of Historical-Critical Discourse* (ed. Caroline Vander Stichele and Todd C. Penner; SBLGPBS 9; Atlanta: Society of Biblical Literature, 2004), 195–210.

24. For attempts to develop Asian ways of biblical interpretation, see the articles in the special issue of *Biblical Interpretation* (2 [1994]: 251–63) edited by R. S. Sugirtharajah as *Commitment, Context and Text: Examples of Asian Hermeneutics*; and Kwok Pui-lan, *Discovering the Bible in the Non-biblical World* (Maryknoll, N.Y.: Orbis, 1995), which raises important and critical issues related to the task of hermeneutics in the Asian world. Sugirtharajah's recent contributions in postcolonial critique and biblical studies in Asia are commented on: *The Bible and the Third World: Precolonial, Colonial, and Postcolonial Encounters* (Cambridge: Cambridge University Press, 2001).

25. For the basic principles behind cross-textual hermeneutics, see Lee, "Biblical Interpretation in Asian Perspective," 35–39. For its application to Chinese creation myths, see Archie C. C. Lee, "Genesis 1 from the Perspective of a Chinese Creation Myth," in *Understanding Poets and Prophets: Essays in Honour of George Wishart Anderson* (ed. A. Graeme Auld; Sheffield: JSOT Press, 1993), 186–98; and idem, "The Chinese Creation Myth of Nu Kua and the Biblical Narrative in Genesis 1–11," *BibInt* 2 (1994): 312–24. I have been asked why I use "cross-textual" rather than "intertextual." Two reasons come

By placing the two texts side by side, cross-textual interpretation signifies the illumination of one text by the other. Through such encounters, new meanings of the biblical text can be engendered, which might never be highlighted in the reading of the Bible alone. Cross-textual interpretation makes multiple crossings between the two texts, engaging them in creative tension. In the process, the two texts should be subjected to a vigorous and critical appraisal of the readers who seek to engage both of them for a renewed configuration of meaning and identity. The aim of such multiple crossings is life-enriching: the transformation of one's life, a process of self-discovery. The result is an "enriched-transformed existence,"[26] which is properly located in a sociopolitical context.

3. Conclusion

In sum, biblical studies in Asia, I propose, should take on board the many non-Christian scriptures and embrace their potentially inspirational nature. Taking the plurality of scripture and the social complexity of Asia as a "text" will eventually broaden the scope and renew the vitality of biblical interpretation in Asia. Cross-textual reading of the Bible will have tremendous implications for graduate biblical studies. It is clear from the experience I have with Chinese postgraduate students that they do not approach the biblical text in a vacuum; rather, they bring with them their own religio-cultural traditions and sociopolitical texts into the understanding of the Bible. The method of cross-textual interpretation intends to read the Bible in Asia seriously, by acknowledging the existence of other Asian texts that are significant to readers. The nonbiblical text represents culture and experience that cannot be divorced from a meaningful and dynamic reading process of the "two texts." In the process, the pluralistic realities of Asia become an abundant textual

---

immediately to mind. First, in the Jewish rabbinical tradition of hermeneutics, the term "intertextual" refers to the relationship between or among texts within the Bible. Thus, the rabbis think that the Hebrew Bible constitutes an organized whole. As such, it is not only consistent from beginning to end, but it also involves cross-referencing and hence cross-expansion in meaning. Second, contemporary literary and biblical scholars have developed this idea even further, as they search for important historical links in literary forms and concepts between texts or chapters of the Bible. See, e.g., Michael Fishbane, *Text and Texture: Close Readings of Selected Biblical Texts* (New York: Schocken, 1979); Daniel Boyarin, *Intertextuality and the Reading of Midrash* (Bloomington: Indiana University Press, 1990); Danna Nolan Fewell, ed., *Reading between Texts: Intertextuality and the Hebrew Bible* (Louisville: Westminster John Knox, 1992).

26. For this term, see Richard Wentz, *The Contemplation of Otherness: The Critical Vision of Religion* (Macon, Ga.: Mercer University Press, 1984), 13.

reservoir for cross-textual reading in Asian biblical hermeneutics. This multi-dimensional understanding of the "religio-cultural texts" and "sociopolitical texts" reflects the religiosity and social locality of Asian people. It is these texts that provide the basic point of departure for cross-textual interpretation.

Social Location: Dis-ease and/or Dis-cover(y)

Yak-hwee Tan

Introduction

Whenever I turn to Channel NewsAsia,[1] an Asian television news channel, their tagline, "Providing Asian Perspectives," is often present on the television screen. Apparently, their tagline serves to remind the viewers of the channel's intention. In the light of ever-changing global issues and developments, Channel NewsAsia seeks to present their Asian insights as reported by their correspondents who are based throughout the Asian region. Hence, "Channel NewsAsia is created for Asians by Asians."[2] The illustration highlights the role perspective plays in media reporting, and perspectives are influenced by one's time and space. To put it differently, events and issues in the world are evaluated and interpreted by the interpreters conditioned by their social location.

Likewise, the notion of social location has been and remains an important factor in the development of graduate biblical education. The rise of biblical scholars from parts of the world other than the West highlights the concept that perspectives on the biblical texts are often influenced by one's social location.[3] As such, social location has a contributory role to play in the standards

---

1. http://www.channelnewsasia.com/about/. Incorporated in March 1999, Channel NewsAsia is owned and managed by Media Corp Pte Ltd., Singapore's largest broadcaster and one of Asia's most renowned broadcasters. Based in Singapore, Channel NewsAsia reports from major Asian cities and key Western cities, such as New York, Washington, D.C., and London.

2. Ibid.

3. See R. S. Sugirtharajah, ed., *Voices from the Margins: Interpreting the Bible in the Third World* (2nd ed.; Maryknoll, N.Y.: Orbis, 1995); Musa W. Dube, *Postcolonial Feminist Interpretation of the Bible* (St. Louis: Chalice, 2000); Yak-hwee Tan, *Re-presenting the Johannine Community: A Postcolonial Perspective* (New York: Lang, 2008); Marvin Suber Williams, "Towards a Cultural Studies Approach to Biblical Interpretation: An Ideological Analysis of Identity Construction in Revelation 21:1–22:5" (unpublished Ph.D. diss., Vanderbilt University, 2006).

of excellence and the transformation of graduate biblical education for the educator-cum-biblical scholar, as well as his or her graduate students.

With respect to my social location as an educator-cum-biblical scholar, there are some questions that I often raise. Who are the constituents that make up my social location? What are the standards of excellence, for someone like me, who has taught and supervised graduate students at Trinity Theological College, Singapore?[4] Should the standards conform to the ethos of a college that is owned and governed by the founding churches, which are evangelical in character?[5] Or should they conform to the ethos of the discipline per se, influenced and challenged by the landscape of the world brought about by globalization?[6]

I moved to Taipei, Taiwan, in August 2008 and began teaching at Taiwan Theological College and Seminary[7] in Taipei, Taiwan. I foresee that the political, socioeconomic and cultural environment of Taiwan[8] will influence my

---

4. Trinity Theological College is an institution sponsored by the Methodist, Anglican, and Presbyterian churches. Its history began when church leaders interned in Changi Prison during the Second World War felt the need to establish an institution to train pastors and church workers. Hence, Trinity Theological College opened its doors on 4 October 1948. In 1962, the Lutheran Church of Malaysia (later known as the Lutheran Church of Malaysia and Singapore) became affiliated with the college.

5. According to the Articles of Union, the college exists "to educate pastors for the church and to train full-time or voluntary evangelists and church workers for religious education or for Christian social service." Thus, the goal of the college is the "equipping of God's people for ministry, for the building up of the Body of Christ."

6. Numerous books have been written with regard to the positive and negative effects of globalization upon the world. See Anthony Giddens, *Runaway World: How Globalization Is Reshaping Our Lives* (New York: Routledge, 2000); Malcolm Waters, *Globalization* (2nd ed.; London: Routledge, 1995); Ankie Hoogvelt, *Globalization and the Postcolonial World: The New Political Economy of Development* (2nd ed.; Baltimore: Johns Hopkins University Press, 2001).

7. In 1872, the Canadian Presbyterian George Mackay initiated a training program that eventually became Taiwan Theological College and Seminary. Taiwan Theological College and Seminary is one of the Presbyterian seminaries affiliated to the Presbyterian Church in Taiwan.

8. For thousands of years, the aborigines of Taiwan (formerly known as Formosa) lived in peace, until the sixteenth century, when settlers from China and Japan began to occupy certain parts of the island. The political history of Taiwan is very eventful and was occupied by foreign powers (the Dutch, the Japanese, and the Chinese) for about three hundred years. In 1949, the Nationalist regime was defeated by the Chinese Communist Party and expelled from China. Since then, Taiwan has been forced to be the refuge of the Republic of China. Taiwan was under martial law for thirty-eight years, and it was only in 1987 that it was lifted. In 1991 and 1992, Taiwanese were able to elect their representatives to congress and the legislative body. Economically, Taiwan is capitalist and state-owned.

social location. When I was teaching at Trinity in Singapore, many of the students came from other countries in Asia and hence, they brought with them their particular social locations. Likewise, when I am in Taiwan, the graduate students come from different regions of Taiwan, bringing with them their own specific social locations. With respect to the relationship between graduate students and biblical studies, some questions are brought to the fore, such as: What are the standards of excellence that I wish to introduce to my graduate students who are doing biblical studies? Is it my own standards that prevail? Or perhaps should we come up with a new type of excellence that will transform graduate biblical education?

The questions surrounding the study of the social locations of the educator-cum-biblical scholar and graduate students bring two words to my mind: dis-ease and dis-cover(y). These two words will form the framework for my discussion in this paper on the theme of social location and transforming graduate biblical education.

The discussion in this paper will be divided into three sections. First, I will outline my social location. Second, I will discuss the question of graduate studies, in particular biblical studies with regard to "rhetoric of space," "rhetoric of location,"[9] and "rhetoric of text." Third, I will share some thoughts concerning the standards of excellence for people who are in the profession of teaching, learning, and research and in so doing, I hope to motivate a transformation of graduate biblical education for the academy and the world at large. However, before I embark on the paper proper, a brief explanation on the rationale for the choice of the two words dis-ease and dis-cover(y) will help us to see the relationship of dis-ease and dis-cover(y) to the concept of social location.

"Ease" means "the lack of difficulty or the state of feeling relaxed or comfortable without worries, problems or pain."[10] In the English language, the antonym for the word "ease" is "unease." However, for this paper, I have intentionally used the hyphenated form, dis-ease, which has been used by critics

---

Most of the people are affiliated with the Buddhism and Chinese religions (Taoism, Confucianism, and folklore). Christianity constitutes 2–3 percent of the population. See Yang En Cheng, "Taiwan," *A Dictionary of Asian Christianity* (ed. Scott W. Sunquist; Grand Rapids: Eerdmans, 2001), 815–17.

9. Susan Stanford Friedman, "Locational Feminism: Gender, Cultural Geographies, and Geopolitical Literacy," in *Feminist Locations: Global and Local, Theory and Practice* (ed. Marianne Dekoven; New Brunswick, N.J.: Rutgers University Press, 2001). Friedman uses "rhetoric of space" and "rhetoric of location" in her discussion with regard to the use of locational feminism.

10. Sally Wehmeir, ed., *Oxford Advance Learner's Dictionary of Current English* (6th ed.; Oxford: Oxford University Press, 2000), 367.

from different academic disciplines to signify the antonym of "ease."[11] Many of us know that the nonhyphenated form of dis-ease is "disease," which has a number of meanings. One of the meanings is "an illness affecting humans, animals or plants, often caused by infection … [or], something that is very wrong with people's attitudes, way of life or with society."[12] In using the hyphenated dis-ease, I am suggesting that social location can be an ailment, a disease that disrupts the ease of some.

In a similar fashion, the verb "discover" could mean to find something that was hidden or that one did not expect to find. In short, "discover" is to become aware of the existence of that particular thing. The noun form of "discover" is "discovery," which is the process of that finding and learning of something that was not known before.[13] I have hyphenated the word "discovery" to dis-cover(y) to denote that another meaning is constructed. That is, the role of social location is something that one is going to find or learn about, and in this case, I hope to uncover its relationship to graduate biblical education.

Therefore, the words dis-ease and dis-cover(y) render assistance to the discussion of standards of excellence for the transformation of graduate biblical education.

My Social Location: A "Shifting" One?

I am a first-generation Chinese Christian raised in the Confucian tradition who received my primary and secondary education in a Presbyterian mission school in Singapore.[14] During the period between the 1950s and 1970s, the school's curriculum followed closely that of the British system.[15] For example,

---

11. For example, see B. A. Keddy, "Dis-ease between Nursing and Feminism: Nurses Caring for One Another within the Feminist Framework," *Issues in Mental Health Nursing* 14 (1993): 287–92; Linda A. Kinnaha, *Poetics of the Feminine: Authority and Literary Tradition in William Carlos Williams, Mina Loy, Denise Levertov, and Kathleen Fraser* (Cambridge: Cambridge University Press, 1994).

12. A. S. Hornby, *Oxford Advanced Learner's Dictionary of Current English* (3rd ed.; London: Oxford University Press, 1974), 332.

13. Ibid., 331.

14. Yak-hwee Tan, "A History of Presbyterian Schools in Singapore and Their Impact on the Education System of Present Singapore" (unpublished paper written for the writer's preacher's licensing examinations; Presbyterian Church in Singapore, 1991). See also Brian Holmes, ed., *Educational Policy and the Mission Schools: Case Studies from the British Empire* (London: Routledge, 1968).

15. In 1819, the British acquired Temasek (present-day Singapore) through a treaty with the local chieftains. The British rule was broken, but only for a short period of three years (1942–1945), when the Japanese occupied Singapore. At the end of the Second World War, Singapore was returned to the British, who continued their rule over Singapore until

the history lessons about the British Empire and its relationship to Southeast Asia from the eighteenth century onward were taught from a British perspective, since the textbooks used were authored by British historians. Similarly, the kind of biblical and theological knowledge I was taught when I was in theological school was mainly Eurocentric, since many of the lecturers were sent by their mission agencies from the West. The narration of these two educational experiences with the West is to disclose that my encounters with the West have produced a "mixed" Yak-hwee—an "in-between" person. The encounter of the native and the colonizer gives rise to a new set of realities for both the native and the colonizer. In my situation, my reality is no longer fixed or essentialized because I embody a conflicting disposition of classes, nationalities, religions and ethnicities. My identity is always "shifting";[16] there is neither a One nor the Other, but "something else besides": a hybridized one.[17] Furthermore, my encounter with the West continued with my doctoral studies in the United States.

When I was teaching in the seminary in Singapore, the majority of graduate students also came from Singapore, although there were also students from other countries in South-east Asia. The students with their distinctive social locations, conditioned by their political, social and religious factors, affected my social location and vice-versa. These encounters shaped my approach towards teaching and research in the area of biblical studies. That is to say, the method and theory I deploy in biblical studies can no longer subscribe to the "methodologically dense, scientific, depersonalized, empirical-factual."[18] On the contrary, the multidimensional context of my experiences as graduate student and professor necessitates interdisciplinary approaches to graduate biblical studies.[19] The univocal reading of the biblical and ancient texts has been challenged, raising the question of the rhetorical function of texts in

---

1959, when Singapore had its first general election. For a detailed study of the history of Singapore, see Constance M. Turnball, *A History of Singapore 1819–1975* (Kuala Lumpur: Oxford University Press, 1977).

16. Homi K. Bhabha, *The Location of Culture* (London: Routledge, 1994), 107.

17. Ibid., 97.

18. Elisabeth Schüssler Fiorenza, "Rethinking the Educational Practices of Biblical Doctoral Studies," *TThRel* 6 (2003): 71.

19. See Fernando F. Segovia, "'And They Began to Speak in Other Tongues': Competing Modes of Discourse in Contemporary Biblical Criticism," in *Social Location and Biblical Interpretation in the United States* (vol. 1 of *Reading from This Place*; ed. Fernando F. Segovia and Mary A. Tolbert; Minneapolis: Fortress, 1995), 1–32. In his essay, Segovia charts an overall view of the shift in biblical criticism with respect to methods and theory and readers.

their past and present contexts, which are imbued with the ideological presuppositions of both writers and interpreters.[20]

Moreover, with my relocation to Taiwan, my social location has been challenged. The political, socioeconomic and cultural environment of the country and the social location of graduate students of the seminary affect both of our social locations. My social location and my approach to graduate biblical education can be illuminated by the terms, "rhetoric of space" and "rhetoric of location." Moreover, the recognition of the relationship between social location and "rhetoric of location" and "rhetoric of space" has ramifications for biblical education which the following discussion seeks to underscore.

"Rhetoric of Space" and "Rhetoric of Location"

"Rhetoric of space" and "rhetoric of location" are two terms that I borrow from Susan Stanford Friedman for my discussion. Friedman's treatment of these two phrases is in light of her discussion on "locational feminism." According to Friedman, "locational feminism," on the one hand, acknowledges its historical and geographical definitions but, on the other hand, it also "changes, travels, translates, and transplants in different spacio/temporal contexts."[21] In short, feminism is not static but is dependent on its location that is conditioned by time and space. Though Friedman's approach concerns feminism, I find her argument on space and location applicable to the conjunction of social location and graduate biblical education. In the articulation of one's perspective on a biblical text, rhetoric is applied but rhetoric is "simultaneously situated in a specific locale, global in scope, and constantly in motion through time and space."[22] In a way, one's perspective is always "locational."

For the past twenty years or more, we have seen that the world is "not as big" as it used to be. Nations are becoming more interdependent, depending upon each other in areas such as politics, economics and culture. Globalization has created inroads whereby borders between nations are becoming more accessible. The accelerating pace of globalization brings about the intensifi-

---

20. See Elisabeth Schüssler Fiorenza, *Rhetoric and Ethic: The Politics of Biblical Studies* (Minneapolis: Augsburg Fortress, 1999). As implied in the title of the second chapter of her book, "Changing the Paradigms: The Ethos of Biblical Studies," Schüssler Fiorenza argues for a turn from a "dogmatic, historical-scientistic or culturally relativist paradigm of interpretation to a critical rhetorical-emancipatory process paradigm." Such a challenge means that readers of the text no longer approach the text either for ecclesial or academic pursuits but for a "more just and radical democratic cosmopolitan articulation of religion in a global context" (57).

21. Friedman, "Locational Feminism," 15.

22. Ibid.

cation of cyber technology and its related processes, contributing "to a shift from temporal to spatial modes of thought."[23] For example, one did not need to be present at Beijing to witness the opening ceremony of the Olympics on 8 August 2008; the ceremony was telecast live for those who could view it. The mode of teleconferencing enables business decisions to be executed without the need of the company's executives to leave their offices. Space and location are no longer seen as solely physical or temporal; they are not fixed, but shifting. Since space and locations are no longer fixed, the meanings of events or issues can be constructed across time and space. Meanings are no longer static but have become fluid because of other determining factors, such as the social location of the interpreter. The interpreter, influenced by his or her historical, geographical and cultural conditions constructs the meaning of the events. The "rhetoric of space" and "rhetoric of location" are related to "rhetoric of texts," such as the biblical text.

"Rhetoric of Text"

Rhetoric is no longer seen as a mode of communication that is simply making statements of facts with the purpose of communicating facts. Rather, rhetoric is understood as "performative language."[24] Rhetoric is more than just persuasive communication. Rhetoric is always situated within a particular location conditioned by history, culture and religion.[25] In light of globalization, historical rhetoric is also influenced and transformed by rhetoric that comes from outside the academy, such as those of the marginalized from the "rest of the world." As such, rhetoric has become polarized, bringing forth diverse and different opinions regarding the construction of one's national history.

When I was in secondary school, I was taught from my history textbook, written by a British historian, that the clash in 1857 between the Indians and the British in India is known as the Sepoy Rebellion. However, friends from India understand and name this clash very differently. To them, it is known as "The British Massacre." The two perspectives show that the rhetoric of historical narrative and other discourses is produced with a pedagogical function in mind.[26] In the words of Schüssler Fiorenza, rhetoric is "best understood as

---

23. Ibid., 18.
24. See Terry Eagleton, *Literary Theory: An Introduction* (2nd ed.; Minneapolis: University of Minnesota Press, 1996), 102–4. Eageleton discusses briefly some aspects and criticisms of speech act theory as propounded by J. L. Austin.
25. Friedman, "Locational Feminism," 17.
26. See Edward W. Said, *Orientalism* (New York: Vintage Books, 1979). Said argues that Orientalism is a discourse invented by European culture to manage and produce the Orient.

epistemic because it reveals an ethical dimension of knowledge production as political practice."[27] To put it briefly, underlying the rhetoric of historical narratives are ideologically-conditioned presuppositions.

Therefore, there is the need to challenge and investigate these underlying presuppositions. This strategy of interrogation is within one's reach because of the fluid nature of space and location which has created a "contact zone" or "social space." A "contact zone" or "social space" is "where disparate cultures need, clash, grapple with each other, often in highly asymmetrical relations of domination and subordination."[28] A further explanation of the term "contact zone" comes from the field of postcolonial theory. The "contact zone" is understood as the process of "transculturation." The "contact zone" is when the colonized or subjugated group of people re-presents information which the colonizers, from their perspective, have selected and designed concerning them.[29]

In the light of the growing number of graduate students doing biblical studies from the once colonized countries and the rest of the world, the "contact zone" is an attractive strategy. This strategy is an avenue whereby such students could engage both the "rhetoric of space," namely their social location, and the "rhetoric of text," namely, the biblical text, and in so doing, articulate their perspectives. The notion that texts are fluid or "hybridized"[30] enables also interpreters, conditioned by their social location, to reinterpret and re-present their own identities and realities anew.

In my personal experience of practicing the "rhetoric of location," "rhetoric of space," and "rhetoric of text," I find such a practice liberative and transformative. It is liberative because it enables me to unearth and therefore, articulate my perspective. For me, this stance is dis-cover(y), and it is transformative because it creates dis-ease. For transformation to take place, dis-ease is necessary. Just like a chrysalis that has to undergo some discomfort and uneasiness in its shell before it transforms into a butterfly, the dis-ease means that such practice in graduate biblical education will be transformative in due time.

The discussion on the "rhetoric of location," "rhetoric of space," and "rhetoric of text" therefore, challenges us to reconsider the practice of biblical

---

27. Schüssler Fiorenza, *Rhetoric and Ethic,* 57.

28. Mary Louise Pratt, *Imperial Eyes: Travel Writing and Transculturation* (London: Routledge, 1992), 4. In her book, Pratt seeks to show the connection between travel writing and forms of knowledge and expressions, how their interaction and intersection have bearing upon the production of "the rest of the world" for European consumption.

29. Ibid., 7.

30. Bhabha, *The Location of Culture,* 97.

studies in the academy in general and at the graduate level in particular. Furthermore, this discussion also raises the question of standards of excellence, especially at a time when globalization (and postmodernism) has encroached upon almost all academic disciplines, and biblical studies is no exception.

STANDARDS OF EXCELLENCE: A GLOCAL PERSPECTIVE OF BIBLICAL STUDIES

In the face of factors such as race, class, sexual orientation, and national identity that create differences and particularities amongst students and teachers, the inevitable outcome is that the practice of graduate biblical studies will encounter challenges both locally and globally. As such, a glocal practice of graduate biblical studies is urgent and pertinent. The practice that I foresee will chart standards of excellence and also work toward transformation in graduate biblical studies.

The term "glocal" is derived from a combination of two words, global and local—a term used in "global and transnational cultural studies to indicate the notion of how the local and global are co-complicit, each implicated in the other."[31] In other words, the particularities of the local, such as its material and culture are not only linked with the local but are also connected politically and economically to that of another, namely the global. Therefore, the tendencies to homogenize one or the other are avoided.[32] In light of intense globalization (note the word "global" in the word) and the rapid processes of cyber and media technology, the interconnection between the global and the local is unavoidable. The identities of some of the graduate students in the courses that I taught at Trinity Theological College reflected the glocal character of the world we live in. The students from the Philippines with their particular identities encountered students from Indonesia, Nagaland and Singapore and in their encounters, an opportunity was provided for engaging their histories that went beyond the local. The association between the local and the global creates the glocal.

Furthermore, the glocal aspect was also reflected in the courses that I taught at Trinity Theological College, Singapore. For example, in the Method and Theory in New Testament course, the graduate students became acquainted with the different approaches toward reading the biblical texts. Instead of employing only a single method towards reading the text, interdisciplinary and multidisciplinary approaches in the discipline were introduced. Many graduate students had only been trained in the historical-critical method of inquiry and were excited when they were introduced to reading strategies

---

31. Friedman, "Locational Feminism," 31.
32. Ibid., 30.

that were akin to their social realities. For example, James Longkumer, a doctoral student from Nagaland, read the parable of the Great Banquet of Luke 15 using the cultural-anthropological approach.[33] The ancient practice of the Feast of Merit has been adapted to the community meal by the Naga Christians, a tribal community of Nagaland who resides in the northeastern region of India. Longkumer illuminated the connection of the Feast of Merit to the Great Banquet of Luke 15. For him, the sharing of a community meal under the ethos of patronal benefaction and honor has some parallels with the parable of the Great Banquet. That is to say, his social location has bearing upon his reading and vice versa.

From my teaching experiences in Singapore and the United States, as well as in Taiwan, two considerations have bearing on the glocal character of biblical studies. These two considerations have significant ripple effects for standards of excellence, stirring the waters of graduate biblical education toward transformation.

The first consideration is social location. The social location of the graduate student or biblical scholar compels him or her to discuss his or her work from the socioreligious location that she or he occupies. Though such location is "locational," it is also "*multipositional*," since she or he no longer inhabits a singular identity but a plurality of identities. She or he belongs to multiple communities in view of his or her race, class or gender; that is, his or her identity is "sometimes overlapping, sometimes contradictory."[34]

When I was studying at Vanderbilt University in the United States, I was one of two Chinese Ph.D. students in the Graduate Department of Religion. Some students in the department often categorized us as the "Chinese." Though Yong Chen and I are Chinese, we are very different. In terms of nationality, he is from Mainland China, and I am from Singapore. We are ethnically Chinese, but we are from different countries. He is male, and I am female. As such, we have a plurality of identities, and our social locations are "multipositional." When I was in Singapore, my social location was also multipositional but different because of my interaction with different cultural and racial communities. Now that I have relocated to Taipei, Taiwan, my social location continues to be influenced by the social locations of graduate students who come from different regions in Taiwan. As a result of our physical mobility and association, our social locations are bound to be multipositional and glocal. With the influx of diverse graduate students and biblical schol-

---

33. The title of James Longkumer's dissertation is "Reversals at the Table: A Reading of the Parable of the Great Banquet with Reference to 'the Poor.'"
34. Ibid., 23.

ars with glocal social locations entering the biblical discipline, the practice of graduate biblical studies is compelled to become glocal, too.

My second consideration is related to the first, and it concerns the practice itself. The glocal nature of graduate biblical education is to be seen with reference to Rebecca S. Chopp's understanding of the "particular." On the one hand, for Chopp, the term "particular" refers to the "concreteness and specificities" of a specific interpretation conditioned by the interpreter's own presuppositions, viewpoints and commitments. On the other hand, she asserts that the particular has more than one meaning. In the light of logic, it "designates a proposition that affirms or denies a predicate to a part of the subject."[35] She affirms that her particular vision for feminist theological practices is that it is "not universal to the whole of theology" but that it can open new ways of discussing theological education.[36] Other practices such as narrativity, ecclesiality and mutuality are blended together for shaping the goals and purposes of such a particular vision for feminist theological education.[37]

Chopp's discussion of feminist practices within the framework of theological education is helpful for my discussion of social location and graduate biblical studies. The practice of graduate biblical studies must seek to be local on the one hand; that is, it must be situated in the "concreteness and specificities" of graduate students and biblical scholars. On the other hand, the practice of graduate biblical studies must be global since the world has become "border-less" whereby people and knowledge intersect through space and text. As such, the combination of local and global gives rise to a practice that should be glocal in character.

A GLOCAL PERSPECTIVE: TRANSFORMING GRADUATE BIBLICAL EDUCATION

For graduate biblical education to become a discipline on the "cutting edge" with respect to academic excellence and transformation, biblical scholars, critics and teachers must recognize and acknowledge the interdependence of the "rhetoric of space" and "rhetoric of location." The interconnection of social location and standards of excellence is aptly described in the words

---

35. Rebecca S. Chopp, *Saving Work: Feminist Practices of Theological Education* (Louisville: Westminster John Knox, 1995), 98.
36. Ibid.
37. Ibid., 99–103. For Chopp, narrativity is the writing of one's life and is an ongoing activity. As such, women are writing new narratives all the time. Moreover, Christian narratives are enveloped by ecclesial practices such as the engagement of women and men on the question of ordination in established denominations and creation of feminist liturgies. The mutual practices of narrativity and ecclesiality could give rise to such a particular vision of theological education.

of Friedman, "thinking glocationally involves understanding how the local, the private, and the domestic are constituted in relation to global systems, and conversely how such systems must be read for their particular locational inflection."[38]

The practice of a glocal nature of graduate biblical education poses some challenges to practitioners of biblical studies, be they graduate students or scholars. For some who are used to the traditional practice of biblical criticism, the role of social location is a disruption of the objective approach to the discipline. For them, social location is dis-ease. However for some, the role of social location spells dis-cover(y) since it expands their horizon in the practice of biblical criticism. The social location(s) of graduate students and scholars is set to transform graduate biblical education now and for the future. For me, this is the way to go with regards to standards of excellence and transformation in the practice of graduate biblical education in Asia and the world at large.

---

38. Friedman, "Locational Feminism," 31.

Taking *Spaces* Seriously: The Politics of Space and the Future of Western Biblical Studies

Abraham Smith

Both [reading and writing] require being mindful of the places where imagination sabotages itself, locks its own gates, pollutes its vision. Toni Morrison[1]

I am trying, then, to take space, geopolitical space, seriously. Enrique Dussel[2]

If what one sees depends on where one stands, social-ideological location and rhetorical context are as decisive as text for how one reconstructs historical reality or interprets biblical texts. Elisabeth Schüssler Fiorenza[3]

Every reader brings cultural, social, and personal perspectives to a text, which always influences interpretation. John Donahue[4]

Introduction

In the wake of postanalytic philosophy, postmodernism, feminist criticism, and a variety of other postmethodological studies (from postcolonial stud-

---

1. Toni Morrison, *Playing in the Dark: Whiteness and the Literary Imagination* (Cambridge: Harvard University Press, 1992), xi.
2. Enrique Dussel, *Philosophy of Liberation* (trans. Aquilina Martínez and Christine Morkovsky; Maryknoll, N.Y.: Orbis, 1985), 2. Quoted in Brian Blount, Clarice Martin, Cain Felder, and Emerson Powery, "Introduction," in *True to Our Native Land: An African American Commentary on the New Testament* (ed. Brian Blount, Clarice Martin, Cain Felder, and Emerson Powery; Minneapolis: Fortress, 2007), 3.
3. Elisabeth Schüssler Fiorenza, "The Rhetoricity of Historical Knowledge: Pauline Discourse and Its Contextualizations," in *Religious Propaganda and Missionary Competition in the New Testament World: Essays Honoring Dieter Georgi* (ed. Lukas Bormann, Kelly Del Tredici, and Angela Standhartinger; Leiden: Brill, 1994), 456.
4. John Donahue, "Guidelines for Reading and Interpretation," in *New Interpreter's Study Bible* (ed. Walter Harrelson; New Revised Standard Version; Nashville: Abingdon, 2003), 2261.

ies to diasporic studies and from queer studies to masculinity studies), few scholars of any professional discipline now adhere to the outmoded notions of unquestionable knowledge or disinterested objectivity.[5] Thus, on the one hand, there is a general acceptance of the social constitution of knowledge in all types of investigative practices, an acceptance that virtually entails "the abandonment of the ideals of certainty and of the permanence of knowledge."[6] On the other hand, there is also the general recognition that scholars are constrained to experience reality through the aspects of reality they choose to observe, the intellectual commitments to which they give assent, and the institutional constraints from which they receive support.[7] Scholars are not hermetically sealed from the cultural legacies of the past or the politics of culture in the present. Rather, scholars labor within professional, disciplinary, and institutional constraints, all of which in varying degrees have been shaped by larger cultural formations, ideological perspectives, and geopolitical currents. The same is true with respect to the biblical studies profession as it has evolved in the West, as a plausible charting of its development reveals.

According to Fernando F. Segovia, critical biblical studies in the West has evolved in three stages, with historical criticism as its first stage; literary criticism and (socio)cultural criticism as its second stage; and cultural studies, its present (and) third stage.[8] As critical biblical research in the West has evolved, moreover, it has had to face three significant changes: (1) a demographic shift;

---

5. This chapter takes seriously the fact that the SBL is an Anglophone academy, despite some efforts to extend itself across different linguistic traditions. I also recognize that there is a fundamental difference in the global wealth of the North over the South, which reinforces the need to restrict the defining parameters of the type of biblical studies of which I am a part and which I know best. Finally, it must be said that Anglophone biblical studies, even if it has much to offer those who speak in non-English language traditions, also has much to learn from them as well.

6. Helen E. Longino, *Science as Social Knowledge: Values and Objectivity in Scientific Inquiry* (Princeton: Princeton University Press, 1990), 232. See also Audrey Smedley, *Race in North America: Origin and Evolution of a Worldview* (Boulder, Colo.: Westview, 1999), 3.

7. Longino, *Science as Social Knowledge*, 221.

8. Fernando F. Segovia, "Cultural Studies and Contemporary Biblical Criticism as a Mode of Discourse," in *Social Location and Biblical Interpretation in Global Perspective* (vol. 2 of *Reading from This Place*; ed. Fernando F. Segovia and Mary Ann Tolbert; Minneapolis: Fortress, 1995), 2, 3. Though critical biblical research in the West is a legacy of the Reformation and the Renaissance, it is the Enlightenment period out of which critical modern biblical criticism arose, particularly in the circles of the historicizing Deists and the studious, though fundamentally pragmatic, Pietists. See Richard Pervo, *Profit with Delight: The Literary Genre of the Acts of the Apostles* (Philadelphia: Fortress, 1987), 12. The Protestant Reformation's *sola scriptura* doctrine gave impetus to the democratic study of scripture and to interest in the historical meaning of scripture. See William Baird, *History of New*

(2) a theoretical explosion; and (3) a "spatial turn."⁹ Thus, Western biblical studies has recently witnessed the growth of nonmale and non-Western individuals in its professional societies. Likewise, Western biblical studies has also witnessed an exponential increase in theoretical positions, resulting not in a consensus but in a state of "radical plurality" and a provisional mode of discourse.¹⁰ Most important, the demographic shift and the theoretical explosion have also yielded a "spatial turn," that is, a deeper appreciation for the ways in which "social location" (a concrete set of material conditions or structures of power) affects the cultural production of texts, the strategies by which such texts are read and interpreted, and the flesh-and-blood readers who appropriate such texts.¹¹ Western biblical studies scholars are thus learning to recognize that there is as much need for a radical (thorough) historicization or contextualization of a reader or reading process as there is a need for the historicization or contextualization of a text. To put the matter sharply, "spaces" matter and need to be taken seriously.¹²

Testament Research (Minneapolis: Fortress, 1992), xvi–xix. The Renaissance humanists provided the earliest and perhaps the crudest tools for biblical interpretation.

9. According to Ahn, since the advent of historical criticism, biblical studies has had two significant critical turns. The first turn, a linguistic one, helped biblical studies move away from historical criticism's positivist orientation (the belief that the language of the text simply reflected a reality waiting to be found) to a belief that language was "constitutive of reality." See Yong-Sung Ahn, *The Reign of God and Rome in Luke's Passion Narrative: An East Asian Global Perspective* (Leiden: Brill, 2006), 6. The second, a "spatial" one, according to Ahn (7), helped biblical studies to appreciate the "materiality" of texts, readings of texts, and the flesh-and-blood readers of texts.

10. Segovia, "Cultural Studies," 4. Stuart Hall (*Representation: Cultural Representations and Signifying Practices* [London: Sage, 1997], 6) provides a practical definition of *discourses*: "Discourses are ways of referring to our constructing knowledge about a particular topic of practice: a cluster (or formation) of ideas, images and practices, which provide ways of talking about, forms of knowledge and conduct associated with a particular topic, social activity or institutional site in society. These discursive formations of, and our practices in relation to, a particular subject or site of social activity; what knowledge is considered useful, relevant and 'true' in that context; and what sorts of persons or 'subjects' embody its characteristics." David Theo Goldberg (*Racist Culture: Philosophy and the Politics of Meaning* [Oxford: Blackwell, 1993], 9) avers that *dominant discourses* are the discursive webs "that in the social relations of power at some moment come to assume authority and confer status."

11. The term "spatial turn" refers to the intellectual commitment by various disciplines, including the sciences (both of the life and social varieties), to the role of real or imagined spatial contexts in the formation of knowledge. See, for example, Diarmid Finnegan, "The Spatial Turn: Geographical Approaches in the History of Science," *Journal of the History of Biology* 41 (2008): 369–88.

12. Blount, Martin, Felder, and Powery, "Introduction," 2.

To reflect on the importance of taking spaces seriously in biblical studies, this chapter initially features brief remarks on the politics of space, that is, on "space" as a site of fluid social/power relations. Then, the chapter examines some of the key "spaces" that bear on our profession.

UNDERSTANDING THE POLITICS OF SPACE

Recent developments in theories on "space" by critical cultural geographers and feminist theorists suggest that space must not be understood as a neutral and static background but as a fluid and "dynamic entity, constituted and reconstituted by the interrelations of real people and real communities."[13] Thus, Doreen Massey writes that "[t]he spatial ... is a way of thinking in terms of the ever-shifting geometry of social/power relations."[14] Likewise, Edward Soja writes that "[s]pace exists ontologically as a part of a transformative process, but always remains open to further transformation in the contexts of material life."[15] Santa Arias and Mariselle Meléndez argue, moreover, that representation or the categorization of spaces also entails dynamics of power,

---

13. Johnathan Mauk, "Location, Location, Location," *College English* 65 (2003): 368–88, esp. 378. The transition from traditional geography to the critical theory known as cultural geography may be stated succinctly as follows: With roots in classical antiquity (from the Chinese Liu An of the Han Dynasty to the Egyptian Ptolemy to the Greek Strabo to the Roman Pliny the Elder), modern traditional geography first established itself as a distinct or independent field of thought in the eighteenth and nineteenth centuries. Claudius Ptolemy (second century C.E.) produced the *Geographia*, which "included instructions for making map projections of the world...; suggestions for breaking down the world map into larger-scale sectional maps...; and a list of coordinates for some eight thousand places" (see Norman J. W. Thrower, *Maps and Civilization: Cartography in Culture and Society* [Chicago: University of Chicago Press, 1996], 23). Although the field of geography began with foundationalist assumptions, it has been challenged relatively recently by "interdisciplinary conceptions of space, which conceive it not as a neutral category but as something that is culturally produced, lived and represented in various ways" (Joe Moran, *Interdisciplinarity* [London: Routledge, 2002], 165). According to Moran, who quotes Derek Gregory (*Geographical Imaginations* [Oxford: Blackwell, 1994], 8), these new conceptions, that is, cultural geography, "undermine any tendency to think of the subject as 'a discipline-in-waiting,' whose formation is determined not so much by the internal logic of intellectual inquiry as the imperatives of an 'external' reality." In its latest versions, moreover, cultural geography (or what is known as the new cultural geography) has sought "to focus on the role of space and place in adjudicating cultural power" (Don Mitchell, *Cultural Geography: A Critical Introduction* [Malden, Mass.: Blackwell, 2008], 58).

14. Doreen Massey, *Space, Place, and Gender* (Minneapolis: University of Minnesota Press, 2001), 4. Quoted from Ahn, *Reign of God*, 9.

15. Edward Soja, *Postmodern Geographies: The Reassertion of Space in Critical Social Theory* (New York: Verso, 1989), 122.

often a violent and intrusive use of power, as certainly was the case with "the cultural production of space in Latin America."[16] That is, spatial configuration (or better, *spatial colonization*) is ideological and fraught with dynamics of "appropriation, domination, contestation, or liberation."[17]

Feminist appreciation of "space" includes not only feminist-informed postmodernists who interrogate Enlightenment ideals such as the notion of a universal subject or that of stable epistemological foundations, but also those who interrogate brands of postmodernism that elide a politics of identity altogether with little or no consideration for the material conditions that shape the experiences of women and other marginalized groups. That is, some feminist-informed theorists (e.g., Judith Butler in *Gender Trouble*) recognize that both the notion of an autonomous self and the notion of positivist claims about knowledge are but constructions that issued out of the "space" or the historical realities of both the Renaissance (from which Anglo-European modernity gained its anthropocentric focus) and the Enlightenment (from which it gained its Cartesian philosophical foundation[18] and its mechanistic worldview).[19] Thus, these are not transcendent, atemporal notions. Nor should they be viewed as bases for positing a stable and already fixed identity category known as "women."

Other feminist-informed theorists (e.g., Radha Hedge, Trinh T. Minh-ha, Susan Bordo, Adrienne Rich, and Chela Sandoval), however, are particularly sensitive about a politics of *spatial* erasure that works within some brands of postmodernism itself. Thus, these theorists advocate the strategic value of a "politics of place" or of positionality theory as a way to honor and acknowledge the different and unequal lived struggles of a plurality of women in an

---

16. Santa Arias and Mariselle Meléndez, "Space and the Rhetorics of Power in Spanish America: An Introduction," in *Mapping Colonial Spanish America: Places and Commonplaces of Identity, Culture, and Experience* (ed. Santa Arias and Mariselle Meléndez; Lewisburg, Pa.: Bucknell University Press, 2002), 15.

17. Ibid., 16.

18. Descartes, coming before the Enlightenment, gave modernity the "supposedly" indisputable philosophical foundation, the idea of the value-free subject, i.e., the autonomous thinking self. See Cornel West, *Prophesy Deliverance: An Afro-Revolutionary Christianity* (Philadelphia: Westminster, 1982), 50–53. On postmodernist feminism, see Judith Butler, *Gender Trouble: Feminism and the Subversion of Identity* (New York: Routledge, 1989).

19. Newton's *Mathematical Principles of Natural Philosophy*, unlike the earlier theories of Descartes, Kepler, and Galileo, gave an explanation for the functioning of the *entire* universe.

effort to move toward a more meaningful coalitional feminist politics.[20] These theorists note, moreover, that the strategies that oppressed groups used in the so-called modernist moments are ripe for use in the present era when Empire seems to have moved beyond the invasion exclusively of territorial and cultural spaces and to have invaded bodily limits through its control of the desires of bodies. As Sandoval writes, "The skills, perceptions, theories, and methods developed under previous and modernist conditions of dispossession and colonization are the most efficient and sophisticated means by which all people trapped as insiders-outsiders in the rationality of postmodern social order can confront and retextualize consciousness into new forms of citizenship/subjectivity."[21]

Altogether, then, *space*, whether one refers to a geographical terrain, a physical abode, a body, or an imagined place or community, is a site for the interrogation of geometries of power, of how these relations of power are secured, and also of how they may be "unmasked."[22] How then might biblical scholars take *our spaces* seriously? Toward some answers to this question, we now turn.

Interrogating the Politics of Space in Biblical Studies

Just as poststructuralists and feminists, particularly those influenced by Michel Foucault, have problematized "the intersections of knowledge and power," cultural geographers have further problematized these intersections with a consideration of space.[23] That is, "space, knowledge and power sit at the heart of the ways that contemporary cultural geographers make sense of society."[24] Thus, on the one hand, cultural geographer Henri Lefèbvre writes, "Every discourse says something about space ... and every discourse is emitted from space."[25] On the other hand, cultural geographer David Sibley notes that "established hierarchies of knowledge" seek to control the production of knowledge through territorial control over a discipline, that is, through knowledge compartmentalization, which "insulates the [established] purveyors of

---

20. See, e.g., Chela Sandoval, *Methodology of the Oppressed* (Minneapolis: University of Minnesota Press, 2000), 36.

21. Ibid., 121.

22. On this point, I am indebted to reflections by Renee M. Moreno in "'The Politics of Location': Texts as Opposition," *College* 54 (2002): 225.

23. David Atkinson, Peter Jackson, David Sibley, and Neil Washbourne, eds., *Cultural Geography: A Critical Dictionary of Critical Concepts* (London: Taurus, 2005), 3.

24. Ibid.

25. Henri Lefèbvre, *The Production of Space* (trans. Donald Nicholson Smith; Oxford: Blackwell, 1991), 132.

knowledge from the threat of challenging ideas;" "scientific hierarchization of knowledges," which gives legitimacy to regulated forms and productions of knowledge and disqualification to others; and "differentiating rituals," which control access and entry into a discipline by requiring would-be members of the discipline's club to use only—or at least primarily—prescribed "methods of analysis, styles of communication, and theoretical consistency."[26]

If biblical studies professionals, then, are to take spaces seriously as we move toward the next decade of the third millennium, it is necessary for us to interrogate some of the key spaces that bear on our profession, namely, public spaces, professional spaces, and pedagogical spaces, for these spaces are intricately tied to dynamics of power.

INTERROGATING THE IMPACT OF BIBLICAL STUDIES ON PUBLIC SPACES

Biblical studies in the West may well seem to be a marginal—if not altogether irrelevant—field of study in many public spaces.[27] This claim is not a simplistic assent to the now defunct secularization theory that once predicted the end of religion in Western societies. Nor is it a solipsistic denial of the longevity of the field or of the creative potential of its recent revitalization, the latter of which emanates from the present guild's wider geo-political constituency along with the new set of questions, concerns, and angles of perspectives that the changing demographics furnished. Rather, the claim of marginality or irrelevance is made because with few exceptions the publications of biblical scholars are simply not known and frankly not missed by most publics. That is, most of our publications do not enter onto what Norman Gottwald calls a "common cultural stage" in tone or content with wider communities, including even the faith communities often addressed in the publications.[28]

---

26. Here, I am drawing widely from several parts of Sibley's *Geographies of Exclusion* (London: Routledge, 1995): on "established hierarchies of knowledge," see 116; on knowledge compartmentalization and its insulating effects, see 122; on "scientific hierarchization of knowledges" and its legitimating and disqualifying effects, see 122–23; on "differentiating rituals," see 125; on the prescriptive quality control regulations of methods, writing styles, and theories, see 116.

27. On the marginality of biblical studies, Tat-siong Benny Liew writes: "the entire discipline of biblical studies is marginal, and has been making very little impact on the larger society and world, regardless of whether it is done in minority or mainstream perspectives" ("When Margins become Common Ground: Questions of and for Biblical Studies," in *Still at the Margins: Biblical Scholarship Fifteen Years after the Voices from the Margins* [ed. R. S. Sugirtharajah; London: Continuum, 2008], 50).

28. On the term "common cultural stage," I am indebted to Norman K. Gottwald, "Biblical Scholarship in Public Discourse," *Did* 16.2 (2005): 7–8.

Recognizing the Insularity of Biblical Studies

To enter onto that "common cultural stage," Western biblical studies professionals must first admit the insularity of our work. That is, we must admit how distant our work seems to be from the issues that might really matter to wider publics. Thus, even if biblical studies has assisted in "theological exposition" for one or more religious communities,[29] much of what we write de facto seems primarily designed for other biblical technicians or directed to the institutional review committees that control our professional mobility.[30] As R. S. Sugirtharajah has noted, even our professional meetings are characterized by jargonistic insularity, with few nonbiblical specialists attending or thinking it worth their while to attend.[31] Thus, our work has not sufficiently moved beyond the physical or virtual classroom and the constricting boundaries of particular disciplines and thus domination is often perpetuated through an arrogant and elitist politics of exclusion.

Often, and most devastatingly, even if we desired to make contributions "beyond the classroom and academic publications," as Norman Gottwald has rightly noted, biblical scholars lamentably recognize that "our training as biblicists has often not included enough of a perspective in the humanities and social sciences for us to feel confident about our views on complicated and disputed public issues."[32] Our training, rather, is steeped in a "Romantic quest for origins," a type of historical retrieval that over-problematizes the distance between us and the ancient past.[33] As Susanne Scholz writes, "Historical

---

29. See Stephen Moore, who argues that "theological exposition" has been one of the "primary preoccupations" of the discipline of biblical studies ("A Modest Manifesto for New Testament Literary Criticism: How to Interface with a Literary Studies Field that is Post-literary, Post-theoretical, and Post-methodological," *BibInt* 15 [2007]: 5). In defining "theological exposition," Moore writes: "I mean the meticulous (and potentially infinite) elucidation of the theological themes, perspectives, and agendas of both the narrative and epistolary literature of the New Testament" (5).

30. On the expression "biblical technicians," see Elisabeth Schüssler Fiorenza, "Rethinking the Educational Practices of Biblical Doctoral Studies," *TThRel* 6 (2003): 66. According to Schüssler Fiorenza, academic socialization, whether in theological schools, divinity programs, or religious studies departments, often produces nothing more than technicians.

31. On the seeming irrelevance of biblical studies in the light of the audience constituency at its annual meetings, see R. S. Sugirtharajah, "Scripture, Scholarship, Empire: Putting the Discipline in Its Place," *ExpTim* 117.1 (2005): 5.

32. Gottwald, "Biblical Scholarship," 2.

33. On biblical studies' "Romantic quest for origins," see Melanie Wright, *Moses in America: The Cultural Uses of Biblical Narrative* (Oxford: Oxford University Press, 2003), 8. I should note that I honor the political act of problematizing the distance if one is seek-

criticism allows interpreters to position biblical literature in a distant past, far removed from today's politics, economics, or religion. Although contemporary exclusion of contemporary questions is not an essential requirement of historical methodology, especially not as understood by many historians during the last decades, biblical scholars often continue using historical criticism in a way that keeps the Bible separate from today's world."[34]

Thus, Western biblical professionals must not carve out an antiquarian space of work nor construct an insular and esoteric set of methodological practices to which the wider public has little access, thus, making the Bible "an object of specialty investigation."[35] Instead, we must participate in "the public sphere of ideas" beginning in our own educational institutions where "curricular isolation" often breeds academic insularity and "curricular incoherence" and moving on from there to wider publics.[36]

Rethinking the Role of Western Biblical Studies

Likewise, to enter onto that "common cultural stage" with wider publics, Western biblical studies professionals must radically rethink our role. What if the larger part of our professional task was not what it has been almost exclusively from the Enlightenment until the recent decades, namely, the examination of a biblical text's sources, or its stages of production, or its final form as the text came to be used by one or more ancient audiences, or even of those various readers/auditors themselves? What if we saw our task fundamentally as the interrogation of myths of innocence, the undressing of "well-dressed imperialisms" in everyday institutions and social practices?[37] As the editors

---

ing to demystify familiarity with the worlds of ancient texts as a given. At the same time, I should add, however, that the political act of problematizing historical distance does not free an interpreter from the biases of his or her own times in the very construction of the past. As Mary Ann Tolbert has noted, "the 'reconstruction' of an ancient reading site must be seen as a construction, a probable fiction, based on modern insights and methods, whose relationship to whatever the actual ancient situation was is never direct or unproblematic" (see "When Resistance Becomes Repression: Mark 13:9–27 and the Poetics of Location," in Segovia and Tolbert, *Social Location and Biblical Interpretation*, 343).

34. Susanne Scholz, "'Tandoor Reindeer' and the Limitations of Historical Criticism," in *Her Master's Tools? Feminist and Postcolonial Engagements of Historical-Critical Discourse* (ed. Caroline Vander Stichele and Todd C. Penner; SBLGPBS 9; Atlanta: Society of Biblical Literature, 2004), 48.

35. Wright, *Moses in America*, 9.

36. On these expressions, see Gerald Graff, *Clueless in Academe: How Schooling Obscures the Life of the Mind* (New Haven: Yale University Press, 2003), 72, 76.

37. On "well-dressed imperialisms" or the ways in which hegemony hides under the cloak of seemingly acceptable practices, see Michael Eric Dyson, *Open Mike: Reflections on*

of *The Bible in the Public Square* have recently written, "As public intellectuals and members of a larger civic conversation broader than the professional guild, biblical scholars have a responsibility to take … [the public square] into their work and use their specialized knowledge for the good of the wider community."[38]

This move from insularity would mean that we would now use our analytical skills—as public intellectuals—to help to expose the full panoply of power arrangements in biblical discourse, whether our attention is devoted to texts, interpreters, or the larger productive processes that seek to control thought, desire, and behavior. Accordingly, our work as public intellectuals could include the interrogation of the *toxic texts* of the Bible, those texts that either condone ecologically irresponsible behavior or promote acts of violence against human formation groups. Given the ways in which the biblical texts we study are enmeshed in the toxicity of empire, we could help to expose how biblical texts often "re-inscribe the structures of domination" even when/if the biblical texts are in some ways also resistant straightforwardly or subtly.[39] For example, Luke-Acts is powerfully alluring. Its notion of powerful reversals strikes a chord within historically victimized persons; the deeper dimensions of Luke's reversal claim, however, remain largely unexplored and often naively accepted. Examples of this phenomenon would be Luke's agonistic reckoning of the universe, and Luke's romanticist complicity with and reification of the dominant discourse.[40] Indeed, the lure overshadows the degree to which the plausibility and seduction of reversal depends itself on the incorporation of certain imperialist images that continue to structure and support forms of oppression. Toward the service of wider publics, then, we would need to demystify the empire in Luke and, as noted by Elisabeth Schüssler Fiorenza, "to investigate and study the interplay of biblical imperial language and ethos with contemporary public discourses."[41]

Well-dressed imperialisms, though, come in other shapes and forms. They also come in the form of *toxic interpretations of biblical texts*. As public intellectuals, then, our role is also to demystify or disrobe the "well-dressed imperialisms" of interpretations that support violence and exploitation. Here,

---

Philosophy, Race, Sex, Culture and Religion (New York: Basic Civitas, 2003), 76.

38. Cynthia Briggs Kittredge, Ellen Bradshaw Aitken, and Jonathan A. Draper, "Introduction," in *The Bible in the Public Square* (ed. Cynthia Briggs Kittredge, Ellen Bradshaw Aitken, and Jonathan A. Draper; Minneapolis: Fortress, 2008), 2.

39. Elisabeth Schüssler Fiorenza, "Reading Scripture in the Context of Empire," in Briggs Kittredge, Aitken, and Draper, *The Bible in the Public Square*, 160.

40. On the luring potential of texts, see Lennard J. Davis, *Ideology and Fiction: Resisting Novels* (New York: Methuen, 1987), 10–23.

41. Schüssler Fiorenza, "Reading Scripture in the Context of Empire," 161.

again though, our focus would not be an antiquarian interest in the biblical texts, but an examination of the ways in which the Bible has been received to support or justify imperial social hierarchies and expansionist/exploitative power configurations.

For example, we could trace the many examples of the use of the Bible to exploit the indigenous populations of the Americas. As Elsa Tamez has noted, indeed the Bible has been used as a tool of exploitation since the time of the conquistadores (or conquerors) who justified their invasion of Abia Yala (the land mass once called the "Good Earth" in the Kuna language but now called the "Americas") with appeals to the so-called conquest of Canaan.[42] Likewise, Robert Warrior, without dismissing the inspirational value of the Exodus story for various liberation theologies (from Latin America to the United States), avers that the Exodus story must also be read from the perspective of the Canaanites.[43] In so doing, one discovers that the deity of the story is not only "God the Liberator" but "God the Conqueror," that is, someone who deploys "the same power used against the enslaving Egyptians to defeat the indigenous inhabitants of Canaan." [44] One also discovers, moreover, that in U.S. history, the Exodus narrative (read in conjunction with the so-called "Conquest" story) supported "America's self-image as a 'chosen people'" even as it justified the genocide of indigenous people, as if the Native Americans were the Canaanites of old.[45]

Similarly, G. E. Thomas has noted not only how the Massachusetts General Court forbade Indians to practice their own religion but also how Jonathan Winthrop, governor of the Massachusetts Bay Colony, justified the

---

42. Elsa Tamez, "The Bible and Five Hundred Years of Conquest," in *God's Economy* (ed. Ross Kinsler and Gloria Kinsler; Maryknoll, N.Y.: Orbis, 2005), 5. Cuna is the language of the Kuna Indians, an indigenous group native to Latin America and now residing mostly in Panama and Columbia. On the Kuna Indians, see Michael Prior, *The Bible and Colonialism: A Moral Critique* (Sheffield: Sheffield Academic Press, 1997), 48. On the conquistadores, note that Genessi Sepulvedae (aka Juan Ginés de Sepúlveda) and others appealed to the Bible (e.g., "the Deuteronomic war codes" that justified Canaanite expulsion) to support war against indigenous people, thus providing a basis for the "future evangelization" of these people and a theological basis for an Iberian settlement that brought forced labor and disease and ultimately "caused a massive fall in the native population," perhaps by as many as 10–12 million (Prior, *Bible and Colonialism*, 55–64). On these codes, see Prior, *Bible and Colonialism*, 65; Luis N. Rivera, *A Violent Evangelism: The Political and Religious Conquest of the Americas* (Louisville: Westminster John Knox, 1992), 237.

43. Robert Warrior, "Canaanites, Cowboys, and Indians," *USQR* 59 (2005): 1–8; also found in Robert Allen Warrior, "Canaanites, Cowboys, and Indians: Deliverance, Conquest, and Liberation Theology Today," *Christianity and Crisis* 49 (1989): 261–65.

44. Warrior, "Canaanites, Cowboys, and Indians," 2–3.

45. Ibid., 7.

exploitation of Native American land in the light of the book of Genesis.[46] He writes that the "Puritan philosophy of land ownership and use was enshrined by law in 1633 when the General Court of Massachusetts ordered that 'what lands any of the Indians have possessed and improved, by subduing the same they have a just right according to that in Genesis.' Implicit was the assumption that any land not so 'subdued' could not rightfully be claimed by the Indians, or kept from the whites."[47]

Furthermore, according to George Tinker, even if some early Christian missionaries (e.g., John Eliot, Juníper Serra, Pierre-Jean De Smet, and Henry Benjamin Whipple) condemned physical assaults against Native Americans, they still supported cultural imperialism and cultural genocide.[48] That is, through the "conquest of conversion," the missionaries were engaged in "the effective destruction of a people by systematically or systemically (intentionally or unintentionally in order to achieve other goals) destroying, eroding, or undermining the integrity of the culture and system of values that defines a people and gives them life."[49] The immigrant missionaries, with a view of themselves "as the New Israel," moreover, reckoned themselves as superior to Native Americans.[50]

Moreover, according to Sylvester Johnson, white colonists questioned the human status of Native Americans (that is, they claimed initially that Native Americans were without religion and thus, in their colonizing logic, not really human) and they regarded the "settlement" territory as an "empty wilderness," both strategies of which helped them to justify the extermination of millions of Native Americans.[51] In *Traits of Resemblance* (1799), as noted by Johnson, Abiel Abbot, a minister, actually read the death-by-disease of thirty thousand

---

46. G. E. Thomas, "Puritanism, Indians, and the Concept of Race," *New England Quarterly* 48 (1975): 5.

47. Ibid., 11.

48. George Tinker, *Missionary Conquest: The Gospel and Native American Cultural Genocide* (Minneapolis: Fortress, 1993).

49. Ibid., viii, 6.

50. Ibid., viii.

51. Sylvester A. Johnson, "New Israel, New Canaan: The Bible, the People of God, and the American Holocaust," *JFSR* 22 (2006): 36–37. On the faulty colonizing logic that declared Native Americans and others to be without religion and therefore not really human, see David Chidester, *Savage Systems: Colonialism and Comparative Religion in Southern Africa* (Charlottesville: University Press of Virginia, 1996). Of course, Christopher Columbus's first assessment of the Western hemisphere inhabitants led him to use this faulty logic, as is suggested by the following: "I think they can easily be made Christians, for they seem to have no religion" (quoted in Tinker, *Missionary Conquest*, 8).

Native Americans as providential, as the deity's work "to make room for … English" just as God had made a way for ancient Israel.[52]

Obviously, the toxic interpretations of the Bible against the indigenous in the Americas in the past is but one example of a hundred stories that could be told of its use to mask over machineries of exploitation or to make the annihilation of "others" appear benign and acceptable. To the list of masked machineries of domination one could add the use of the Bible to support British and Boer settlements in southern Africa, to (try to) induce docility in enslaved Africans in North America, to authorize the disfranchisement of women in the U.S., to de-Judaize the German church in support of Hitler's Nordic Aryan policies against the Jews, to corral options of sexuality under the restrictive regulating ideals of heteronormativity, or to support the so-called prosperity gospel movement that seductively packages capitalist values and preys on the poor and vulnerable throughout the world.[53]

Yet another type of "well-dressed imperialism" would be the seductive productive processes of the market's forces, processes that seek to control the desires, orientation, and values of a variety of publics. To understand these processes, though, a few words are in order about the changing face of Western empire-building. As Fernando F. Segovia has noted, since the sixteenth century, Western empire-building has roughly witnessed three periods: early imperialism, a mercantilist phase from the sixteenth through eighteenth centuries; high imperialism, a monopoly capitalism phase that lasted from the nineteenth to the mid-twentieth century; and late imperialism, a neo-imperial and neo-colonial phase lasting from the mid-twentieth century to the present.[54] From roughly 1959 to 1989, late imperialism stripped wealth from and controlled the fortunes of many poor countries in Latin America through

---

52. Johnson, "New Israel, New Canaan," 33–34.

53. On the British and Boer settlements in southern Africa, see Prior, *The Bible and Colonialism*, 71–105. On the use of the Bible to support slavery, to sanction the subordination of women to men, and to endorse heteronormativity, see Mary Ann Tolbert, "A New Teaching with Authority: A Re-evaluation of the Authority of the Bible," in *Teaching the Bible: The Discourses and Politics of Biblical Theology* (ed. Fernando F. Segovia and Mary Ann Tolbert; Maryknoll, N.Y.: Orbis, 1998), 172–73. On the use of the Bible to dejudaize the German church, see Susannah Heschel, *The Aryan Jesus: Christian Theologians and the Bible in Nazi Germany* (Princeton: Princeton University Press, 2008). According to Robert Franklin, "The 'gospel of prosperity' refers to the cultural ideology or message that suggests that the accumulation of material possessions, wealth, and prosperity are morally neutral goods that are necessary for human happiness" (*Crisis in the Village: Restoring Hope in African American Communities* [Minneapolis: Fortress, 2007], 117).

54. Fernando F. Segovia, "Postcolonial and Diasporic Criticism in Biblical Studies: Focus, Parameters, Relevance," *Studies in World Christianity* 5 (1999): 183.

U.S. support of unjust military-led governments in these countries and eventually through U.S. controlled financial organizations (such as the IMF, the WTO, and the World Bank) that imposed structural adjustment programs on countries that were saddled with foreign debt.[55] Late imperialism now also supports neo-liberalism, a set of policies ideologically presupposing an unlimited faith in the market, materially favoring free trade in a globally integrated economy, and politically ceding control over a nation-state's economy and labor force to transnational corporations, the latter of which often operate with impunity and "present themselves as patrons of a 'global village'" despite their excessive production demands, exploitative workplace conditions, and horrendous environmental abuses.[56]

Moreover, the new imperialism also supports the "marketization of the Bible," that is, the production and dissemination of "niche market Bibles."[57] Ostensibly, the recent Bible boom seeks to meet the needs of specific age-groups or specific ethnic groups. In truth, however, the values endorsed are often Western and individualistic, with one Bible (*Revolve*, designed for teenage girls) actually offering fashion tips based on Bible passages.[58] Furthermore, the market knows well how to foster what Rebecca Todd Peters asserts is "a superficial celebration of ethnicity," with the market simply trading "on the exchange of cultural capital" for a profit without moving to a "deeper and more nuanced approach to engaging difference."[59] As public intellectuals, then, biblical scholars will need to unmask the latest round of "well-dressed imperialisms," to examine what may only appear to be an innocuous attempt to celebrate diversity but at a deeper level is simply another attempt to export values and turn a profit.

---

55. For late imperialism's effect on Meso-America (Mexico, Central America, and the Caribbeans, and I think one could extend the parameters to much of the larger category of Latin America), I am indebted to Jorge Pixley, "Exodus," in *Global Bible Commentary* (ed. Daniel Patte, J. Severino Croatto, Nicole Wilkinson Duran, Teresa Okure, and Archie Chi Chung Lee; Nashville: Abingdon, 2004), 17.

56. On these comments on neoliberalism, I am indebted to Rebecca Todd Peters, "The Future of Globalization: Seeking Pathways of Transformation," *Journal of the Society of Christian Ethics* 24 (2004): 105–33. For the quote on transnational corporations, I am indebted to Gerald West, "Disguising Defiance in Rituals of Subordination: Literary and Community-Based Resources for Recovering Resistance Discourses within the Dominant Discourses of the Bible," in *Reading Communities Reading Scripture: Essays in Honor of Daniel Patte* (ed. Gary A. Phillips and Nicole Wilkinson Duran; Harrisburg, Pa.: Trinity Press International, 2002), 199.

57. Sugirtharajah, "Scripture, Scholarship, Empire," 9.
58. Ibid., 10.
59. Todd Peters, "The Future of Globalization," 111.

INTERROGATING THE PROFESSIONAL SPACES OF BIBLICAL STUDIES

Professional disciplines in the West cannot be read apart from the historical context and spaces of modernism in which they arose and developed. Thus, an interrogation of the professional spaces of biblical studies in the West requires first a few words about modernism. Despite whatever good has come out of modernism, as its defenders would purport, it cannot be dismissed that modernity—from Descartes (1596–1650) to the Enlightenment (1688–1789) and to positivism's rise in the late nineteenth century—has had an "underside," that is, that it has been connected to hegemonic cultural ideals and brutal/racialist practices.[60] Unquestionably, modernism in the West did bring about freedom from some of the dogmatic practices of the medieval past. With the "Cartesian turn to subjectivity" (the inward turn to the knowing subject) and a celebration of human reason,[61] a new Archimedean point became the basis for knowledge in the West, a point that replaced traditional authorities like "the Bible, the church, and or the philosopher."[62] Furthermore, modernism has indeed brought "impressive advances in universal education, literacy, and learning," technological innovations that have reduced the proliferation of disease, and has spawned various democratic revolutions.[63]

On the underside, however, the Enlightenment's celebration of reason also "collapsed differences of culture, race and religious orientation into a uniform and Eurocentric mode of being, valuing and knowing by generating theories that were taken to be universally true and socially efficacious."[64] The result was that the West now had ostensibly a legitimate, epistemological base for maintaining "the hegemony of the West over the other traditions that Europeans were beginning to encounter in Asia, in Africa, and in the Americas."[65] In Foucault's words, non-Western traditions became "subjugated knowledges,"

---

60. Carol Wayne White, *Poststructuralism, Feminism, and Religion: Triangulating Positions* (Amherst, N.Y.: Humanity Books, 2002), 7; on some of the discrete stages of modernity, see 4–6. On the dates for the Enlightenment, see Cornel West, "Race and Modernity," in *The Cornel West Reader* (New York: Basic Civitas, 1999).

61. White, *Poststructuralism, Feminism, and Religion*, 4.

62. Ibid. Joining this new epistemology or basis for knowing was Kant, as given in his *Critique of Pure Reason*, for he celebrated reason and placed value in the human subject as opposed to "traditional religious thought" (ibid., 5).

63. Ibid., 6.
64. Ibid., 8.
65. Ibid.

that is, ways of knowing that were deemed to be epistemologically inferior to Western ways of knowing.[66]

Similarly, in seeing its own Enlightenment ideals as superior, the West also looked on non-Westerners as "uncivilized," dependent, and exploitable. So, even if the West supported a doctrine of "liberal humanism" (with the idea of "the universal rights of humans"), the West's view of itself as superior and "civilized" "spawned a distinct set of discursive formations and cultural practices that justified unjust capitalist social relations in the West and their extension, via colonialism and imperialism, to other societies."[67] Thus, (Western-based) reason became racialized.

As Cornel West has noted, the racialized discourse assumed by the writers of the Enlightenment period was possible because three earlier historical processes fused, namely, "the scientific revolution, the Cartesian transformation of philosophy and the classical revival."[68] The scientific revolution (in the work of Copernicus, Kepler, Galileo, Newton, Descartes and Leibniz) "signified the authority of science;" the Cartesian transformation gave the important "gaze" of the value-free subject; and the classical revival furnished an ideal or standard against which to judge contemporary values.[69] The fusion gave authority or a "normative gaze" to those disciplines (phrenology and physiognomy) that used skin color to support an essentialist and hierarchic distinction between European people (based on classical ideals of beauty) and non-European others.[70] The consequence for such Enlightenment writers as Montesquieu, Voltaire, Hume, Jefferson and Kant, according to West, was the ready assumption that their racist views needed no proof.[71]

Yet the racialized discourse not only affected phrenology and physiognomy. According to Shawn Kelley, race affected all "the humanistic disciplines that study culture: history, philosophy, and literature."[72] For Kelley, moreover, these latter disciplines directly affected the emergence of biblical studies.[73] Thus, biblical studies emerged in the web of racialized discourse; as such, it is understandable that recent empire-critical thought, whether advanced by feminist critics, postcolonial critics, or others, has noted the geometries of

---

66. See Foucault's *Power/Knowledge: Selected Interviews and Other Writings*, (ed. Colin Gordon; trans. Colin Gordon et al.; New York: Pantheon, 1980), 81–82.
67. White, *Poststructuralism, Feminism, and Religion*, 8–9.
68. Cornel West, *Prophesy Deliverance*, 50.
69. Ibid., 50–53.
70. Ibid., 57–59.
71. Ibid., 61.
72. Shawn Kelley, *Racializing Jesus: Race, Ideology and the Formation of Modern Biblical Scholarship* (London: Routledge, 2002), 30.
73. Ibid.

power in Western professional biblical discourse outside of the space of the U.S. That is, one can raise questions about the emergence of biblical studies in the West roughly at the same time that discourses of domination arose in the so-called Enlightenment to justify "the political position of imperial Europe."[74]

Given the racist "Western imperialist practices" that ranked the "mental and moral capacities" of human beings in accordance with rigid essentialist taxonomies "all under the guise of objective scientific 'knowledge' about race, sex, and sexuality,"[75] Paul, for example, was separated from his own native Judaism and assumed to be the creator of a *superior* "new, universal, and spiritual religion," namely, Christianity, while Judaism itself, at least in the tradition of Georg Wilhelm Friedrich Hegel's (and biblical scholar F. C. Baur's) racialized discourse, was seen as the separatist, parochial, and *inferior* "other."[76]

Furthermore, D. F. Strauss's two-volume *Life of Jesus* (1835–1836), reaction to which set off a spate of "lives" of Jesus, was written "as a part of a national, German program."[77] Similarly, Ernest Renan, a French specialist in philology, wrote his own life of Jesus (*Vie de Jésus*, 1863) in the context of official trips to Palestine supported by the French government.[78] As Halvor Moxnes notes, "Renan's travels to the country of the Gospels were immersed in a context of empire, with French military and political presence and domination in the area."[79]

Yet, within the U.S. (or what eventually became known as the U.S.), the geometries of power have also operated in biblical criticism with a "civilizing" if not also an "orientalist" function. Acknowledgment of this early history

---

74. Ibid. Cf. Elisabeth Schüssler Fiorenza, *Jesus and the Politics of Interpretation* (New York: Continuum, 2000), 20–25, 89; R. S. Sugirtharajah, *Postcolonial Criticism and Biblical Interpretation* (Oxford: Oxford University, 2002), 26.

75. Denise Kimber Buell and Caroline Johnson Hodge, "The Politics of Interpretation: The Rhetoric of Race and Ethnicity in Paul," *JBL* 123 (2004): 239.

76. Richard A. Horsley, "Introduction," in *Paul and the Roman Imperial Order* (ed. Richard A. Horsley; Harrisburg, Pa.: Trinity Press International, 2004), 1. On Hegel and Baur, see Kelley, *Racializing Jesus*, 76–77; John M. G. Barclay, "'Neither Jew nor Greek': Multiculturalism and the New Perspective on Paul," in *Ethnicity and the Bible* (ed. Mark G. Brett; Boston: Brill, 2002), 197.

77. Halvor Moxnes, "Renan's *Vie de Jésus* as representation of the Orient," in *Jews, Antiquity, and the Nineteenth Century Imagination* (ed. Hayim Lapin and Dale B. Martin; Bethesda, Md.: University of Maryland Press, 2003), 88.

78. Ibid., 89.

79. Ibid. As studies of archaeology attest, moreover, the evolution of that discipline was not a "natural" pursuit. Rather, the discipline developed to support "myths of origins," especially "during the nineteenth century, the heyday of nation-building in Europe" (Philip L. Kohl, "Nationalism and Archaeology: On the Constructions of Nations and the Reconstructions of the Remote Past," *Annual Review of Anthropology* 27 [1998]: 223–46, esp. 228.

is important for the future of biblical studies in the U.S. because the history bespeaks the need for biblical studies to pay attention to the ways in which its professional products and methodologies are not free from spatial orientations and configurations of power.[80] Thus, the reconstruction of the past of U.S. biblical criticism—even what is surely a contested and imagined past and not history in a moralistic *Grand Tradition* key—may reveal the ways in which the seemingly ordinary and natural products and productions of our profession are already tied to culture-specific relations of power.[81]

Professional biblical criticism in the United States is largely a product of the U.S. higher educational system as that system evolved from the first colonial colleges to the development of professional schools to the emergence of

---

80. The late public intellectual Edward Said scrutinizes the whole institution of Orientalism (the colonial and imperial process by which Westerners legitimated nationalistic hierarchies over Arabs and Indians or others in the ideologically constructed "space" called the "Orient") and its supportive infrastructure of foundations and centers. Said exposed the connection between power and knowledge, i.e., the ways in which Western canonical cultural productions of knowledge (e.g., Joseph Conrad's *Heart of Darkness*) were solidly tied to colonial structures of domination and subjugation. See Edward Said, *Orientalism* (New York: Vintage, 1978), 301–2. According to Kelley (*Racializing Jesus*, 24), Said demonstrated the "dissemination of racist thought into the very fabric of high European culture." According to Tat-siong Benny Liew, moreover, Said exposed the cultural violence of colonialism as it works its way through discourses that construe colonized subjects as inferior. Still, in some ways, Said did not go far enough. First, he focused on British and French productions of legitimation, not on German or U.S. forms. Second, as Liew argues ("Postcolonial Criticism: Echoes of a Subaltern's Contribution and Exclusion," in *Mark and Method: New Approaches in Biblical Studies* [2nd ed.; ed. Janice Capel Anderson and Stephen D. Moore; Minneapolis: Fortress, 2008], 214), Said "offers few if any alternatives for or accounts of resistance," which is one of the reasons that Gayatri Chakravorty Spivak's postcolonial work is important. That is, her work highlights "the agency and resistance of the rural peasantry in India against British colonialism" (214). See Gayatri Chakravorty Spivak, *In Other Worlds: Essays in Cultural Politics* (New York: Methuen, 1987).

81. Obviously, a different story could be told if one traced the history of biblical studies in Canada or another part of the West or if one examined the history of Roman Catholic biblical scholarship. Both the page limits for the chapter and the spaces in which I have been taught limit my ability to offer a respectable history for these other dimensions of Western biblical studies. See, however, these important works: John S. Moir, *A History of Biblical Studies in Canada: A Sense of Proportion* (SBLBSNA 7; Chico, Calif.: Scholars Press, 1982); Gerald P. Fogarty, *American Catholic Biblical Scholarship: A History from the Early Republic to Vatican II* (San Francisco: Harper & Row, 1989). For a critique of the moralistic *Grand Tradition* view of history, the view in which a historian thinks that history has a transcendent moral truth hidden in it, see David Harlan, *The Degradation of American History* (Chicago: University of Chicago Press, 1997), xviii.

the modern U.S. university.[82] Accordingly, in the first phase, from the founding of the earliest liberal arts colleges such as Harvard (1636), William and Mary (1692), and Yale (1701) to the rise of yet several other such colleges from the 1740s roughly to the mid-eighteenth century, biblical criticism was largely inchoate in its infancy and a part of a so-called "civilizing" ideal.[83] That is, the limited biblical criticism that obtained in school coursework served the interests primarily though not exclusively of a white, male Protestant clergy, and featured training in textual criticism and classical and biblical language

---

82. Yet another way to write the history of the introduction of biblical studies in the U.S. is traced by J. Albert Harrill. He asserts that the intellectual environment of the fermentation of biblical studies in the late nineteenth century had already been seeded by several cultural factors: (1) Deism; (2) Unitarianism; (3) the rise of the natural sciences; and (4) an often neglected factor in historical treatments of the subject: responses to slavery ("The Use of the New Testament in the American Slave Controversy," *Religion and American Culture* 10 [2000]: 149–86).

83. Time will not permit me to mention in detail the "civilized" mindset that accompanied the English to the so-called New World. That is, in the mid-sixteenth century, the English had already viewed the Irish as "savages," and the English brought that mentality with them to the so-called New World. On the English colonization of the Irish, see Peter Mancall, *Envisioning America: English Plans for the Colonization of North America, 1580–1640* (Boston: St. Martin's, 1995). On the English Anglo-Norman Protestant view of the Irish as "savages," see Audrey Smedley, *Race in North America: Origin and the Evolution of a Worldview* (Boulder, Colo.: Westview, 1999), 84–88. Given that higher education in what would become the U.S. began in Puritan New England, a word is in order about the Puritans. Inspired by Calvin and other "magisterial reformers," the sixteenth- and seventeenth-century English Puritans sought to purify the Anglican church from all vestiges of the Roman Church that could not be warranted by scripture. See Mark Valeri and John F. Wilson, "Scripture and Society: From Reform in the Old World to Revival in the New," in *The Bible in American Law, Politics, and Political Rhetoric* (ed. James Turner Johnson; SBLBAC 4; Chico, Calif.: Scholars Press, 1985), 13. Armed with a covenantal theology (a belief that God had established a covenant with them as with ancient Israel) and a typological reading of the Bible, they first sought to make a New Israel in Old England in the so-called Old World. When their efforts failed there, however, they set their sights on the so-called New World and crossed the Atlantic to realize their religious and political program in New England (Valeri and Wilson, "Scripture and Society," 21). According to George M. Marsden, moreover, the Puritans established Harvard six years after beginning their Massachusetts settlement because "[h]igher education was for them a high priority in civilization building" (*The Soul of the American University: From Protestant Establishment to Established Nonbelief* [New York: Oxford University Press, 1984], 33). Marsden also notes that the founders of Harvard were "an old-boy network of Emmanuel graduates" (one of the colleges in Cambridge, England, in which the Puritans of England sought "to push the English settlement to a more Calvinistic conclusion") and that the key theological textbook, the *Medulla Theologica*, in which Harvard's first students were trained was written by a militant Puritan, William Ames (39).

acquisition (and grammatical and linguistic analysis)—all of which were in the service of erudition, political persuasion and disputation, anti-Romanist and Protestant vindication, "orientalist" fascination, and "gentlemanly" status distinction.[84] As a discourse, then, biblical criticism in this initial phase instrumentally supported relations of power as mostly eastern elite males defined themselves culturally (and thus *spatially*) apart from all "others."[85]

---

84. According to Marsden, for a little over a hundred years after the founding of Harvard College in 1636, Harvard and Yale (established in 1701) were "all there was to [U.S.] American higher education" (*Soul of the American University*, 48); on the formation of other schools in and beyond the colonial era, see 57; on the interests served in the colonial era colleges, see 50. On the training in the first U.S. colleges, see Thomas Olbricht, "Biblical Primitivism in American Biblical Scholarship, 1630-1870," in *The American Quest for the Primitive Church* (ed. Richard T. Hughes; Urbana: University of Illinois Press, 1988), 82. On the elitist and "gentlemanly" social functions of the earliest U.S. colleges, see Caroline Winterer, *The Culture of Classicism: Ancient Greece and Rome in American Intellectual Life, 1780-1910* (Baltimore: Johns Hopkins University Press, 2002), 10-29, esp. 20-21. On the use of early biblical criticism to vindicate "the Protestant movement against Roman Catholic claims," see Judith A. Berling, *Understanding Other Religious Worlds: A Guide for Interreligious Education* (Maryknoll, N.Y. : Orbis, 2004), 50. It should be stated, moreover, that the New Englanders saw themselves as a part of English Protestantism. As Anders Stephanson has stated: "English Protestantism, early on, had developed a notion of England as not only spatially but also spiritually separate from the European continent, as the bastion of true religion and chief source of its expansion: a place divinely singled out for higher missions. The Separatists who crossed the Atlantic [into New England] were part of this tradition, only more radical. Old England, in their eyes, had not broken in the end with the satanic ways of popery" (*Manifest Destiny: American Expansionism and the Empire of Right* [New York: Hill & Wang, 1995], 3-4). On the "orientalism" of the colonial period, Malini Johar Schueller writes: "Harvard College from its very inception, required the study of such languages as Chaldee and Syriac. Such learning did much to awaken interest in the oriental churches in Syria and Lebanon, leading to the first foray of missionary activity in the region in the early nineteenth century" (*U.S. Orientalisms: Race, Nation, and Gender in Literature, 1790-1890* [Ann Arbor: University of Michigan Press, 1998], 24). As for the figures of biblical criticism in this period, they are few and would include such persons as Charles Chauncy (great-grandson of one of the early presidents of Harvard College by the same name) and Jonathan Mayhew. See Jerry Wayne Brown, *The Rise of Biblical Criticism in America, 1800-1870* (Middletown, Ct.: Wesleyan University Press, 1969), 6.

85. If the Church of England, in its sacralization of history, saw itself as an elect people and their nation as an elect nation chosen by God, New England Puritan immigrants desacralized England and saw their migration across the Atlantic as an exodus. For those who established settlements in Virginia, however, the biblical type was not Exodus but Gen 12:1-3, for they retained their view of England as elect, with their migration simply being an extension of "England's mission in America." On these ideas and the quoted material, see Avihu Zakai, *Exile and Kingdom: History and Apocalypse in the Puritan Migration to America* (Cambridge: Cambridge University Press, 1992), 56-68.

In the second phase, beginning in the late eighteenth century but mostly in the early nineteenth century, U.S. schools witnessed an era of professionalization.[86] Thus, there emerged several professional schools (medical schools, law schools, technical schools [for example, military academies, or engineering schools], teachers colleges, and seminaries).[87] In the case of seminaries, which were the first true professional schools to emerge, some of them developed as free-standing, separate institutions (such as Andover Theological Seminary); others developed as divinity schools attached to larger educational institutions (as in the case of Harvard Divinity School or Yale Divinity School); and some later evolved into larger liberal arts institutions (as in the case of Drew and Dubuque).[88]

Aided by or positioned against the innovations of "higher criticism" (historical criticism) in Germany, many of these schools offered biblical criticism to defend their denominational and doctrinal perspectives.[89] Thus, for example, when the Unitarians gained control of Harvard College over the moderate Calvinists, the Congregationalists formed Andover Theological Seminary, a school whose major biblical scholar, Moses Stuart, and one of his students, Edward Robinson, who taught at Andover and Union, would play a pivotal role in the shaping of biblical studies in the U.S. for years to come.[90]

---

86. Burton J. Bledstein, *The Culture of Professionalism: The Middle Class and the Development of Higher Education in America* (New York: Norton, 1976), 80–92.

87. For this list, see Christopher Jencks and David Riesman, *The Academic Revolution* (Garden City, N.Y.: Doubleday, 1969), 199–236. See also William Warren Sweet, "The Rise of Theological Schools in America," *American Society of Church History* 6 (1937): 260.

88. Marsden, *Soul of the American University*, 211. On this evolution, see Jencks and Riesman, *The Academic Revolution*, 211. Sweet ("Rise of Theological Schools in America," 260) notes that the first law school was established the same year as the founding of the first theological school but at the time "the courses [for the law school students] were loosely organized and there was no definitely prescribed amount of work required for graduation and no academic requirement for the practice of law." Neither the first law school nor the first seminary (New Brunswick Theological Seminary) were graduate institutions. The first graduate theological seminary was Andover Theological School (now Andover-Newton after its merger with Newton Theological Seminary in 1965). See Sweet, "The Rise of Theological Schools in America," 266.

89. Olbricht, "Biblical Primitivism," 88–91.

90. On the forces in the formation of Andover Theological School and on Stuart's pivotal role, see Olbricht, "Biblical Primitivism," 88–94. On the moderate Calvinists, see Marsden, *Soul of the American University*, 182. The story of Andover Theological Seminary, of course, must be told in the light of the liberal criticism at Harvard. That is, New England biblical criticism in that period largely went in two directions: a liberal tradition, espoused by Joseph Stevens Buckminster (Harvard's first Dexter Lecturer of Biblical Criticism, 1811), William Ellery Channing, Edward Everett (who would later become a President of

In the second place, moreover, the interests of these two influential biblical scholars were not solely for the advancement of scholarship. Certainly both men advanced biblical scholarship, often with meager resources and under difficult circumstances. Both men were also distinguished biblical scholars who drew on German scholarship to support their conservative positions.[91] As professors at Andover, however, both scholars were also required to take a pledge that mandated each professor's work to be—in the words of the pledge—"in opposition not only to atheists and infidels ... but to Jews, Papists, Mahommetans, Arians, Pelagians, Antinomians, Arminians, Socinians, Sabellians, Unitarians, and Universalists, and to all other heresies and errors, ancient and modern, which may be opposed to the gospel of Christ or hazardous to the souls of men."[92]

More tellingly, both scholars were also members of the American Oriental Society, which "was established in Boston for 'the cultivation of learning in the Asiatic, African, and Polynesian languages.'"[93] This learned society, as indicated in the opening address of its first president, John Pickering, a Hebrew and Greek specialist, was linked both to missionary activity and to a "civilizing" orientation. Thus, on the one hand, in his address to the "Gentlemen of the American Oriental Society," Pickering writes: "in the wisdom of Providence has it happened, that, while the propagation of Christianity, on the one hand, is opening to us new sources of information in different languages-which are the essential instruments of all knowledge-on the other hand, the progressive acquisition of those languages is constantly placing in our hands new means of disseminating religious instruction."[94] On the other hand, he also writes: "It is also our intention to extend our inquiries beyond the East-

---

Harvard University), Andrews Norton, and George R. Noyes; and a conservative (moderate Calvinist) tradition, espoused by Moses Stuart and his students, Edward Robinson and Josiah Willard Gibbs. See Brown, *Rise of Biblical Criticism*, 8.

91. On Moses Stuart, see John H. Giltner, *Moses Stuart: The Father of Biblical Science in America* (SBLBSNA 14; Atlanta: Scholars Press, 1988). On Edward Robinson, see Jay G. Williams, *The Education of Edward Robinson* (New York: Union Theological Seminary, 1997).

92. The creed is mentioned in Henry K. Rowe, *History of Andover Theological Seminary* (Newton, Mass.: Todd, 1933), 18; quoted in Robert James Branham and Stephen J. Harnett, *Sweet Freedom's Song: "My Country 'Tis of Thee" and Democracy in America* (Oxford: Oxford University Press, 2002), 56.

93. Quoted in Philip J. King, *American Archaeology in the Mideast: A History of the American Schools of Oriental Research* (Philadelphia: American Schools of Oriental Research, 1983), 6. Edward Robinson, moreover, would form and edit two biblical journal series, *Bibliotheca Sacra* and the *American Biblical Repository* (King, *American Archaeology in the Mideast*, 2).

94. John Pickering, "Address," *JAOS* 1 (1843): 2.

ern Continent to the uncivilized nations, who inhabit the different groups of islands in the Indian and Pacific Oceans, from the eastern coast of Asia to the western coast of America; comprising that region of the globe which has been called Polynesia."[95] According to Malini Johar Schueller, moreover, the Society's "attempt to seek knowledge was related to national self-definition. The society saw itself as representative of the reach of the new, potentially expanding nation and in competition with the powers of Europe."[96]

Thus, in this second early phase as before, biblical criticism in the U.S. would continue its "orientalist" interest. Its early proponents presupposed that they were civilized agents preparing other civilized Christians in the U.S. with the necessary tools (linguistic and otherwise) to propagate Christianity to an "uncivilized" world.

In the third phase, beginning in the late nineteenth century, higher education in the U.S. saw the emergence of the university, and with it increased professionalization, specialization, and disciplinary rituals of certification.[97] Although Harvard College became a university in 1780 (and Yale College awarded the first Ph.D. in 1861), "it was not until the 1880s that anything like a modern university really took shape in [U.S.] America."[98] That is, not until this period were there "permanent postgraduate training programs" offering the Ph.D. degree in the U.S.[99] Likewise, women, who had entered U.S. colleges in great numbers in 1870, also entered graduate programs in the 1890s though in many fields "the pattern of recruitment remained highly irregular until the 1920s."[100] In the same period, moreover, Harvard's institution of an elective system "facilitated the assemblage of a more scholarly and specialized

---

95. Ibid., 5.
96. Schueller, *U.S. Orientalisms*, 146.
97. Donald G. Tewksbury, *The Founding of American Colleges and Universities before the Civil War* (New York: Teachers' College, Columbia University, 1932), 32. According to Richard Ohmann, "Professions affixed themselves to, or grew out of, universities toward the end of the nineteenth century, when modern universities themselves first came into existence. Professionalism seems to have been an integral growth within advanced capitalism, which first offered the opportunity for such specializations of knowledge, status, and power" (*Politics of Knowledge: The Commercialization of the University, the Professions, and Print Culture* [Middletown, Ct.: Wesleyan University Press, 2003], 66. On the disciplinary rituals of certification, see 68–84.
98. Jencks and Riesman, *The Academic Revolution*, 13. On the founding of Harvard as a university, see Tewksbury, *Founding of American Colleges*, 32. On Yale offering the first Ph.D. in the U.S., see Jencks and Riesman, *The Academic Revolution*, 13.
99. Winterer, *The Culture of Classicism*, 152.
100. Helene Silverberg, "Introduction: Toward a Gendered Social Science History," in *Gender and American Social Science: The Formative Years* (ed. Helene Silverberg; Princeton: Princeton University Press, 1998), 9.

faculty"; colleges and universities developed academic departments that compartmentalized knowledge; and various learned societies published journals, fostered extra-institutional independent research, advocated recruiting procedures and training protocols, and advanced the methods (or "disciplined language-sets") and specific investigative interests of their own disciplines.[101]

Accordingly, in this third phase, the Society of Biblical Literature (and Exegesis) would emerge in 1880. The members of the society would also establish a journal, *The Journal of Biblical Literature and Exegesis*.[102] While the substance of the first journal articles largely featured technical text critical subjects, the articles also reveal the Western "civilizing" orientation of the contributors. That is, several articles from the first twenty years of publication used the expression "heathen" to classify non-Israelites, non-Jews, and non-Christians. In part, this terminology may be a function of the English Bibles used at the time, but in part it is also a function of the larger culture's "missionary" view of foreigners as persons who are not necessarily non-religious but who did not have the same deity as Jews and Christians. Likewise, the articles deploy the terms "civilized" and "savages," thus again expressing their Western "missionary" spatial orientations.[103]

Of the Society's founding thirty-two members moreover—all white, male, and Protestant—seven received their training at Andover Theological and four at Union, thus ultimately showing the dominant influence of Moses Stuart

---

101. Jencks and Riesman, *The Academic Revolution*, 13–14. On Harvard's elective system, introduced by Charles W. Eliot, see Marsden, *Soul of the American University*, 182. On seeing methods as "disciplined language-sets," see Burke O. Long, "Planting and Reaping Albright," in idem, *Politics, Ideology, and Interpreting the Bible* (University Park: Pennsylvania State University Press, 1997), 9.

102. As Philip J. King (*American Archaeology in the Mideast*, 10) writes, "Since 1962 the Society of Biblical Literature and exegesis has been known as the Society of Biblical Literature."

103. For example, Willis J. Beecher, "Ark in Josh. xvii. 15, 18, and Ezek. xxi. 24, xxiii. 47," *JBLE* 2 (1882): 128–33, esp. 130; R. P. Stebbins, "Servant of Jehovah: Isaiah lii. 13–liii," *JBLE* 4 (1884): 65–79; John E. Todd, "The Caper-Berry (Eccles. xii. 5)," *JBLE* 6.2 (1886): 13–26, esp. 15; Henry M. Harman, "The Optative Mode in Greek," *JBLE* 6.2 (1886): 3–12; Crawford H. Toy, "On the Asaph-Psalms," *JBLE* 6.1 (1886): 73–85, esp. 74; Frederic Gardiner, "Various Topics," *JBLE* 8 (1888): 142–51, esp. 147, 150; Crawford H. Toy, "Analysis of Gen ii, iii," *JBLE* 10 (1891): 1–19, esp. 13; Marcus Jastrow, "Light Thrown on Some Biblical Passages by Talmudic Usage," *JBL* 11 (1892): 126–30. Perhaps the most telling example is found in H. Ferguson, who writes that it is likely that the "worshippers of Dagon, or some other of the heathen divinities, practiced these crimes as a religious ceremony, as the Thugs in India used to murder as an offering to their goddess" ("The Historical Testimony of the Prophet Zephaniah," *JBLE* 3 [1883]: 42–59, esp. 54).

over the Society's beginning.[104] Anna Rhoads Ladd in 1899 would become the Society's first female member, while Elleanor D. Wood (1913) and Louise Pettibone Smith (1917) became, respectively, the first female to present a paper at the Society and the first to publish an article in the *Journal of Biblical Literature*.[105] Although blacks and other ethnic/racial minoritized persons would not become members of the Society until well into the twentieth century, the first four black biblical scholars to receive doctoral degrees (Pezavia O'Connell [1898, Ph.D., Pennsylvania University]; James Leonard Farmer [1918, Ph.D., Boston University]; Willis J. King [1921, Ph.D., Boston University]; and WilliamYancy Bell [1924, Ph.D., Yale University])[106] would do so before the end of the first quarter of the twentieth century.[107]

Thus, what this brief historical account reveals is the need for more self-assessment, the scrutiny of our profession's products. Notwithstanding its protestations, biblical criticism in the U.S. has never been "objective." Rather, its scholars have been influenced by the larger imperial and cultural determinants of their times and such determinants have shaped the sociolinguistic currents through which the discourse of biblical studies has been communicated and the largely male constituency of the profession itself. Periodically, then, as biblical studies proceeds toward the future, it needs self-assessment to explore how deeply entangled its professional products are to such cultural determinants. The field of biblical studies is not separate from its various cultures; it is both *in* them and it contributes to the maintenance and operations of such cultures.

---

104. Olbricht, "Biblical Primitivism," 94.

105. I owe this information to Elisabeth Schüssler Fiorenza, "The Ethics of Biblical Interpretation: Decentering Biblical Scholarship," *JBL* 107 (1988): 6.

106. For these names, I am indebted to Robert Fikes Jr., "African Americans' Interest, Experiences, and Scholarship in Middle Eastern Cultures," *Western Journal of Black Studies* 28 (2004): 303–11, esp. 304. Note, however, that Fikes incorrectly lists James Leonard Farmer as John Leonard Farmer. James Leonard Farmer (Sr.) is the father of the civil rights activist James Leonard Farmer Jr. Also, see Robert Fikes's "Black Scholars in Middle Eastern Studies," *The Journal of Blacks in Higher Education* 43 (2004): 112–15.

107. The Society of Biblical Literature and Exegesis was not the only learned society that developed for biblical scholars in this period. The American Schools of Oriental Research began in 1900, many members of which were drawn from the ranks of its two parent organizations, the Society of Biblical Literature and Exegesis and the Archaeological Institute of America (which was formed in 1879). For this information, I am indebted to King, *American Archaeology in the Mideast*, 10; on the AOS as a parent of ASOR, see 6.

INTERROGATING THE PEDAGOGICAL SPACES OF BIBLICAL STUDIES

On the one hand, as educational theorists have long noted, the physical or virtual classroom is a primary pedagogical space for scholars, and activity in the classroom speaks volumes about the spatial dynamics of power. Thus, the interrogation of pedagogical spaces would require socially engaged biblical scholars to unmask hegemony's strategies of pedagogical manipulation inherent in such things as hierarchical spatial arrangements, rigid teaching formats, and poor student involvement in course formation and knowledge distribution.[108]

Notwithstanding the multiple critiques of top-down pedagogical models espoused by educational theorists, however, graduate biblical education continues to operate as if knowledge production is unilateral, and with little or no attention given to the ways in which knowledge and power relate. Accordingly, as Elisabeth Schüssler Fiorenza has noted, academic socialization, whether in theological schools, divinity programs, or religious studies departments, often produces nothing more than technicians.[109] Implicit in this pedagogical model is a view of knowledge as something that can be scientifically packaged and separated spatially from the subject so as to render reason untainted and unadorned by human subjectivity.[110]

On the other hand, pedagogical space is not confined to the physical or virtual places from which our academic labor is put to service. That is, the tools we deploy, especially the canons we endorse, the cartographical frames we deploy, and the critical theories we embrace, also speak volumes pedagogically about the spatial dynamics of power. These tools, to cite Sibley again, are "regulated forms and productions of knowledge" that seek to control what is counted as legitimate within our discipline.[111]

---

108. William B. Kennedy, "Ideology and Education: A Fresh Approach for Religious Education," *Religious Education* 80 (1985): 336–44.

109. Schüssler Fiorenza, "Rethinking the Educational Practices," 66.

110. Ibid., 71. For many of us whose heritage stems back to these subjugated nations or whole continents, our ancestors were the first of many generations to be affected by this instrumental use of reason. Moreover, if these pedagogies are culturally patterned, how do they help us at a time when we so desperately need to honor diverse cultures and ways of living, being, and working in the world? This view of the self, moreover, has been used instrumentally in history for nationalistic purposes, that is, to render some nations as superior, mature, and civilized conduits of reason, while other nations were castigated as inferior, childlike, and primitive conduits of emotions.

111. Sibley, *Geographies of Exclusion*, 122–23.

CANONS AND "SPACE"

Canons, by virtue of the spaces to which they give prominence (or by which they are deemed to give prominence), indicate the *spaces* that matter to those who endorse those canons (or judgments about those canons) as norms, guides, or the focal point of their labor. Thus, on the one hand, biblical scholars must critique traditional canons (or our readings of those canons) when the "production-in-use" or even the production of such canons exclude the spaces inhabited by large groups of persons.[112] Accordingly, even if the Bible since the advent of European colonialism has often been appropriated/reconstituted to inspire hope and proffer resistance among exploited communities, it has also been used to establish bases for European and U.S. American exploitation. What is needed in part then is a pedagogical intervention that shows the long history of discursive traditions in biblical interpretation and their roles in supporting exclusion. To intervene, biblical scholars must seek to hear erstwhile residual voices in biblical texts[113] and the voices of persons whose spaces of habitation have been previously "structured into silence" in the traditional biblical texts that have largely received our attention.[114]

On the other hand, the task must go further. That is, there is a need to decolonize Western "scriptural imperialism" altogether, that is, radically to critique the whole machinery that promotes Jewish and Christian scriptures to an ascendancy over other scriptures, foundational narratives, or charter stories that operate outside the pale of Western cultures.[115] What is needed is the acknowledgment that the declaration of any canon is an assertion of power.[116] Most graduate biblical studies students, though, are only trained to know intimately and thoroughly Jewish and Christian scriptures, and the various languages associated with them. Few have had any sustained and substantive training to help them engage the "scriptures," charter stories, and

---

112. On the term "production-in-use," I am indebted to Wright, *Moses in America*, 7.

113. Marcia Landy, *Film, Politics, and Gramsci* (Minneapolis: University of Minnesota Press, 1994), 30.

114. Pierre Macherey, *A Theory of Literary Production* (trans. Geoffrey Wall; London: Routledge & Kegan Paul, 1978). Silenced voices, though, need not mean passive.

115. On "scriptural imperialism" as opposed to territorial imperialism, see R. S. Sugirtharajah, *The Bible and the Third World: Precolonial, Colonial and Postcolonial Encounters* (Cambridge: Cambridge University Press, 2001), 52. Vincent Wimbush seems to treat a similar idea. See his "'Naturally Veiled and Half Articulate' Scriptures, Modernity and the Formation of African America," in Sugirtharajah, *Still at the Margins*, 56–68.

116. On canons and power, see Charles Mabee, *Reading Sacred Texts through American Eyes: Biblical Interpretation as Cultural Critique* (Macon, Ga.: Mercer University Press, 1991), 9–10.

foundational narratives of other non-Western cultures—from the canonical texts of Chinese Buddhism to the Hindu Vedas to the Mayan Popol Vuh.[117]

Few may also have had any courses treating the various strategies of scriptural imperialism, from the encroachment of Western readings of biblical ideas into languages where such ideas do not exist to the denigration of specific non-Western local cultures for their oral/aural orientation as opposed to the Western text-based biblical hermeneutics.[118] As Musa Dube has stated, moreover, colonizers have often imposed the Bible's literary canon and its (assumed and real) values (in the language of the colonizers) onto the colonized through a variety of mission institutions and with an insistence that the Bible is a "universal standard for all cultures."[119] And in settler colonies (that is, among colonizers who settled onto lands [or actually invaded lands] first inhabited by others [as in the cases of Australia, Canada, South Africa, New Zealand, and the United States]), moreover, much of their biblical interpretation has followed in the vein of "conquest exegesis."[120] Yet, the failure of biblical studies to give sufficient attention to other "scriptures" is not simply a disciplinary politics of omission. It is pragmatically also a failure to read the "signs of the times" in a world that is increasingly shrinking through mass communications and massive migrations, in a world in which there has never been a more dire need to appreciate what other cultures offer in the spaces outside of Europe and North America or in the spaces of aggrieved groups within Europe and North America.

Cartographical Frames and "Space"

Cartographical frames, even those based on the revolutionary techniques of recent satellite technologies and sophisticated computers, are not simply visual impressions of the earth's material surfaces.[121] And although "much of the power of the map … is that it operates behind a mask of seemingly

---

117. The exception here may be the Qur'an. For information on the "interconnectedness of [different sacred] texts and integrative practices," see Sugirtharajah, "Scripture, Scholarship, Empire," 3.

118. Sugirtharajah, *The Bible and the Third World*, 63–73. A bit of irony about such practices is that Jewish and Christian scriptures did not themselves originate in the West, though they have been used instrumentally by the West for exploitative practices.

119. Musa W. Dube Shomanah, "Post-colonial Biblical Interpretations," in *Dictionary of Biblical Interpretation* (ed. John H. Hayes; 2 vols.; Nashville: Abingdon, 1999), 2:299–300.

120. Ibid., 2:300.

121. On recent technology in cartography, see Denis Cosgrove, "Mapping/Cartography," in Atkinson, Jackson, Sibley, and Washbourne, *Cultural Geography*, 27–33.

neutral science, as cartography theorist J. B. Harley has noted,[122] maps are not "mirrors of nature."[123] Rather, maps are both conceptual instruments that organize knowledge and the means by which spaces are created, reified, contested, or otherwise negotiated by cartographers. Maps thus may be used to colonize, as indeed they were used in the seventeenth and eighteenth centuries.[124] Likewise, as in the case of what is now known as the African continent, maps may be used to assign ostensibly homogenous identities to groups of persons. Accordingly, the name Africa, which since the fifteenth century has been applied to a whole continent, was once used by the Romans only to refer to a smaller land mass, namely, "the land of the Afri,"[125] the "Roman province created after the conquest of Carthage in 146 BCE," or what we now know as Libya.[126] Thus, the idea of "Africa" is an invention.[127] Most important, maps are also cultural projects, and thus the type of map deployed in a publication already assigns a cultural value to its type over other possible mapping traditions where maps may be construed through cosmological mandalas (as in Hindu cultures), songlines (as among Australian aborigines), and charcoal sketches (as among Koreans and the Japanese).[128]

The discourse of biblical studies is rife with colonizing cartographic constructions of spaces, whether one speaks of the "mental maps" of the biblical texts themselves or the biblical atlases of modern interpreters.[129] With respect to the mental maps of the biblical texts, the recent empire-critical orientation of biblical studies should suggest to biblical scholars not only the biblical writ-

---

122. J. B. Harley, "Deconstructing the Map," *Cartographica* 26 (1989): 7.

123. See J. B. Harley, "Maps, Knowledge and Power," in *The Iconography of Landscape: Essays on the Symbolic Representation, Design, and Use of Past Environment* (ed. Denis Cosgrove and Stephen Daniels; Cambridge: Cambridge University Press, 1988), 277–312.

124. Moran, *Interdisciplinarity*, 168.

125. According to Rodney S. Sadler Jr., "Afri" is "the plural form of the term 'Afer,'" a Berber "group that hailed from the North African region around what is now Libya" ("The Place and Role of Africa and African Imagery in the Bible," in Blount, Martin, Felder, and Powery, *True to Our Native Land*, 23).

126. John Parker and Richard Rathbone, *African History: A Very Short Introduction* (New York: Oxford University Press, 2007), 5.

127. It should be stated, however, that Europe also was invented. Gerald Delanty writes: "To speak of Europe as an 'invention' is to stress the ways in which it has been constructed in a historical process; it is to emphasize that Europe is less the subject of history than its product and what we call Europe is, in fact, a historically fabricated reality of ever-changing forms and dynamics" (*Inventing Europe: Idea, Identity, Reality* [New York: Martin, 1995], 3).

128. Cosgrove, "Mapping/Cartography," 30.

129. On "mental maps," see Douglas R. Edwards, *Religion and Power: Pagans, Jews, and Christians in the Greek East* (New York: Oxford University Press, 1996), 72.

ers' resistance to empire but their incorporation of empire's "spatial" strategies as well. Thus, Luke's listing of persons from various locations in the ancient world in Acts 2 may not simply indicate the ubiquity of the apostles' way of life. Rather, perhaps it also is the adoption of the imperialistic strategy of placing cities throughout the *oikumene* in a list to indicate implicitly the power of the apostles' movement over those cities.[130]

With respect to the biblical atlases of modern interpreters, one does not have to deploy a vindicationist hermeneutics of return or be in full solidarity with the bold though otherwise limited perspectives of card-carrying nineteenth-century Afrocentrist scholars to see the politics of race and space in such atlases. Clarice Martin has noted, for example, the modern ideological bias of those biblical atlases that omit the "region south of Palestine and Egypt."[131] Likewise, Randall Bailey has noted that many modern maps de-Africanize what we now know as Africa by referring to "African territories" as the Near East.[132] Rodney Sadler has argued, moreover, that the designation of *biblical lands* as "the Near East" or "the Middle East" reflects a Eurocentric orientation. He writes, "It is only from a European orientation that these imprecise designations have meaning."[133]

Critical Theories and "Space"

Far too often the terms of the discussion about critical theories have been focused on the utility or lack thereof of traditional methods, especially historical criticism. And there is some merit in critiques of historical criticism as it has been practiced because of the instrumental way in which it was used for nation-building, its emphasis on the retrieval of so-called originary moments, and the unconvincing views its adherents have had about history as an objective possibility. Little attention is given, however, to how the terms of most discussions on critical theory seem to reflect an intra-sibling Western rivalry

---

130. Gary Gilbert, "The List of Nations in Acts 2: Roman Propaganda and the Lukan Response," *JBL* 121 (2002): 497–529.

131. Clarice Martin, "A Chamberlain's Journey and the Challenge of Interpretation for Liberation," *Semeia* 47 (1989): 105–35.

132. Randall C. Bailey, "Beyond Identification: The Use of Africans in Old Testament Poetry and Narratives," in *Stony The Road We Trod: African American Biblical Interpretation* (ed. Cain Hope Felder; Minneapolis: Fortress, 1991), 146–84.

133. Sadler, "Place and Role of Africa," 25. In agreement about such designation is Philip J. King, who writes: "With unbecoming provincialism, they [Western geographers] divided that vast expanse [of so-called non-Western lands] into three parts—Near, Middle, and Far East—in reference to their own perspective" (*American Archaeology in the Mideast*, xi).

between old guards and vanguards. Postcolonial studies, while not hermetically sealed from the Western discussion, at least raises geopolitical questions about practices of colonization, questions that expose the West's long history of colonizing discourses as yet another form of appropriation. To take spaces seriously, though, is to go a step further, namely, to recognize that the primary objective many Westerners bring to biblical texts—for example, seeking a fairly circumscribed meaning—already presupposes a Western view of *subjectivity* (an individuated self) and thus may not at all reflect the ways in which non-westerners approach any canon that matters to them.[134] In effect, then certain theories erase heterogeneity, evoke a new form of colonizing violence, and advance alien "styles of reasoning" that parade as universal modes on and for all others.[135]

With respect to biblical studies, then, "critical theorists" are often shortsighted to the colonial implications of their theoretical approaches, to the culture-specific spatiality of their theories and to the culture-specific bases of their denigration of other readings as eisegesis whenever other readings depart from the regiment and prescriptions of the so-called universal "critical" methods.[136] Accordingly, without resorting to a romanticist approach toward colonized subjects, biblical studies must see the inherent value of a

---

134. Clear evidence of the ways in which our theories are imbricated in Western epistemologies is found in the work of Chidester, who argues that the notion of comparative religion is not something "natural." Rather, it developed as Western colonializing powers sought to categorize and control the colonized (*Savage Systems*).

135. On "styles of reasoning," see Arnold I. Davidson, *The Emergence of Sexuality* (Cambridge: Harvard University Press, 2001), 126–41. I do not wish to deny the value of the Western liberal subject. As Benjamin Valentin has noted, "this conception helped Western societies to deal with the crisis of authority and the sectarian strife engendered by the religious wars of the sixteenth and seventeenth centuries" (*Mapping Public Theology: Beyond Culture, Identity, and Difference* [Harrisburg, Pa.: Trinity Press International, 2002], 92). It also "has served invaluably to emancipate human and social thought from the chains of uncritical submission to tradition" (92). What he finds problematic is that this conception "has also served to generate a radical individualism, an enchantment with private life, and an ahistorical understanding of reason that has eventually served to constrict the meaning of public life" (92). That is, if a human being is defined as "ontologically prior to society" and construed as self-made, the need for others becomes only a "matter of protecting and maximizing individual interests" (93). Hence, this view "has served to weaken the sense of and desire for connection between the self and the other…; it has encouraged a one-sided enchantment with private life that values being in private—alone with ourselves, family, and intimate friends—as an end in itself, and … [it] has weakened the desire to value those bonds of association in the *respublica*, where we must live in the 'company of strangers'" (93).

136. Dube Shomanah, "Post-colonial Biblical Interpretations," 2:299–300.

wide variety of reading strategies practiced by colonized groups—from indigenous reading practices (as, for example, with Native Americans in the U.S., the Maori in New Zealand, and the Aborigines in Australia) to decolonizing reading practices (that often begin with the experience of the oppressed, expose the non-Mediterranean currents of early Christianity, and relativize all religions in general) to migrant reading practices (as with the diaspora reading projects of Fernando F. Segovia or the guerrilla exegesis of Obery Hendricks).[137]

Conclusion

Biblical criticism in the West has recently received revitalization through the inclusion of non-male and non-Western scholars in its professional societies. And there are some—though not nearly sufficient—signs that minoritized scholars will continue to infuse Western biblical criticism in ways that could not have been imagined just fifty-five years ago, when the U.S. Supreme Court handed down its rule against segregated schools, or even forty-one years ago when C. Shelby Rooks, the Fund for Theological Education (FTE) former director of black doctoral students in religion, lamented that only eighteen blacks were "enrolled in religious studies doctoral programs [in the U.S.] nationwide."[138] For example, in 2005, the FTE, in partnership with the SBL, the AAR, the Institute for Leadership Development and the Study of Pacific and Asian North American Religion (PANA), and the Hispanic Theological Initiative (HTI), sponsored a recruitment conference that brought together thirty racially and ethnically diverse students to "identify and encourage African American, Hispanic, Asian American and Native American graduate students to consider doctoral study in religion, biblical studies and theology."[139] The SBL also sponsored several recruitment conferences (1996, 1998, 2000) held at Union, Vanderbilt, and Pacific School of Religion with similar goals directed toward undergraduate and graduate students. These conferences "represent"

---

137. All of these practices and the places in which the practices have occurred are noted in ibid., 2:300–302. I would add to the list of practices Delores Williams's *proto-gesis* hermeneutics. See her "Hagar in African American Biblical Appropriation," in *Hagar, Sarah, and Their Children* (ed. Phyllis Trible and Letty M. Russell; Louisville: Westminster John Knox, 2006), 171–84. According to Williams (174), *proto-gesis* (as opposed to exegesis) draws on cultural studies, uses pertinent genre-specific interpretative strategies to unearth a biblical cultural deposit or cultural memory deeply sedimented in one's own community, and yet remains in dialogue with historical-critical discussions.

138. Quoted in Sharon Watson Fluker, "Diversity Delayed, Excellence Denied," *Diverse* (6 April 2006): 1.

139. *Vocare* 9 (2006): 7.

as Jean-Pierre Ruiz notes, "efforts to address the problem of under-representation of racial and ethnic and racial minorities in doctoral programs and in the professorate over the long term."[140] Various mentoring programs (such as the Hispanic Theological Initiative), journals (such as the *Journal of Asian and Asian American Theology* and the *Journal of Hispanic/Latino Theology*), SBL program units featuring minoritized perspectives on the Bible, multiple anthologies by women biblical scholars, and the prolific work of scholars such as Elisabeth Schüssler Fiorenza, Fernando F. Segovia, Randall Bailey, Mary Ann Tolbert, Tat-siong Benny Liew, and R. S. Sugirtharajah, among others, all reveal, in the words of Sharon Ringe, the "changing demographics in biblical studies," and that, too, is a cause for celebration.[141]

These signs, though, are not enough because simple acknowledgment of them may well only replicate the neo-imperial strategy of mixing and stirring without providing the true structural changes that will allow the SBL and other largely Western-influenced biblical societies to appreciate difference, to take spaces seriously. This chapter, thus, has charted a few ways in which Western biblical criticism might take its "spatial" turn seriously. Acknowledging demographic shifts will not alone resolve the geometries of power that remain because these geometries are historically long in their development, geopolitically forceful in their reach, and seductively satisfying in their differentiating appeal. Any step forward then must always demand an examination of the spatial configurations from the past lest we replicate what many of us would easily condemn (perhaps) if we could see clearly how our productions of knowledge reinforce a politics of exclusion even though to some extent Western biblical criticism's beginnings also emanated out of a desire to be more inclusive, that is, to carve out some democratic space for larger groups of persons to control the course and flow of biblical interpretation.

Any step forward also means as well that we must be more specific in naming the geo-political dynamics that inform biblical studies, whether one speaks of the normativised geo-political "cultural" gaze that directed eighteenth century German biblical criticism or the extent to which insufficient credit is given today to the insights (and "innovations") of non-Western interpreters of the Bible and other sacred texts. With respect to the latter, it is interesting to note that much of the ethos of empire-critical thought that pervades Western biblical scholarship was already acutely influencing Latin American biblical scholars who could easily read empire in the Bible because

---

140. Jean-Pierre Ruiz, "Tell the Next Generation: Racial and Ethnic Minority Scholars and the Future of Biblical Studies," *JAAR* 29 (2001): 653.

141. Sharon H. Ringe, "Changing Demographics in Biblical Studies," *SBL Forum*; online: http://www.sbl-site.org/publications/article.aspx?ArticleId=54.

they lived under the dominance of yet another "empire" every day. Could the campesinos living in dire poverty not have understood empire? Thus, according to Ernesto Cardenal who compiled the comments of these rural Nicaraguans in the archipelago of Solentiname, these peasants portrayed Jesus in the garb of the campesinos and they discussed important biblical concepts in the light of their own needs.[142] Accordingly, sin becomes selfishness; the Eucharist becomes paradigmatic sharing; the incarnation becomes the manifestation of God's wrath against injustice; and resurrection becomes the anticipated birth of a (this-worldly) new order after the demise of economic oppression. Thus, the idea that politics and religion do mix (a staple of empire-critical biblical studies) was already an assumption in the creative art of these Nicaraguans who could not have imagined life otherwise. Could the biblical scholar Néstor Míguez who lived through the military dictatorship period in Argentina not have understood empire? Given the secret meetings he had with students and social workers all of whom were reading the Bible for liberation in the face of police visits, possible torture or even death, it is with little wonder that he would be able to understand Paul's artful and anti-imperial use of political diction in 1 Thessalonians (as indeed many empire-critical biblical scholars now do).[143]

Any step forward also means that biblical criticism will need to explore the dynamics that so often force us to read *against* others or *for* others rather than *with* others. That is, although we may wish to say that we have acquired certain skills that then generate "better" readings of the biblical texts, we often fail to acknowledge how much we depend on the rituals (or "lie") of differentiation to be able to justify the unquantifiable amount of time we spend in research and writing, an amount that in many societies can only be called an unaffordable "luxury." Convinced of the "lie," we may go on with business as usual, with the insider jargon and club-talk that matters very little to anyone else. Yet, if we continue to do so, especially at a time when the severity of economic woes—for the old and now the new poor—has never been greater, we do so at our own peril. In Morrison's words, there is a need to be cognizant "of the places where imagination sabotages itself, locks its own gates, pollutes its vision."[144]

---

142. Ernesto Cardenal, *The Gospel of Solentiname* (trans. Donald D. Marsh; Maryknoll, N.Y.: Orbis, 1982).

143. Néstor Míguez, "La composicion social de la iglesia en Tesalonica," *Revista bíblica* 51 (1989): 65–89.

144. Morrison, *Playing in the Dark*, xi.

Biblical Studies and Public Relevance: Hermeneutical and Pedagogical Consideration in Light of the Ethos of the Greater China Region (GCR)

Philip Chia

There appears to be a serious concern, particularly in the academic arena, for the overuse, if not misuse or abuse, of the Bible by conservative Christians in American political discourse. In this view, conservative "biblical" discourse has had undue influence within the Bush administration, and it has played a role in shaping public policy in America, especially after the events of 9/11. Former Director of the Center for American Political Studies at Harvard University, Theda R. Skocpol, voiced her concern: "we live in a time when religiously motivated Christian activists are playing major, highly visible, and contentious roles in shaping U.S. public debates, tipping electoral outcomes, and demanding shifts in public policy."[1] If this is a fair reflection of American public politics, then the exact opposite is true in Asian political realities, where the presence of the Bible and Christianity has occupied at most a very minimal place in the public sphere, given the short span and relatively recent appearance of the Christian church within the long histories and storied cultures of Asia. The Bible and Christianity play far too dominant a role in American public discourse, while Asian Christians may be worried that those implementing public policies ignore their legitimate concerns. Both Americans and Asians have their legitimate, albeit very different, concerns over the appropriation of the Bible and its relevancy to their societies. Since "traditional" Christianity takes the Bible very seriously even in its interaction with

---

1. In his foreword to the book by Hugh Heclo, *Christianity and American Democracy* (Cambridge: Harvard University Press, 2007), viii; Heclo "feels the successful American confluence of Christianity and democracy has been under grave threat since the 1960s," as Mark Noll comments.

the general public, one of the central issues facing Christians today seems to be the "Bible and its public relevance" or frame in terms of academic culture, and may well be the issue of "biblical studies and its public relevance." In turn, the different problems encountered in the relationship between Christianity and biblical elements in American and Asian public spheres challenge the future of the discipline of biblical studies with regard to its place in public life. This problem is particularly pressing with regard to graduate biblical education, since the next generation of scholars is in the midst of forming its research agendas and disciplinary habits.

This essay[2] attempts to address the problematic relationship between *biblical studies* and *public relevance* with hermeneutical and pedagogical consideration in light of the ethos of the Greater China Region (GCR, i.e., Mainland China, Hong Kong, Macau and Taiwan), while hoping to interact, wherever appropriate, with Elisabeth Schüssler Fiorenza's works.[3] The interest of this study is to explore, understand, delineate, and compare the "ethos" of biblical studies from different *social locations*, with interest in how their *standards of excellence* are constructed and operate. These standards are found to use varying instruments of measurement, and may be constructed with the covert intention of challenging any existing paradigm of biblical studies that requires innovation.

I will begin by sharing my experience in teaching biblical studies at different social locations within the GCR and Southeast Asia over the last twenty-five years to different student groups, undergraduate and graduate, at various levels of academic quality. In the course of addressing this topic, I would also like to raise the question of the relations between biblical studies and public relevance (with a special interest in developing some sort of biblically-based public theology, or perhaps a public-based biblical theology). This concern forms part of my on-going research interest: namely, situating the world of the public sphere within my overall social location, whereby the current general ethos of the GCR as a public domain has formed the context of my concern. The GCR's ethos has also encouraged my interaction with Schüssler Fiorenza's idea of "ethical-political turn" and her proposed "rhetorical-emancipatory paradigm" which "seeks to situate biblical scholarship in

---

2. An earlier form of this essay was presented at the 2005 Society of Biblical Literature International Meeting in Singapore.

3. Materials by Elisabeth Schüssler Fiorenza from the previous session at the International Meeting in Cambridge, England, were very helpful in understanding the rationale of the project. Cf. Elisabeth Schüssler Fiorenza, "Rethinking the Educational Practices of Biblical Doctoral Studies," *TThRel* 6 (2003): 65–75; and "Key Questions Regarding Departments/Programs" developed for the session at the 2004 SBL Annual Meeting.

such a way that its public character and political responsibility become an integral part of its contemporary readings and historical reconstructions,"[4] although I am well aware that my appropriation needs to be flexible, since the American ethos is very different from that of Asia.

ETHOS OF BIBLICAL STUDIES IN THE GCR

It will be beyond the scope of this study to trace a detailed historical description of the entire development of the "discipline" of biblical studies in GCR, especially pre-1949, due to the volatility and complexity of the GCR history of this period. At that time, biblical studies was closely related to Western missionary activities and colonial power, the rise of nationalism and political ideologies, geopolitical effects of WWI and WWII Europe, regional geopolitics (especially that of relationship with Japan) and internal politics (the declining end of the Qing Dynasty, 1644–1912), which all triggered a series of nationalistic and anti-religious movements that were led by intellectuals of the new-era China. Much has been written on this period of Chinese history, and for the purpose of our task, elements of it may be mentioned wherever relevant in the course of this study. However, it is worth mentioning here that the most common use of the Bible among Christian communities in pre-1949 China was in revival or evangelistic meetings that are familiar to the West, with very minimal attempts to interact with indigenous intellectual communities, such as Chinese Buddhism and Confucianism. The other element that would also be useful to this study (yet properly belongs to a separate independent study) is the history of biblical translation in the GCR.

Traditionally, the ethos of biblical studies in post-1949 GCR, may be understood in three general modes: (1) the *precritical mode*, characterized by the use of the Bible exclusively for devotional, spiritual or allegorical readings; (2) the *enlightened mode*, characterized by the development of expositional and sermonic materials from biblical texts (in Chinese or English) that emphasize religious/spiritual teachings and require minimal interpretative and analytical skills for reading biblical texts, but not necessarily training in biblical languages; and (3) the *critical-exegetical mode*, characterized by biblical exegesis interacting with critical scholarship mainly from the English-speaking world, though European Continental scholarship also has its place. The first two modes are common at Bible colleges or pastoral/missionary training centers and thus normally operate at undergraduate or high-school levels (as such, these are of lesser concern for our study). These practitioners are gener-

---

4. *Rhetoric and Ethic: The Politics of Biblical Studies* (Minneapolis: Fortress, 1999); idem, "Rethinking the Educational Practices," 69, 73.

ally locals and missionaries. The third mode is commonly employed at the graduate level in seminaries or universities, mostly prompted by Western missionaries who introduced locals to their graduate biblical education. There has been an expanded interest in this mode of biblical studies since the 1970s due to the increase in graduate students in the society at large. Although pre-1949 China also witnessed missionary efforts to establish Christian religious studies at higher educational institutions, there has been a hold on this process due to the political transformations that occurred after 1949. Lately, there has been the fourth, "hermeneutical-postmodern"[5] (to use Schüssler Fiorenza's term) mode of reading and teaching the Bible, focusing on the hermeneutical aspect of textual production of meanings, employing gender-race-cultural models, that decentralizes and destabilizes the traditional "Scriptural-doctrinal" modern scientific paradigm. This mode of biblical study encounters certain strong reservations and resistance from both the church and the academy alike in the GCR.

To consider the operative *standards of excellence* that are assumed by these modes of "biblical studies," one would need to ask the question: Whose interest does each mode of biblical studies serve? Unlike the more established system of quality assurance that is metonymically associated with accreditation bodies in Western higher education, which reflects an objective and systematic ideal established over a few hundred years of educational development, the modern Western higher educational system has only existed in the GCR for about a century. Thus when it comes to the discipline of biblical studies, it rests mostly upon untrained specialists without "objective" standards or precise technical formulas to decide what schools are "better" or "worse." That is, the community of believers (or, in economic terms, the "market") must decide on their own standards of excellence by which they may judge biblical studies programs.

Whose interests are served by each "type" of biblical education? First, the pre-critical mode obviously serves the interest of the individual Christian within the *ecclesia* community, and exists mostly for self-enrichment in the spiritual sense or for edification in personal conduct, whereby post-1949 individuals outside of the mainland China find comfort and consolation in the teaching of the Bible as they settle in a foreign land. Their teachers are normally clergy or pastors, whose educational qualification may not be at the seminary level, though there are some exceptions.

---

5. Considering this as the third paradigm of biblical studies, Schüssler Fiorenza felt that "it also cannot address the increasing insecurities of globalized inequality nor accept the constraints that the ethical imperative of emancipatory movements places on the relativizing proliferation of meaning" ("Rethinking the Educational Practices," 73).

Pre-1949, Bible teachers looked much like Dr. John Sung (1901–1944), the most influential evangelist and revivalist in the GCR and Southeast Asia in the 1920s and 1930s. He earned a doctorate degree in chemistry from the Wesleyan University of Ohio and Ohio University before returning to China, but his biblical teaching did not conform to Western academic styles or present any intellectual challenges, perhaps for the sake of the culture of his audience. Church activities and revival and evangelistic meetings constituted the basic channels of communication on biblical teachings in various forms up until the 1970s in the GCR.

Rev. Robert Alexander Jaffray (1873–1945), who founded the first "Bible magazine" in 1913, was one of the earliest Christians to publish in pre-1949 China, specializing in biblical studies in the loose sense of the term. The magazine was one of the most influential publications in Chinese church history; it has as its focus study of the Bible and continues to publish today, though in a slightly different format.

Jia Yu-ming (1880–1964) was another Bible teacher whose biblical commentaries are still available today in Chinese Christian bookstores in the GCR. He focused mainly on the ethical and spiritual aspects of the biblical teachings and operated a spiritual, devotional school in mainland China.

The other contribution worth mentioning from Western missionaries is Young John Allen (1836–1907), who introduced advanced Western scholarly approaches (such as those published under the auspices of the Methodist Society for the Diffusion of Christian and General Knowledge among the Chinese) through newspaper publication (the *Wan Guo Gong Bao*, or *Review of the Times*) and helped established higher education institutions (such as the Anglo-Chinese College and Suzhou University) in mainland China, which nurtured many intellectuals whose effort is remembered in the GCR today. These few examples offer a glimpse of the general ethos of biblical studies in pre-1949 China; even until the 1970s, however, the general tenor of biblical studies in the GCR remained relatively consistent.

The second segment of biblical studies in the GCR, the *enlightened mode*, found emphasis in the church or general Christian communities who were, or are, in need of establishing their *ecclesia* identities. These communities emphasize biblical teachings as a method of enhancing their doctrine of faith; thus, the standards of excellence used to judge their scholarship are the *doctrinal* and *political* outworking of such scholarship. The enlightened mode is mostly operative in denominational Bible colleges or seminaries. The influence of Western missionaries in graduate biblical education is evident in this mode, and it has effectively nurtured future local biblical scholars in each respective denomination. Taiwan Theological College and Seminary and Tainan Theological College and Seminary are among the earlier seminaries established in Taiwan. Founded in the late nineteenth century by the Presbyterian denomination, these schools have nurtured many locals including the famous Choan-Seng Song, who has developed the unique contextualized cultural biblical theology of Taiwan.

Third, we find the *critical-exegetical* mode, which is mainly practiced in the academic arena following the ethos of "scientific positivist paradigm."[6] Serious practitioners are normally those who are educated in the West, though unfortunately only a handful are involved in the community of international academic scholarship. Today, most practitioners of critical-exegetical biblical studies in the GCR teach in the few seminaries or universities that offer graduate biblical education.

In pre-1949 GCR, there already existed Chinese scholars trained in ancient Near Eastern philology. Subsequently, a handful of biblical scholars who earned their doctorate degrees in biblical studies from the West returned to the GCR, and have helped in laying the foundation for establishing seminary and graduate biblical education in post-1949 GCR. Due to political transformations in the GCR for the first half of the last century, graduate biblical education has been slow in developing. Largely responsible is the fact that modern higher education remained available only to the privileged few until the late 1960s and 1970s. In post-1949 GCR biblical scholarship, Ronald Fung, a student of F. F. Bruce, is among the few Chinese biblical scholars in Hong Kong who gained recognition in Western academia through his English publications. His exegetical studies of New Testament texts are comparable to the best exegetical scholarship among his Western contemporaries. However, relatively few GCR scholars have excelled in biblical scholarship according to Western standards. Though they act as role models for future students of the Bible, generally these critical-exegetical scholars do not reflect the general ethos of biblical scholarship in the GCR, due to their limited number.

Fourth, there is a small number of scholars who work in the *hermeneutical-postmodern mode*, which emphasizes theories of textual production of meanings as they apply to biblical studies. This is a relatively recent development and only has begun to gain substantial followers in the GCR since the late 1980s; in general, it is still approached cautiously if not resisted by both the church and the seminary academy at large. The practitioners of this method are, for the most part, those who were educated in the West since the 1980s.

---

6. See her discussion on "Professionalization of Biblical Studies" in "Rethinking the Educational Practices," 69–71.

In general, the ethos of biblical studies in the GCR, unlike in the West, is still largely a phenomenon oriented toward the church-public.[7] This is true mainly because of the so-called "market" power at play, whereby the communities of "consumers" exercise a deciding power over the product cycle and the construction of standards of excellence. Rarely is biblical studies part of the university[8] education program, undergraduate or graduate alike, perhaps due to the nature of the public tertiary or university education system in the GCR, since these societies do not have Christianity as a normative culture (the Chinese University of Hong Kong is an exception due to the historical nature of its formation).

However, since the late 1970s, even within the church-public there have been attempts to go beyond the traditional modes of biblical studies due to the return of a substantial number of Western-trained biblical professionals who were influenced by scholarly biblical criticism. Biblical studies in the GCR is neither comfortable to remain at home with the precritical mode, nor does it adopt freely and whole-heartedly the Western scientific positivist paradigm. This is partly due to the fear of being labeled unintelligent or nonacademic if one remains within the first two modes of biblical scholarship, yet one also runs the risk of being accused of not edifying the church-public if one pursues the third mode of biblical studies. The shift in interest is also due to changes in the social-intellectual demography of the GCR and the *ecclesia* communities. Thus, standards of excellence have varied greatly and there is a decided lack of a standard scheme or authoritative body that would allow for objective evaluation. Perhaps two key accreditation bodies, the Asia Theological Association (ATA) and The Association for Theological Education in South East Asia (ATESEA), could constitute some academic standards of excellence for seminaries and theological colleges, whereby admission to membership means mutual recognition of academic excellence and thus, credit transfer among member institutions could be facilitated. At present, the GCR is far from having active promoters and facilitators of academic excellence, particularly for the discipline of biblical studies. The lack of reference journals in biblical studies within the GCR and the nonrequirement for faculty mem-

---

7. The church as *ecclesia* in its original sense is an open assembly, a public in its classical sense. In fact, the Scottish public theologians talk about three publics; the church being a public (Pc), the academy being another public (Pa), while the general population of the society is the Public (P) with a capital P. Thus, the church and academy are two publics in one public society P. See Andrew R. Morton, "Duncan Forrester: A Public Theologian," in *Public Theology for the Twenty-First Century: Essays in Honor of Duncan B. Forrester* (ed. William F. Storrar and Andrew R. Morton; London: T&T Clark, 2004), 28–31.

8. As pointed out by Morton: "That the modern university is a public more than a community need hardly be argued" ("Duncan Forrester," 30).

bers to publish in some institutions constitutes yet another set of problems for establishing some scheme of measuring standards of excellence in colleges and seminaries; universities, on the other hand, have their own policies.

Regardless of whatever mode is being employed as the hermeneutical tool for engaging biblical studies, the general ethos is largely an inward-looking religious practice, addressing the individual Christian's personal or spiritual needs, serving mainly Christian communities. Seldom would any biblical scholar cross over to consider the public sphere in general as an arena of direct discourse or engagement. Historically in pre-1949 China, Western imperialism and colonialism coupled with aggressive missionary activities had invited reactive measures from the Chinese intellectual community, such as the May 4th movement of 1919 and the anti-Christianity movement of the 1920s. In post-1949 GCR, also as a form of reaction to the social-gospel movement of the West from the conservative evangelical Christians, a strong and unique sense of sacred/secular and private/public dualistic world view settled in. This ethos continues among Chinese Christian communities today. Thus, biblical studies is basically a church-public oriented enterprise, with the exception of only a handful of academic institutions that engage critical exegesis. By doing so, they may risk dissociating the discipline from the general church-public. Academic standards of excellence in the "scientific or theological positivist" sense are the concern of none but a handful or small circle of academic scholars or institutions.

In Whose Interest? For Which Public?

In whose interest does the discipline of biblical studies serve in the GCR? The church public (Pc) and academia (Pa), as two distinct "publics," are what the discipline of biblical studies has been serving, at least historically and traditionally in the GCR. Standards of excellence varied greatly according to their distinct "public" interest.[9] Thus, the ecclesial and the academic form two distinct publics, and the politics and power relations within these two publics

---

9. The term "public" here serves better than the term "community," as demonstrated in the thought of Duncan Forrester, the Scottish public theologian, that, "[w]hereas 'community' places strong emphasis on what is common to its members, shared by them, 'public' puts more emphasis on what is not common, not shared" (Morton, "Duncan Forrester," 29). He notes that, "[i]n a public, as distinct from a community, there is space or distance in the sense of difference and either disagreement or absence of agreement ... a space which allows and indeed encourages encounter with that which is different.... a public would not be a public unless its members had something in common. At the very least a public has a common language and form of discourse.... What is shared in a public is space more than substance; there is some togetherness but with large spaces in it; its weave is open."

play an important role in the formation of the ethos of biblical studies and the development of the authority for setting standards of excellence. Despite the difference in the two "public" interests, they still fall primarily within the inner circle of interests of the religious community. This reality of inward religious public interest constituted a lack of concern for the general social public (P) as well as the inability to engage in general public discourse on issues of public interest. Consequently it has ultimately challenged the very core of their confessional doctrine of creation and salvation, whereby humanity and creation are the ultimate concern and interest of the God of the Bible.

The common religious languages of the church public (Pc) and learned terminologies of the academic public (Pa) have also contributed to their inability to actively engage in public (P) discourses. Thus, biblical studies, in advocating the message embedded within the ancient texts or normative documents of the biblical religions, needs a paradigm that can adequately address the relevancy of its text to contemporary general social public interests, can engage in public discourses, and can contribute responsibly towards the advancement of human civilization, which has been seriously threatened as humankind enters into the twenty-first century. With the emerging of new generations of publics who are used to new modes of acquiring knowledge in the age of telecommunication technology and globalization, biblical studies in particular and Christian/religious studies in general have been seriously challenged with a call for the discipline's public relevance and market value, thus situating the discipline at the crossroads of human inquiry.

Schüssler Fiorenza has rightly pointed out that even as the hermeneutical-postmodern paradigm of biblical studies has "successfully destabilized the certitude of the scientific objectivist paradigm in biblical studies, it still asserts its own scientific value-neutral and a-theological character ... [and] *cannot address the increasing insecurities of globalized inequality.*"[10] To this I would reinforce it with the concern that, biblical studies should seriously consider taking on a "public turn" to make public relevance a primary task of its intellectual discourse and expand its capability of engagement in public interests, as a response to Schüssler Fiorenza's proposal of an "ethical-political turn." In fact, earlier in her argument, she has already pointed out that "[t]his call for a public-ethical-political self-understanding of biblical studies has become even more pressing today."[11] Although the concerns may be different in the U.S. and the GCR, the reason is the same, namely, the nonusage and the abuse

---

10. "Rethinking the Educational Practices," 73, emphasis added.
11. Ibid., 69. She also points out that "this is especially urging in view of the Moral Majority in the 1970s, the Christian New Right in the 1980s, resurgence of religious fundamentalism in all major religions in 1990s."

of the Bible in public discourse. Perhaps this call for a self-understanding of biblical studies also voices out a sense of identity crisis within the discipline: In whose interest and which public do we serve? How should we position the discipline? It is imperative that the new paradigm must be able to address a variety of public-ethical issues concerning humanity's well-being, engaging public discourses in areas such as global economy, global warming, environmental ecology, life-science such as stem cell research, DNA manipulation projects, life cloning, and so on. This, in fact, also posed one of the greatest challenges to biblical studies in the GCR because of the cultural heritage embedded within its history of understanding the concept of human value (biblical concepts as compared to the Taoist or Buddhist concepts). Biblical studies needs to see itself as a "public discipline," in that its professionals are "public intellectuals" (e.g., like William Barclay, C. S. Lewis, or perhaps even Susan Sontag),[12] using the biblical text as their primary resource.

The Challenge of Public Relevance for Biblical Studies

As the GCR increasingly opens up its doors for knowledge and social transformation (since the 1980s) and as impacts of information technology and changes in social intellectual demography are taking effect in the region, biblical studies in particular and theological or Christian studies in general can no longer remain as a privatized educational program. They cannot limit themselves to the church public where members share common faith and where job markets consist only of *ecclesia*-related institutions. In the academic public, students of theological and biblical studies can no longer limit themselves to church members or religious people who share a similar faith. Nonchurch intellectuals trained in social sciences and humanities, regardless of their religious faith, are increasingly interested in taking on the task of studying Christianity. Often, these scholars point to the search for religious value in nation building and modernization as their reason for studying this field. Thus, teaching biblical studies to students of non-Christian faith is becoming a common reality, at least in the GCR.

Constantly, in courses of biblical studies, I find myself being challenged with regard to its contemporary and public relevance. As pointed out by Jürgen Moltmann, "Christian theology ought to get itself involved in public affairs of the society."[13] Thus, it is only natural and relevant that students of

---

12. See Richard A. Posner, *Public Intellectuals: A Study of Decline* (Cambridge: Harvard University Press, 2001).

13. Jürgen Moltmann, *God for a Secular Society: The Public Relevance of Theology* (Minneapolis: Fortress, 1999), 1: "Its subject alone makes Christian theology a *theologia*

biblical studies want to know how biblical studies or religions can contribute as a resource for discourses in public issues, social development, nation building and global responsibility. They challenge the usage of exclusive language of the church public in biblical or Christian studies, which in itself creates a communicative barrier for public discourse. Biblical texts not only serve as a normative document for biblical religions (Pc), they are increasingly demanded and expected to serve as a collection of ancient texts,[14] like any other Chinese classics, that would provide wisdom for human inquiry and advancement. The challenge from academia for the "public character"[15] or "public-ness" of biblical studies is also increasingly matched with the demand from within the Christian public for the relevance of biblical teachings, urging the ability to engage in public discourse on pressing public and global issues with a sense of hope to contribute values of biblical teachings towards the development of a healthy public policy and nation building.

Having highlighted the above, however, the use or abuse of the Bible in its appropriation for the public domain also largely rests upon the responsibility of academia within the discipline of biblical studies. Ancient and classical philological study related to biblical texts no doubt is important for biblical studies, and so is the historical-descriptive and analytical-linguistic-literary study of the biblical text. But if the discipline remains an inward-looking descriptive, linguistic, historical, dogmatic, literary discipline, it might continue to engender the nonuse, misuse, or abuse of the biblical text in public discourse. The urge to take on a "public-turn" in biblical studies may not sound necessary in the American scene, due to the impression that too much of it already exists in public policy debates since 9/11. It is possible that it is precisely the alienation and absence of responsible biblical studies in the gen-

---

publica, a public theology. It gets involved in the public affairs of society. It thinks about what is of general concern in the light of hope in Christ for the kingdom of God." See also Philip Knight, "Pragmatism, Postmodernism and The Bible as a Meaningful Public Resource in a Pluralistic Age," in *Biblical Interpretation: The Meanings of Scripture—Past and Present* (ed. John M. Court; London: T&T Clark, 2003), 310–25.

14. Schüssler Fiorenza points out, "The same rhetorical tension remains.... Should it be viewed as a collection of ancient texts or as a normative document of biblical religions?" ("Rethinking the Educational Practices," 72).

15. Schüssler Fiorenza argues that "[s]ince the socio-historical location of rhetoric as the public of the polis, the rhetorical-emancipatory paradigm shift seeks to situate biblical scholarship in such a way that its public character and political responsibility become an integral part of its contemporary readings and historical reconstructions. It insists on an ethical radical imperative that compels biblical scholarship to contribute to the advent of a society and religion that are free from all forms of kyriarchal inequality and oppression" (ibid., 73).

eral Christian public that leads to the misappropriation of the Bible becoming more prominent in general public discourse. The responsibility of and challenge to the scholars in America and Asia alike is the demand for responsible Bible usage and application in the public arena for the health of global nations.

From Public Relevance to Public Theology: Hermeneutical Consideration

As a reader and teacher of the Bible, I have been keen to read and teach the biblical text in a manner identifiable to the people of the GCR. To identify my reading strategy with the ethos of the GCR is to interact with the public interest of the GCR and to engage the social, political, economic and cultural aspects of the GCR with the text. This engagement itself inevitably drives the result of my readings of the biblical text into formulating some sort of a "localized" biblical theology or public-based biblical theology. In a way, this contributes towards the development of a kind of critical public-biblical theology that is based on critical biblical scholarship and contemporary hermeneutics, as compared to philosophically based or politically based theology in Western Europe. In this way, there is a meeting of biblical studies and public theology.[16]

The ethos of biblical studies and the ethos of the GCR are, and should be, closely related to each other, if social location means anything to biblical studies or its reading strategies. When detached, biblical studies is merely a scientific positivist academic exercise without its context or social location to form the field of context for practice or application of the text if it is to have any real life effect at all. Perhaps this also forms the difference between pragmatic and ideological approaches to the biblical text. The split between exegesis and application is unhealthy and irresponsible, if not unethical, as Schüssler Fiorenza has rightly pointed out, that "the once reigning hermeneutical division of labor between the exegete who describes what the text meant and the pastor/theologian who articulates what the text means has been seriously challenged in the past two decades and been proven to be epistemologically inadequate."[17]

---

16. I must confess that it was not until recently that my pedagogy has been the "scientific-theological positivist" paradigm, adopting standards of excellence from the West. It is also my continuous interest to develop some kind of a critical public biblical theology to form as the platform for contextual public engagement with biblical studies.

17. In "Rethinking the Educational Practices," 69, she also speaks of "how the seven critical feminist hermeneutical strategies could overcome the split between exegesis and application, between what the text meant and means, between history and hermeneutic/theology, which can also become fruitful for shaping doctoral education."

To engage biblical studies with the public relevance of the GCR, one needs to delineate the ethos of the GCR public (P). The ethos of the GCR is a complex phenomenon given the effect of globalization, political economy and market economy on any social location in the twenty-first century, not to mention the political history of the GCR for the last century.

To highlight simply and summarize forcefully, the ethos of the GCR and its primary public relevance and/or interest, as demonstrated by various academic and intellectual traditions, has been for the last century, and still is, the issue of political and legal systems or constitutional orders and the rule of law.[18] This is evident also in the recent economic and political developments of the GCR, where such interest has since sharply escalated both at the local and global level. The relation between mainland China and Taiwan has posted as a constant challenge not only to the stability of the region, but also to international politics, dragging Japan, the United States, and Korea into the troubled muddy water. North Korea and Tibet are yet other problems. If not handled well, the already unstable situation of the current political climate will become traumatic, and human life in the region will be at stake.

How, then, should biblical studies be relevant and engage in public discourses of various scales of magnitude? How should the "public character" or "public-ness" of biblical studies be delineated? Hermeneutically, the biblical text is the primary resource, historical scholarship must be acknowledged, multiple interpretive models ought be engaged, and standards of excellence ought be shifted from the scientific-positivist paradigm to the *public-ethical paradigm*, evaluating its ability and effectiveness in critical engagement with its scholarship on discourses of public issues. The functional aspect of the discipline in engaging with public issues should not be undermined either.[19]

---

18. I have been in constant dialogue with legal professionals, church and nonchurch, faith and nonfaith, intellectuals of public concerns, on issues of constitutional order, given the disparateness of the GCR particularly in their social and political systems. I continuously met with requests for contribution from biblical studies/scholarship in discussion on the issue of constitutional order or rule of law, knowing the effect of biblical traditions, e.g., the concept of covenant, on the formation of the federation of the United States.

19. I would take the creation in Genesis as a point of departure and work its way through the biblical text, from Old to New Testaments, constructing some sort of a "critical Sino-public biblical theological" model that could form a basis for further engagement in public issues. Such a theological construction is informed by both historical-critical scholarship, as well as the hermeneutical-postmodern paradigm, though not limiting itself to those paradigms. It takes seriously issues of public relevance as a focus of its interpretive reading strategy.

Pedagogical Consideration: A Critical-Public Intellectual Model

In order for biblical studies to engage in public discourse, pedagogical models must be considered, especially in graduate and/or doctoral studies. Since "competence in biblical criticism does not entail the ability to engage in a critical theoretical interdisciplinary meta-reflection on the work of biblical studies," as already pointed out by Schüssler Fiorenza,[20] the challenge to pedagogical consideration is on what model of graduate biblical education should the discipline engage and develop, that could yield the effect of achieving the goal of producing and shaping future "critical public intellectuals" of biblical scholarship. Pedagogically, departments/programs could consider including as its goal, the training of future "public intellectuals" who are equipped with the ability to critically draw on resources of historical-critical-biblical scholarship, while strategically producing contemporary readings of the text with public relevance, for which the intention of engaging their wealth of knowledge rhetorically in discourses of public issues are expected to contribute constructively towards the well being of humankind. The challenge to grasp with significant understanding of any public contexts in such a mobilized and volatile global reality of our daily living experience will post as a threat to modern contextual biblical interpretation because constant updating of one's general common knowledge is almost a must for adequate interaction with informed realistic contemporary social location. This may very well be the global challenge of public contexts to contemporary biblical studies.

The critical-public intellectual model also assumes the contribution of the master-apprentice model,[21] but given the reality of globalization and information technology, public discourse in the form of electronic digitized mode must be taken into serious consideration as complimentary tools to the hardcopy publishing industry, whereby the production and dissemination of knowledge can reach its utmost effect. This in turn will affect the traditional model of establishing standards of excellence for the discipline. The virtual public (Pv) may constitute perhaps the largest public social population than any existing form of public realm. The one commonly shared element of the

---

20. "Rethinking the Educational Practices," 72.

21. "Rethinking the Educational Practices," 69. This is the most common ancient model in the history of the production of Chinese intellectuals. See Jerome B. Grieder, *Intellectuals and the State in Modern China: A Narrative History* (New York: Free Press, 1981). Such a model of the ancient Chinese educational system placed a high value on the relationship between education/knowledge and personal/public human virtue, as in contrast to the modern economy-commercial and market-value oriented interest of current educational models. Not to mention the popular television series, *The Apprentice*, by Donald Trump.

virtual public is the exchange of information in the quantity and speed that human history has never encountered before. Knowledge no longer is the exclusive privilege of only a few scientific positivist elite solidly grounded at higher educational institutions. If the goal is for the advancement of common human wellness, and the production of knowledge in biblical scholarship has for its goal addressing public issues of equality, justice, love and responsibility, biblical studies should then consider departing from being a discipline of "purely technical and value-neutral science."[22] The historical educational ethos of the GCR perhaps could contribute positively and constructively towards the search for a pedagogical model for graduate/doctoral biblical education globally.

---

22. In "Rethinking the Educational Practices," 70, she notes that "[s]cientific knowledge was to serve the people and to be used for redistributing knowledge and wealth. It is this notion of science that needs to be recaptured by graduate biblical education."

2. Cultural-National Locations of Graduate Biblical Studies

Graduate Studies Now: Some Reflections from Experience

Athalya Brenner

Let me begin with a little story by way of an introduction. The original version of this paper was written for presentation in the "Graduate Studies: Ethos and Discipline" session of the Society of Biblical Literature Annual Meeting in San Diego (November 2007). I finished it in Haifa, Israel, a week before the conference. Just before sending it to the session's organizers and this book's editors, Elisabeth Schüssler Fiorenza and Kent Harold Richards, I decided to watch a little television for relaxation while pondering whether additions or changes were necessary.

Almost immediately, there appeared a commercial on the screen. A young, handsome-in-a-design-way male painter was shown in his untidy atelier, with a huge empty canvas on the wall, and a male voice, a *basso profundo*, started speaking. The voice said:

> **In the beginning, there was chaos** (tohu va-bohu). **Just water. And then there was light.** *The painter puts some water and light on the canvas.* **Then the water was divided.** *The painter divides the water on the canvas.* **Then dry land appeared, and vegetation.** *The painter paints wonderful flowers and shrubs.* **Then the sun, and the moon and stars;** *duly painted in another corner.* **Then the animals, big and small.** *Painted as well.* Then came humankind. *Ditto.*

> **And then**, said the voice, **it was time to rest.** *And the painter sits down with a smile and sigh, and takes out of his pocket a chocolate bar, and eats it slowly, completely relaxed and absorbed, with an expression of bliss on his face.*

The television channel was a regular commercial Israeli channel, presenting both news and entertainment. The story was told in English with Hebrew subtitles, although the chocolate bar was an Israeli product. I take it therefore that an American advertisement was adapted locally, hence this commercial was shown originally outside Israel. A few years ago, my initial response would have probably been, "How cheap, how dare they?" But this time, after the initial amazement, all I could think about was, "Let me have this, and let me know what caused this creative outburst, and let me start from here when I teach Genesis. For this is what we have; this represents the *Zeitgeist* well, and at least gives the Bible some transparent afterlife in popular culture. And this is the cultural wave I would like to join, we should join, if we want to have students, including graduate students, and show social responsibility." And so on. How exactly to do it, how now, this is another matter entirely. And the business of the reflections I shall offer below.

The mandate of the session was to recommend directives for the future of graduate studies of the Bible. But, before doing that, it is perhaps advisable to refer to the recent past and to the present. My personal experience here may be significant, I think, since it is derived from several locations and various cultural traditions. In the last ten years I have taught Biblical Studies in four places that are different from each other geographically, religiously and culturally: Israel, The Netherlands, Texas, and Hong Kong. I can therefore compare the situations in those different locations, using firsthand observations.

In the Netherlands and in Israel there has been a dwindling of interest and student numbers for Jewish studies, Religious Studies and theology, which used to be the natural homes for Biblical Studies. This process has now gone on for about two or three decades. In the Netherlands, this has happened not only in so called secular universities, like the University of Amsterdam, but also in religiously affiliated universities, both protestant and Catholic. As a result, and for economic reasons, market policies were applied and mergers effected. In the Netherlands, two moves were undertaken: toward consolidation of church education in certain locales, on a national basis, and similar action for nonchurch but confessional institutions (in this connection, the forced merger of the Catholic University of Utrecht with the Theological University of Tilburg is a good example); and in "secular" institutions, the consolidation of traditionally independent theology and Religious Studies "disciplines" into hardly distinct segments of a larger, often subordinate, unit. Thus, when I came to the University of Amsterdam in 1994—first as a visiting professor, then as full-time faculty—there was there a fully-fledged Faculty of Theology and Religious Studies, including a department of church instruction, with Biblical Studies as a department in it. In 1996 the Church withdrew its support and localized its training and recognition at a limited number of other universities. Concurrently, the university's decentralized structure was centralized by fusing many former mini-faculties into larger units. This faculty was therefore discontinued as such and made into a department within a new Faculty of the Humanities. Theology was duly dropped from the department's title and Religious Studies was defined as a subdepartment within the Humanities' Department of Art, Religion, and Culture (in that order). Individual sections such as Biblical Studies, each with its own professorial chair, remained organizationally distinct as a sub-sub-sub unit, each having its own M.A. mini-program. But as of this academic year, this too is gone. There is one subsection, Religious Studies, and one M.A. program. Students can still specialize in the trajectory of their choice but there is no adequate course supply—on the undergraduate or the graduate level—in many subjects, apart from the fashionable ones: mysticism and Islam. Needless to say, the demand for studying original biblical languages was dropped up to and sometimes including the Ph.D. level. In August 2008, after I had retired from the Amsterdam Hebrew Bible/Old Testament Chair, the chair itself ceased to exist. Biblical studies is taught by entry-level teachers, at times without a Ph.D.; the same fate awaits the New Testament Chair and other branches of Religious Studies, such as Church History or Sociology/Psychology of Religion. Instead, a general position of a Religious Studies Chair has been created and presumably fills also the needs for Biblical Studies.

In Israel, a similar picture is beginning to emerge. At the secular Tel Aviv University, where I now teach since retiring from Amsterdam, Biblical Studies and other subjects stopped being independent departments two years ago and are now bundled together in a Department of Hebrew Culture. (In other places in Israel, Bible is still a stand-alone, but the change is certainly coming, since similar subjects have been clustered together for a while now. A case in point is the merger of Jewish History and Jewish Thought, including Talmud, into one department already years ago). To turn to the Chinese University of Hong Kong: the wonderful Hebrew Bible Ph.D. program that Prof. Archie Lee has created for Chinese students, as well as the M.A. and B.A. classes, are all given within a Department of Culture and Religion (in that order), although in close cooperation with the Divinity School—since the college, Chung Chi College, is basically a Christian college. Let me add that in recent years I have also taught graduate students at Brite Divinity School, which is part of Texas Christian University, where students introduce themselves quite often by saying, "My name is so-and-so and I am a Disciple [of Christ]." Even there, Biblical Studies is now limited by comparison to what it was, and the divinity/theology programs get more attention, and more budgets and positions, than the once independently thriving Biblical Studies program.

What is being described here is probably the inevitable result of market forces as well as the creation of a new market situation. The Bible appears to be once more the legitimate portion of religious, not to say orthodox, circles. If you go into church training, Jewish or Christian, you will have to take a few Bible courses, but not too many by comparison to pastoral, doctrinal, and other courses. If you are interested in religious phenomena from an ethic point of view, you will probably opt for more fashionable subjects like mysticism—the New Age connection is here unmistakable—and/or Islam, which seems to carry a tag that reads: "urgent understanding needed and will solve intercultural problems."

Biblical studies aficionados can rant and rage or protest politely, according to their personal temperament: This is unfair, the Bible is with all of us even in a so-called "secular" culture—whatever "secular" means, "soft secular" or "hard secular."[1] The Bible continues to be used, misused, and abused variously. It is present in life even when ignored, certainly in the fashionable Islam as well as in culture generally. One can also speak eloquently about the failure of Biblical Studies practitioners, especially teachers, to make their subject more attractive to newcomers.[2] A *mea culpa* attitude and apportioning the blame is always fun to do. So let me continue from here.

The wheel of fashion may turn back, as it often does. Classical Biblical Studies may return—together with its well known hallmarks: original languages, higher and lower criticism, historical criticism, study of form and genre and lexicography and grammar, and so on. This might happen, but I doubt whether it will happen soon. And, meanwhile, there are certain things to foreground. Classical Biblical Studies, as developed from the eighteenth century onwards, were motivated by the Enlightenment spirit but remained for the most part the product of scholars with some confessional attitude. It was never innocent of ideologies. It remained largely the domain of interested religious parties, mostly male and Protestant and European then American and Caucasian, even in the academic world. Therefore even now, when the world polarizes in between secularism and neo-orthodoxy, when "classical" Biblical Studies is still insisted upon by church-training institutions and divinity schools, this insistence, and the praxis itself, is not free of ideology. Of

---

1. My use of "soft" versus "hard" secular harks back to a recent Israeli debate concerning a work published in Israel in 2007: Yirmiyahu Yovel and Yair Tsaban, eds., *Encyclopedia of Jewish Culture* [Hebrew] (5 vols.; Jerusalem: Keter, 2007). The heated public debate concerned, among other points, the declared "secular" bias of the work as a whole and the (non)usefulness of such a bias for doing justice to its topic. In this debate, "soft" would imply a nonconfessional but nonviolent attitude to religion, sometimes tinged with respect; "hard" would imply a combatant, totally nontolerant atheism and anticlericalism.

2. In Israel there has been a decade-long debate about the quality of Bible study in the state-run (secular) education system in all levels up to university level. A common claim is that, because of the teachers' low pay and low level, Bible study (which is part of the obligatory curriculum packet) has lost so much status that it has become an unpopular academic destination for prospective students, who have the choice of applying to more practical and/or attractive subjects.

course, this is neither interesting nor greatly attractive for "secular" students. This may be regrettable but is a fact. It is also a fact that biblical study has always been tainted by intent and target, even within academic institutions, which is far from ethical, notwithstanding the type of direction or intent. At the risk of being unpopular, let me state that the only Biblical Studies that are relatively ethical, in my experience, have been and still are conducted in academic institutions that have no overt religious affiliation (read: dependency).

So what to do? I would like to suggest that the only option that we have now is to adjust to the *Zeitgeist*, which would mean to bow to the need to teach Bibles as cultures and within the interdisciplinary (rather than conventionally "disciplinary") frameworks now being developed all over, as shown. Whether we wish for Bible, and religion, to be subsumed under "culture" as a (semi) discipline or not, this is the situation now. My guess is that in future years this will become the trend more and more: people, including graduate students most of whom will prepare themselves to teaching careers, would be more and more interested in the Bible's afterlife in their own culture and in other contemporary cultures, as relevant subject as well as strategy. Therefore, this is perhaps not just an ethical choice but it is pragmatic and a means of endurance. We had better exploit the trend before it is too late. When media studies are more attractive than Greek philosophy or medieval theology, I would rather join forces with the former, for my own purposes. When mysticism is popular and conceptualized as a pre–New Age phenomenon, I would rather inject some ancient magic and ritual into the discussion, thus appropriating it, rather than disparage the subject (which is in fact what I would really like to do).

In Amsterdam, when we became part of the Faculty of the Humanities, we dreamt up two M.A. programs, or trajectories, in our field. One was named Bibles and Cultures, the other Jewish Cultures. Let me say a few words about the first one, which is more relevant to the present topic, because in my opinion it represents an attempt at embracing the new while preserving something of the old and also aims to serve the changing community.

You may notice that the program title contains a double plural: Bibles and cultures. Indeed, notions of plurality are central to it. Our basic premise is that various communities' "Bibles" are as different as their cultures, even if they all call it The Bible irrespective of creed or its lack thereof, and that we as teachers have to let our graduate students integrate that pluralistic perspective into their worldview. Handpicked courses on the afterlives of the Bible in cultural—diachronic and synchronic—reception, Bible and/in media, theoretical approaches to Biblical Studies, and Bible and visual arts, are specifically designed to appeal to the students' current interests as well as to be text-based. We teach Hebrew Bible and New Testament together and refer to the Qur'an and Islamic traditions as much as we can, starting to do that already on the undergraduate level. We do suffer, since university policy does not require graduate students to study Hebrew or Greek on the M.A. level, but we have found that working with at least three translations—for instance, the JPS, NRSV, and perhaps the NAB or the New Dutch translation, and tracing their differences and the difficulties that produce the differences, as directed by the teacher—does help. Other possible classes deal with religion, power and violence or additional subjects relevant to contemporary life, and there are research programs tracing the politicization of Bibles and similar trends.

Formally our Ph.D. students were members of the faculty's research schools—either ASCA (Amsterdam School of Cultural Analysis) or the ICH (Institute of Culture and History). In keeping with the European tradition, they do not have to attend Ph.D. classes apart from a general graduate seminar, in which all Ph.D. students from cultural and related studies participate. In recent years, we have found that students who complete the M.A. program tend to continue as Ph.D. students with us, if this is at all possible.

So, please ask me, does it work well? Do you get enough students, do they do good work, are they satisfied, do they find work and what kind of work? My answer is, not really so far. After four or five years of practice, the graduate student number still does not justify a separate and solid program of Biblical Studies. I can cite various reasons: we do not give enough grants; we have no undergraduate program in Biblical Studies; other Religious Studies topics are more fashionable; we offer no specific professional future to our students. Reasons for failure and also excuses can be stated, but this is not my purpose. I remain convinced that this is a "right" way since the rewards are beginning to come in, as Ph.D. students. The work currently undertaken by Bible Ph.D. students is interesting and varied and combines classical Biblical Studies with Cultural Studies in a way that would have been unthinkable only a few years ago. At this time, each of the Hebrew Bible Ph.D. students has decided to study Hebrew and the New Testament students are taking Greek. Each one of them has decided to focus on a segment of biblical text, as in the past, but to add a cultural lens to it, be it media or film or book history or literature or music or philosophy studies, or a combination of the above. We see this as an encouraging sign, especially since we went through several years of no new Ph.D. students, and our grant budget is as severely limited as it is for M.A. students.

At this time, I know that the University of Amsterdam does not have enough patience and faith and strength to invest, as an institution, in a specific graduate Biblical Studies program within its framework. (Within the Religious Studies undergraduate programs only several courses are offered, although a minor in Biblical Studies is possible.) We should also be mindful of another ethical aspect, namely, turning out (so to speak) graduate students on any level who can find work. This is part of our responsibility. Exclaiming that we educate them for understanding contemporary culture is good but hardly practical. Perhaps on the M.A. or equivalent level, at least, a solid pact with any university's teacher training program is advisable, even mandatory. Not all M.A. graduates will continue to the next, Ph.D. level; those who do not and who are not affiliated with a religious institution or calling might wish for another career option. A program along this line is actually being implemented currently at Tel Aviv University: an interdisciplinary program in Hebrew Studies, with or without Bible at its center, tailored especially if not solely for high school teachers.

These notes are written, and spoken, from a space that is felt as a minoritized space. By this I do not point to my being Jewish/Israeli or a feminist. My space is a Third Room, if you wish, to use Homi Bhabha's famous idiom. In my case, this is the nonreligious, nonfaith, nonbelieving room, if you want this to be presented negatively, or the secular, a-believing room, if you want it positively. In my view, you might have guessed, the only way and just way and responsible way of saving Biblical Studies, for graduate students and for others, is by transporting them from Religious Studies to Cultural Studies, consciously so, at least for the time being and with all the responsibility that this entails.

Graduate Biblical Studies in India

Monica Jyotsna Melanchthon

The Doctoral Program in India: A Historical Note

This brief paper on graduate biblical studies in India begins with an outline of the history of the Board of Theological Education of the Senate of Serampore College (BTESSC), which is an association of Protestant theological schools based in India. The history recognizes William Carey as the founder of the Serampore College, which was integrated by a royal charter in 1827 with rights and immunities of a university and the power to confer degrees. In 1845, this Danish settlement was transferred to the British government, which made provision for the continuation of the chartered rights and powers of the college. The first convocation of Serampore College was held in 1915 when the Degree of Bachelor of Divinity was conferred. The Bengal Legislative Act IV of 1918 enlarged the Council of Serampore College and constituted the Senate of Serampore College (SSC). From its inception, the SSC was ecumenical in character, comprised of representatives from various Christian communities in India. In the year 1919, several theological colleges were affiliated with the Senate of Serampore College. At the convocation held in January 1930, the degree of Doctor of Divinity (HC) was conferred for the first time. In 1949, the location of the Council of Serampore College was transferred from London to Serampore, India.[1]

The Board of Theological Education of the Senate of Serampore College

In 1975 the SSC joined the Board of Theological Education (BTE) functioning under the auspices of the National Council of Churches in India (NCCI),

---

1. See Samson Prabhakar and Ravi Tiwari, "Hope Challenges and Priorities of Ecumenical Theological Education: A Regional Perspective from India," in *Ecumenical Theological Education in Changing Context: Problems, Challenges, Priorities* (ed. A. Wati Longchar; Jorhat: ETE-WCC/CCA, n.d.), 41.

for the purposes of strengthening and broadening the ecumenical dimension of theological education in India. Thus was created the Board of Theological Education of the Senate of Serampore College (BTESSC) with the objective to change and renew theological education. This was done in response to the challenge of the context, to meet the demands in ministry and create new patterns of ministry, and to be an agent of change in structures of theological education for the sake of the mission of the church. It was also hoped that it would enable the church to engage more vigorously in reflection, articulation, and communication of faith in Christ in the midst of the concrete life situation in South Asia. Today the BTESSC, with representation from fifty theological institutions in India, Sri Lanka, Nepal, and Bangladesh, of varied confessional leanings (all Protestant), is one of the major representative bodies of churches, legally constituted and responsible for administering theological education in India. "It stands as a unique example of ecumenical participation of the churches and theological institutions in curriculum planning and evaluation towards common degree programs and in their quest for holistic training for ministry."[2]

SOUTH ASIA THEOLOGICAL RESEARCH INSTITUTE

In the 1980s the BTESSC felt the need for an advanced research center in the country to develop, coordinate, and facilitate research at doctoral and nondegree levels emphasizing its indigenous and contextual character. A national consultation held in 1987 with participation of several related partners resulted in the establishment of the South Asia Theological Research Institute (SATHRI) in 1989 in Bangalore. SATHRI then became the research wing of the BTESSC with the aim to promote contextualized theological research both at the degree and nondegree levels to promote faculty development, to strengthen member institutions as centers for research, to produce basic tools for theological education and to arrange programs that would strengthen the relationship between the church (Protestant) and theological education and to deal with the publication of research works.[3]

In 1999, the BTESSC recognized centers for doctoral research, namely, the United Theological College, Bangalore; the Gurukul Lutheran Theological College, Chennai; the Federated Faculty for Research in Religion and Culture (FFRRC) in Kottayam, Kerala; and the North India Institute of Post Graduate Theological Studies (NIIPGTS) in Kolkata. Subsequently the Tamilnadu Theological Seminary (TTS) in Madurai, Tamil Nadu, and the Union Biblical

---
2. Ibid., 42.
3. Handbook of SATHRI (Bangalore: SATHRI, 2005).

Seminary (UBS) in Pune, Maharastra, have been added to the list. These are institutions that have been identified to have the capacity, facilities and the infrastructure to develop doctoral programs according to the criteria given by the BTESSC from time to time. SATHRI continues to coordinate and guide formal research at the doctoral level under the guidance of the Committee for Research and with the cooperation of the doctoral centers.[4]

Doctoral studies are becoming increasingly significant in the shaping of both theological educators and pastors and leaders in the church. There was a time when higher theological training and studies were pursued only by those who wanted to become seminary teachers, but today more and more individuals are opting for doctoral studies and returning to serve as pastors in the church. The doctoral program in India is aware that it needs to equip individuals with skills and knowledge that will enable them to effectively serve the academy, the church and the world as critical interlocutors between the Christian faith and the society/world.

Ninety-nine percent of the students are financially supported by SATHRI through funds that it receives from partners, mainly from overseas.[5] It continues to monitor the standard of the doctoral program of all the centers through the Committee on Research (which is comprised of all the Deans of doctoral Research of member institutions and others). At the national level, it functions as a liaison between member institutions and the World Council of Churches (WCC), the Christian Conference of Asia (CCA), the Association of Theological Education in South East Asia (ATESEA), the Regional Committee of the Solidarity fund, and works closely with the Association of Theological Teachers in India, and the Association of Theologically Trained Women in India (ATTWI) thus enhancing ecumenical theological education through its academic programs, financial stewardship and facilitation of mutual cooperation. In addition SATHRI continues to depend upon resource persons drawn from outside, both Protestant and Catholic institutions as well as from secular universities to enable research programs of BTESSC, especially in areas such as social analysis, communication, liturgy, Christian education, women's studies, and other emerging areas.

The records of the BTESSC show that between 1970 and 2007 there have been 125 graduates in various disciplines, seventeen of whom are women. The first woman graduated in 1993. The records of the office of SATHRI (November 2008) show that there are currently 107 registered students, of which twenty-four are women at the various centers pursuing research in varied

---

4. *Report of the Director of Research and SATHRI 2004–05* presented to the BTESSC, at its meeting in Jorhat, Assam (February 2005), 1.

5. Ibid., 3.

disciplines but more particularly Old Testament, New Testament, Christian theology, Christian ethics, history of Christianity, religions, communication, Christian ministry, women's studies, and social analysis. Ten of these will receive their degrees in the 2009 convocation, one of whom is a woman.

Theological education imparted through the BTESSC is based on the hope that it would promote the formation, equipment and empowerment of the leadership personnel for the ministry and mission of the church in the world and for theological education of the church as a whole. It is envisaged that the theological education thus imparted would promote a creative, comprehensive and critical knowledge of the context and the content of ministry and mission of the church in the contemporary religious, social, economic, political and cultural realities. This overall objective of theological education is applicable to all courses offered by the BTESSC.

Hence, the stated aim of the Doctor of Theology program of the Senate of Serampore College is to form and equip "leadership personnel for the ministry and mission of the church in the world and for the theological education of the Church as a whole."[6] The aim therefore points to the formation of personnel who can function both within the academy and the society at large. An individual holding a Doctor of Theology degree "should have a creative, comprehensive and critical knowledge of the context and the content of the ministry and mission of the Church in the contemporary religious, social, economic, political and cultural realities."[7]

The objectives of the program are: (1) "to promote critical and creative research in specialized fields of knowledge related to the life, heritage and mission of the Church as well as contextual Christian faith, and to advance the frontiers of knowledge"; (2) "to promote the formation of well-equipped Christian teachers, leaders, communicators, writers and scholars"; (3) "to provide leadership for shaping the self-understanding and structures of the Church, which are relevant for fulfilling its God given vocation in the world"; and (4) "to encourage independent and original research using integrated and interdisciplinary approach in theological education."[8]

The perspectives that a candidate is encouraged to adopt in his/her research should be those that are committed to "justice, dignity and a life worthy of all humanity"[9]; the cultural, ideological and religious plurality of our societies, the ecumenical dimension of all Christian thinking, church, and

---

6. Senate of Serampore College, *Regulations Relating to the Degree of Doctor of Theology (D.Th.)*, (2005): 7.
7. Ibid.
8. Ibid., 7–8.
9. Ibid., 8.

life and one that takes seriously the context of Asia, its languages, culture, and patterns of thought and behavior.

GRADUATE BIBLICAL STUDIES IN INDIA

Four of the six centers offer the doctoral program in biblical studies, but not necessarily in both Testaments: UTC (Old Testament and New Testament); Gurukul (Old Testament); UBS (Old Testament); FFRRC (Old Testament and New Testament). Hebrew and Greek are prerequisites and proficiency in German is also required. Students are expected to attend a four-week-long course on research methodology conducted by SATHRI which is a prerequisite. The methodology seminar is conducted in order to expose and introduce the student to the aims and objectives of research in the discipline and the varied methodologies in the discipline. This is accompanied by some practical sessions enabling the student to apply the method that is introduced. Since it is assumed that a holder of a master's degree has learned how to do research, this four week formal introduction to research methodology at the beginning of doctoral training is considered sufficient.

During the first year of the program, besides exhibiting proficiency in languages, the student goes through a period of assessment during which he/she is required to write three to four research papers on different areas within the discipline (methodology, theology, etc). The titles of these papers are pre-approved by the Committee on Research and the submissions are evaluated by a team of three examiners, two internal (from within the center) and one external reader appointed by the Committee on Research. Upon satisfactory completion of the papers, the student presents a thesis proposal, which is reviewed by the doctoral committee at the center where he or she is registered and later by the Committee on Research. The student then works in close consultation with the appointed advisor and upon completion of the project, the dissertation is submitted to SATHRI, which appoints two readers besides the advisor. There is a public defense of the dissertation. The completed research cannot be published without the permission of SATHRI. These, in brief, are the requirements of the doctoral program.

I do not have the figures for those who have completed the doctoral program in biblical studies before the establishment of SATHRI, but between 1989 and 2007, nineteen individuals graduated with degrees in biblical studies (seventeen men and two women): eight in Old Testament studies (six men and two women) and eleven in New Testament studies (all men). Currently there are approximately twenty-five students doing research in the area of biblical studies, thirteen in Old Testament studies (three women and ten men) and twelve in New Testament studies (nine men and three women).

As of now there is no database containing or listing the abstracts or the titles of dissertations completed. Judging by the titles of the research projects of those that I have been able to find, from a sampling no doubt, one is able to discern the fact that most of the topics are a study of biblical themes.[10] Despite the efforts of SATHRI, which encourages students to be contextual and interdisciplinary, the titles do not reflect such an effort except for a few exceptions. The few dissertations I was able to browse through revealed that the majority of them employ traditional methodologies with the classical historical critical and literary methods dominating Old Testament studies and redaction criticism dominating New Testament studies. Many of them also claim to use insights gained from the sociological approach to the study of the Bible to supplement or strengthen their conclusions. The perspective, method, and hermeneutic in vogue today is the postcolonial one.

---

10. New Testament: (1) The Rich and the Poor in the Parables of Luke; (2) The Nature and Function of the Paraclete in the Farewell Discourse in John 13:1–17, 26: An Enquiry; (3) Temple Criticism in St. Mark's Gospel: The Economic Role of the Jerusalem Temple during the First Century CE; (4) Nature of the Parables of Mark: An Inquiry into the Use of Nature Images in Chapter 4 with Special Reference to Their Significance for Ecological Concern; (5) Galatians 1:11–2:21—Paul's Understanding of the Gospel and Its Impact on the Relationship between Jewish and Gentile Christians; (6) The Concept of the Church in Matthew; (7) The Inheritors of the Kingdom of God according to Lucan Perspective; (8) The Role of Women in the Portrayal of Salvation in the Gospel of Luke; (9) The Importance of the Christological Confessions in the Fourth Gospel—A Critique of Johannine Christology; (10) Diversity in Paul's Eschatology and Its Determinants: A Study of the Selected Eschatological Themes in Paul's letters; (11) A Socio-narrative Analysis of the Characters in the Lukan Infancy Narratives (Luke 1:5–2:52); (12) Theocentricity in Lukan Theology: An Exploration into the Portrayals of God in Luke-Acts; (13) Pauline Concept of Soma in Relation to the Saving Work of Christ: A Study of Select Texts from the Letters of Paul.

Old Testament: (1) Legal Protection for the Poor in Ancient Israel and Its Significance for Mizo Study; (2) The Impact of the United Monarchy on the Peasantry in Ancient Israel; (3) The Identity of "the Enemies" according to Job 4:27; (4) The Motif of the Righteous Sufferer in the Psalms of Individual Lament; (5) The Preferential Option of the Poor in Prophetic Literature of Israel in the Socio-political Context of Eighth Century BCE; (6) The Relationship between Election and Israel's Attitude towards the Nations in the Book of Isaiah; (7) The Process of the Formulation of Liberative Hebrew Scripture as a Paradigm for the Formulation of a Scripture for the Liberation of Dalits; (8) The History and Significance of Manual Labour in the Hebrew Bible: A Sociological Approach; (9) Portrayals of Woman in the Book of Proverbs: A Reading from the Perspective of a Mizo Woman; (10) The Worldview of the Yahweh Speeches in the Book of Job; (11) Theology of Hope in Deutero-Isaiah: A Quest for a New Identity of the People of God.

CHALLENGES TO CRITICAL STUDY AND INTERPRETATION OF THE BIBLE IN INDIA

Studies by scholars on the expansion of Christianity in Asia have shown that Christianity was present in the west coast of India even in the first century C.E.[11] Yet the rich history of the Bible in India has had little impact on biblical research and interpretation in India. Graduate biblical studies in India are affected by several internal and external challenges.

1. In the last two decades the face of the Serampore college family and therefore the character of theological education in India have radically changed. From its inception, theological education has been an endeavor of and for the church. An ecumenical and mainline theological and ideological institution has given membership to increased populations of evangelical and Pentecostal groups and institutions. Students from many and varied Christian denominations and ideological persuasions, cultural contexts, social locations are seeking training for leadership in churches, the academic community and the secular society at large. The theological community has not fully grasped the extent of the challenge this poses both to our teaching methods and the content of our teaching. The wide range of denominational and confessional leanings within the Serampore family makes it almost impossible to effectively introduce new methods or ideologies that would be appreciated by all. Not all agree or approve with the concept of biblical interpretation for the purposes of social transformation. But more importantly new perspectives being offered by women, Dalits, the *adivasis* and tribals are received with suspicion. The differences and diversity inherent within the Serampore family has therefore not been sufficiently dealt with nor has it been tapped to enrich theological education in India. Hence there is often a distinction made between "liberal and progressive" colleges and "evangelical and charismatic" ones. The Bible and its interpretation has become a sensitive issue and arguments are made in favor of maintaining the authority of the Bible. But is it really a question of the authority of the Bible? Duraisingh says it well:

> The claim of the absolute and sole authority of the Bible in doctrinal matters in protestant churches is a dubious and dangerous one. It is dubious because if one is honest, one has to accept that the ultimate authority for Protestants

---

11. John C. England, *The Hidden History of Christianity: The Churches of the East before 1500* (Delhi: ISPCK, 1996); Hugh Moffett, *Beginnings to 1500* (vol. 1 of *A History of Christianity in Asia*; rev. ed.; Maryknoll, N.Y.: Orbis, 1998).

is not and never has been scripture alone, but scripture as interpreted in the tradition of their respective denomination or school of thought.[12]

A majority of institutions are therefore not willing to sufficiently expose their students to the critical study of the Bible which to them is against the doctrine of the inerrancy and verbal inspiration of Scripture. However, this uncritical approach is not because Indian interpreters have not sufficiently developed scientific minds in order to be able to look at the Bible critically. One major reason is that some of our theological institutions are headed by individuals and graduates of similar schools from abroad. Hence a collaborative effort to bring about integration and intellectual excellence by using this rich denominational diversity in scriptural interpretation is still to be explored.

2. This issue of Indian students not being critical of the Bible has to be also understood within the context of the history of the reception of the Bible in India. A majority of the Christian populace belongs to the Dalit communities who were, by virtue of their status as "unclean" and "untouchable", denied access to scripture, not only to read and reflect but to even hear it being recited. The Bible when it was made available to them became an icon, a meta-symbol of the colonialists and the *Vedas* for the Christian Dalit communities.[13] Accessibility to the Christian sacred Scriptures enabled them to "embrace a central religious symbol that was denied to them by Hinduism."[14] The Bible functioned in a subversive manner, for it replaced the worldview of the Hindu Scriptures and displaced the Hindu Vedas. The Bible became the Christian "Veda,"[15] filling a void and supplying the Dalits with a framework for knowledge that they did not have to begin with, and which they desired. A possible concomitant result of this history is the Indian interpreter's (particularly the Dalit) inability to question and critique Scripture.

3. The thought-world of India and that of the Bible are similar. The similarities in the culture(s) of the Bible and the Indian culture(s) in some ways contribute to the inability of the Indian interpreter to be critical of the biblical text. Any comprehension of things Indian requires acquaintance with the Hindu worldview. Here one does not mean so much the abstractions of Hindu philosophy, but rather the popular interpretations and norms of con-

---

12. Christopher Duraisingh, "The Authority of the Bible in the Modern Period," *IJT* 33 (1974): 75.

13. Sathianathan Clarke, "Viewing the Bible through the Eyes and Ears of Subalterns in India," *BibInt* 10 (2002): 245–66.

14. Ibid., 256–57.

15. Thomas Thangaraj, "The Bible as Veda: Biblical Hermeneutics in Tamil Christianity," in *Vernacular Hermeneutics* (ed. R. S. Sugirtharajah; Sheffield: Sheffield Academic Press, 1999), 138–39.

duct. Many of these have long been accepted or assimilated by the non-Hindu minority, and many practices that have been challenged by civil law owe their impunity to convergences in Hindu and Muslim attitudes and traditions. The ethical and social ideas compactly contained in the law books of Manu and Moses, namely, the Manusmriti and the Torah, illustrate in a systematic manner the rules of life that prevailed in the Aryan and the Hebrew society. Both exhibit the cultural stratification of the principles of the social, ethical/moral and cultic/religious life of the Aryans and the Hebrews, respectively, and they contain the "rules of life" of the traditions concerned, and both continue to have a determinative influence on Hindu and Christian morality. They are jointly affecting the Indian Christian community but more particularly the roles and the status of Indian Christian women and other marginalized groups. The commonly understood biblical position surrounding, for example, the hierarchical societal structures, the treatment of women, slaves (read "Dalit"), and people of diverse faiths to name a few, resonate with the Indian Christian reader's experience of life and culture. Scripture and culture collude, hence a questioning of scripture is considered redundant.

4. The student is hesitant and is often unable to be critical of the vast amount of available knowledge. This needs to be understood culturally. Learning in the Indian context is a collaborative exercise, an expression of the valuing of the communal and familial over the individual. Deference to authority is valued and expected, and similarly a general attitude of obedience to and respect for the more senior. These are aspects of valuing of hierarchy over equality. The student is therefore more at home in learning situations where the teacher is the expert, with ascribed authority as well as achieved authority. Such students expect the teacher to transmit knowledge to them in a more or less banking style. This is the dominant pedagogy in the Indian educational system and the student is often unprepared and ill equipped to handle research which requires skill, individual initiative, evaluation of sources, and the identification of a hermeneutical framework.

5. The doctoral degree in biblical studies is normally earned over three to seven years and culminates in a single research thesis. The emphasis is on research achievement, with the thesis representing an original contribution to knowledge. Against this background, an emphasis is placed on the role of the degree as research training. D.Th. students pursue a formal training program in research methods, intended to provide a grounding in theory and techniques which will be of long-term value to them, beyond the completion of their D.Th. theses. Similarly, D.Th. students are now encouraged to acquire and to use a broad range of more generic skills. The emphasis is also being placed on a multidisciplinary approach and experience and on the development of life-long skills both relevant to the subject being studied but also of

more general value, such as skills in technology, communication and languages, and presentational skills.

The training component of the doctoral degree program provides the academic and methodological schooling necessary with respect to work on the doctoral dissertation, but doctoral education in India has not been oriented toward the training of professors/teachers for higher education, that is, university teaching and scientific research. The D.Th. as it stands today represents training for many potential consumers of graduate education; yet it is too little training for its traditional role of preparing future faculty/teachers.

I am advocating that research centers have a structured educational program that would equip them with a comprehensive knowledge of the field. I would think that future employers expect doctorate holders to have a broad orientation as well as disciplinary depth. In other words, the educational part of the doctorate should prepare doctoral-degree holders both for functions within universities, research institutes, and resource and development functions as well as for other functions in a variety of societal organizations. An important challenge will be to provide a course program which combines both the objective to prepare students to become the next generation of biblical interpreters and that of preparing them for other career destinations.

6. There is the lack of access to and paucity of published material and financial restrictions. The Indian student has access to only a fragment of the material that might be available in the West, although the Internet and Web-based research is providing some help. Information literacy skills are an important part of doctoral studies and librarians in India are not playing a substantial role in the doctoral research process. This is because librarians in India lack the subject expertise to assist them with finding literature relevant to their research topic. Involving librarians more directly in the dissertation research process in an effective way to help students develop information literacy skills is an urgent need. Funding is a major problem and students are unable to afford the purchase of books or travel to research sites which may hold the material required for their research.

7. Because of the legacy of colonialism and Christianization, many of us have been taught to devalue our heritages to the extent that our Indian religious and cultural resources are either unfamiliar or have not been emphasized in doing theology. A simple example would be the ease with which students of mine see themselves as the descendants of the Israelite community and have little concern about their ignorance of their Indian ancestry, their traditions or culture. Most cultural resources that are made available to Indian interpreters are often mediated through Western scholarship and heavily influenced by racism and orientalism. Another issue is that in the last few decades the concern of biblical interpretation in India is the contextualization of the Christian

message in India. Yet the works by Indian scholars are rarely reflected in the syllabi or in the bibliographies of research projects—works of Indian biblical scholars, namely, E. C. John, Gnana Robinson, M. Vellanickal, George Soares Prabhu, Maria Arul Raja, J. J. Kanagaraj, George Mlakuzhyil, S.J., C. I. David Joy, Sam P. Matthew, Michaelsami Arockiam, T. Job Anbalagan, Takatemjen Ao, D. Jones Muthunayagom, Paduthottu G. George, P. P. Thomas, M. Gnanvaram, Pratap Chandra Gine, L. H. Rawsea, and R. L. Hnuni, to name a few.[16] A majority of these articles by Indian scholars are found, as can be seen, in

---

16. E. C. John, "Life and Death in Old Testament Research," *BTF* 9 (1977): 13–27; "Theological Research and the Churches in India: Old Testament," *BTF* 10 (1978): 6–11; "Israel and Inculturation: An Appraisal," *Jeevadhara* 14 (1984): 87–94.

Gnana Robinson, *Let Us Be Like the Nations: A Commentary on 1 and 2 Samuel* (International Theological Commentary; Grand Rapids: Eerdmans; Edinburgh: Handsel, 1993); *The Origin and Development of the Old Testament Sabbath: A Comprehensive Exegetical Approach* (Frankfurt: Lang, 1988); *Critical Use of the Bible* (Chennai: CLS, 2000).

M. Vellanickal, "Jesus: The Bread of Life," *BiSh* 4/1 (1978): 30–48; "Drink from the Source of the Living Water: A 'Dhvani' Interpretation of the Dialogue between Jesus and the Samaritan Woman (Jn 4:4–26)," *BiSh* 5 (1979): 309–18; "The Johannine Concept of Righteousness or Dharma," *BiSh* 6 (1980): 382–94; "The Society of the Future according to the Book of Revelation," in *The Indian Church in the Struggle for a New Society* (ed. D.S. Amalorpavadass; Bangalore: National Biblical Catechetical and Liturgical Centre, 1981), 689–701; "Understanding the Gospel of John in India," in *Theologizing in India* (ed. M. Amaladoss et al.; Bangalore: Theological Publications in India, 1981), 368–80; "St. John and the Advaitic Experience of the Upanishads," *BiSh* 11 (1985): 68–74.

George Soares Prabhu, "Good News to the Poor: The Social Implications of the Message of Jesus," *BiSh* 4 (1978): 193–212; "And There Was a Great Calm: A 'Dhvani' Reading of the Stilling of the Storm (Mk 4, 35–41)," *BiSh* 5 (1979): 295–308; "The Kingdom of God: Jesus' Vision of a New Society," in Amalorpavadass, *Indian Church*, 579–608; "Towards an Indian Interpretation of the Bible," *BiSh* 6 (1980): 151–70; "The Historical Critical Method: Reflections on Its Relevance for the Study of the Gospels in India Today," in Amaladoss et al., *Theologizing in India*, 314–67; "Interpreting the Bible in India Today," *The Way, Supplement* 72 (1991): 70–80; "The Table Fellowship of Jesus: Its Significance for Dalit Christians in India Today," *Jeevadhara* 22/128 (1992): 140–59; "Two Mission Commands: An Interpretation of Matthew 28:16–20 in the Light of a Buddhist Text," *BibInt* 2 (1993): 265–82.

Maria Arul Raja, "The Authority of Jesus: A Dalit Reading of Mk 11:27–33," *Jeevadhara* 25/146 (1995): 123–38; "Towards a Dalit Reading of the Bible: Some Hermeneutical Reflections," *Jeevadhara* 26/151 (1996): 29–34; "Some Reflections on a Dalit Reading of the Bible," *Indian Theological Studies* 33 (1996): 249–59; Exorcism and the Dalit Self-Affirmation: A Reinterpretation of Mk 5:1–20," *Vidyajyoti Journal of Theological Research* 60/12 (1996): 843–51; "Assertion of the Periphery: Some Biblical Paradigms," *Jeevadhara* 27/157 (1997): 25–35.

J. J. Kanagaraj, *The Gospel of John: A Commentary* (Secunderabad: OM Books, 2005).

George Mlakuzhyil, S.J., *Abundant Life in the Gospel of John* (New Delhi: Views/ISPCK, 2007).

Indian publications, but students first look for Western scholarship/publications rather than those by Indian publications/journals or books. Also it needs to be borne in mind that the effort/attempt to contextualize biblical interpretation has not metamorphosed sufficiently into a discipline that can be categorized as "Indian" biblical interpretation.

8. As per the regulations, accreditation is given to those institutions that have at least two qualified faculty persons in the concerned discipline/area. Even individual centers that do not have two faculty persons then name a person from an institution nearby who is willing to work with a student, who has been, in most cases, approved by the research committee. Theological institutions do not pay attention to the specific areas of specialization of faculty that is hired to provide for a balance in the area of discipline.

9. India lacks sufficient expertise in biblical languages and other Semitic languages and little attention is paid to extracanonical material, namely, the intertestamental literature; the Qumran scrolls, the Nag Hammadi texts, and the like. Feminist, Dalit, and adivasi insights and contributions to biblical interpretation are met with some suspicion.

10. A majority of those who read the Bible read it in an Indian language. Biblical studies and interpretation in India will be of much service if more effort is put also into transferring biblical thought and vocabulary into the

---

C. I. David Joy, *Revelation: A Postcolonial Viewpoint* (New Delhi: ISPCK, 2001); *Not By Might, but by My Spirit: A Collection of Sermons* (New Delhi: ISPCK, 2008); *Paul Examined* (New Delhi: ISPCK, 2001).

Sam P. Matthew, *Temple Criticism in Mark's Gospel: The Economic Role of the Jerusalem Temple during the First Century* (New Delhi: ISPCK, 1999).

Michaelsami Arockiam, *The Concept of Joy in the Johannine Literature* (New Delhi: ISPCK, 2002).

T. Job Anbalagan, *Redemptive Names of God* (New Delhi: ISPCK, 2003).

Takatemjen Ao, *The Banquet Is Ready: Rich and Poor in the Parables of Luke* (New Delhi: ISPCK, 2003).

D. Jones Muthunayagom, *The Relationship between Election and Israel's Attitude towards the Nations in the Book of Isaiah* (New Delhi: ISPCK, 2000).

Paduthottu G. George, *The Rod in the Old Testament* (New Delhi: ISPCK, 2003).

P. P. Thomas, *Jeroboam II the King and Amos the Prophet: A Social-Scientific study on the Israelite Society during the Eighth Century BCE* (New Delhi: ISPCK, 2003).

M. Gnanvaram, *Poverty and Wealth in the New Testament* (New Delhi, ISPCK, 2003); *Treasure in Heaven and Treasure on Earth: Attitude towards Poverty and Wealth in the New Testament Communities and in the Early Church* (New Delhi: ISPCK, 2008).

Pratap Chandra Gine, *Law in Context: Philo, Galatians and the Bengali Bible* (New Delhi: ISPCK, 2001).

L. H. Rawsea, *Differing Interpretations of the Torah in Mathew's Gospel* (New Delhi: ISPCK, 2003).

various Indian languages. Biblical scholarship and research should also help to meet the need for new Bible translations or for the revising of existing translations. So far, grammars, lexicons, and commentaries prepared in the West are being used. But there is no doubt that Semitic languages can be better learned and taught through the medium or use of Indian languages which have verbal endings, inflections and a more readily recognizable grammatical structure than does English. There is therefore a need for research in this area and preparation of grammars and lexicons using one or more of the Indian languages.

Future Prospects

Indian Christianity has benefited tremendously from the cumulative labor of Western scholars. It has created awareness to the questions being raised about the Bible and which are pertinent to serious biblical research today. At the same time, the increasing desire among some Indian scholars to make biblical studies relevant should be seen as contributing to the history of enquiry into the nature and contents of the Bible. Indian religion and culture which has shaped the lives of our fore fathers and mothers to a large extent still continues to shape life in India. Biblical scholars in India must therefore take cognizance of the particular spiritual, cultural, and intellectual milieu of the non-biblical world that is India to which they are addressing themselves. They cannot come to the text in a personal vacuum, but rather with awareness of the concerns stemming from their cultural background, contemporary situation and responsibility to the faith and community.

India with its diversity is a complex entity, and yet if one takes seriously this complexity of gender, caste, culture, colonial history, class, and language and debunks the autonomous dominant caste masculine and transcendental subject, it will have much to offer to biblical studies globally. Its communal understanding of existence, its embodied way of knowing as well as practicing religious life equips the interpreter with a multiple subject position, enabling the interpreter to imagine a layered and multiaxial biblical and theological hermeneutics that will do justice to the many layered experiences inscribed in both the written texts and oral traditions and to lift up the suppressed and silenced voices.

> The basic thrust now is not the declaration of the gospel in an Asian style but discerning it afresh in the ongoing broken relationships between different communities and between human beings and the created order. The task is seen not as adapting the Christian gospel in Asian idioms, but as reconceptualizing the basic tenets of the Christian faith in the light of Asian realities.

The new mood is not to assume the superiority of Christian revelation but to seek life enhancing potentialities also in the divine manifestations of Asia.[17]

A section of Indian biblical scholarship has recognized this and hence has affirmed that

> The curriculum in theological colleges should be so oriented that the student should get a basic knowledge of the world around him [sic] and of the forces at work in the world. The study of the historic faith and contemporary society are both vital. This would enable him [sic] to be sensitive to the hopes, fears and frustrations of the people among whom he [sic] is to work. The Christian Gospel, if it is true to its genius, should meet the people at the point of their elemental needs and struggles.[18]

To this end, the following commitments have been named.

Contextual integrity and sensitivity. The complex social reality in India is made up of its diversity, religiosity, the abject poverty of the majority and affluence of the minority, violence, religious fundamentalism, communalism, as well as the inner reality of caste and gender discrimination. This complex Indian context presents many challenges and offers many resources for authentic Indian biblical interpretations.[19]

The poor and the marginalized. There is a commitment to the reading and interpretation of texts from the perspective of the poor and the marginalized. The oppressed and the marginalized, namely, the women, the Dalits, children, the Tribals, those infected and affected by HIV/AIDS, the physically and mentally challenged, are people who have been noticeably absent in biblical interpretation due to their position in the margins. It is the place where the "other" produces meanings and nuances, illustrations and images, conceptual ideas and ideologies, methods and interpretations. The margin is the place where arguments and controversies, where critical and creative discourse can occur. A radical commitment to the marginalized and oppressed communities is imperative in a context where the majority live in abject poverty owing to social institutions and structures such as caste, and gender.

Liberation, life, and community. Graduate biblical studies must be committed to critical modes of reading the Bible, which develop a critical

---

17. R. S. Sugirtharajah, "Introduction," in *Frontiers in Asian Christian Theology: Emerging Trends* (ed. R. S. Sugirtharajah; Maryknoll, N.Y.: Orbis, 1994), 5.

18. Theological Education in India: Report of a Study Programme and Consultation 1967–68, 17.

19. Sam P. Matthew, "Indian Biblical Hermeneutics: Methods and Principles," unpublished version, 5.

consciousness, which questions the status quo and analyzes the biblical text. Since biblical interpretations and the text itself are not devoid of ideology that results in political, cultural, economic and gender bias, these biases need to be unmasked in order to ensure that the hermeneutical process is liberating and not oppressive. The interpretation must contribute to personal and social transformation, life in all its fullness and foster community. In order for this to happen, there needs to be an ongoing dialog between the text and its context on the one hand, and the interpreter and his or her/community's context on the other.

Faith. Biblical interpretations need to be able to engender hope against all death-dealing forces. A religious experience would give grounds for hope and the vision of overcoming a system that is oppressive. Exegesis of Scripture in accordance with the rules of interpretation needs to result in the transformation of the exegete. Indian tradition affirms that "no hermeneutic by itself will yield truth in its fullness without purification of the mind, transformation of the heart and discipline of the body."[20] An effective hermeneutic is one that is based on a faith response. This perspective will help us to be cautious in our use of tools that sift the text of the Bible for meaning irrespective of the method that we use. In India, the study of the bible is a matter of faith. Biblical research is not merely an intellectual exercise but ultimately a means to respond to God and God's demands and this provides both the motivation and goal in all aspects of biblical research.

Methods, approaches, relevance. Both "anglicism" and "orientalism" as described by Sugirtharajah as the manners by which biblical studies were introduced in India[21] have had drastic effects on biblical scholarship in India. The influence of anglicism is so widespread and deep that we are in a situation now where we need to find ways to discover our own literary and cultural heritage. The orientalist methods and principles of interpretation are almost alien and attract few subscribers.

With the advent of Pentecostal and charismatic groups into the Indian academy, higher criticism has become controversial. New and growing movements such as the Dalit and feminist have also expressed dissatisfaction with Western historical critical methods of reading the text contributing to varied positions on the issue that range from an almost obsessive adherence to the

---

20. S. J. Samartha, "The Asian Context: Sources and Trends," in *Voices from the Margin: Interpreting the Bible in the Third World* (London: SPCK, 1991), 309.

21. R. S. Sugirtharajah, "Biblical Studies in India: From Imperialistic Scholarship to Postcolonial Interpretation," in *Teaching the Bible: The Discourse and Politics of Biblical Pedagogy* (ed. Fernando F. Segovia and Mary Ann Tolbert; Eugene, Ore.: Wipf & Stock, 1998), 283–89.

historical critical method to a total rejection of the method as being almost irrelevant or blasphemous.[22]

Among the traditional methods of scriptural interpretation, the most well known is the dhvani method. The word dhvani literally means "sound, tone, echo" or "evocation," which lays a stress on the suggestive meaning rather than the expressed meaning of the text. The method calls for the interpreter to be in tune with the evocative nature of the text and respond to what the text might evoke in him or her.[23] Yet methods such as this are not well known, nor do students know how to employ them effectively. In fact, our syllabi do not call for familiarity with these traditional philosophical systems or methods of interpretation.[24]

It is becoming more and more certain that Indian biblical hermeneutics and methods can only grow out of a combination of traditional Indian and Western methods of interpretation.

> Biblical interpretation in India and Asia is a cross fertilization of both traditional Indian methods of textual interpretation and modern scientific methods set within the context of Indian reality. Relevance is a major issue and the applicability of the interpretative result is crucial to determining the relevance.[25]

Indian interpreters are becoming increasingly aware that it does not help to be dogmatic about one's approach and methodology on a purely ideological basis but to be contextual, discerning when, where and by whom a particular approach and method can be applied.

Indian Contribution to Biblical Studies and Interpretation

The toleration of diversity has also been explicitly defended by strong arguments in favor of the richness of variation, including fulsome praise of the need to interact with each other, in mutual respect, through dialog. Hence an authentic Indian contribution to biblical studies would be possible if the interpreter transcends the textual, historical, and religious boundaries of Christian tradition and cultivates a deeper contact with the mysterious ways in which people of other religious persuasions have defined and appropriated humanity and divinity. It is an approach that tries to use indigenous literary and nonlit-

---

22. Prabhu, "The Historical Critical Method," 314–67.
23. M. Vellanickal, "Drink from the Source of the Living Water," 309–18.
24. It is interesting to note that it is Catholic scholarship in India that experiments much more with Indian philosophical systems and traditional methods of interpretation.
25. Prabhu, "Towards an Indian Interpretation of the Bible," 151–70.

erary resources for theological enquiry.[26] The rich and multifaceted religious and cultural heritage of India calls for the integration of the religious wealth of its neighbors of faith through dialogue with them, a dialogue that looks for the liberating factors that these religious traditions contain and to discover new insights into its own biblical tradition that may come from the encounters with these age-old religions. Hence methodologies such as the intertextual,[27] extratextual,[28] cross-textual,[29] dialogical imagination,[30] and the contrapuntal or reading in juxtaposition[31] allow for the placement of scriptures side by side, the biblical text and a native text, and letting them speak for themselves without judgment or effort to prove the superiority of one or the other. Such an approach it is hoped will shed light upon some of the great religious problems with which humankind has been concerned, at many times and in many places.[32]

Conclusion

Graduate biblical studies in India need to become bolder, both in method and in content, in their attempt to make the Bible relevant for the Indian people and their lives. The Bible needs to be approached with freedom, originality

---

26. See Samuel Rayan, "Wrestling in the Night," in Sugirtharajah, *Frontiers in Asian Christian Theology*, 109–129.

27. Jean Delorme, "Intertextualities about Mark," in *Intertextuality in Biblical Writings: Essays in Honor of Bas van Iersel* (ed. Spike Draisma; Kampen: Kok, 1989), 35; see also A. Maria Arulraja, "Breaking Hegemonic Boundaries: An Intertextual Reading of the Madurai Veeran Legend and Mark's Story of Jesus," in *Voices From the Margin: Interpreting the Bible in the Third World* (ed. R. S. Sugirtharajah; 3rd ed.; Maryknoll, N.Y.: Orbis, 2006), 103–4.

28. Samuel Rayan, "Wrestling in the Night."

29. Archie Chi Chung Lee, "Cross Textual hermeneutics in Asian Context," *PTCA Bulletin* 5 (1992): 5.

30. Kwok Pui Lan, "Discovering the Bible in a Non-biblical World," in *Voices from the Margin: Interpreting the Bible in the Third World* (ed. R. S. Sugirtharajah; London: SPCK, 1991), 305.

31. R. S. Sugirtharajah, "Postcolonial Criticism and Asian Biblical Studies," in *Critical Engagement in the Asian Context: Implications for Theological Education and Christian Studies* (ed. Preman Niles; Hong Kong: Asian Christian Higher Education Institute, 2005), 78; see also R. S. Sugirtharajah, "A Postcolonial Exploration of Collusion and Construction in Biblical Interpretation," in *The Postcolonial Bible* (ed. R. S. Sugirtharajah; Sheffield: Sheffield Academic Press, 1998), 94; idem, *Asian Biblical Hermeneutics and Postcolonialism: Contesting Interpretations* (Maryknoll, N.Y.: Orbis, 1998), 116ff.

32. Goeffrey Parrinder, *Upanishads, Gita and Bible: A Comparative Study of Hindu and Christian Scriptures* (London: Sheldon, 1975).

and Indianess, always cognizant of the voices and experiences of those at the periphery—the women, the adivasis, the Dalits, and the HIV/AIDS-affected. Our graduate program needs to do more to encourage this for the sake of the future of Christianity in India and for its people and the transformation of the individual and society.

Biblical Study in Korea in the Twenty-First Century

Kyung Sook Lee

1. Introduction

When I took part in the international conference about "Feminist Exegesis and the Hermeneutics of Liberation," which was held in Ticino, Switzerland, on 2–7 July 2000, it was so interesting for me to hear the voices of women from different contexts.[1] For example, Nancy C. Pereira from Latin America said that, in Latin America, the Bible has been used as a tool of oppression by the colonizers.[2] She quoted that there were five seasons in Latin America: winter, spring, summer, fall, and massacre.[3] According to the historical record, much of the season of massacre has been executed in the name of Christianity. Christianity arrived in Latin America as a gun, as a sign of power; it has functioned and still functions there as a religion of oppression. In response, women in Latin America now want to see a resurrection of the Bible, and, in order to liberate the Bible from an oppressive system, Latin American women want to develop a new method of hermeneutics using the concepts of their own folk religion.

In Hungary, in the former Eastern Europe, the situation was quite the opposite. The Hungarian women there said that they were able to survive because of the Bible during the very difficult time under Communist dictatorship. For them the Bible was their hope and salvation. Also, a number of African American women said that without the comforting stories of the Bible they would never have been able to survive their oppression. They read

---

1. The symposium volume: Silvia Schroer and Sophia Bietenhard, eds., *Feminist Interpretation of the Bible and the Hermeneutics of Liberation* (JSOTSup 374; Sheffield: Sheffield Academic Press, 2003).

2. Nancy C. Pereira, "Changing Seasons, About the Bible and Other Sacred Texts in Latin America," in Schroer and Bietenhard, *Feminist Interpretation of the Bible*, 48–58.

3. Manoel Scorza, quote from ibid., 48.

the Bible with the knowledge that their ancestors, who were in slavery, found strength and courage in the Bible. They read the Bible as one of the sacred books among others and thus maintained a continual interreligious dialogue.

When I heard all of these stories, I could understand these situations very well, because we Koreans had a similar oppressive experience with the Bible under the Japanese colonial occupation (1910–1945) and during the Korean War (1950–1953). Many Korean Christians were persecuted by Japanese occupiers because of their refusal to participate in forced Shinto Shrine worship[4] and others were killed by Communists during the Korean War. Even today, all these experiences co-exist in Korea. The situations of Christians in Korea are very diverse, and likewise, their ways of reading the Bible are also very diverse. Reading the Bible can offer comfort, hope, and even empowerment for poor people, but at the same time, the Bible can be a tool of oppression and exploitation—especially when used by an imperialistic colonial church. Now, it seems that everybody reads the Bible differently, although many still have in common the desire to read and discuss the Bible, thus maintaining its active force in culture. Christians generally believe that the Bible is God's textbook for hope and liberation. How, then, can we read the Bible as God's word for hope and liberation for all as Asians in the twenty-first century? What is the aim of biblical study in theological seminaries, universities, and churches in Asia?

Is it true that, as Silvia Schroer writes, "a responsible interpretation of biblical tradition cannot be globalized; it cannot be uniformly defined worldwide; it can, however, be discussed globally"?[5] Every "context" involves a different "history with the Bible" that has shaped this context and that has influenced and will continue to influence the interpretation of biblical texts.[6] It is also impossible to generalize the situation of Asia into one homogenous field. Even the situation in Korea is extremely diverse, separated according to denominations and regions. Nam-Soon Kang urges respect for these groups: "They have real difference in experience, perspective and knowledge, and these differences require developing varied strategies for participation and transformation."[7] In this sense, I will just suggest some ideas of developing a local strategy for Korean church and society.

---

4. Yang-son Kim, "Compulsory Shinto Shrine Worship and Persecution," in *Korea and Christianity* (ed. Chai-Shin Yu; Studies in Korean Religions and Culture 8; Seoul: Korean Scholar Press, 1996), 87–120.

5. Silvia Schroer, "We Will Know Each Other by Our Fruits," in Schroer and Bietenhard, *Feminist Interpretation of the Bible*, 3.

6. Ibid.

7. Nam-Soon Kang, "Creating Dangerous Memory: Challenges for Asian and Korean Feminist Theology," *The Ecumenical Review* 47 (1995): 21; idem, "Who/What Is Asian?" in

What is the Bible? How can we "see a resurrection of the Bible"? How should we teach it at theological seminaries and universities? Before I handle all of these problems, I will give a short survey of the history of the church in Korea and the history of biblical interpretation. Then, I will reflect on how we can teach the Bible in our universities and theological seminaries to prepare our future in Korea and in Asia.

2. Korean Church History from the Minjung's Perspective

2.1. At the Beginning (1885–1953)

Unlike many other Asian countries, Christianity was not brought to Korea by Western colonizers but rather by Koreans in the late nineteenth century. The Bible had been already translated into Korean in China and Japan when it was brought to Korea by a progressive young generation who desired social and cultural change during the last stage of the Chosun dynasty.[8] Joong-Eun Kim elaborates: "In particular, some Korean intellectuals who wanted to enlighten Korea were interested in Christianity because they understood that Christianity represented modern Western civilization, which held sufficient power to strengthen Koreans for a fight against Imperial Japan."[9] It is very extraordinary that Koreans themselves wanted to import Christianity into Korea from abroad.

Christianity was spread very quickly in Korea in the late nineteenth century through the lower-class Minjung. In this period, Korean people had experienced "inequality, oppression, and infringement of human rights under the patriarchy."[10] Christianity became so popular among the poor—and especially the women among the lower class—because Christianity proclaimed the equality of all humankind, especially the equality between the aristocracy and the lower class and between male and female. Those women whose husbands had many concubines, or widows whose remarriages were banned were among the first people to receive the Christian gospel. Men and women

---

Postcolonial Theologies: Divinity and Empire (ed. Catherine Keller, Michael Nausner, and Mayra Rivera; St. Louis: Chalice, 2004), 108–14.

8. Joong-Eun Kim, *Die Geschichte der Übersetzung des Alten Testaments ins Koreanische* (Europaeische Hochschulschriften 23/114, Bern: Lang, 1979).

9. So-young Baik, "The Protestant Ethic Reversed: A Study in the 'Elective Affinity,' between Neo-Liberalism and Christian Fundamentalism," *Madang: International Journal of Contextual Theology in East Asia* 9 (2008): 33.

10. Duk-joo Lee, "An Understnading of Early Korean Christian Women's History," *Ewha Journal of Feminist Theology* 2 (1997): 21.

attended Christian worship together and sang gospel songs together in the church: it was the real "good news" for Korean Minjung at that time.

During Japanese colonialism, Korean Christians were compelled to worship at Japanese Shinto shrines, and some of those who refused to do so were put in jail, persecuted, and killed.[11] Also, many Christian educational organizations were closed, and others went through hard times. Korean Christian men and women had to respond to the reality of the Japanese oppression together in the church, and they, men and women together, strove to overthrow Japanese colonial domination. This unity of men and women had been impossible in feudal Confucian society before Christianity.[12] So in the early stages of Christianity in Korea, the Bible was not only regarded as a spiritual and religious book, but also as a basic textbook in the struggle against oppression and colonialism, as well as against the inequality between men and women, the rich and the poor. In this respect, early Korean Minjung experienced firsthand the essence of the gospel.

Since the 1930s, Korean churches have experienced conflicts between fundamentalism and liberalism stemming from the beliefs of several pastors of Presbyterian churches who did not accept Mosaic authorship of the Pentateuch. In 1934, Rev. Chun-bae Kim appealed for the ordination for women and insisted that Paul's passages against women's ordination had been written two thousand years ago and Korean Christians should not follow Paul's contextual ethical teachings word by word.[13] In addition, Rev. Young-ju Kim wrote an article in 1935 stating that the book of Genesis was based on old Hebrew mythologies and that Moses was not the real author of the Pentateuch.[14] Both of them underwent religious trials and had to withdraw their opinions and apologize for themselves, otherwise they would have been expelled from their denomination. In 1930 the *Abingdon Bible Commentary* was translated into Korean, only to be accused of heresy; as a result, the fifty-three translators

---

11. Yang-son Kim, "Compulsary Shinto Shrine Worship and Persecution," in *Korea and Christianity* (ed. Chai-Shin Yu; Studies in Korean Religions and Culture 8; Seoul: Korean Scholar Press, 1996), 87–120.

12. Duk-joo Lee, "An Understanding of Early Korean Christian Women's History," *Ewha Journal of Feminist Theology* 2 (1997): 23–24.

13. Chun-bae Kim wrote an editorial in the *Presbyterian Weekly* in 1934 advocating a better status for women in the church. See Jung-min Suh and Ho-ik Huh, *The Thirty Years History of Korea Association of Christian Studies* (Seoul: The Christian Literature Society of Korea, 2001), 43–44.

14. Young-ju Kim has reported officially to the assembly as saying that the book of Genesis was not authored by Moses himself (ibid., 42–43).

underwent many hardships.[15] These were the beginnings of the fragmentation of Korean churches.

During the Korean War (1950-1953), Korean churches suffered severely from the ideological conflicts between the United States and the Soviet Union, and in turn, South and North Korea. Many Christians in North Korea fled from the communist massacre to South Korea seeking religious freedom.

2.2. AMERICAN INFLUENCE AFTER THE KOREAN WAR (1953-1970)

After the Korean War (1950-1953), the center for Korean Christians in Pungyang had disappeared, and Seoul became the center for all Korean Christians, who established many theological seminaries there. Korean Christians became more conservative, fundamental, and puritan after experiencing the religious oppression during the Korean War. There were hot debates in the 1950s on the acceptance of historical criticism in the Presbyterian churches. The conservative and fundamental Christians who fled from North Korea did not like to accept historical criticism, unlike other liberal theologians. So in 1956, the Presbyterian church of Korea was divided into two denominations: the PROK (Presbyterian Church of Republic of Korea) and the PCK (Presbyterian Church of Korea). The former accepted historical critics, while the latter rejected them. This segregation still exists and the conservative PCK group became the majority and fragmented further into many small groups. The Methodist churches in Korea tabled debate, neither rejecting historical criticism nor fully accepting it.

In the 1960s, South Korean society rapidly industrialized, and Korean churches developed quickly as well. On the other hand, helpful Christian traditions and actual social contributions such as resisting oppression slackened as the church grew rapidly; this is, in part, a result of developing a powerful social and financial basis.

Most professors who taught biblical studies in the theological seminaries in 1955-70 were educated in the United States or in Germany and were thus strongly influenced by Western theologies. They thought that Koreans should adopt Western logic and culture in order to understand the Bible and to make progress within Korean society and churches. So, many theologians who regarded themselves as pioneers of modernization have tried to import Western theology as much as they could. The curricula of Korean theological seminaries and schools were replicas of Western theological schools, and the students had to learn Western terminology, concepts, and history along with Hebrew and Greek, the biblical languages as well as the English and German.

---

15. Ibid., 44-47.

No wonder, then, that they ignored Korean culture and heritage for they had neither will nor time to learn them. Many American missionaries and Korean theologians at that time thought Korean culture did not allow for modern ways of life and thinking. This was the time when the identification of Christianity with the spirit of modernity emerged, and the "elective affinity" between capitalism and Christian fundamentalism started.

2.3. Minjung Theology and the Recovery of the Liberation Tradition (1970–1990)

In the 1970s, when Korean society began to develop economically, most Korean people lived under the control of the military regime and their government-controlled labor unions. The people of Korea began to protest against the dictatorship in order to reclaim their freedom. In particular, university students were not only politically critical but also very much aware that the suffering of the Minjung people stemmed from unequal economic distributions. They protested strongly against the military government, and many of them were put in jail and gravely tortured.

To reflect on and respond to this serious situation, some liberal theologians came together and started to read the Bible again from a Korean perspective. This was the starting point of Minjung theology.[16] The pioneer of this stream was Prof. Ahn Byung-mu, the New Testament scholar who began to read the Bible from the perspective of the Korean Minjung, the oppressed people, and said the Minjung were the *ochlos* in the New Testament.[17] Jesus was the savior because he was on the side of the *ochlos*, the oppressed. Prof. Ahn and other Minjung theologians read passages from Exodus,[18] the books of the prophets in the Old Testament,[19] and the teachings of Jesus in the New Testament from a new perspective, interpreting Minjung's power very positively. In this manner, these scholars developed Minjung theology—a theology of the people, for the people. Because of their radical theology and explicit support of student demonstrations, Minjung theologians were also put in jail and fired from their schools.

---

16. Committee of Theological Study, KNCC, ed., *Minjung and Korean Theology* (Seoul: Korea Theological Study Institue, 1982); David Kwang-sun Suh, *The Korean Minjung in Christ* (Hong Kong: Commission on Theological Concerns, 1991).

17. Byung-mu Ahn, "Jesus and Ochlos," in Committee of Theological Study, *Minjung and Korean Theology*, 86–103.

18. Jung-jun Kim, "The Old Testament Reference to Minjung Theology," in Committee of Theological Study, *Minjung and Korean Theology*, 29–57.

19. Hi-suk Mun, "My People from the Perspective of Micah," in Committee of Theological Study, *Minjung and Korean Theology*, 104–32.

Many other conservative theologians did not agree with these Minjung theologians and criticized them, some assuming Minjung theologians' support for the North Korean regime and communism in general. Conservative Christians said that religion and politics should be separated and that Christians who criticized the military government of South Korea or interfered unnecessarily with political matters must be communists. Fortunately, Minjung theologians had support from overseas—for example, from organizations such as the World Council of Churches, and from many churches in Germany, the United States, and Japan, among others.

Minjung theology was not mainstream Korean theology at that time, but in the 1990s, due to Minjung theologians' and university students' struggles and efforts, political democratization, freedom of labor unions, the reunification movement and the consciousness of a national identity progressed slowly in Korean society. In other words, Bible reading itself related deeply to the sociopolitical context of Korea has changed Korean history and contributed much to its society. Due to its needed influence, Minjung theology could conceivably even attain a world-wide reputation for its engagement in social justice issues inside and outside of Korea.

2.4. The Current Situation (1990–present)

Minjung theology and the liberation theology are still at work in some corners of the Korean church, especially concerning the issue of reunification of Korea; in general, however, it is not so powerful as it once was. This is in large part because our context has changed since the 1990s. Military concepts such as "mission," "growth," "conquer," and "crusade" have been key words of the Korean church for the last twenty years, and such words as "blessing," "success" and "prosperity" are commonly what Christians seek, as opposed to "justice" or "peace." Most church pastors are male-oriented, authoritarian, conservative or fundamental, and many of them are juxtaposing themselves to the neo-liberal church business-managers. Though they believe they are serving God, they have stopped becoming the "light and salt" of society. Now, having their own money and power, many Korean churches lost interest in feminism and Minjung, just like other traditional Korean religions, such as Shamanism, Buddhism and Confucianism. Women are 70 percent of all churchgoers, but they are oppressed again as a subsidiary class and still forced to be silent, obedient, and supportive of the male leaders. Now, how can we keep advocating for the liberation of these women and Minjung in the church? We need another theology that can change the authoritatian patriarchal system in the church, which is deeply imbued with capitalism, neo-liberalism, and neo-imperialism.

Neo-liberalism, which permeates Korean churches, is linked with conservative theology, and one of the important factors for ethical decline is an inappropriate biblical hermeneutic. Therefore, biblical interpreters and professors have to ask ourselves this question: Have we interpreted the Bible properly, or have we just played word-games that are irrelevant to the Korean churches? It is a real problem that the dichotomy between scientific research in theological seminaries and application in the church becomes ever wider.[20] Now is the right time to find a new paradigm to interpret the Bible in order to narrow or eliminate this gap.

3. Suggestions to Deconstruct the Absolutism of the Bible

3.1. Using All Kinds of Methods for Deconstruction

Many conservative church leaders regard the Bible as absolutely normative, and they take everything quoted from or interpreted in the Bible as the absolute truth itself. In this sense, the Bible could be used as a tool to oppress and exploit naïve Christians. Here we must raise the question: How normative is the Bible to Asian Christians?[21] What does it mean that the Bible is the canon of Christianity? Does only the Bible have the truth? Or, should Christians humbly admit that our claims are not the truth itself?[22] The majority of Korean churches still tend to interpret the Bible literally without consideration of its historical, social and cultural backgrounds. In order to make it clear that the Bible did not fall from heaven, but was written by particular people in a certain period of time under certain circumstances, we must use the historical-critical method of biblical interpretation, since it is still useful to deconstruct claims that the Bible is the one and only absolute truth.

The Bible is not a "mythical type" but a "historical type" of God's word.[23] In other words, God has used many voices to express God's diversity, and we can hear many different voices from different contexts and times in the Bible.

---

20. Elisabeth Schüssler Fiorenza, *But She Said, Feminist Practices of Biblical Interpretation* (Boston: Beacon, 1992); idem, *Wisdom Ways: Introducing Feminist Biblical Interpretation* (Maryknoll, N.Y.: Orbis, 2002); Sandra Harding, *The Science Question in Feminism* (Ithaca, N.Y.: Cornell University Press, 1986).

21. Hope S. Antone, *Religious Education in Context of Plurality and Pluralism* (Quezon City, Philippines: New Day Publishers Christian Conference of Asia, 2003), 51–68.

22. Ibid., 52.

23. Elisabeth Schüssler Fiorenza, "Emerging Issues in Feminist Biblical Interpretation," in *Christian Feminism* (ed. Judith L. Weidman; San Francisco: Harper & Row, 1984), 42; idem, *Bread Not Stone: The Challenge of Feminist Biblical Interpretation* (Boston: Beacon, 1984).

As such, we question if Korean biblical scholars can say already that the era of historical criticism is over, or is our work a true methodological discourse among scholars in the First and Two-Thirds worlds?[24] I think, in Korea, we cannot yet discard this method in theological seminaries and universities. Of course, we must reject the arrogance of Western biblical scholars when they assume that their research is value-neutral and objective. But it is also absurd if we deny entire methods just because they were developed in Europe in the nineteenth century, coinciding with European colonialism in bloom.

I think the best way for Asians to read the Bible critically is to use all kinds of critical methodologies; otherwise, we cannot deconstruct the "mythical" glorification of the Bible. The insight that the world of the Bible was very much characterized by a plurality or multiplicity of cultures and religions could have been explored wholly through the historical, social, and cultural-critical methods. The multifaith situation of the times of Moses, the prophets, and Jesus should be explored by all these methods. In the era of the postmodern or postcolonial, it matters a lot how we apply these methods and perspectives to interpret the Bible from an Asian context without assuming the Asian situation is the same as that of the United States or Europe, where the historical-critical method has been prevalent and dominant for many centuries.

Thus, Asian theologians are expected to put off imperialistic and colonial clothes that were laid upon the Bible by the Western missionaries and the conservative theologians. Jesus, for example, is an Asian in the view of Minjung theology.[25] The image of Jesus was tainted by Western theology, and we have to use any scholarly tools at our disposal to deconstruct the imperialistic, mythical authority of the Bible. In order to deconstruct the absoluteness of the Bible and the concept of one fixed interpretation, we should expand the "critical" reading of the Bible with the "suspicion" or "comparison" with Asian pride. In this sense, we should use all kind of comparative studies available; historical-critical, literary, inter-cultural, inter-textual, or postcolonial approaches.

3.2. Confluence of the Bible with Asian Cultural and Religious Heritages

One of the greatest achievements of liberation theology, such as Minjung theology, is the awareness of Korean history and culture, which is shown in

---

24. Sung-hee Kim, "Mark, Women, and Empire: Ways of Life through a Korean and Postcolonial Perspective" (Ph.D. diss., Drew University, 2006), 44.
25. Yong-bok Kim, "Asians Meet Jesus the Asian: A Historical Reflection," *Quest: An Interdisciplinary Journal for Asian Christian Scholars* 4 (2005): 17–40.

the inclusive attitude of Christianity since the 1970s. Folklore, mask dances,[26] classical dramas, folk music, liturgy, novels and so on began to be interpreted from the perspective of the people's movement and were compared with the Jesus movement. Many Minjung theologians have thoroughly studied Korean history again and tried to include it within Christianity.[27] They thought that Jesus was the model for the revolutionaries in Korea since Jesus is always with the Korean people, though anonymously so. Minjung theologians said that Jesus is our savior because he liberates the people from the bondage and yoke of oppression. This kind of interpretation of Korean history gave great power to the anti-military dictatorship movement, and empowered both Christian and non-Christian student demonstrations.

According to Minjung theologians, God worked in Korea even before Christianity came to Korea. Of course the biblical God did not care about the history of Korea directly, but Minjung theologians believe that the Christian God has been very much interested in peace and harmony in the Korean peninsula. In this way, Prof. Nam-dong Suh and Prof. Yong-bok Kim have endeavored very seriously to encounter Korean history with the biblical stories, or, conversely, tried to understand biblical stories within the frame of Korean history.[28] This kind of interpretation, called the "confluence of the Bible with the history of Korea," gave us deep insight into Korean history from the perspective of liberation.

Minjung theologians also remembered that Asians have their own classics and literary traditions; these are very unique, profound, and precious goods. Until the 1970s, we did not consider them as precious goods, but disregarded these treasures as disturbing legacies. Until 1980, doctoral papers handling themes related to Korean culture and history were not regarded with high esteem. There might be various reasons for this, but now we should appreciate these treasures by carrying out comparative studies, and thus enlarging our interpretations of the Bible. In this manner, our interpretations can have an impact on the rigidity of Korean churches and society in general.

Perhaps Asians have more advantages in understanding the Bible, because we are already living in a multireligious society. This is especially clear if we

---

26. Young-hak Hyun, "The Theological Interpretation of Korean Mask Dances," in *Mask Dance of Jesus* [Korean] (Seoul: Korea Theological Study Institute, 1997), 56–78. He has interpreted Korean mask dances theologically in his many articles since 1973. A Korean dance mask became the logo of the CCA Assembly (Suh, *The Korean Minjung*, 159–74).

27. Suh, *Korean Minjung*, 17–86.

28. Nam-dong Suh, "Confluence of the Two Stories," in Committee of Theological Study, *Minjung and Korean Theology*, 237–76; Yong-bok Kim, "Messiah and Minjung," in Committee of Theological Study, *Minjung and Korean Theology*, 287–301; Suh, *Korean Minjung*, 9–83.

think of our history in comparison to the history of Christianity throughout the world. Christianity came to Korea via Palestine, Rome, Europe in general, China, or America. In Rome in particular, Europe in general, and America, the Bible has been used mostly to expand their imperial holdings or their territories. But in Palestine, the birth place of Christianity, we cannot find this imperialistic character, so we do not need to add this character arbitrarily to the Bible. We want to go back to the origin, the essence of the Gospel of Jesus. Asian Christianity seeks to be radically discontinuous from the Western colonial mission in Asia and also from Western, imperial Christianity. Korean Christians do not need to be involved much in Western elements of Christianity such as their doctrines, philosophical concepts, and traditions. Instead, we must use Asian resources and cultural heritages to understand the Bible newly with our own eyes. Now is the time for a paradigm shift!

We can borrow the concepts of many other Asian religions, such as the humble and cautious living attitude of Buddhism, the concepts of the spiritual transcendence like "nirvana," and "anubhavam" in order to understand the concepts of "life" and "peace." We can also borrow the concepts of reverence, piety, and T'ien from Confucianism to understand biblical concepts such as "fear of God"[29] and the folktale elements from Shamanism for a better understanding of the ancient, inexplicable stories in the Bible. We need a hermeneutics of inclusion or a hermeneutics of diversity in Asia for this postcolonial era. Christianity itself cannot be fixed, but flows hand in hand with changing interpretations of the Bible. We, therefore, should open our minds and start to learn our classics and traditions very carefully and use them to interpret the Bible with a creative "dialogical imagination."[30] In this sense, the concepts of "dialogical imagination," "multifaith hermeneutics" and "postcolonial critics" are very helpful for the building of a methodology on Asian biblical hermeneutics.

Here I will raise another important issue, namely, the relationship between the Bible and other sacred Asian classics. Before Minjung theology, many theologians said that the text, the Bible, was more important than the context. Here, the Minjung theologian said no! Context is as important as the text—or even more important! Nevertheless, the question concerning the

---

29. Kyung Sook Lee, "God in Wisdom Literature from the perspective of Asian Feminist Theology," *Quest: An Interdisciplinary Journal for Asian Christian Scholars* 3 (2004).

30. S. Wesley Ariarajah, *The Bible and People of Other Faiths* (Geneva: World Council of Churches, 1985), 45–47; Kwok Pui-lan, "Discovering the Bible in the Non-biblical World," *Semeia* 47 (1989): 25–42; idem, *Discovering the Bible in the Non-biblical World* (Maryknoll, N.Y.: Orbis, 1995).

relationship of the Bible and other sacred Asian texts is not so easy to answer.[31] We should not romanticize and overestimate Asian sacred texts. We must be very careful not to lose that balance between the Bible and other sacred Asian texts, otherwise we could not only stop the misuse of the Bible, but we also could lose our identity. Christianity itself is not fixed, but is moving forward according to the proper interpretations of the Bible. The question of biblical study is not whether we need the Bible or not, but how we Asians interpret the Bible as well as Christianity and keep them alive for the people's hope and liberation.

3.3. Liberation from Empire[32]

Korean Minjung theologians began to reread Korean history with our own eyes, from the perspective of the people, the Minjung, the poor, the weak and the marginalized, such as women, who have been invisible throughout our history. Minjung theologians could start to interpret the whole history of Korea as a part of Asian Christian history[33] and believe the Christian God was very much interested in the peace and harmony of the Korean peninsula. What is the main obstacle for Koreans to a life of peace and harmony? What was the pivotal reason that the Korean people were oppressed, divided, and fragmented? The answer can be seen as sexism, colonialism, and imperialism in Korean society, but many people believe the division between the North and the South is instead the heaviest burden for the Korean society.

In Korea, reconciliation and reunion have been the fundamental aspirations of the Korean people throughout their history, so it is no surprise that the reunification movement became a central issue for all Korean Christians. The most critical issues theologians have concentrated on were peace with independence, and self-determination without interference from the outside powers of the United States, the Soviet Union, China, and Japan. These four imperial powers destroyed the common prosperity and human security of all people in Korea. Not only theologians, but also many politicians and other peace experts think that without the peaceful reunification of the Korean people, there can be no true peace in Asia or in the world. In this sense all theologians in Korea should endeavor to help the reunification of Korea and its liberation from empire.

---

31. R. S. Sugirtharajah, *Asian Biblical Hermeneutics and Postcolonialism* (Maryknoll, N.Y.: Orbis, 1998), 100–101.

32. Ninan Koshy, "The Empire: Some Preliminary Reflections," *Quest: An Interdisciplinary Journal for Asian Christian Scholars* 3 (2004): 65–82.

33. See note 27.

There are many new forms of empire, such as sexism, neo-liberalism, neo-nationalism, and Christian fundamentalism, all of which are equipped with global media systems such as satellite dishes, online programs, and books. We must think about how to disrupt all these new forms of empire so that we may live in peace. Jesus spoke out against imperialistic, oppressing power and also against colonial hegemony. He was always supportive of life-giving, life-sharing, peace-making, and peace-cultivating, and he preached humility, togetherness, and inclusiveness. We may call it, in modern terms, an "alternative way of living." How can we revitalize this message of Jesus for our postmodern world in the twenty-first century and surmount all kinds of imperialistic power around us? Now we must try to develop our own methodology of reading the Bible so we may use it as an instrument to break down the imperialistic, oppressive power and to begin the peace-making process in Korean society.

4. Suggestions to Reconstruct a New Biblical Study

4.1. New Curriculum

Now is the proper time to create a proper curriculum of Bible interpretation for Korea in particular and Asia in general. In retrospect, our education in biblical studies has not been so beneficial to those over whom it has influence. Moreover, we are living in this rapidly changing, global new world with electro-communication, bio-technology, and neo-capitalism. Our world is now a world of flux: every year approximately one thousand jobs are disappearing and about one thousand new jobs are created.

In Korea, more and more theological students want to major in pastoral counseling, not in biblical theology. These are the real challenges for biblical studies. So to survive in this new world, we should educate our students multidimensionally, not just recycle outdated curricula. It means that the students who want to serve the church and society should create new types of ministry and pedagogy using technology such as the internet, and artistic expression such as visual arts, film, music and dancing. All of these fields will be useful tools in the future, so we should be very flexible with our curricula. Otherwise, not only biblical professors but also our students will always be left behind and become increasingly irrelevant.

To create our own curriculum for biblical studies, we should clarify our multireligious cultural background. Is "theology" a term just for Christianity, or do other religions also have their own theologies? How can we co-exist with other religions? Why has Christianity often caused wars in order to conquer the non-Christian world with the Bible? What does it mean to talk about the policies of "religious freedom," "just war" and "war for freedom"?

We should also be clear about our status and experience.[34] We should know the political, economical, and psychological analysis of our society. Therefore, we need first of all an interdisciplinary system of curricula in seminary courses. It would be very good to have colloquia with other disciplines, for example, political and geopolitical science, world history, Korean history, economics, psychology, bio-technology, medical science, and pedagogy. Through these interdisciplinary courses and colloquia, we can analyze the imperialistic patriarchal structure of society more clearly and suggest new alternative ways of thinking and acting.

The necessity of historical thinking to our project of analyzing our Asian situation cannot be overemphasized. Why were we colonized by Western and Japanese empires? Was Jesus a Western colonialist, a white racist and also a male chauvinist, or just presented as such by certain Western theologians? Who has the imperialistic power over us now? How can we liberate ourselves from this power? We should try to answer all these questions historically and geo-politically. It will be also good to promote solidarity with other Asian scholars and have free discussions in colloquium style in various levels as often as we can.

The problem which we face now, however, is the lack of competent professors who can take care of these kinds of interdisciplinary research. At some point, we can have a team with progressive professors in various levels and in various disciplines, including among the doctoral and master program candidates. We should transform the old "master-disciple" system or the classical university education system based on departmental studies into team-learning or team-teaching systems, composed of doctoral candidates and learning professors, who are open-minded and have a creative view of the future. In this team teaching, everybody can mutually learn and teach. Otherwise how can we educate students with a wide scope and power to have influence over the whole society? One broad theme, such as life, wisdom, nationalism, terror, or war in the Bible, can be handled in various ways and fields. Multiple professors who are intrigued by a similar problem can evaluate this team research. The most important thing is that this study be creative, alternative, and world-relevant.

4.2. Global Ethics

Here we should also be clear that finding an alternative way of reading the Bible is imperative not just for scholars, but also for the church and for society.

---

34. Elisabeth Schüssler Fiorenza, "Rethinking the Educational Practices of Biblical Doctoral Studies," *TThRel* 6 (2003): 65–75.

There are theories upon theories dedicated to the academic circle of scholars' intellectual play, but what really matters is not their degrees or positions but this question: For what purpose are all these theories developed? Of course, every theory has its own contribution to make, but we should avoid so-called chauvinistic academic play, which does not help anyone except the writer. What is crucial is the fact that our research is for critical thinking, social change, global ethics, and world peace-making. It is, therefore, imperative for biblical research to show its abilities to criticize, deconstruct and rethink the patriarchal and imperialistic system. At the same time, it should also reconstruct the liberation tradition, and the life-giving, peace-making, and empowering spirit.

I think any biblical research that does not have any impact on a "global ethic," be it directly or indirectly, is not good research. Biblical study is not pursued just for a display of philological-philosophical Western scholarly languages unfamiliar to Asian, African, or women's life-giving languages, but rather it exists for its emancipatory spirit and its ability to inspire a paradigm-shift. Biblical study should be good for thinking, analyzing, scrutinizing, and criticizing capitalism, imperialism, fundamentalism, and patriarchy, which are so destructive at present. Biblical study should not be word-play for a scholars' league of their own, but for the liberation and inspiration of spirit for global ethics.

5. Conclusion: Dream of Some Korean Theologians

Finishing my paper, I will introduce our dreams with an example of a new type of doctoral or postdoctoral course of study in Korea that is in the process of construction. Some progressive theologians in Korea (especially Yong Bok Kim)[35] are planning to establish a new type of graduate school in the near future to prepare for the global era. They are thinking of an "Asia Pacific Graduate School for the Integral Study of Life," which is designed as an alternative to and continuation of theological seminaries and graduate schools. It is at the same time an alternative to the present academic system. It combines the Eastern way of learning and the Western academic system through an integral and holistic approach. It is an attempt at a synthetic, integral fusion of "East" and "West" in search of a creative convergence of wisdom for fullness of life. It is a search for ways to realize a new civilization of common life for all living beings, overcoming the forces of death inherent in globalization, and the domination of the Western super-power imperialism.

---

35. They send their news in the name of "Zoesophia." Their e-mail address is: oikozoe@gmail.com.

The graduate school should be designed to carry out comprehensive and integral studies on the life of all living beings in the universe. As an alternative to the prevailing academic system of specialization and compartmentalization, it pursues integral studies based on the establishment of a new academic paradigm, the integral study of living, using a methodology of multidisciplinary integration. Thus, the theology of life (the gospel of Jesus) will find its concrete expression within the integral study of life.

In this graduate school, doctoral students and scholars alike learn how to develop intellectual skills of investigation, ethical criteria of evaluation, and hermeneutical frameworks. The professors will not be seen as mere knowledge-delivery systems but as creators of new perspectives and knowledge. The point is to train Asian thinkers, intellectuals, and professional leaders in Asia who would lead their people to self-determination and liberation from the colonial powers as well as from the patriarchal dominant powers. Here we would take seriously the experiential wisdom of Asia's religions and cultures, and its historical resources for social, political, and economic life.

How much success they will have in establishing this kind of graduate school as an alternative to the normal academic system remains in question. At present, they have some financial support from some progressive theologians from Korea and Japan, but need more support from all over the world. It would be wonderful if we could find the resources we need to successfully train new types of Asian leaders; this is the hope of some Korean theologians, including myself. The other problem is this: the scholars who will have been educated here might face difficulties finding jobs in our current universities and seminaries. So, on the one hand this new kind of graduate school should train the "new" scholars in the old frame of academia, but on the other they should build a truly new academic system. In this regard, our work is a real challenge!

The Practice and Ethos of Postgraduate Biblical Education: A Glance at Europe and in Particular Switzerland

Gabriella Gelardini

INTRODUCTION

The following account originates from a paper given in the context of the 2006 Society of Biblical Literature International Meeting in Edinburgh.[1] By invitation of Elisabeth Schüssler Fiorenza, I was given the opportunity to present in one of the seminars co-chaired by her and Kent Richards entitled "Ethos of Biblical Studies." I am sincerely grateful to both for inviting me to contribute to the present publication as the sole voice from Europe. This fully revised version of my original paper begins with reflections on the relation between state and religion in nineteenth-century Europe, during which time the canon of religious education and its institutional configurations were determined. Following a discussion of graduate and postgraduate programs in theology, including biblical studies, I turn to the ethos of New Testament studies as personally experienced, agonized over (yes, we Europeans are also afflicted by our intellectual heritage), adopted, and applied in my own research. In conclusion, I formulate proposals for both a new and inspiring as well as transformative practice and ethos of future biblical studies in Europe. These proposals draw from the contexts of my national location and Schüssler Fiorenza's seminal article "Rethinking the Educational Practices of Biblical Doctoral Studies."[2]

---

1. I am grateful to Dr. Mark Kyburz for proofreading this essay.
2. *TThRel* 6 (2003): 65–75.

1. Educational Practice

1.1. European Policies on Relations Between State and Religion in Comparison with the United States

As is generally known, Europe and the United States underwent different processes of secularization, which resulted in different perceptions of how state and religion ought to interrelate. Essentially, two lines of argumentation can be distinguished: state-controlled (or centrist) and market-controlled. The former describes a trajectory from Thomas Hobbes over Max Weber to Carl Schmitt that considers the state's exclusive regulatory force as the prerequisite for the peaceful co-existence of rivaling religious communities. That is, state monopoly is necessarily based on jurisdiction. The latter relies upon a peaceful contest in the context of a cultural pluralism guaranteed by this very competition.

The "old" European model, which is still effective in Europe, derives from the Roman Empire. In Imperial Rome, the state authoritatively ascertained which cults and *collegia* were admissible, and, by contrast, which were prohibited. The latter labeled especially those formations that failed to satisfy the central precondition for legitimate religion, namely a public rather than a covert cult practice. Thus, the state functioned as adjudicator, thereby introducing a claim for religious neutrality on the one hand, and the possibility of proximate and convergent state and religious power in the form of a state church on the other. Such a state church not only acted as the sole representative of particular state (social) politics, but also remained assured of privileged access to public resources. Such convergence first occurred in the late Roman Empire, between Constantine and Christendom.

The Reformation marked the second and decisive interference of the hegemony of the one Christian church, which had lasted for centuries until then. Suddenly, European empires and states found themselves confronted not with just one but multiple Christian communities. These were locked in bitter rivalry, waging brutal wars over competing and exclusive claims to truth. New, practicable political theories concerning the relations between state and religion were called for. Such theories arose in the course of the French Revolution, and resulted in new articulations and the enforcement of state monopoly on the basis of rational jurisdiction. In view of the former religious wars, such monopoly entailed the complete banishment of religion from the public sphere and its restriction to the private. While the privatization of religion based on anticlerical and atheistic motives did not oust religion from society, it clearly undermined its development and growth by imposing rigid structures on the modern derivatives of the old centrist Roman model, albeit now in relation to nation states and as such national and ethnic religious communities. Claus Leggewie has shown that these developments led to merely three models in nineteenth-century Europe: laicism, the state church, and pillarization.

The laical republics France and Turkey declared religion to be an entirely private affair and banned it from public life by erecting a high wall between state and religious institutions, characterized by far-reaching state control of religious communities. By contrast, nations opting for the state church model, similar to late antiquity, officialized and privileged a certain confession and church, whose dignitaries entered a more or less overt symbiosis with state authorities. Thus, Russia and Greece privileged Orthodoxy, Poland, Austria, Italy, Spain and Portugal the Catholic Church, England the Anglican, and Germany the Lutheran Church. Concordance democracies, such as the Netherlands and Switzerland, introduced the model of pillarization, arranging religious groups like pillars side by side. Granted extensive autonomy, these religious communities could represent civil society as largely free of the state, and co-existed with other groups endorsing different worldviews.

These different models of regulation had in common that the constitutions of western democracies in principle guaranteed both positive and negative religious freedom; irrespective of the historic hegemony of the Christian faith, such freedom always includes members of non-Christian confessions. States and their representatives can no longer determine what counts as religion and what not, even when the approval of associations, for instance in Germany, implies the extension of a so-called "religious privilege," whereas public utility is denied under fiscal law when a religious community is deemed to be primarily pursuing commercial activities. Whether this centrist model measures up to twenty-first century Europe in light of an increasingly globalized world comprised of transnational societies due to vast flows of migration is currently the subject of various debates.

Contrary to the European, state-controlled concept, the market-controlled concept of religions evolved in the United States instead. It did so on account of a more radically implemented secularization process, wherein the *Bill of Rights* implied a "wall of separation between church and state" (as understood by Thomas Jefferson) and is often interpreted and confirmed as such by the Supreme Court. This measure aimed to prevent the privileging of any single confession as well as the possible suppression of others. Consequently, religiosity prospered more in individual and loose structures of competing religious communities rather than in a few complex and dominant institutions receiving church taxes collected by the state—as in Europe—or offered religious education at public schools or even social services performed under the direction of churches.

Precisely because no religious community held a monopoly in the spiritual representation of the American people, secularization and modernization in the United States—unlike in Europe—amounted neither to the ousting of (a dominant) religion from the public sphere nor to its depoliticization. Since the emancipation of the individual citizen in the United States was not borne by anticlerical or atheistic motives, this people in its versatile entirety was represented by all religious communities. Such equal representation and resulting peaceful co-existence in turn provided the guidelines for the development of American civil religion.[3]

The above arguments prompt the following conclusions. (1) Unlike in the United States, religious education in Europe, including graduate and postgraduate studies in theology, is—with exceptions such as laical France and Roman Catholic Italy—almost invariably offered by public (or state) universities. Since the predominant number of graduates still aim to become pastors (or priests) in one of the large state churches, theological faculties have developed traditional-pragmatic yet monopolistic relations with these religious institutions. (2) Unlike their counterparts in the United States, European theological faculties and their members are not held in high esteem, neither in the larger university context nor in the public sphere. The recurrent calls issued by other disciplines to "abolish theology" from higher education are a perennial symptom of a discipline under ideological suspicion.

1.2. Graduate and Postgraduate Education in Theology in Europe and Switzerland

In general, biblical studies for most of Europe including Switzerland form part of the theology programs offered by the faculties of theology of public (or state) universities, the equivalents of Christian divinity schools in the United States. In Europe, universities are prestigious and often century-old institutions. Founded in 1460, the University of Basel is the oldest university in Switzerland.[4] Together with its theological faculty,[5] it will celebrate its 550th anniversary in 2010.[6] Quite often, such time-honored institutions owe

---
3. Claus Leggewie, "Zweierlei Säkularisierung: Globalisierung und Euro-Islam," in *Theoriebildung im christlich-jüdischen Dialog: Kulturwissenschaftliche Reflexionen zur Deutung, Verhältnisbestimmung und Diskursfähigkeit von Religionen* (ed. Gabriella Gelardini and Peter Schmid; Judentum und Christentum 15; Stuttgart: Kohlhammer, 2004), 71–82, esp. 71–74.
4. Online: http://www.unibas.ch.
5. Online: http://theolrel.unibas.ch/.
6. Universität Basel, ed., *Portrait Universität Basel* (Gelterkinden: Seiler, 2008), 3; Susanne Schaub, ed., *Universität Basel: Theologische Fakultät* (Basel: Gremper, 2008), 4.

GELARDINI: ETHOS OF POSTGRADUATE BIBLICAL EDUCATION 157

their very existence to a theological faculty. Consequently, the Bologna process—ratified by forty-six European countries since 1999—bears relevance to theological faculties. The process, named after the oldest university of Europe, aims to introduce a three-cycle degree system across Europe by 2010. The new system will comprise bachelor's, master's, and doctoral (postgraduate) programs, thereby forming the European Higher Education Area (EHEA). The goal of this continent-wide operation is to improve attractiveness but also mobility, employability, and compatibility in Europe and the rest of the world.[7] Swiss universities have thus introduced not only bachelor's but also master's programs while also adapting their academic calendar.[8] They are currently on the verge of implementing Bologna III, that is, the new doctoral programs. Bologna III plans to extend the privilege of rights to all doctoral students in the future, so that they may be perceived and appreciated not merely as students but also as young professionals making essential contributions to gaining new knowledge.

Although located at public universities, most German-speaking theological faculties of Switzerland maintain close relationships to Protestant confessions, as observed above.[9] This does not mean that denominational seminaries do not exist. Rather, they are few and far between and in a weaker structural position than university-based faculties. Various reasons account for this difference, be it because church-sponsored seminaries were founded to serve temporary means such as a shortage of pastors for generations with high birth rates, or because Roman Catholic seminaries have only little career options to offer—in particular for women, and finally because evangelical seminaries[10] commit themselves to anti-modern and fundamentalist theologies, and are therefore neither accredited nor can their religious communities offer decent salaries.[11] On the other hand, however, and given patchwork biographies and diverse educational careers nowadays, faculties have entered into local and basic pragmatic relations with seminaries located nearby. Such

---

7. The current website for 2007–2010 is: http://www.ond.vlaanderen.be/hogeronderwijs/bologna.
8. The so-called summer semester (April–September) has been commuted into a spring semester (February–July); the former winter semester (October–March) is now an autumn semester (August–January).
9. In Switzerland, most theological faculties also lean toward the Evangelical-Reformed Church, such as in Basel, Bern, Geneva, Lausanne, Neuchâtel, and Zürich. Conversely, the Fribourg and Lucerne faculties lean toward the Roman Catholic Church, while Bern additionally leans toward the Christian Catholic Church.
10. One example of an evangelical seminary in northwestern Switzerland is the Staatsunabhängige Theologische Hochschule Basel (STH): http://www.sthbasel.ch.
11. Schüssler Fiorenza, "Rethinking the Educational Practices," 66–67.

arrangements enable seminary students to have prior achievements accredited at our theological faculty in Basel and to complete their higher education with a fully recognized degree.

Postgraduate training in biblical studies usually begins with the successful completion of graduate studies in theology over the course of a minimum of five years (until the 2004 summer semester, this led to a licentiate in theology; since the 2004/2005 winter semester, successful candidates are awarded a bachelor's and master's in Theology).[12] On the one hand, this program traditionally includes historical-exegetical fields, such as Old and New Testament as well as church history and the history of church dogmatics; on the other, it comprises systematic-theological fields, such as dogmatics and ethics, and finally practical theology. Subject to faculty developments, further fields complement the University of Basel program, including the study of ecumenical science and Christian mission, religious studies, Jewish studies, and gender studies.[13] Nearly 70 percent of our graduates in Basel pursue a career as pastors in the Evangelical-Reformed church. In German-speaking Switzerland, the ordination of pastors requires the completion of a churchly education alongside a degree in theology, comprised of an ecclesiological-practical seminar over the course of five months; following theological education, such training also comprises a one-year vicariate in a parish, and concludes with a practical examination. Such churchly education, organized by the concordat of the churches in cooperation with the universities, provides students with access to practical experience, including preaching, only in its final, vicariate-based year.[14] Subject to the prevailing political-cultural circumstances, the political sermon has enjoyed popularity, for instance during the two World Wars and in the 1970s and 1980s, but less so now, it seems.

Within the Bologna process, as mentioned, postgraduate programs have neither been introduced in Europe nor in Switzerland. Graduates aiming to continue their studies after earning a licentiate or master's degree in Theology will thus enroll for a doctorate in theology. Depending on individual career plans, candidates may embark on a doctoral dissertation with or without a churchly education and practical examination. Although a few European universities have started to abolish the *Habilitationsschrift* in the humanities, applying for a vacant chair without presenting a second book or at least a

---

12. Schaub, *Theologische Fakultät*, 7.
13. Ibid., 3, 8–17.
14. Online at: http://theologie.unibas.ch/index.php?id=1734; Schüssler Fiorenza, "Rethinking the Educational Practices," 67: Hence our students seldom find themselves in the schizophrenic situation of pursuing critical studies and having to deliver a biblicist sermon.

cumulative qualifying postdoctoral thesis is still unthinkable. Furthermore, such a thesis remains highly relevant in German-speaking Europe for structural reasons, since universities currently have few salaried positions to offer professionals "only" holding a doctorate.

The employment situation for individuals holding a *Habilitation* in biblical studies and in nearly any other field of research is precarious. This is mainly because higher education has either disguised or ignored the ever-changing circumstances of the employment market for decades now. On the one hand, writing two academic books on a meager research associate's salary, together with the desire or need to start a family, takes a long time—and is full of privations; on the other, applying for a vacancy involves the daunting prospect of as many as two hundred other competitors. Under these circumstances, an application process is protracted; in view of widespread age discrimination, however, no one can afford to be judged as "too old." Put differently, since supply exceeds demand, everyone pursuing a career in theology is into the risk business. The application process is further complicated by so-called "pseudo-competition": although in-house appointments are scorned, being on familiar terms with important members of the search committees almost always improves a candidate's chances, regardless of his or her qualifications. Often, selection decisions hinge on irrational factors, such as shared experiences, relations, nationality, and, yes indeed, gender. I find it utterly disturbing when female candidates, even at my own faculty, are judged and hence dismissed due to a "lack of character qualities," even more so when statistics show that of approximately 55 percent female graduate students only 9 percent in German-speaking Europe are appointed professors.[15]

Admittedly, the problems delineated here have been recognized. Various strategies and structural changes promise a better future. First of all, no one enters postgraduate studies naively; responsible career planning includes more than one option. It is unwise, for instance, to apply for only one specific teaching or particular research position within the university system. Many extramural opportunities exist, too: as a pastor or positions in church management, undergraduate instruction, government bodies, media, the arts and culture, or highly specialized IT and publishing. With the Bologna process, European universities are also undergoing structural changes, which are

---

15. Jutta Dalhoff, "Berufungs- und Karrieretraining für Wissenschaftlerinnen—Ausgangspunkt, Entwicklung und Perspektiven," in *Anstoß zum Aufstieg—Karrieretraining für Wissenschaftlerinnen auf dem Prüfstand* (ed. Jutta Dalhoff; CEWS Beiträge: Frauen in Wissenschaft und Forschung 4; Bielefeld: Kleine, 2006), 11–25, esp. 12–13; Inken Lind, "Wissenschaftlerinnen an Hochschulen: Analyse der aktuellen Situation," in Dalhoff, *Anstoß zum Aufstieg*, 142, esp. 143.

evaluated ambivalently by nonprofessorial faculty. Although new and unusual positions are introduced, such as tenured and nontenured junior and assistant professorships and lectureships, these changes aim to reduce overall teaching budgets, and will eventually lead to a reduction of the number of positions available at professorial level. The Swiss National Science Foundation (SNSF) plays an important role in supporting the upcoming new generations of scholars. For instance, it offers funding for individuals at graduate, postgraduate, and postdoctoral levels, establishes so called SNSF-professorships (equal to nontenured assistant professorships but sponsored entirely by SNSF-funding), runs finance mentoring programs for women, and, finally and not insignificantly in view of age- and gender discrimination, speaks of an individual's "academic age" as against the previously common "biological age."[16]

1.3. Postgraduate Biblical Education in Switzerland and in Particular in Basel

Whoever enrolls at the Basel Faculty of Theology to pursue graduate or postgraduate training joins the country's oldest full-faculty university, as mentioned above. Notwithstanding state funding from the cantons Basel-Stadt and Basel-Landschaft, the University of Basel was part-privatized in 1996 and subsequently became self-managed. Notwithstanding its student body of 11,000,[17] including 2,000 doctoral students and 1,300 academic staff, of which 320 are professors (with a higher-than-average 15 percent share of women), the University of Basel is a smaller institution by European standards; it nevertheless ranks among the top hundred of the world's leading universities and belongs to the top ten in German-speaking Europe. Only 1 percent of the University's students are enrolled at the Faculty of Theology, as opposed to 28 percent at the Faculty of Humanities, 22 percent at the Faculty of Science, 18 percent at the Faculty of Medicine, 13 percent at the Faculty of Law, 10 percent at the Faculty of Business and Economy, and 8 percent at the Faculty of Psychology.[18]

In comparison with other theological faculties, Basel has nine professors (six from Germany), ten research associates (five from Germany and one from Russia) and a few lecturers, making it a smaller, yet together with Bern and Zürich one of the leading theological faculties in Switzerland. In the

---

16. Online: http://www.snf.ch.
17. Of the total figure of students, 55 percent are female and 20 percent from abroad.
18. Universität Basel, *Portrait Universität Basel*, 3–4; Beat Münch, ed., *Jahresbericht 2007 der Universität Basel* (Basel: Steudler, 2008), 4–5, 88–102; online: http://www.unibas.ch/doc/doc_download.cfm?uuid=7F40BF2A3005C8DEA380AF9BA5094954&&IRACER_AUTOLINK&&.

German-speaking area, Basel is considered the most progressive faculty and is on the verge of developing into a research faculty, as evidenced by statistics: out of 170 students, as many as 37 are working on a doctoral dissertation. For some obscure reasons, these figures exclude candidates undertaking a postdoctoral thesis (*Habilitation*). Structurally, the faculty is also undergoing transformation: in the 2007 autumn semester, a second department of religious studies—combining theology *and* humanities—was incorporated; this will eventually comprise all religion-related studies at the university, ranging from religious over Jewish to Islamic studies in the future. Furthermore, the faculty is currently engaging in various interdisciplinary and across-universitary projects, such as the Zentrum für Religion, Wirtschaft und Politik (ZRWP),[19] one of whose core activities will be to design master's programs and research-related lecture courses.[20] Besides these new departmental and interdisciplinary activities, the faculty will considerably expand opportunities for interdisciplinary approaches to theology in the context of the already existing bachelor and master of arts in theology.[21] Whether the faculty—apart from the inherent and traditional tensions in theology between historical and systematic fields—will be able to bear the ideological tensions between theology and supposedly value-free religious studies remains to be seen.[22]

Graduates admitted to doctoral studies in Basel have usually pursued a first career,[23] have either studied theology in Switzerland or Germany (and are hence Swiss or German nationals), have mostly been socialized into a Protestant denomination, and 50 percent of enrollees are females. Depending on professorial networking, a few doctoral students from Eastern Europe and Asia are attracted as well.[24] The demography of those working on a postdoctoral thesis (*Habilitation*) is similar. For most, the motivation to enroll in doctoral studies is to pursue an academic career. Whether this ambition can be achieved depends on individual working conditions. There are basically three feasible possibilities. (1) Doctoral or postdoctoral work is undertaken within the context of research associate's position, under the supervision of

---

19. Online: http://www.zrwp.ch.
20. "Bericht der Theologischen Fakultät über das Studienjahr 2007," 1–33, esp. 1, 3; online: http://theolrel.unibas.ch/index.php?eID=tx_nawsecuredl&u=0&file=fileadmin/theorel/redaktion/Dekanat/Jahresbericht_Theologie_2007_Eingabe.pdf&t=1278348694&hash=39bc33170eb56aa0ecf4817e84c32e8a.
21. Schaub, *Theologische Fakultät*, 7.
22. Schüssler Fiorenza, "Rethinking the Educational," 66.
23. Ibid., 67.
24. Ibid. It can therefore be concluded that, although the overall demography of students at the faculty has changed, the demography of students enrolling in doctoral programs for theology has remained similar, apart from the increased participation of women.

a professor holding a chair in the candidate's research field of inquiry. While candidates are quite free to choose their research topics, many decide to determine theirs in consultation and correspondence with their supervisors. Research associates are given fixed-term 50–75 percent contracts by the university—four years to complete a dissertation and six years to complete a *Habilitation*—on the basis of wages close to the poverty level. The idea in this setup is to work *for* the university at the percentage level agreed upon in the contract, and to conduct one's *own* research beyond that time frame. Essentially, working for the university means teaching two to four hours and assuming various duties in the faculty's and university's self-administration, including committee work. (2) Doctoral or postdoctoral work is undertaken in the context of mostly SNSF-funding *ad personam* (scholarships) or funding related to specific research projects initiated by one or several professors. The duration of such grants depends on the type of scholarship and the dimensions of the project; the choice of topic is free in the first case and project-related in the second. No further obligations beyond research are imposed. (3) Doctoral or postdoctoral work is undertaken alongside employment unrelated to the research project. Here, too, candidates are free to determine their research topics, and work independently of institutional commitments and timeframes. Without any doubt, research associates are afforded the best chances for an academic, since they are the fortunate ones "invited" by a professor to take up one of few such positions, on the basis of an outstanding licentiate/master's or doctoral thesis. While such arrangements lead to rich experience at an early stage of one's professional life, they slow down individual progression through the ranks.

Graduates who have completed a licentiate or master's in theology and who have enrolled for at least two semesters in Basel are eligible for a doctoral degree at the Basel Faculty of Theology. The university's doctoral studies regulations define the goal of a dissertation as follows: "The dissertation ought to be an independent and exhaustive investigation on a certain topic in theology."[25] In the best case, such an "independent investigation" offers a real and coherent contribution to a research field. In principle, this short and general description allows for much freedom, but its handling needs to be learned. Unlike in the Anglo-Saxon system, earning a doctorate involves no coursework, but this will change with the introduction of Bologna III.[26] Informally, however, doctoral students are expected to attend the national, German-speaking doctoral

---

25. "Universität Basel 446.160: Ordnung der Theologischen Fakultät Basel über die Erwerbung des Doktorgrades (9. Juni 1937)," 1.

26. Schüssler Fiorenza, "Rethinking the Educational Practices," 67.

colloquium in New Testament, co-sponsored by the faculties of Basel, Bern, Chur, Fribourg, Luzern, and Zürich.

Irrespective of the working circumstances outlined above, all doctoral students are supervised by a professor representing the research field in question. Female candidates, moreover, can acquire further expertise in mentoring through one of several national or local mentoring programs. The first such program was launched in Switzerland in 2001.[27] Its success led to the introduction of several successors. Upon submission of the completed dissertation, the faculty decides whether the dissertation ought to be accepted or not, based on the internal supervisor's report and at least one second external report.[28] Usually, these proposals are approved, yet the contrary can, and has occurred, generally due to a dispute between two or more antagonized professors. Upon grading, candidates are admitted to the oral examination, the *Rigorosum*. Subject to the final grade earned for the graduate course, this comprises either three or five individual examinations, each containing three themes beyond the topic of the dissertation. The examination in the main (that is, dissertational) field of the three-field *Rigorosum* lasts one hour and is chaired by the principal supervisor; the two examinations in the subsidiary fields lasts forty-five minutes, and candidates are examined by the professorial representatives of those fields. Among the theological fields, candidates must by necessity opt for either the Old or New Testament; the other examinations can be taken either in church history, along with the history of church dogmatics, systematics, practical theology, ecumenical science and Christian mission, comparative religious, or Jewish studies.[29] The dissertation and the oral examinations each make up half of the final grade, and one of the following predicates is conferred on the candidate's overall performance: *summa cum laude, insigni cum laude, magna cum laude, cum laude*, or *rite*.[30] Only upon submitting four printed and bound copies of the dissertation to the faculty is an official doctoral degree certificate presented, bearing the Latinate predicate awarded. Publishing the dissertation thereafter requires the faculty's permission.[31]

On the one hand, the range of topics available within theology and in combination with other disciplines is in principle unlimited, as long as a professorial faculty member is capable of assessing a dissertation in association with one external supervisor. On the other, however, those pursuing an aca-

---

27. Online: http://www.academic-mentoring.ch/.
28. "Universität Basel 446.160," 1.
29. Ibid., 1–2.
30. Ibid., 2.
31. Ibid., 2–3.

demic career will make sure that at least either their doctoral or postdoctoral dissertation focuses on a mainstream topic, preferably an exegetical one; a contrary choice certainly diminishes a candidate's academic employment prospects. With regard to New Testament studies, such core topics are the exegesis of one central New Testament text (such as a Gospel, Acts, a Pauline Letter, Revelation, and lately the book of Hebrews). Or such topics include an historical investigation of Jesus, Paul, or early Christianity; methodologically, they would adopt a philological-linguistic or intertextual approach, a sociohistorical, archaeological or anthropological approach, a theological and hermeneutical, or reception-historical approach.[32]

Personally, I did not conform to the typical demography of a doctoral student in theology. For one, I pursued theological studies as my second career, studying in Switzerland and in the United States. Born in Switzerland to immigrant parents, I have dual Swiss and Italian citizenship. I therefore changed my religious affiliation from Roman Catholic to Evangelical-Reformed, because I had been chiefly socialized into the latter. Finally, when I enrolled in doctoral studies back in 1999, women were still a minority. My motivation to pursue postgraduate training was clearly a future academic career, so I was all the more delighted when my licentiate thesis on the structure of the book of Hebrews[33] obtained the approval of the local professor of New Testament, who encouraged me to develop it into a doctoral dissertation. Since no research associate positions were available at that time, I applied for, and received, a one-year SNSF postgraduate scholarship for "prospective researchers." Given the requirement to conduct research abroad, and through my professor's contacts, I was able to spend the 1999/2000 academic year with the greatest benefit at Harvard Divinity School (HDS). During that year, I was invited to apply for the meanwhile vacant position as a part-time research associate for New Testament at Basel, which I held from 2001 to 2004 and during which I completed my dissertation in due time.[34] With equal benefit, I had the opportunity to attend a two-month archaeological course (*Lehrkurs*) throughout Israel and Jordan in summer 2001, sponsored by the Evangelical Church of Germany (EKD) and organized by the German Protestant Institute of Archaeology (DEI)[35] along with the German Archaeological Institute (DAI). Since

---

32. Schüssler Fiorenza, "Rethinking the Educational Practices," 66. The thematical restriction to "bread and butter" topics in regard to the job market is not any different in Europe than it is in the United States.

33. "Der konzentrische Stufenrhythmus: Eine Strukturanalyse zum Hebräer" (Lizentiatsarbeit, Theologische Fakultät der Universität Basel, 1998).

34. The dissertation was published in 2007 under the title: *"Verhärtet eure Herzen nicht": Der Hebräer, eine Synagogenhomilie zu Tischa be-Aw* (BibInt 83; Leiden: Brill, 2007).

35. Online: http://www.deiahl.de.

2004, I have held a 70 percent position as a Senior Research Associate working on my postdoctoral thesis (*Habilitation*) bearing the working title "The Role of Ethnicity and Religion in the New Testament in the Formation of a Collective Christian Identity."

My personal evaluation of my doctoral studies in the context of a research associate's position is positive, notwithstanding various challenges. This is due to some fortunate circumstances, since the "research associate" model by no means guarantees success, that is, a completed dissertation after four years. Initially, I found daunting, the prospect of offering curricular teaching without any prior research or university teaching experience. Fortunately, I soon realized that teaching fertilizes research, and vice versa. With the help of the university's in-service teaching skills program, I was not only able to professionalize my teaching but also determine my own course of themes, such as exegetical methods, feminist biblical hermeneutics, biblical archaeology, Hellenistic-Jewish texts, and historiographical theory. Multitasking also proved challenging, since faculty interests required me to teach well, plan and host international symposia and publish their proceedings, reliably assume administrative duties within a self-managed department, advance my own research, engage in side projects, attend to alternative publications, enroll in advanced training, and network. None of this benefited from a supportive environment; in my experience, faculties are not places where friends are made, but rather the site of fierce and frequent competition. Fortunately, I was blessed by a marvelous working relationship with my (male) supervisor and, in the context of a mentoring program, with my second (female) supervisor. Both granted me the unlimited freedom I needed for my research, teaching, continuing education, related projects, and involvement in the Society of Biblical Literature. Both were always available for questions, supported and even contributed to my projects, and helped to find loopholes when the university suddenly cut wages by 20 percent. Such outstanding supervision was by no means a matter of course, since sad and sorry tales of professors who employ staff on a part-time basis but require full-time output, or curtail their research associates' intellectual freedom, or downright abuse their research findings without, however, giving them due credit are the order of the day, not only in Switzerland but even at our university.

Unlike a doctoral thesis, a postdoctoral *Habilitation* aims at qualifying candidates for the *venia legendi*. This "right to teach" is conferred upon candidates who hold a doctoral degree, have submitted a second book in a specific area of theology, and with a proven publishing record; mostly recently, candidates are also required to have obtained a certificate in academic teaching skills. If the materials submitted are considered sufficient by the faculty, candidates are required to deliver a trial lecture, followed by a colloquium reaching beyond the theme of their postdoctoral work in front of the faculty and two representatives of the university president. Once these requirements have been met—and this is mostly the case—the faculty petitions the university to confer upon the candidate the *venia legendi* in their designated field and discipline; this, too, is mostly a formality.[36] Upon conferral of the *venia legendi*, candidates are appointed *Privatdozent* (PD); pursuant to a medieval tradition, they are required to offer a gratuitous two-hour lecture each semester until hired by another university. In the best case, candidates will qualify for the academic employment market in their mid-thirties; should they fail to do so by their mid-forties, the reality of being unemployable looms.

2. The Acquisition and Application of Ethos

2.1. The Acquisition of Ethos

After discussing the practice of graduate and postgraduate education, I now turn to the ethos of biblical education, namely, by acknowledging what Elisabeth Schüssler Fiorenza has repeatedly argued—that education never takes place in value-free zones—and by inquiring where the *topoi* of ethos acquisition lie.

Apart from continent and country, the university's location and immediate surroundings are certainly relevant to its ethos. The city of Basel, the second largest city in Switzerland, located in its northwestern tip and pitted in epic enmity against the financial capital Zürich, which Basel perceives as elitist, takes pride not only in a rich and Protestant cultural heritage developed in exchange with neighboring France and Germany but also in a long-standing liberal political tradition.[37]

Other than location, the faculty and its educational goals, formulated with regard to the introduction of bachelor's and master's degrees in theology in 2005, are central to the formation of ethos: "The Faculty of Theology of the University of Basel engages scientifically with the *history* and *present* of Christendom. It actuates theology therefore as the *historical investigation* of the historical reality of Christianity as well as a *search for the meaning* of the Christian tradition for the individual and society in the present and with regard to its *practical implementation*."[38] Studies are thus undertaken in a

---

36. "Universität Basel 446.170: Ordnung über die Habilitation an der Theologischen Fakultät der Universität Basel (8. Mai 1943)," 1.
37. Online: http://www.basel.ch.
38. "Wegleitung für das Bachelor- und Masterstudium Theologie (2005)," 3 (my translation, emphases added).

spirit of ecumenical-interreligious openness,[39] adopting an emic-theological as well as an etic-religious-scientific perspective. Other than interpersonal skills, coursework leading to academic degrees aims to build core philological, historical, critical-hermeneutical, and practical-theological skills.[40] Although these definitions sound progressive, they leave ample space for interpretation, since ethical criteria for measuring these core skills are not laid down.[41] Regardless of these noble intentions, unprepared and passionless teaching is nevertheless offered, questionable socio-pedagogic skills are apparent, and fierce antagonism amongst colleagues abounds, at times degenerating into trivial yet energy-consuming faculty wars.

Without doubt, postgraduate students acquire ethos in the contexts of their particular discipline, in my case New Testament studies, and above all of a specific professorship, usually the chair held by their supervisor. A premodern-doctrinal paradigm is no longer effective in German-speaking Europe and was replaced by a modern-scientific paradigm in the twentieth century, when, as Oda Wischmeyer ascertains, the still widely accepted historical-positivist and literary-structuralist approaches were adopted instead.[42] Teaching focusing on the present remains rare,[43] and it mostly involves professors affected by May 1968, who acquired a postmodern-hermeneutical approach, like my supervisor. Together with others, he tirelessly engaged in a political-ethical struggle to help establish an anti-anti-Jewish hermeneutic of biblical exegesis in light of the Holocaust. The political fruits of these endeavors were to help facilitate Christian-Jewish dialog and the establishment of Jewish studies at the University of Basel.

The second most important place of ethos acquisition is the aforementioned Swiss-German doctoral colloquium. Upon attending, I soon realized that the various disciplinary paradigms did not work there in the interactive and complementary fashion that I was used to from Basel; rather the historical-positivist paradigm was repeatedly enforced in a hegemonic fashion upon the group by the most senior and most distinguished scholar (who has mean-

---

39. Schüssler Fiorenza, "Rethinking the Educational Practices," 65: An international and interreligious dialogue as Schüssler Fiorenza calls for is hence integrated.
40. "Wegleitung für das Bachelor- und Masterstudium Theologie (2005)," 4–5.
41. Schüssler Fiorenza, "Rethinking the Educational Practices," 65.
42. Oda Wischmeyer, "Die neutestamentliche Wissenschaft am Anfang des 21. Jahrhunderts: Überlegungen zu ihrem Selbstverständnis, ihren Beziehungsfeldern und ihren Aufgaben," in *Herkunft und Zukunft der neutestamentlichen Wissenschaft* (ed. Oda Wischmeyer; Neutestamentliche Entwürfe 6; Tübingen: Francke, 2003), 245–71.
43. Oda Wischmeyer, "Das Selbstverständnis der neutestamentlichen Wissenschaft in Deutschland: Bestandesaufnahme, Kritik, Perspektiven," *ZNT* 5/10 (2002): 13–36, esp. 19, 22, 28.

while retired).⁴⁴ Unfortunately, this was the place where doctoral students presented portions of their work for the first time. Harsh criticism was meted out to those failing to comply with the dominant paradigm, if necessary in the guise of reproval regarding methodological or formal aspects. Looking back, I could never report an edifying learning atmosphere in that context, and the increasing silence of newer, younger, and especially female students along with chronically bad attendance seem to have been symptomatic. Scientific dictatorship is less prevalent nowadays, but some professors are still known to forbid their students from citing their opponents. In the course of my experience at Harvard Divinity School, I was fortunate enough to discover another, transformative paradigm, the rhetorical-emancipatory one, which I readily acquired in the unconstrained meetings of the Society of Biblical Literature, along with the familiar scientific-hermeneutical paradigm.⁴⁵

2.2. The Application of Ethos in the Context of my Dissertation

In view of my own research, the paradigms acquired needed to be implemented, but which one should underpin my own research efforts? I had learned that every scientific quest, every primary text to be scrutinized, needs its own set of methods. Did I have the courage to disappoint the hegemonic demands of my colleagues at the doctoral colloquium? No problem. But what about my supervisors? The capacity to evaluate intellectual capital and methods in view of competing paradigms is one matter, but implementing what has been discerned as the proper venue, perhaps against the grain and even against the views dear to my supervisors, is another. This does indeed require courage, and courageous scientific integrity also needs to be learned.

Investigating a century of research on the book of Hebrews provided an important precondition for this courage. Certain works called for my unrestrained admiration, others bored me profoundly, and others provoked downright anger. The tediously gathered synopsis of this research field helped me understand that not only new methods but also new hermeneutical frameworks complied with specific socio-historical needs, and that therefore certain interpretations remained irrevocably popular for decades. So much for scientific objectivity. Influenced by French structuralism, the French-Catholic school drew attention to the structure of Hebrews at the beginning of the twentieth century. According to their understanding, the center of the text,

---

44. Schüssler Fiorenza, "Rethinking the Educational Practices," 68, 72: Inspiring collaboration remains a desideratum.

45. Ibid., 65, 69, 72–73. Thereby I am aware that acquiring political-ethical approaches has a somewhat accidental character.

and along with it the main theological emphasis, was the high priest Christ. Could it be that this new aspiring elite was in search of a "strong man" after the tussle of the First World War, moreover one who was priest, like themselves? In the 1940s, the German school emphasized the paraenetic aspects of Hebrews, considering its author a cautious counselor. Could it be that a war- and crisis-ridden country needed precisely this message? In the early 1980s, the American school directed attention to the theocentric and covenantal theology of Hebrews. Could it be that only a Theology after Auschwitz had made it possible to finally acknowledge the Jewish character of the text rather than solely a "Christian-supersessionist" interpretation?

I opted to read against the grain of so many German and Swiss anti-Jewish authors indebted to the old school of Tübingen, even more so as my personal structural analysis led me to a theocentric and covenantal interpretation of Hebrews. And since the mentioned archaeological *Lehrkurs* allowed me to visit dozens of ancient synagogues, even those dating to the first century, I followed those authors that came to perceive the book of Hebrews as an ancient synagogue homily. Based on extensive intertextual comparison and socio-historical analysis of ancient synagogue liturgy, I was able to furnish evidence that Hebrews is a homily based on the torah reading Exod 31:18–32:35 and the prophet reading Jere 31:31–34 (as quoted in Hebrews) and for the most important day of fast, Tisha be-Av, which up to this day commemorates the destruction of both Jerusalem temples. This kind of reading understands covenant renewal as an integral part of ancient Jewish (-Christian) synagogue liturgy and not as a socio-religious indicator that God expelled the Jews and renewed the broken covenant in favor of Christians. I was aware that this retraction of a covenant renewal motive to Jewish ends would not please every apologetic Christian reader. First reader reactions then confirmed the old cliché that innovation—at least in theology—first needs to experience sanction in America before being accepted in Europe twenty years later.

I subjected my own reconstruction to a critical-hermeneutical evaluation, since it had become important to me to assume responsibility for my findings in the context of a rhetorical-emancipatory paradigm (with an astonishing outcome). Not only had I experienced the ethical evaluation of biblical texts as a liberating process, since from my postmodern background I had come to perceive biblical texts as problematic and partially even as a disastrous cultural heritage of which no useful theological remains could be gained; the critical-hermeneutical and rhetorical-emancipatory approach, moreover, unlocked for the first time the (positive) theological potential of biblical texts for me.

Conclusions

In view of educational practice, I formulate the following proposals to improve biblical studies. Research associates should become organized in labor unions so that their female members can also afford to have families. Furthermore, Swiss postdoctoral staff should be perceived by their universities not as cheap labor for implementing the Bologna process for free and at their own expense, but as the upcoming and new generation of scholars. They should be treated accordingly, that is, they should be paid commensurately and receive appropriate and abundant career advancement aid.[46] Finally, one can hope that the introduction of Bologna III will further minimize the abuse of research associates' labor by their supervisors.[47]

In view of the ethos discussed, it would be appropriate if educational goals were made measurable through the explication of ethical benchmarks. Likewise beneficial would be the alignment of inter- and transdisciplinary approaches to the relevant problems or needs in society, along with the permanent implementation in course syllabi of transformative, political-ethical paradigms in content, method, and didactics. Only such measures will unshackle German-speaking New Testament scholarship from its provincial erudition, enable it to once again participate in international discourses within the discipline, and facilitate participation in larger discourses, such as literary studies and social and cultural-anthropological research.

Most significantly, may the implementation of necessary reforms and desirable proposals heed Wilhelm von Humboldt's axiom, formulated at the end of the eighteenth century for the welfare of higher education and research, and which I do not want to see endangered under any circumstances: freedom, and abundantly so, if you please.

---

46. Francesco Benini, "Unis wollen Zustrom deutscher Professoren bremsen," *Neue Zürcher Zeitung am Sonntag* 6/51 (23 December 2007): 1; idem, "Unis wollen eigenen Nachwuchs fördern," *Neue Zürcher Zeitung am Sonntag* 6/51 (23 December 2007): 9; "Schweizer Unis tun zu wenig für Professoren-Nachwuchs," *Neue Zürcher Zeitung am Sonntag* 6/51 (23 December 2007): 17.

47. Schüssler Fiorenza, "Rethinking the Educational Practices," 67–69.

3. New Voices from the Margins

BIBLICAL STUDIES: A VIEW FROM THE FEMINIST MARGINS AND THE JEWISH FRINGES

Cynthia M. Baker

My graduate training in biblical studies took place far from the field's center(s) (wherever it—or they—might be) and almost entirely along its sharp feminist edges and its dangling Jewish fringes. Moreover, my own academic center of gravity is not biblical studies, per se, but rather ancient Jewish and Christian studies by way of feminist cultural history. That said, I do teach biblical studies at the undergraduate level and have sent a number of gifted students on to graduate biblical studies. In considering how to articulate the most valuable insights afforded me by my training and what I might offer to a conversation about the desirable future of graduate biblical studies, I find myself drawing from a deep wellspring of passionate engagement with both feminism and classical rabbinic Judaism. What I find I have to offer is a handful of visions—elements of practice from the widening feminist margins and Jewish fringes of biblical studies—that might enliven our institutions and nurture our succeeding generations. Since I was invited to contribute reflections on my own training and what it has taught me, this essay necessarily swings back and forth between confession and proposition. I offer it in the hope that these personal ruminations might echo convictions and visions larger than my own.

I trained in scriptural studies at the master's level at Harvard Divinity School in the mid-1980s. My strongest New Testament training was with Elisabeth Schüssler Fiorenza, and my richest Hebrew Bible training was with Mieke Bal—then a visiting research associate in HDS's Women's Studies in Religion program (whose public lecture on the book of Judges was very noticeably avoided by the resident—older, white, male—Hebrew Bible scholars of Harvard University).[1] The foundations of my graduate biblical study,

---

1. Bal's groundbreaking work in biblical studies appears in *Death and Dissymmetry: The Politics of Coherence in the Book of Judges* (Chicago: University of Chicago Press, 1988)

then, were laid by two pioneering feminist scholars whose work contributed significantly to revolutionizing biblical studies in the late twentieth century.

While pursuing a doctorate in History of Judaism at Duke University, I fully expected to continue working in biblical studies—and I did, with a material-culture bent, on the one hand, and through a midrashic lens, on the other. (I had first fallen in love with rabbinic midrash during undergraduate studies in Jerusalem.[2]) Although I had also expected to pursue a formal doctoral minor in biblical studies, I ended up fleeing the tour of nineteenth-century German Christian scholarship that constituted the requisite methods course at the time. My feminist and critical cultural studies continued primarily through a secondary doctoral concentration, through close work with Duke's women's-studies program, and through very regular extracurricular reading-and-discussion soirées hosted by Elizabeth Clark. These latter, off-campus gatherings truly formed the heart of my professional training—although you will not find them on any transcript. Thus, my graduate-level training in biblical studies took place almost entirely along its edges and fringes but also, to a very real extent, in a kind of "woman-centered university" akin to that invoked by Adrienne Rich in her classic essay.[3] The result is a peculiar mix of perspectives on the problems and potentials of a field that both is and is not my own.

Both feminism and rabbinic midrash have drawn me to swim in a never-ending stream of questions without fear of drowning or of being swept away to unfamiliar shores. They have trained me both to trust my ability to ask important questions and to grasp the significance and possibilities inherent in others' questions, as well. From its earliest years, feminist biblical scholarship has embraced what Elisabeth Schüssler Fiorenza has called a "hermeneutics of suspicion" that approaches biblical texts and historiography with countless queries born of silences, absences, and contradictions—particularly those involving women.[4] That and related feminist hermeneutics continue to serve biblical studies well as our investigations and our understandings of the subtle workings of sex/gender/race/class/nation complexes and their queer poten-

---

and *Lethal Love: Feminist Literary Readings of Biblical Love Stories* (Bloomington: Indiana University Press, 1987).

2. "Midrash" refers to classical rabbinic Jewish patterns of biblical exegesis. Significant elements of this "rabbinic hermeneutics" will be discussed below.

3. "Toward a Woman-Centered University," in idem, *On Lies, Secrets, and Silence: Selected Prose 1966–1978* (New York: Norton, 1979).

4. *Bread Not Stone: The Challenge of Feminist Biblical Interpretation* (Boston: Beacon, 1984), 15–18.

tialities become ever more sophisticated.[5] At the same time, the worlds and dimensions that feminist questioning opens up in biblical studies become, in turn, places of re-imagined possibilities—of old (and new) stories seen through Other eyes and spoken by Other tongues.

The midrashic drive to question arises from a somewhat different, but not incompatible, impulse. It grows from a conviction that hard questioning about the "whys" and "whats" of Scripture leads to deeper insights. Further, it recognizes in multiple answers—and the multiple voices that speak them— sources of knowledge and wisdom that can stand in creative tension with one another. From a midrashic perspective, one need not single out, from among a rich multitude of viewpoints, possibilities, and responses, the one "correct" (or even a "best") interpretation. In our age, such "midrashic polyphony" can embrace the broadest possible cultural diversity as significant readings and renderings of biblical texts emanate from all quarters of the globe, all levels of society, and all manner of persons. The practice of midrash, moreover, has taught me that asking challenging questions of biblical texts is, itself, a sacred act and a gesture of faith. Students of Scriptures often find themselves buffeted between a Western Enlightenment imperative to question all religious claims, on the one hand, and, on the other, an orthodox reflex against unfettered inquiry as an assault on faith and a diminishment of the sacred. As a religious ideal, a midrashic conception of biblical study avoids this stark binary and invites a reconsideration of both common understandings of faith and assumptions about humanistic engagement with texts that some hold to be sacred.

In the same vein, both feminism and rabbinic Judaism have led me to the conviction that suspicion, horror, delight, dismay, curiosity, anger, disgust, amazement, grief, compassion, and wonder all have an honorable place in a practice of biblical study that acknowledges that scholars are whole persons— intellects and hearts, individuals and community members, genuinely capable and frighteningly needy. The extent to which a biblical-studies program is a place of persistent grappling with ever-multiplying questions, perspectives,

---

5. In *Bread Not Stone*, Schüssler Fiorenza outlines a fourfold path of feminist biblical interpretation, adding to her "hermeneutics of suspicion" hermeneutics of "proclamation," "remembrance," and "actualization" (15–22). See also her *In Memory of Her: A Feminist Theological Reconstruction of Christian Origins* (New York: Crossroad, 1983); *The Power of the Word: Scripture and the Rhetoric of Empire* (Minneapolis: Fortress, 2007); and her edited volume *Searching the Scriptures: A Feminist Introduction* (New York: Crossroad, 1993). The latter volume offers remarks on additional feminist hermeneutics, including Alicia Ostriker's "hermeneutics of indeterminacy" (8), Schüssler Fiorenza's "hermeneutics of re-vision" (11), Rita Nakashima Brock's "hermeneutics of wisdom" (64–75), and Kwok Pui-Lan's "multifaith hermeneutics" (110–11).

and insights (rather than a purveyor of packaged information and potted formulas) and the extent to which it supports and helps sustain whole persons (instead of disembodied intellects) can determine the difference between a thriving and vital program and one that strangles the desires that continue to draw people to this field of study.

Collaboration and dialogue as constitutive practices of feminism and rabbinic Judaism have played a significant part in my own training and practice. The active listening and coming-to-voice that marked the rise of feminism, and the *hevruta* (or dialogue-partner) model that characterizes traditional rabbinic study both tap into a profound human need for meaningful connection. Biblical study comes most alive when it embodies that desire and connection and is institutionally framed and nurtured as the communal, collaborative, dialogic endeavor that it is. The practice of dialogue that lies at the heart of traditional rabbinic patterns of biblical study is not an abstract addressing of questions from scholar to text; nor is it a silent searching of the Bible for insights about history, ethics, theology, and the like; nor is it even the honored Socratic method of master-challenging-disciple. It is, rather, a dynamic peer-to-peer encounter that draws on the lived experiences of students/scholars who meet each other regularly, face to face, to grapple with a range of biblically inflected subjects and texts.

The most gratifying and edifying moments in my biblical training involved such sustained and intimate discussion of texts, material artifacts, and ideas with peers and teachers outside—as well as in—a classroom setting. Dialogue is neither sermon, nor lecture, nor drill. Although these latter might have a place in biblical-studies training, one goal of that training at the graduate level is to assist students in becoming respected colleagues, professional partners, and public intellectuals capable of engaging effectively in broader cultural conversations and policy debates. The most practical and effective (not to mention pleasant) way to pursue this end is to build collaborative and dialogic models and means of learning into program design from the outset. Crucial among such means are *spaces*—material and ideological, within and outside the academy walls—for dialogue, debate, and collaborative teaching and learning to take place.

One of the more difficult skills to develop in biblical study, but also, to my mind, one of the more necessary and desirable, is a finely attuned sense of humor and delight in the subjects we engage. A good ear for the puns and ironies that abound in biblical texts, for example, is a skill that too few biblical scholars ever develop and fewer still can teach. The ancient rabbis were masters of this art, and the sheer pleasure that many took in the play of biblical words, images, and meanings is palpable in their own patterns of speech and debate. In a similar vein, feminism, which taught many of us the power of laughter and lampoon in resisting the foibles of patriarchal society, has produced a number of scholarly wordsmiths capable of enlightening through verbal delight.

Mary Daly, for one, awakened many in my generation to the serious potential of playful language.[6] More recently, Catherine Keller's verbal dexterity has been a rare gift dazzling her readers to new levels of comprehension.[7] Caught tightly between the rabbis and such feminists, among the puns and wordplays and the joy to be had in engaging a finely crafted text, my scholarly training somehow afforded me both the permission and the means to approach the august task of reading and teaching Holy Writ with an intact sense of humor and playfulness. Such a sense seems sorely lacking in much of the academy as a whole and in biblical studies, in particular. The sense of gravity and earnestness that our students (and many colleagues) bring to biblical studies would be well tempered or complemented by a greater openness to the wit and wryness intrinsic to the objects of our scholarly devotion. Such openness and mindful humor might also be key to disarming some of the deadly potential of a scriptural authority wielded far too often as a weapon in conflicts at home and around the world.

So much of my own joy in biblical study derives from the deep resonances and polysemous nature of biblical language itself. Greek has its moments, to be sure, but for me there is little in biblical study that is quite so pleasurable as tumbling headlong into Hebrew words and phrases as they open out into their myriad dimensions and possibilities, vibrating with the echoes embedded in the very fabric of that language. The *adam* of *adamah*—the *human* of rich red *humus*, breathing/blowing/inspiring the breath/wind/spirit of living/being—is a genesis of endless possibility to me. And countless more such wonders are to be found in the simple words and phrases of the ancient Hebrew texts—wonders so often erased by clumsy translation and imposed orthodoxies of meaning. A midrashic sensibility and a healthy feminist suspicion of "traditional" translations and interpretations can provide an impetus for discovering (through intimate attention to words) and magnifying (through a willingness to hear their echoes and multidimensional meanings) the beauties and terrors that these texts encode.

---

6. Daly's etymologically sensitive and cleverly deconstructive use of language is on display in all her works, including *Beyond God the Father: Toward a Philosophy of Women's Liberation* (Boston: Beacon, 1973); *Gyn/Ecology: The Metaethics of Radical Feminism* (Boston: Beacon, 1978); *Pure Lust: Elemental Feminist Philosophy* (Boston: Beacon, 1984); and *Webster's New Intergalactic Wickedary of the English Language* (Boston: Beacon, 1987).

7. Keller's *Face of the Deep: A Theology of Becoming* (New York: Routledge, 2003), to my mind, epitomizes the potential of well-chosen and skillfully crafted words to open up depths of insight into biblical texts and their reception histories.

Regardless of the original language(s) of composition, cultures and subcultures will always read their own and others' Scriptures in their own native language(s). They will do so as part of an inevitable process of reading themselves into, and constructing their selves through, those Scriptures. Earliest rabbinic Judaism and Christianity were, as much as anything else, modes of biblical translation, appropriation, and creation. Competence in original biblical languages and their cognates is the foundation of modern biblical-studies training and must remain a core element. But it has become clear to me, through my own training in and teaching of biblical studies, that critical attention to the politics and poetics of biblical translation (or, put another way, to how biblical texts "signify" within and between cultures) is also a vital and indispensable part of an ethically and socially responsible—and responsive—practice of biblical studies.

As a scholar of the ancient and modern Middle East, I have come to appreciate the extent to which all biblical scholarship is inevitably ideologically laden and can be harnessed in pursuit of local and global political agendas, regardless of the conscious intentions of those who generate that scholarship. In both modern feminist movement and ancient rabbinic movements I find progressive, ethically grounded enterprises that engage biblical study from a stance of conscious and conscientious advocacy.[8] Neither movement ever pretended to be disinterested or value-neutral; indeed, at their best, both have provided potent tools for the unmasking and disabling of claims to objectivity on the part of all manner of orthodoxies—secular or religious. Biblical scholarship is, always has been, and likely always will be politically promiscuous and potentially powerful. Although scholars cannot control how our scholarship comes to be used, we can be aware of, and appropriately reflective about, whose interests it most serves and whose interests we desire to serve. We can and do make choices about both how to frame our work and to how extensive and diverse a community we consider ourselves responsible. It seems imperative that training in biblical studies provide a place and tools for sustained, critical reflection on the ethics and ethos of biblical studies as a discipline, and on the many cultural movements in which biblical scholars—willingly and unwillingly, intentionally and unintentionally—play a part.

Among the most visible and powerful cultural movements in evidence today are scriptural fundamentalisms with overt political agendas and attendant militaristic elements. Their reach is global, and their numbers are growing. A biblical-studies paradigm in which many possibilities, perspec-

---

8. The phrasing "feminist movement" is that of bell hooks, whose *Feminist Theory: From Margin to Center* (Boston: South End, 1984) remains an important text in the development of feminist and womanist practice.

tives, voices, and questions are perpetually at play is the diametrical opposite of a fundamentalist paradigm of unquestioning allegiance to a forcefully circumscribed and authorized version of singular scriptural truth. Academic biblical studies, on the model envisioned above, can serve as an important, even crucial, counterweight to scriptural fundamentalisms. But in order to do so effectively, biblical-studies programs need actively and constructively to engage fundamentalisms in several ways.

First, fundamentalist voices and perspectives need carefully and critically to be analyzed as part of an encompassing biblical-studies curriculum—and not to be excluded as irrelevant or beyond the realm of proper scholarly training. Second, fundamentalisms have to be addressed, in part, on their own terms and in their own particular terminologies. This is not an impossible task for the creative, flexible, and multivocal fringe of the discipline of biblical studies, although it clearly exceeds the capabilities of a magisterial "old school" whose rigid and paternalistic claims to authority are matched only by those found in fundamentalist institutions themselves. Finally, biblical-studies programs need to take seriously the training of students to be visible public intellectuals prepared to participate in popular forms of discourse and to weigh in on issues of religion in civil society and the public sphere. Scriptural fundamentalisms answer human needs for community, meaning, and identity in ways that are profoundly problematic and often extremely dangerous. They will continue to answer those needs for growing numbers of people as long as there are few scripturally coherent, humane counternarratives widely available as alternatives to meet those deeply felt desires and needs.

It should go without saying that critical and cultural agility in biblical knowledge production is of a piece with a theory of pedagogy that values facility in the use of a range of analytical tools and in the conscientious crafting of knowledge. A pedagogical model based merely or primarily on the reception of disbursed information and doctrinal or disciplinary consolidation will accomplish very little that is not, in this day and age, better left to computers and other such storage devices. In my own training it has been, once again, my encounter with feminist and ancient rabbinic Jewish practices that has, in large measure, shaped my pedagogical ideals as they apply to biblical studies.

Feminist pedagogy, from the time of its emergence within the second wave of feminist movement, has sought to develop and implement antihierarchical, anti-authoritarian models of teaching and learning in which all patterns of oppression and objectification are actively scrutinized, resisted, and transformed.[9] It has sought ways to put into practice at every level the key

---

9. The literature on feminist pedagogy is extensive. Notable titles include Frances A. Maher and Mary Kay Thompson Tetreault, *The Feminist Classroom: Dynamics of Gender,*

insights that the personal is political and all knowledge is situated. Given the power—both for good and for grave ill—exercised explicitly in the name of biblical authority, all members of biblical-studies programs ought to take very seriously our own exercise of power and the models of power and authority embedded (and thereby legitimated and perpetuated) in our faculty governance and pedagogical practices. Feminist theories and modes of pedagogy provide, to my eyes, the best tools for examining and intervening in structures of oppression as local as our own seminaries, graduate schools, and classrooms and as diffuse as nations and transnational corporate enterprises.

Rabbinic Judaism also offers some excellent pedagogical models and insights for biblical study that are (perhaps surprisingly) consistent with feminist theory and practice. At the heart of traditional rabbinic patterns of biblical study is the *hevruta*, or dialogue method, described above. In addition, the very nature of classical rabbinic texts and traditions is such that they lend themselves far more explicitly to a process-based pedagogy than to a content-based one. As any modern student of midrash can attest, the very fact of encountering a plethora of competing, even contradictory, interpretations of Scripture, collectively preserved and presented as "words of the living God" shaped by generations of learners, conveys a deep sense that it is the ongoing process—and no single product—of biblical exploration that is to be embraced. Midrash does not work well as dogma, doctrine, or prescription— its thoroughgoing pluralism militates against these.[10] Instead, midrash works as a multimethod exemplum and invitation to all learners to participate in the creative unfolding of biblical learning. Moreover, within a rabbinic worldview that honors all manner of competing exegetical claims and insights, the realm of practical application is held to privilege the teachings of those who love peace, who treat others—including their opponents—with respect, and who teach the traditions of others along with their own.[11] Such a privileging of the ethical does far more than forestall a potentially paralyzing relativism of

---

Race, and Privilege (Lanham, Md.: Rowman & Littlefield, 2001); bell hooks, *Teaching to Transgress: Education as the Practice of Freedom* (New York: Routledge, 1994); and Maralee Mayberry and Ellen Cronan Rose, *Meeting the Challenge: Innovative Feminist Pedagogies in Action* (New York: Routledge, 1999).

10. I am well aware, of course, of Jewish fundamentalisms and orthodoxies that circumscribe understandings of midrash and rabbinic pedagogical practices within the narrowly wrought confines of a religious and/or nationalistic ethnocentrism. What I wish to argue for here is not an embrace of rabbinic Judaism—much less its fundamentalist orthodox versions—but rather a modern, progressive appropriation of what I take to be the underlying dynamics inherent in the traditional rabbinic models.

11. See b. Eruvin 13b and Yebamot 14b. See David Stern's fine discussion of these rabbinic traditions and their ethical implications in *Midrash and Theory: Ancient Jewish*

interpretation and meaning; it presents the compelling proposition that an inclusive pedagogy and a commitment to peace are the conditions by which those who claim to speak with authority on biblical matters are to be measured and judged.

As I began this essay by identifying the locales—institutional and ideological—of my graduate training, it seems appropriate to conclude by describing the environments within which I have researched and taught for the past decade. For several years my academic home was a Catholic university in Silicon Valley, California, an epicenter of major cultural dynamics associated with globalization. I lived and worked in one of the most ethnically, linguistically, nationally, and religiously diverse population centers in the world, embedded within what is arguably the most politically progressive region in the largest existing global superpower, whose local economy is fueled by transnational business technologies and the design of weapons of mass destruction undergirded and serviced by international migrant labor from all over the Pacific Rim. At present I teach in a small, secular, New England liberal-arts college whose egalitarian ethos goes back to its founding by abolitionists as a coeducational seminary in the nineteenth century and whose location in an economically depressed old mill town links it, in some respects, to countless other such small communities throughout the world.

Notwithstanding the vast differences between these two academic environments and the perspectives that each affords, I find that my vision of the desirable future of biblical studies remains constant. It appears to me to lie with those who are trained at, and can teach from, the margins and fringes (feminist, Jewish, and otherwise) toward a center that must grow to encompass a globalized and fragmented world. In addition to reading the many tongues of our ancient texts, we need to become fluent in the disciplinary languages of theology, sociology, history, and cultural theory as well as in the many languages of local and global politics, evangelical imperialism, anti-imperial resistance, and intercultural dialogue. Perhaps most urgently of all, we should be training our students—and a larger public—to analyze critically and challenge compassionately the fearsome narratives of scriptural fundamentalisms that are running rampant worldwide and feeding the power of oppressive nationalist and corporate regimes. If biblical scholars do not publicly and effectively challenge biblical fundamentalisms (of both the global North and South) on their own terms as well as beyond those terms, it is uncertain who else can. The only worthwhile and viable future for biblical studies, in my view, is one that grows out of an ethical commitment to work

---

Exegesis and Contemporary Literary Studies (Evanston, Ill.: Northwestern University Press, 1996), 19–22.

against all forms of oppression and on behalf of peace and justice worldwide, and one that pursues these ends through a genuine multidisciplinarity and a political/ideological/analytical sophistication suffusing research and teaching at all levels.

On the Fringes of the "Big Tent" of Graduate New Testament Studies

Thomas Fabisiak

I should begin by saying that I am not studying in a New Testament studies department, but rather am a Ph.D. candidate in a recently formed Comparative Literature and Religion program at Emory University, where I am in the midst of completing my exams and dissertation proposal. Most of my research is in the "history of interpretation" of ancient apocalyptic texts in the modern era. This work does not merely consist in collecting and cataloguing moments in texts' reception history, however: instead, I aim to highlight subversive readings of apocalyptic texts that go against the grain of right wing Christian and mainstream American eschatologies and apocalyptic visions. In that vein, my dissertation work will focus on a number of inverted, parodic readings of early Christian end-times figures and scenarios in the nineteenth and twentieth centuries,[1] readings that take back fantasies of eschatological violence from the political and religious right and reconstitute them as mandates for social transgression and political radicalism. The project offers a consideration of the ways in which "secular" anti-institutional philosophies and subcultures have emerged through an interpretation of Christian eschatological ideas and even through exegesis of New Testament texts. Ideally, it will

---

1. My dissertation will likely remain confined to the nineteenth century, focusing in particular on certain young Hegelians and early anarchists' readings of apocalyptic texts. However, I have been struck by a remarkably widespread tendency among subversive readers of New Testament apocalyptic texts, including and beyond these nineteenth-century exegetes, to subject Christian eschatological figures to a series of inversions ("God-man"/"man-God," Christ/antichrist, martyrdom/suicide-homicide, universal annihilation/individual death) on the basis of a contrast with some idea of mainstream or, more recently, right-wing fundamentalist Christian eschatology. In the twentieth century I would include, as particularly compelling examples, the occultist Aleister Crowley, the industrial-goth rocker Marilyn Manson, the metal vocalist Karyn Crisis, and the comic-book writer Jhonen Vasquez, though there are certainly others.

suggest legitimate rereadings of a significant portion of the New Testament within the literary and historical context of disturbing and visionary eschatological politics, philosophy, or literature.

I am aware of three or four major New Testament studies departments in this country that would accept and support in its entirety a dissertation project along these lines. What follows is a modification and extension of a presentation given at the Graduate Biblical Studies: Ethos and Discipline section at the SBL in 2005; in it, I want to take some time to explain why I believe few programs would support my project. Then I will try to discern and evaluate the disciplinary constraints, spoken or unspoken, according to which this relative exclusion is maintained.

To begin with, I will mention some of my work from a course taught by Elisabeth Schüssler Fiorenza during my first year at Harvard Divinity School. For my final project in her New Testament studies class, I emailed a number of different professors in well-known New Testament studies and related programs in, for example, early Christianity, with a description of my project as I conceived it then. At that time, which was four years ago, I was considering eventually writing a dissertation exploring certain striking continuities between ancient apocalyptic literature and what I termed "literature produced by and for misfit adolescents," which consisted of pop-culture texts including music, mostly in the metal genre, as well as zines and comic books.

By focusing especially on the "sense in both groups of texts that the world is so utterly flawed it can only be deeply transformed or destroyed," I anticipated that the study "would in its very nature reflect rather overtly on contemporary social issues through a detailed analysis of ancient texts."[2] I asked professors whether I could do this kind of work at their university and asked them to evaluate, as thoroughly as possible, why or why not. I ended the email by suggesting why I thought it ought to be possible to do this kind of work in the field: "There is no reason that the careful study of Biblical texts should not explicitly reflect on modern society since it already does so implicitly." Now, I would probably formulate this statement differently by suggesting, for example, that truly rigorous historical and exegetical work on ancient religious texts needs to account for the forms and functions of both ancient literature and modern scholarship in the contemporary era in which the ancient world is produced and reproduced.

In what follows, I hope to show that it is the underlying commitment, in both of these formulations, to acknowledging and transforming the stakes and possibilities of research in and around New Testament studies that makes

---

2. All personal correspondence cited here was from April 2004. I have kept the emails that I received anonymous.

my work, then as now, incommensurable with the prevailing and conservative attitudes toward historiography that continue to shape graduate training in the discipline.

Why the Project Doesn't "Fit" in the Field of New Testament Studies

There were only three definite yes responses to the email I sent out four years ago, and the majority responded by saying no. I want to begin here by looking at some of these no responses.

One respondent wrote, "As a rule we encourage cross-disciplinary work, but I think your proposed study—very interesting as it is—is probably *more* cross-disciplinary than we (well, I) would be willing to take on, in part because *both* aspects of the study are full time careers for grad students." Here the respondent divides my project into two separate disciplines, which in turn correspond to two distinct "aspects," which I take to mean "fields of inquiry." Another respondent was more explicit about this, writing: "I don't know that any of us is especially knowledgeable about the interpretation of contemporary literature of the sort that concerns you." Other respondents clarified this in turn by distinguishing between the modern and ancient as disciplinary objects, for example in the following:

> It sounds like an interesting project to me, but I wonder if it really belongs in a Biblical Studies program, especially since you say that your purpose is to use biblical texts as a window into modern society. It seems to me, therefore, that your real interest is modern society. One of our rubrics for Ph.D. work here is "Religion and Modernity," and it seems to me at first glance that this project would fall more under that rubric than under New Testament.

One respondent similarly wrote, "I'm afraid the answer would be 'no' because our department has always focused on ancient evidence and parallels rather than on modern comparanda." Another explained, "If you were to come to our department, a dissertation in biblical studies would have to demonstrate ability to contextualize early Christian literature within ancient studies."

As with many of the other responses that I received, there is not a lack of interest in the project per se; instead, their authors reject it on methodological grounds that remain more or less implicit in their responses. They suggest that there is a division between the "ancient" and the "modern," a division along which are distinguished two exclusive methods of interpretation and bodies of data. The potential project is conceived in terms of mastery of these sets of data and corresponding methods, and therefore quantitatively in terms of the time it would take to achieve that mastery.

Another respondent wrote,

> I certainly think that the discipline "New Testament studies" is a big enough tent to include your project, but I doubt that [our university] is the best place for you to do it (as long as indeed you want to be in "NT studies" rather than, say, "Religion and Literature" or the like) because our NT and early Christianity faculty ... are pretty relentlessly historical in our work and would have to be your primary advisors.

Here, the respondent's rejection is rendered in terms of the relative "historicality" of our work: their faculty is "relentlessly historical," while my project would have been, I suppose, anachronistic. Another respondent confirms this suspicion, writing,

> It sounds like your project is more suited to Religion and Literature than biblical studies or early Christianity. It might even fall under American Studies since your interest is in "adolescents," a category of persons that did not exist in antiquity; as far as I know it is an invented category of modern Western (especially American) culture, dating from the 1950s.

According to this respondent, only those categories that are intrinsic to the ancient context should concern the student of early Christianity. As in other responses, he distinguishes between the ancient and modern as given, which is to say by no means "invented," and exclusive objects and sets of categories, to which correspond two distinct disciplines.

To sum up, these emails give the impression that Ph.D. work and scholarship in the various fields of New Testament studies, early Christianity, and the like is guided by an anti-anachronistic objectivism in which one masters a body of knowledge that is defined in terms of a field that is given in advance, a field that is circumscribed temporally as a historical era and spatially as a set of geographical, textual, and cultural contexts. Since the goal of research in the field is the correct representation of these given texts and contexts, it is critical that training should remain exclusively focused on objects and categories that are proper to those temporal and spatial boundaries. The discipline has nothing to do with modernity or contemporary literature, which are construed as given and cordoned-off objects in their own right and are left to the disciplines of American studies, religion and literature, comparative literature, and the like. Conceived in these terms, work in the discipline is done either in ignorance of or in opposition to the notion that "the study of Biblical texts should ... reflect on contemporary culture explicitly because it already does so implicitly" and consequently excludes the kind of project I had anticipated doing four years ago.

A cursory glance at the websites of the various departments in question, among others, confirms this impression. The emphasis in both Ph.D. examinations and coursework almost across the board is on ancient texts, ancient cultural contexts, philological expertise, and training in interpretive and historical methods. According to the descriptions of the fields of early Christianity, New Testament studies, ancient Christianity, and ancient Mediterranean and/or Near Eastern studies on the websites of their respective programs[3] at UNC at Chapel Hill, in Brown's Religion in the Ancient Mediterranean area of study, in Yale's New Testament field of study, at Duke, Chicago Divinity School, Emory University, Indiana University, Claremont Graduate University, and Rice University, preparation for a Ph.D. degree emphasizes some combination of these areas of competence. I think I would be right to assume that training in these four areas is aimed at developing accuracy in interpreting sets of data. The proper linguistic expertise, range of texts, hermeneutical tools, and evidentiary excavations are cultivated and anticipated in order that texts, religions, and historical eras might be correctly understood and represented. Students do not appear to be required to consider how they produce and transform the objects under consideration, and certainly are not required to consider the stakes, condition, or possibilities of that production. Thus not one of the above websites mentions theory or methodology as a requisite part of Ph.D. training.

Of course, there are a few programs where methodology and theory are designated as part of graduate training, including Brown's Early Christianity field of study and Yale's Ancient Christianity area of study, and at biblical studies programs at Vanderbilt, Drew, and the Graduate Theological Union. Even here, however, there is always the possibility that "methodology" or "theory" are simply reduced to the study of tools to be "applied" under the auspices of an interest in "methodological diversity" or historical and exegetical accuracy, whereby they are then brought under the scope of "training in interpretive and historical methods."[4] Thus for example Drew emphasizes "methodologi-

---

3. These were all accessed during the months of June and July 2008.
4. One ought to distinguish here between "training in methods" and "methodology" (I am grateful to Elisabeth Schüssler Fiorenza for pointing out a distinction along these lines in a course I took with her a few years ago), with the latter meaning something like "an inquiry into the stakes, condition, or possibilities of research." "Methods," on the other hand, are tools that are put to work for the unspoken interests of the discipline, usually for the sake of historical or hermeneutical "accuracy" in the case of historiography at large and New Testament studies in particular. Some methods, for example feminist or marxist hermeneutics and cultural studies, tend to be inherently "methodological," insofar as they reflect on the context and stakes of their interpretive work. Even in these cases, however, they still always risk being uncritically applied in the interests of historical accuracy or

cal multiplicity and theoretical eclecticism,"[5] and the Graduate Theological Union seeks to develop "skill in the application of particular methodological approaches to biblical texts."[6] At Vanderbilt, "Our approaches include the more traditional types of analysis as well as various literary, sociological, and anthropological methods. Through continual work with the ancient texts students gain familiarity with methodological tools and learn to appraise their limitations critically."[7] There is no indication of what, exactly, those limitations would consist of, or to what end these "tools" are directed. Thus the stated objective of methodological training according to these websites is not that students should account for the stakes, functions, condition, and institutional and disciplinary constraints related to these tools, but that they should develop mastery in their "application."

This lack of interest in methodological rigor is confirmed by the apparent lack of interest in the contemporary condition of ancient literature and scholarly research: I could not find any programs where students were required to consider the functions of biblical-historical scholarship, on the one hand, or of biblical or ancient literature, on the other, in the modern context. I think it's consequently fair to say that a project like mine, which is explicitly devoted to exploring and transforming those functions, is beyond the range of mainstream work within the discipline. More generally, it is fair to say that Ph.D. students in the field are by no means expected to become competent in taking account of the ways in which their work and their objects of study are complicit in and structured by modern social, political, and religious needs and interests.

The Functions and Interests of "Relentlessly Historical" Work

Within the field of New Testament studies and related programs in which training is circumscribed by the focus on interpretive and historiographical methods, ancient cultural contexts, and ancient texts, there are certainly very different areas of emphasis. Rice, for example, emphasizes texts outside the New Testament canon, while Duke and Emory emphasize the canon and theological expertise, Chicago emphasizes historical contexts, and Brown

---

some arbitrary notion of "theoretical sophistication" and thereby divested of their "methodological" form and functions.

5. Drew Theological School, Graduate Division of Religion, "Biblical Studies and Early Christianity"; online: http://www.drew.edu/gdr.aspx?id=16039.

6. Graduate Theological Union, "Biblical Studies"; online: http://www.gtu.edu/academics/areas/biblical-studies.

7. Vanderbilt University, Divinity School and Graduate Division of Religion, "New Testament and Early Christianity"; online: http://www.vanderbilt.edu/divinity/gradnewtest.php.

and UNC emphasize comparative work on ancient cultural contexts and religions. There is, that is to say, a whole spectrum of research interests, running the gamut from a canon-based, theologically-oriented focus to a focus on material culture and a wide array of ancient religions and literature. There is a distinction, perhaps a related distinction, to be made between work that develops methodological and evidentiary diversity as a means of representing variegated perspectives on the cultures and texts in question, and work that emphasizes traditional historical-critical methods as the means to a final and thorough rendering of texts' meanings or religions' characteristics.[8]

It would be reductive and unfair to suggest that all of this work is the same. It has been my impression, however, that these seemingly antagonistic interests collude in maintaining the same methodological orientation and fostering the same set of exclusions and blind spots. Across the board the historiographer's work is determined by the telos of accuracy in representation, an accuracy that is achieved primarily through the ritual divestiture of all forms of "anachronism" and the cultivation of a set of historical "skills," or "methods." The text, context, or accumulated evidence is envisioned as a set of objects that one excavates and describes, albeit, in some cases, from a kaleidoscopic multiplicity of perspectives.

The more "sophisticated" version of research, in which one heuristically entertains a variety of points of view and methods, is still understood in terms of scientific accuracy: it is more scientifically correct to tentatively represent the object in a proliferation of its ancient diverse functions and aspects than to lock it down into one final or definitive meaning. Such research still proceeds as if the attack on all forms of anachronism is an essential prerequisite for the possibility of a liberated, objective encounter with the riches of history.

In the work that I envisioned doing four years ago, as with the work that I will continue to do, I have started from the contrary notion that anachronism is the condition in which historiography becomes possible, and that the objects under consideration proceed from the procedures by which we represent and transform them. These procedures are determined and constrained by a whole set of institutional and cultural apparatuses to which we are constantly held accountable and against which we can always engage in forms of resistance. As such, our work of understanding the ancient past is a progressive or conservative force that demands subtle allegiances and performs disruptive takeovers in the present.

---

8. This is the distinction that Elisabeth Schüssler Fiorenza makes between the "scientific positivist" and "(post-)modern cultural" paradigms in biblical studies in "Changing the Paradigms: The Ethos of Biblical Studies," in idem, *Rhetoric and Ethic: The Politics of Biblical Studies* (Minneapolis: Fortress, 1999), 31–55.

As long as work is perceived as strictly or "relentlessly" historical it tends to have a conservative and domesticating function, in which the potentially destabilizing effects of historiography are contained by the consignment of historical events to a kind of menagerie of fascinating and pacified discoveries. In this mainstream approach to history there's a sense that now that the struggle for access to the resource that we call truth is over and won by our "enlightenment forebears" we can afford the luxury of a museum curator's view of history. Hayden White characterizes this attitude towards history as "gentlemanly aestheticism," adding,

> These attitudes inevitably involved respect for the "individuality," "uniqueness," and "ineffability" of historical entities, sensitivity to the "richness" and "variety" of the historical field, and a faith in the "unity" that makes of finite sets of historical particulars comprehensible wholes. All this permits the historian to see some beauty, if not good, in everything human and to assume an Olympian calm in the face of any current social situation, however terrifying it may appear to anyone who lacks historical perspective. It renders him receptive to a genial pluralism in matters epistemological, suspicious of anything smacking of reductionism, irritated with theory, disdainful of technical terminology or jargon, and contemptuous of any effort to discern the direction that the future development of his own society might take.[9]

Such attitudes serve two predominant interests: on the one hand, they serve the interest of the expert for whom access to certain forms of cultural distinction are guaranteed by the claim to have comprehended a body of knowledge or unearthed a trove of historical riches. On the other hand, they serve the function of keeping history from threatening or compromising the status quo. Correspondingly, they help to develop a certain amount of cultural capital among those for whom putting their luxury time to work in viewings at museums or on the history channel is a mark of prestige.

None of this is to say that historical research is *passé* or unnecessary or even that there is no difference between a more or less correct application of the procedures for verifying reality within historical and sociological discourse. In many cases, a scientific and positivistic focus on data and accuracy can even be a necessary accessory to transformative historical work.

It bears keeping in mind, for instance, that historicists can, at times, challenge our preconceived notions about the ancient world. Such reframing can even transform our views of the present.

---

9. Hayden White, *The Content of the Form: Narrative Discourse and Historical Representation* (Baltimore: Johns Hopkins University Press, 1987), 71.

I suspect that many "relentlessly historical" scholars would still want to see their work in that light if they were pressed to account for its social purpose. Nevertheless, it has been my experience that the passion for correct and complete representation tends to overtake any struggle against forms of conservatism, and that this passion transforms the telos of correct representation into the apparently inevitable, timeless, and necessary goal of the discipline. Thus training is not seen as a subversive alienation from forms of apparent self-evidence, but as the definitive movement beyond the obscuring mists of modernity that makes an unmediated, simple, or disinterested encounter with the categories and objects proper to the ancient world possible. Inasmuch as this mystical or objective apprehension of the past becomes the goal of disciplinary training and research, it neutralizes the real work of history, which is to be a critical mediation in our encounter with the imminent present: "To be sure, we need history, but we need it in a manner different from the way in which the spoilt idler in the garden of knowledge uses it, no matter how elegantly he may look down on our coarse and graceless needs and distresses."[10]

To that end, there is no reason why even the most antiquated, "theological," or traditional methods cannot be transformative if taken on in self-consciously perverse or deconstructive ways, or if directed towards emancipatory ends. In the history of the study of the New Testament, there have been many moments in which exegesis and historical study were not seen as ends unto themselves, but as transgressive acts of insurgency.

Bruno Bauer, who features prominently in Schweitzer's *Quest of the Historical Jesus*, imagines that his work and that of his peers, including his work on the Synoptic Gospels and D. F. Strauss's *Leben Jesu*, were part of the precipitation of a "hellish discharge" from which "Church and State would be shaken to the core."[11] It is upsetting to see the degree to which we have become fixated on historical correctness, one might even say historical "propriety," at the cost of any subversive legacy our discipline, among others, might have retained from these earlier scholars. Bauer was far less interested in the freedom to collect historical baubles than in the disruption of the loci of taken-for-granted authority; and where twentieth century New Testament scholars have wanted to see D. F. Strauss's work as part of an emerging desire for "free" or "disinter-

---

10. Friedrich Nietzsche, *On the Use and Abuse of History for Life* (trans. Ian Johnston); online: http://records.viu.ca/~johnstoi/Nietzsche/history.htm.
11. Bruno Bauer, *The Trumpet of the Last Judgment against Hegel the Atheist and Antichrist: An Ultimatum* (trans. Lawrence Stepelevich; Studies in German Thought and History 5; Lewiston, N.Y.: Mellen, 1989), 94.

ested" inquiry, a more serious and careful review of his work shows that the real struggle there was against political and social conservatism.[12]

Really, it is a testament to the coercive strength of mainstream discourse in general that perspectives that are radical in a certain context wind up being sacrificed to some newly fetishized object that develops out of them. In the case of Bauer and Strauss the radicalism of the New Hegelians was sacrificed to a glorified notion of "history," now alienated from the local struggles against authoritarianism in which it had developed, and complicit in new forms of authoritarianism about which Bauer, Strauss, and others remained largely ignorant. I have noticed that the same process seems to be happening now in the occasional celebration of "theoretical sophistication" among many of the most progressive biblical scholars. The very notion of "theoretical sophistication" smacks of the "gentlemanly aestheticism" of the "spoilt idler," and in practice it usually amounts to little more than the assimilation of otherwise radical theories to the conservative study of ancient history.

This is not to attack theory or to suggest a return to some kind of taken-for-granted historical-critical approach. On the contrary, it is to say that where many biblical scholars do become interested in theory it is only insofar as they can justify it as another set of "methods" or "tools" in the hunt for historical riches. The elaboration of new perceptual grids, focalizing devices, and historiographical languages should do more than just make for creative and in some cases more accurate new ways of describing ancient phenomena. While this work is also useful and necessary, of course, it does not in itself challenge the fetishized nature of history as a "beautiful object" protected, sanctified, and sanitized by mainstream interests. Even when the languages and devices in question might have unleashed some disturbing charge into a battle for the terms of what constitutes truth in another context, there is no reason to believe that they will do so when haphazardly applied to the study of ancient Christianity. In many cases, they do just the opposite: developing a modicum of theoretical expertise can wind up being a pious and conservative exercise in doing the "right" kind of research for the "right" group of texts, all in the pursuit of greater degrees of accuracy or value-neutrality.

THEOLOGICAL, SECULAR, AND APOCALYPTIC HISTORIOGRAPHY

I suspect that the *de rigueur* expectation that one should have a superficial interest in theory among certain historians of early Christianity or ancient

---

12. See Marilyn Chapin Massey's important study to this effect, *Christ Unmasked: The Meaning of* The Life of Jesus *in German Politics* (Chapel Hill, N.C.: University of North Carolina Press, 1983).

Mediterranean religions is part of a widespread apologetic tendency to want to present work on ancient Christianity as legitimate or "scientific" research. I believe that scholars may be adopting the research methods of other disciplines in order to show that they are, in fact, up to date on whatever passes for "cutting-edge," which is to say as far as possible from the "dogmatic" study of the New Testament. I understand that the study of the Bible, along with the study of religion in general, remains suspect within the mainstream world of the humanities and the social sciences, and that to make their work acceptable to historians, social scientists, literary scholars, and classicists, biblical scholars have worked very hard to divest themselves of any air of "theological bias." At this point, however, rather than confirming this widespread misunderstanding about the study of religion by distancing ourselves from theologizing, I think our energy should be devoted to transforming the mainstream logic of "secularism vs. religion" and demanding an accounting of the stakes and condition, even the religious condition, of academic research in general.

At the same time it ought to be noted that while many "progressive" and "secular" scholars have sacrificed hermeneutical rigor in an effort to be as scientific as possible, certain more theologically oriented scholars have moved in the opposite direction: because such scholars feel constrained by the implications of biblical research in the religious work of ministers and theologians, they have often worked harder than their "relentlessly historical" counterparts to take account of the modern context of historical work. In a class I took in Emory's New Testament area of study, for instance, this meant that we grappled with the reading and interpretive practices of early and medieval biblical interpreters as a way of finding resources to disrupt taken-for-granted modern modes of inquiry into the texts, thereby expanding the possibilities for exegetical and historical work. The exacting focus on reading techniques forced us to think in surprising and unexpected ways, against the grain of most enlightenment and modern exegesis and historiography, about the work done by early interpreters and about the texts being interpreted. Such work is one example among others of research founded on sensibilities that have developed more or less on behalf of pastors and theologians, yet this research has a number of similarities to the kind of work that I want to do on the history of interpretation of apocalyptic literature.

In spite of such examples of hermeneutical seriousness, however, it seems to me that programs and professors that develop theological expertise tend by and large to limit their methodological inquiry to making their historical and exegetical research useful to the dominant modes of ministerial and theological work. At the same time, they generally tend to eschew methods from other disciplines, for example from the sociological and comparative study of ancient religions, in favor of more traditional modes of exegetical and historical analysis, in large part because of their emphasis on the canon.

Thus, for example, Duke's New Testament program writes of itself: "Areas of strength in the Duke program include Paul, the use of the Old Testament in the New, the Synoptic Gospels, the Jewish cultural context of the New Testament, and biblical theology. The faculty has expertise in historical, exegetical, literary, and theological methods of interpretation." Because the emphasis in these cases tends to be even more unproblematically "historical," and because the objects of research are even more unproblematically "given" (e.g. "Paul" as a departmental "area of strength"), training continues to focus on ridding students of anachronizing perspectives in order that they can properly recover the objects or texts that are then handed over to theology.

What is more, insofar as it restricts hermeneutical meticulousness to overseeing the relationship between historical-exegetical research and the Christian community, theologically-oriented scholarship is allied with "relentlessly historical" research in ignoring the stakes of such research in the wider culture. In my work, on the contrary, I have begun from the premise that the study of ancient apocalyptic literature is not only implicated in the ongoing life of Christian communities, but in the wide swath of religious, political, economic, and philosophical eschatologies and apocalyptic visions that are articulated in, around, and against those developed by mainstream, confessional Christianity.[13]

Among these eschatologies and apocalyptic visions are those pertaining to scholarly, historical research. It has always seemed strange to me that, in spite of the well-known and longstanding relationship in the modern era between biblical exegesis, philosophy, literature, and scholarship in general, and in spite of the well-known fact that modern modes of exegetical, historical, and philosophical thought and inquiry largely developed out of the study of the Bible, the prevailing, usually taken-for-granted notion guiding most historical work now is that the predominance of confessional, religious modes of scholarship have entirely faded along with the apparent self-evidence of the religious world-view to which they corresponded. Underlying the anti-theological and anti-anachronistic tendency among biblical scholars, for example, is the conviction that we are now faced with the possibility of either ignoring or finally demystifying churchly hierarchies, eschatological utopian schemes, and Christian images of paradise lost. I believe that it is, on the contrary, in the

---

13. American twenty-first-century culture is constantly threatened and encouraged by its own human-made apocalypses, from the neo-conservative vision of a transformed Middle East, to the threat of environmental or nuclear apocalypse, to the subjective mystical apocalyptic ascent of celebrities into a realm of glossy or digitally recorded immortality.

absence of a reckoning with our own theological and apocalyptic eschatological predilections that these tendencies constrain and develop our scholarly discourses even more coercively: the fetishized and glorified "ancient world" divested once and for all of its obscuring veil of anachronistic illusions, for instance, rather easily becomes its own impending New Jerusalem; there is even a kind of scientific mysteriology here, in which a "relentless" and ascetic historiography grants the initiate unmediated access to a vision of the naked and illuminated ancient world in its original and pristine purity. Even without this conceit of some unconscious apocalyptic image underlying mainstream historical work, we would still have to account for the ways in which practices of historical representation and deduction are derived from and complicit in their own peculiar eschatologies and soteriologies. Notions of truth and historical periodization, the belief in the independent and self-identical existence of historical objects, practices of close reading, and the notion of comprehensive or encyclopedic work are all informed by and formative of notions of the apocalypse as the final judgment, the absolute unveiling, the book in which the world's secret history is contained, or the correct rendering of the obscure remains of the ancient past.[14] Whether such unveilings or readings are seen as definitive and singular or as part of a heuristic and many-faceted representation of a partly-knowable totality they are still mystical, apocalyptic practices: the only difference between them is whether their practitioners seek after unique or polymorphic manifestations of the "ancient world" and its treasures.

I do not want to suggest that we should have to, or are even able to, simply put aside these eschatological methods or denounce, once and for all, our mythologizing and theologizing proclivities; nor do I think that there will be a full reckoning or final judgment by which we can determine the totality of the stakes and interests of our research at any given moment and thereby exercise a god-like control over the means and ends of biblical scholarship. I do think, however, that we ought to risk distinguishing between two modes of inquiry: the first, which is dominant in the fields of New Testament studies, early Christianity, and ancient Mediterranean religions, calmly conforms to the logic of its own apparent self-evidence by sedately consigning history to the halls of museums. The second still has enough fervor, perhaps even theological or apocalyptic fervor, to disturb and dislocate the historical and historiographical work of silencing and exclusion that will be perpetuated in

---

14. See to that effect Jacques Derrida, "Of an Apocalyptic Tone Recently Adopted in Philosophy" (trans. John P. Leavey Jr.), *Semeia* 23 (1982): 25–71. Since Nietzsche's *Genealogy of Morals*, the, as he says, "ascetic" religious qualities of notions of truth always remain to be scrutinized.

the imminent onset of the status quo. As I see it, the conservatism in New Testament studies does not lie in the continued dominance of the historical-critical method, but in the absence of this passion on behalf of the possibility of a radically transformed future.

A "Big Enough Tent"?

Perhaps I did not give enough credit above to the amount of work that has been allowed within the field that is dedicated to methodological inquiry and transformative scholarship. As I mentioned earlier, when I sent out emails a few years ago, there were some yes responses, from professors at Drew, Claremont, and Vanderbilt, and two of the professors even went so far as to say that they saw the work of biblical studies in the same way that I did. One of the no respondents still suggested that New Testament studies might be a "big enough tent" to include work like my own. Another professor replied with what I could only characterize as a "maybe" response and wrote, "Whereas my other senior colleagues in NT studies … are pretty much straight-forward historical critics, my own work does bring in modern ideology and culture, hermeneutical theory, and cultural studies approaches." He went on to say that he was overseeing a dissertation on the relationship between certain nineteenth- and twentieth-century philosophers and New Testament scholars, adding, "Whereas some of my colleagues might not feel that is enough of a 'real New Testament dissertation topic,' I do, and so admitted the student and have advised his dissertation." I have also worked with professors and students in the field of New Testament studies who were receptive to and supportive of my own work, and I have found that the professors in Emory's New Testament program have been willing to include me in their classes and work with me on my exams and dissertation.

There is perhaps some room for optimism here: New Testament studies might, in fact, be a "big enough tent" to include work like my own. I remain suspicious, however, for two reasons. The first is that the majority of Ph.D. programs in the field would not admit work like my own, including the program from which I received the email about the "big tent," in the first place. The fact that professors are willing to work with people like me in fields outside of New Testament studies is no indication that they would be responsible for a dissertation like my own in their own field.

The more important reason, however, is that it does not matter if specific instances of work like my own are "allowed," "brought in," or "admitted" alongside the dominant modes of historiography and exegesis if this does not entail any widespread recognition of the significant methodological shifts and questions upon which my research is founded. It bears keeping in mind, for example, that, in the same email in which the respondent suggested my work might find a place within "the big tent," he remained able to distinguish between my own work and "relentlessly historical" work. In other words he either ignored or misunderstood my claim that "biblical studies should ... reflect on contemporary society explicitly since it already does so implicitly."

As I see it, historiography remains in the hands of the treasure-hunter and the "spoilt idler in the garden of knowledge" as long as it does not self-consciously include work that accounts for the modern contexts within which the ancient world is imagined, explored, represented, and produced. A genuinely "relentless" historiography would be as rigorous in accounting for its own position within those contexts as in reporting on ancient objects. The anachronistic inquiry into the modern manifestations and functions of ancient literature and contemporary scholarship is, that is to say, not an accessory to a thoroughgoing historiography, but is the condition of its possibility. Any willingness to tolerate work like my own, work that is founded on these methodological conditions, is meaningless if there is no recognition of the way in which such conditions are incommensurable with the forms and interests of mainstream work within the discipline. Unfortunately, the appeal to the "big tent," like so many other well-meaning liberal or ecumenical gestures, becomes a means by which this divergence is neutralized while a superficial appearance of pluralism is maintained for the sake of good taste, politeness, and, ultimately, complacency.

GIVING AN ACCOUNT OF A DESIRABLE SUBJECT: CRITICALLY QUEERING GRADUATE BIBLICAL EDUCATION

Joseph A. Marchal

1. A STUDIED DESIRE

Desire might seem like an odd place to begin a series of reflections about graduate biblical studies. Desire is something felt in and through our bodies, while graduate work has been more typically characterized as primarily involving tasks of the mind and, thus, dissociated from crude, bodily impulses. Indeed, graduate work is *work*, serious and strenuous, requiring considerable efforts so that one can attain a sophistication generally described in elitist and exceptionalist terms (such as, "Most cannot do such work"). In a narrative common to such work, gaining a doctorate takes ample ability and arduous application in order to achieve advancement. Contrary to this rather cold and calculated view of the solitary individual objectively mastering mass quantities of information, it is important to highlight how crucial the activation and management of desire(s) are to graduate education, particularly in biblical studies.

Simply pursuing enrollment in such programs, for example, requires extensive desire. This desire develops always-already in a scene of considerable constraints—from economic and cultural conditions to the peculiarly conflicted social status of "the scholar." As a result, interested students often try *not* to pursue further studies in religious or theological areas; desires of this sort are deferred or denied. People will often do everything but pursue graduate biblical studies at first, which in turn also means that we have colleagues with impressive nonacademic resumes and rich "interludes" between periods of (more formalized) study and scholarship. This indicates that such desires are already viewed as odd: academics are often viewed skeptically, even suspiciously, as effeminate, disloyal, and/or foreign to "normal" (increasingly nationalist) citizens. If advanced studies are already characterized queerly, how much more so does graduate biblical studies occupy a series of uncommon positionalities as neither science nor belief, not quite history or theology, incorporating tasks from philology to ideology. As a field, it certainly involves adopting a queer position with an eccentric assemblage of analytic skills and interpretive possibilities.

In order to negotiate, or potentially bypass, this distinct sociocultural point of view regarding study, then, the prospective graduate student often requires a desire in excess of the norms that prioritize different modes of cultural authority and market-based utility.[1] A particular, even peculiar desire is not only the precondition of such a vocation, but it also marks a range of processes from application to acceptance, to study and socialization, and in advising and advancement. Graduate biblical education entails the desire for specific knowledges, along with the company of partners and peers whose desires are oriented in homologous or overlapping ways. The student-scholar aspires to a transformation in terms of both being and becoming, yet this transformation is most commonly affected through a master-disciple model of pedagogy where the scholar becomes (enough) like an advisor as an adequate, if not exemplary, representative of the norms of the field.[2] The process of becoming such a representative, an "expert," requires very specific forms of mastery, most typically of the standardized historiographic theories and stances developed by previous practitioners and accepted as legitimate by those currently holding positions of scholarly authority. Comprehensive (or general) examinations, for example, test graduate students' abilities to reproduce this information, giving the standard answers to those issues prioritized by the historical-critical malestream in biblical studies. Despite their names, such exams are far from comprehensive; of course, it is impossible to "know everything."[3] Rather, they are indicators of whether a scholar-in-the-making

---

1. Most of these reflections on the sociocultural tendency to view advanced study as strange denote these evaluations in North America and Western Europe, the site of most graduate biblical studies. Though operating with some differences in terms of assumptions and suspicions toward academia, students from migrant, historically underrepresented minorities, or first-generation collegiate contexts are also often (and perhaps especially) encouraged to value more socially recognizably statused fields such as medicine, law, or business, even as the humanities' irrelevance is similarly marked in typically erotically aberrant ways. See, for example, Kwok Pui-lan, "Jesus/the Native: Biblical Studies from a Postcolonial Perspective," in *Teaching the Bible: The Discourses and Politics of Biblical Pedagogy* (ed. Fernando F. Segovia and Mary Ann Tolbert; Maryknoll, N.Y.: Orbis, 1998), 69–85, 71.

2. On the master-disciple model of learning, see Elisabeth Schüssler Fiorenza, *Wisdom Ways: Introducing Feminist Biblical Interpretation* (Maryknoll, N.Y.: Orbis, 2001), 30; and idem, "Rethinking the Educational Practices of Biblical Doctoral Studies," *TThRel* 6 (2003): 65–75, esp. 66–68.

3. The dual study processes of preparing for exams and developing dissertation research at times require almost contradictory impulses: to know just enough about gener-

can explain the "state of the field," narrating what others have done and are doing, all to demonstrate that they know how to be a normal, typical (if not always average) biblical scholar.

The transformation, then, into an "educated person" is intimately involved with processes of normalization. It becomes essential, then, for scholars to learn more effective negotiations of such norms if we are to do more than simply replicate ourselves in a cycle of self-conceit. Indeed, such a stance denotes my own particular desire for biblical scholarship, while also indicating that any and every vision of what graduate biblical education should be or become (as many, if not most of the contributions of this volume likely reflect) involves particular developments of desire.

Thus, desire is already with us from the start, not only in a passion for study, engagement, and analysis, but also in any program to assess and transform the practices of graduate biblical education. With other feminist, postcolonial, and queer scholars, then, the aim of my own particular intervention on this occasion is to contribute to the transformation of the scholarship, curriculum, and public activities of biblical scholars to speed the development of safer practices of textual intercourse.[4] Though the debts of this reflection to a range of approaches will likely be clear, I will especially stress and draw upon the eclectic resources of queer studies for several reasons, including: (1) its relative circumscription in biblical studies (in comparison to both "traditional" historiographic approaches and recent feminist, postcolonial, and race-critical advances), (2) its relevance and utility for engaging particular issues at hand like desire, legitimacy, and normativity in contexts academic and public, and (3) the symptomatic example it provides for why and how biblical studies must be increasingly and critically transdisciplinary to maintain an ethical, political, and social accountability. For these reasons (and more), this essay will begin the task of giving an account of a desirable subject. Here the desirable subject is both the subject each of us might seek to become (the biblical scholar?) and the subject we study and instantiate (biblical studies?).

---

ally "everything" (all potential exam topics and questions) and to know generally everything about just enough of something (a research topic) to make it interesting. An oft-traveled, if pessimistic, aphorism that circulates in doctoral programs in the humanities about these programs is that scholars simultaneously learn to tell you "nothing about everything and everything about nothing."

4. For this phrase, see Ken Stone, *Practicing Safer Texts: Food, Sex, and Bible in Queer Perspective* (London: T&T Clark, 2005), 8–14. For my own previous reflections and applications of this concept as it relates to the future of biblical studies and "public health" modes of interpretation, see "Responsibilities to the Publics of Biblical Studies and Critical Rhetorical Engagements for a Safer World," in *Secularism and Biblical Studies* (ed. Roland Boer; London: Equinox, forthcoming).

As the phrase adapted for this task indicates, the essay will draw upon Judith Butler's recent ethical-political reflections on moral philosophy in order to think through the conditions and norms of the subject in/of biblical studies.[5] Such a strategy offers an opportunity to conceptualize how one could simultaneously learn the norms of an education as well as the modes to question and resist these norms, advancing as well as qualifying the "public health" aspects of biblical scholarship. Since too often biblical (or at least biblical-sounding) arguments have been used to move against the safety and survival of the disempowered and dominated, considerations of desire and "health" must lead to the interrogation and contestation of dominating dynamics across space and time. Toward this end we will consider examples of exploitation and subordination—including but not limited to the normalizing operations of contemporary homophobia—in order to indicate specific rationales for critically queer challenges and changes that should, in the end, be able to address more than might be expected. Such focused reflections should enable us to question, evaluate, and reposition to what uses our pleasure(s) and pain(s) are put in and through graduate biblical education.[6]

2. A Brief Account of a Butlerian Accountability

In order to redeploy Butler's reflections on the ethical life to our own scene of desire in biblical studies, we must first concisely describe key elements of Butler's argument on this occasion. Butler's work in *Giving an Account of Oneself* seems especially relevant to feminist, postcolonial, and queer forms of biblical studies since it reflects upon the relation of ethics to social critique (and vice versa). In doing so, Butler (like Foucault before her) focuses on the process of ethical self-making and its simultaneous delimitations.[7] Ethical deliberation needs to foster critique, but critique must consider how the subject who is doing the deliberating emerges and lives by and through a negotiation of norms.[8] Her project questions the identity of the "I" that pre-

---

5. Judith Butler, *Giving an Account of Oneself* (New York: Fordham University Press, 2005).

6. On the management of desire in ancient Greek contexts, see Michel Foucault's second volume of *The History of Sexuality: The Use of Pleasure* (trans. Robert Hurley; New York: Vintage, 1985). For further reflections on the use or the strategic "improper use" (*catachresis*) of biblical argumentation, see my conclusion in *The Politics of Heaven: Women, Gender, and Empire in the Study of Paul* (Paul in Critical Contexts; Minneapolis: Fortress, 2008), especially 121–23.

7. See, for example, Butler's thoughts on *The Use of Pleasure* in *Giving an Account of Oneself*, 15–19.

8. Ibid., 7–8.

scribes a course of action, just as we might wonder about the "I" we seek to create in graduate biblical studies. Yet, this I, this subject (in whatever field of human endeavor) emerges in the context of norms and always in relation to others.[9] These norms and the relations they both express and constitute are not fully "mine," and are, thus, disorienting. Though the I exists and operates in the constraints of these conditions, making it only partially transparent, the I is still responsible.[10] Furthermore, these disorienting, "not fully mine (or mine alone)" conditions can become a scene of critical assessment: we learn to address the other in the way that we are being addressed.[11] At the heart of the I, then, is the relationship between the other and myself: "*I am only in the address to you.*"[12] These relationships can become "relationships" with the object(s) of our affection, signaling how the project of ethical self-formation also gives rise to our desires.[13]

As she proceeds toward the close of her argument, Butler describes the condition of the I in ways that might delineate, to me at least, a most desirable kind of human (who could also be a biblical scholar).

> To be human seems to mean being in a predicament that one cannot solve....
> If the human is anything, it seems to be a double movement, one in which we assert moral norms at the same time as we question the authority by which we make that assertion.[14]

This conception of a doubly moving subject, vacillating between norming and critical activities, would be worth recalling for a number of contexts in graduate biblical education, for admittees, advisors, and administrators. Engaging in these practices should also highlight how the dynamics of normativity function to frame who and what is recognizable,[15] whether we are consider-

---

9. Ibid., 21, 26, 64, 131.

10. Ibid., 36–40, 88–91. Butler elaborates that "my own foreignness to myself is, paradoxically, the source of my ethical connection with others" (84).

11. Ibid., 49, 66.

12. Ibid., 82, emphasis original.

13. These desires also manage to "undo" us, further loosening firm ties between the desiring subject and the "mineness" of my desire. See Butler, *Giving an Account of Oneself*, 77–78; as well as idem, *Precarious Life: The Powers of Mourning and Violence* (London: Verso, 2004), 19–49, esp. 23–27; and idem, *Undoing Gender* (New York: Routledge, 2004), 2–4, 17–39, 131–51.

14. Butler, *Giving an Account of Oneself*, 103.

15. Ibid., 30, 132. Butler has been persistently turning to considerations of these conditions or "frames" for recognizability and speakability in contemporary contexts of conflict (militarized and gendered). See *Precarious Life*; *Undoing Gender*; and the following, most recent articles (likely to reappear as or to influence in altered and/or extended form a forth-

ing what is un/speakable in biblical studies or what is deemed il/legitimate or un/persuasive in the public uses of biblical argumentation. These limiting frames make clear that the conditions of being and doing also act as costs in the constitution of an ethical self.[16] With these costs and risks, though, come opportunities for transformation within constraints and accountability within conditions: "a certain self is risked in its intelligibility and recognizability in a bid to expose and account for the inhuman ways in which 'the human' continues to be done and undone."[17] Again, while there are constraints on and in the subject, there also remains responsibility and the possibility for taking norms to an ethical elsewhere. The sociality that inheres in the definition of human and in her participation in ethical interaction exposes the agent to "an anguish, to be sure, but also a chance."[18] This opportunity in a context of risk, even danger, reminds us of the development of "public health" modes of biblical interpretation utilized by Krister Stendahl, Elisabeth Schüssler Fiorenza, and Ken Stone, among others.[19] Stendahl proposed that biblical studies adopt the mentality of a department of public health, since "the whole scriptural tradition has had a clearly detrimental and dangerous effect."[20] Schüssler Fiorenza has argued that the contents of biblical texts should be marked with the label: "Caution, could be dangerous to your health and survival."[21] Stendahl and Schüssler Fiorenza took these positions and made these proposals in the face of typical ways of doing historical-critical work in biblical studies, insisting that those topics not traditionally considered as legitimate (especially the

---

coming Butler collection tentatively titled *Frames of War: When Is Life Grievable?* (London: Verso, 2009): "Photography, War, Outrage," *PMLA* 120 (2005): 822–27; "Torture and the Ethics of Photography," *Society and Space* 25 (2007): 951–66; and "Sexual Politics, Torture, and Secular Time," *British Journal of Sociology* 59 (2008): 1–23. For the unthinkability (or "impossible desires") of a queer female desiring subject in the postcolonial contexts of both nation and diaspora, see Gayatri Gopinath, *Impossible Desires: Queer Diasporas and South Asian Public Cultures* (Durham, N.C.: Duke University Press, 2005).

16. Butler, *Giving an Account of Oneself*, 120–22.
17. Ibid., 133–34.
18. Ibid., 136.
19. For another recent and more extended reflection on these three scholars in the context of a "public health" approach to biblical studies, see Marchal, "Responsibilities to the Publics."
20. Krister Stendahl, "Ancient Scripture in the Modern World," in *Scripture in the Jewish and Christian Traditions: Authority, Interpretation, Relevance* (ed. Frederick E. Greenspahn; Nashville: Abingdon, 1982), 201–14, here 204.
21. Elisabeth Schüssler Fiorenza, *Rhetoric and Ethic: The Politics of Biblical Studies* (Minneapolis: Fortress, 1999), 14. For further reflections on the potential of a public health aspect to biblical interpretation, see Schüssler Fiorenza, "Rethinking the Educational Practices," 69.

status and roles of women and Jews) should not only be included but prioritized, given the public and private uses of biblical literature and scholarship.

Even as both of these scholars refuse to ignore the negative effects of traditional uses of these materials, they also do not argue for abandoning or rejecting the Bible because of these risks and dangers. Rather, it is their insistence on combining ethical evaluation with persistent critique (not abandonment) that Stone later connects to the wonderfully apt pun of his recent title, *Practicing Safer Texts*, and that still might connect to the reflections of Butler above.[22] This "public health" approach, then, can be extended by way of an analogy to the "safer sex" approach of contemporary AIDS activists, since safer sex also offers a route besides denying the risks of certain practices for HIV transmission or rejecting sexual activity absolutely.[23]

Stone's concept of "safer textual practice" helps to refashion where the perils and problems lie in the process of interpretation. Safer sex emphasizes that HIV transmission is not attributable to the gender, number, or location of one's partners, but to very specific practices in particular situations. To make both sexual and textual practices safer, one should attempt to avoid or modify only these particular practices and cultivate safer practices of textual intercourse. Just as one might question the absolutism of the practices of denial or relinquishment, Stone argues that one cannot invest this practice with the hope of providing total safety.[24] Hence, the emphasis is upon making interpretation "safer." In fact, any argument that claims to offer complete safety or security is an argument worthy of suspicion. Not only might it function as a reinforcement of a particular imperially classed and racialized arrangement (refracted through norms of gender and sexuality), but any actual and complete removal of risk would also dissolve the meaningful joys of human existence. Stone observes, "'safer sex' approaches acknowledge that pleasure always exists in relation to some degree of risk, and that attempts to reduce any risk whatsoever are not only naïve, but too frequently result in the elimination of pleasure as well."[25] Butler's anguished chance and Stone's evocation of safer textual intercourse clarify that finding any desirable course of action involves risks, dangers, and difficulties.

Hence, there might be a variety of ways to rather idiosyncratically link Butler's insights to the project of transforming graduate biblical education. It seems vital to begin giving an account of ourselves as individuals

---

22. Stone, *Practicing Safer Texts*, 12–13.
23. Ibid., 8–9, 13
24. Ibid., 13.
25. Ibid. For further reflections on risk, as it relates to the uses of both food and sex, see 10–11.

yet inevitably socialized within "biblical studies." Butler's account recasts human responsibility in light of the not-fully-transparent self.[26] Similarly, biblical scholars are still responsible for how our field, our actions, and our arguments operate, *even if* (or *as*) we do not have any absolutized authority or mastery over all of its materials. As Butler argues, our accountability exists in a context of conditions and constraints, historical and cultural. As student-scholars we enter into a centuries-long conversation that has done discernible and demoralizing damage to humanity. Though we may not have been present for some of the field's most horrific forms of complicity and cooptation, we are nonetheless conditioned and socialized into those norms that developed in and out of these forms; they still frame what it means to be recognizable as a biblical scholar.

Our processes for establishing comprehension and comprehensiveness involve learning a set of norms that should be known and somehow become "mine," even as they are "not fully mine," or at least "not fully mine alone." Indeed, in becoming the "I" (biblical scholar) and gaining legitimacy as such a subject (expert in biblical studies), the subject is constituted by the tension between embodying norms that are "mine," but "not fully mine (alone)." This tension presents the subject ethically deliberating over the impact of her education and ascribed expertise with "an anguish, to be sure, but also a chance."[27] Since the norms are mine, the scholar must be responsible for the legitimizing and delegitimizing operation of the norms and all the attendant effects of their operation. The task must fall to us, if we are constituted as biblical scholars. Yet, since the norms are also "not fully mine," an I initiated into the subjecthood of biblical studies has a unique vantage point from which to expose the particularized oppressive operation of these norms, within and without the subject (biblical studies). Finally, since these norms are not fully mine alone, as a member of the human community the I (that might also be a biblical scholar) exists always only in social interrelation with others, reminding the critically reflective I that justice for me is ineluctably tied to justice for others.

Given these conditions for the emergence of the I who becomes a "biblical scholar," then, it seems crucial to continuously and consistently pair critique of such norms with ethical deliberation about their impact. In doing so, we must attend to subject-formation in our discipline and the norms that both delimit and still might make possible critical opportunities for change.[28] In

---

26. See her argument throughout, but esp. Butler, *Giving an Account of Oneself*, 83.

27. Ibid., 136.

28. For the importance of a genealogical understanding of the field, see Schüssler Fiorenza, "Rethinking the Educational Practices," 69–72; and Kwok, "Jesus/the Native," 75–80.

education we cannot but help to assert norms (indeed, my consideration of normativity here could itself be seen as another norm to be desired), but to queer this education we must also question the authority and utility of our norms and their various effects on the subject. Graduate biblical education must find a way to enact this doubled, if tensive activity: learning the norms while establishing a critical stance in relation to these norms. Que(e)rying biblical education requires us to ask why and how norms are enacted in order to recognize under what constraints or conditions we operate.

The example of comprehensive/general exams and their relation to advanced coursework in graduate biblical education is one locale for critically examining the function and operations of such norms. As a process the exams work in normalizing ways, directing the student to become a biblical studies expert through the reproduction of the conventional content sanctioned by an established, historical-critical, pale malestream. In advance, students are schooled in what kinds of answers are legitimate to the typical questions, illustrating that only certain standardized topics are relevant and expected to be known. From these norms flow the coursework in doctoral and, perhaps, advanced years of masters' programs; the best preparation for the rigors of exams entails coursework only in those areas, approaches, and topics covered on exams. By its structure, then, the program of study can obscure why certain questions are foregrounded or specific tasks pursued. Historically this explains how graduate biblical education was able to ignore the roles of women, the poor, and the racially and colonially dominated in both ancient history and contemporary society. Even now, the dynamics of gender, sexuality, race, ethnicity, and empire are most often treated as peripheral to the "real work" of biblical scholars, or given only cursory attention en route to "core concerns" for biblical studies. Through such operations, then, one can see not only how certain modes become legitimized and normative, but also how all other modes are marginalized or excluded.

Within all of this, though, we must also recall that the difficulties and dangers of ethical-political interpretation are not predetermined or fated as particular conclusions. The desirable subject (here both the biblical scholar and biblical studies) is still evolving and is constantly being remade. Echoing Butler's most famous work, to engender resistance and transformation we would do well to recall that the subject is also a practice, a doing: a repeated stylization of our bodies and the bodies of work we produce(d).[29] The subject in and of biblical studies is not yet foreclosed. If we are still to fashion a more

---

29. Butler challenged most received notions of the gendered body by asserting: "Gender is the repeated stylization of the body, a set of repeated acts within a highly rigid regulatory frame that congeals over time to produce the appearance of substance, of a natu-

desirable subject, we must account for the still manifest costs and risks for those whose safety, survival, and social justice have been traditionally and even more recently threatened in the use of biblical argumentation.

3. Accounting For Impact in an Education

One path for considering how to adopt and adapt strategies from Butler's reflections on ethical accountability to graduate biblical studies would be to reflect further on particular instances of the damaging potential of biblical argumentation, in contexts both academic and public. Discourses of health and disease recur in these dynamics and provide a fitting occasion to evaluate what forms graduate biblical education might still take.

Certainly, the rhetorics of contagion, filth, disease, and impurity operate in a variety of ways in biblical literature, including those oft-cited texts that are purportedly "about" homosexuality. The Sodom story (Gen 18–19) involves divine judgment executed through an act of "sweeping away" the inhabitants of the city, preparing the way for Abrahamic possession. The Levitical Holiness Code condemns behavior that violates certain social boundaries meant to maintain an internal communal purity against defilement, protecting the audience from the contagion brought in by or as outsiders. Paul's letters labor to define and shore up certain views of communal belonging, through claims about the depravity of certain desires and practices. For Paul, true followers are cleansed of such impurities and passions and must remove anyone from the community who violates these norms. Biblical scholars, and Pauline interpreters in particular, have proudly claimed to "reproduce" these rhetorical practices and, as a result, adopt contemporary positions in apparent continuity with the texts and the heteronormative traditions built up around them. From such a perspective, Paul's instructions to the ancient community at Rome or Corinth are simply taken to be instructions to the communities (typically of the devotional variety) to which scholars belong, given the proper, expert coding.

Such claims that Paul guides the community by protecting them against the external threat represented by a libidinous and unchecked "paganism" echo the equally problematic scholarly narratives that celebrate Jesus "saving" women from oppressive Judaism.[30] Just as the latter displays an inept and

---

ral sort of being." See Butler, *Gender Trouble: Feminism and the Subversion of Identity* (New York: Routledge, 1990), 33.

30. See Judith Plaskow, "Anti-Judaism in Feminist Christian Interpretation," in *A Feminist Introduction* (vol. 1 of *Searching the Scriptures*; ed. Schüssler Fiorenza; New York: Crossroad, 1993), 117–29; Ross Shepard Kraemer, "Jewish Women and Christian Origins:

ahistorical caricature of Jews as legalistic and backward, the former projects a historically and ethically troublesome view of the "opponents" to these developing communities. Both happen to tell us more about the cultural views of biblical scholarship of our times than the ancient contexts of the first century assemblies. Not only do we have a considerable history of anti-Semitism with which to deal, but continuing characterizations of Paul's "outsiders" as depraved pagans also reflect and reinforce persistent imperial justifications for the civilizing mission of Western (Christian) colonial powers. As Kwok Pui-lan has highlighted, in recent colonial discourse racialized populations are identified as modern pagans, since they lack the religion and civilization symbolized through the particularized erotic austerities promulgated by normalizing biblical traditions.[31] Thus, failure to interrogate the exclusionary practices of both the biblical text and biblical interpretation perpetuates a damaging and dominating ideology of legitimacy not just in terms of gender and sexuality, but also race, ethnicity, religion, and empire.

For the various members of LGBTIQ communities, these kinds of arguments are all too familiar. Of course, as any informed person knows about contemporary public uses of biblical literature, the four aforementioned texts (Gen 18 and 19; Lev 18 and 20; Rom 1; and 1 Cor 5 and 6) are the typical "bashing" texts used in homophobic proclamations. Beyond these, though, LGBTIQ subjects are often acquainted with the rhetorics of purity, health, and cleanness in general, since they have been deployed historically and presently as strategies of differentiation and condemnation against them in communities academic, religious, personal, regional and/or national in orientation. Furthermore, the projection of the sexual problems onto Gentile outsiders by Pauline interpreters is no great comfort to Christian queers seeking to become or remain insiders by suggesting an ancient parallel to the "inclusion of the Gentiles" in Paul's first-century activities.[32] With only a few recent exceptions, most biblical scholarship has done little to address and undercut the public authority of these various argumentative practices targeting queer populations for pathologization and/or exclusion. As a result, one could say that being

---

Some Caveats," in *Women and Christian Origins* (ed. Ross Shepard Kraemer and Mary Rose D'Angelo; New York: Oxford University Press, 1999), 35–49; as well as the special section on feminist anti-Judaism in *JFSR* 7 (1991): 95–133.

31. See Kwok Pui-lan, "Sexual Morality and National Politics: Reading Biblical 'Loose Women,'" in *Engaging the Bible: Critical Readings from Contemporary Women* (ed. Choi Hee An and Katheryn Pfisterer Darr; Minneapolis: Fortress, 2006), 21–46, esp. 43–44.

32. See, e.g., the strategy presented by Jeffrey S. Siker, "Homosexual Christians, the Bible, and Gentile Inclusion: Confessions of a Repenting Heterosexist," in *Homosexuality in the Church: Both Sides of the Debate* (ed. Jeffrey S. Siker; Louisville: Westminster John Knox, 1994), 178–94.

queer in the study of "Christian origins" involves embarking on a relationship dangerous to one's health. One could argue, with Amy-Jill Levine, that just as we need more Jews and/or scholars of formative Judaism in graduate theological education in order to combat academic anti-Semitism, there should be a greater (explicit) LGBTIQ presence and/or scholarly expertise in ancient sexuality in order to challenge scholars' heterosexism.[33] For if it is often harder to maintain anti-Jewish views when one has contact or courses with Jews, one might also note a reduction of biblically endorsed homophobia when in the open and acknowledged presence of LGBTIQ people. In most of her reflections, Levine links the "rot" or the "virus" of academic anti-Judaism to the ahistorical bend of some of the more recent approaches developing in biblical studies. Whether the culprit is multiculturalism, postcolonialism, or cultural studies in general, Levine maintains that a shift toward newer approaches or concerns and a corresponding deemphasis on historical approaches in curriculum and writing leads to anti-Judaism in scholarship.[34] Here Levine's arguments might parallel the confidence scholars such as Jacques Berlinerblau and Dale Martin have in various historicizing projects. Berlinerblau's approach to a secular kind of hermeneutics seems to assume that the destabilizing effects of normative historical-critical approaches, untethered from devotional moorings, will be sufficient aid for people to intelligently negotiate issues like intermarriage and same-sex relations.[35] More recently, Martin has argued for a peculiar historicist methodological shift that ends up re-emphasizing the patristic and pre-modern contexts of church history (rather than the potentially riotous multiplicity of the opening centuries of these communities) in order to better understand biblical literature.[36] Again and again, such

---

33. See, e.g., Amy-Jill Levine, "Lilies of the Field and Wandering Jews: Biblical Scholarship, Women's Roles, and Social Location," in *Transformative Encounters: Jesus and Women Re-viewed* (ed. Ingrid R. Kitzberger; Leiden: Brill, 2000), 329–52, esp. 334, 346; idem, "Multiculturalism, Women's Studies, and Anti-Judaism," *JFSR* 19 (2003): 119–28, particularly 121, 124, 126; idem, "Theological Education, the Bible, and History: Détente in the Culture Wars," in *Early Christian Families in Context: An Interdisciplinary Dialogue* (ed. David L. Balch and Carolyn Osiek; Grand Rapids: Eerdmans, 2003), 327–36, esp. 327, 329–30, 332–34; and idem, "The Disease of Postcolonial New Testament Studies and the Hermeneutics of Healing," *JFSR* 20 (2004): 91–99.

34. Levine, "Lilies of the Field," 334, 346; idem, "Multiculturalism," 121, 126; idem, "Theological Education," 327; and idem, "The Disease," 91, 96.

35. See, e.g., the format of Jacques Berlinerblau, *The Secular Bible: Why Nonbelievers Must Take Religion Seriously* (Cambridge: Cambridge University Press, 2005).

36. See, e.g., Dale B. Martin, *Sex and the Single Savior: Gender and Sexuality in Biblical Interpretation* (Louisville: Westminster John Knox, 2006); and idem, *Pedagogy of the Bible: An Analysis and Proposal* (Louisville: Westminster John Knox, 2008).

scholarly proposals maintain a focus on the historical horizon, even when they grapple with contemporary challenges in the areas of gender and sexuality. This is, indeed, odd and a marker of how little queer approaches have gained an audience among "progressive" biblical scholars (whether Christian, Jewish, or nonbeliever): the current implications and manifest directions of queer studies are hardly (let alone primarily) historical.

Recognizing that "public health" is often created through the management and elimination of such threats should give us collective, if temporary, pause about adopting public health as a mode for biblical studies. Though I find myself in frequent solidarity with the proposals of Stendahl, Schüssler Fiorenza, and Stone, it is crucial to grapple with how health as a concept has been differentially ordered along the intersecting lines of gender, sexuality, race/ethnicity, and imperial-colonial placement. No less a figure than Angela Davis has detailed the way health as a concept (here, reproductive health) can operate to reflect and reinforce a sexist, racist, classist and even transnational order.[37] Certainly, Stone's adaptation of the "safer sex" educational practices of activists and public health workers is meant to counteract the (often "Christian" and Bible-quoting) vilification and judgment heaped on especially urban American gay males at the height of the AIDS crisis of the 1980s.[38] Nevertheless, queer subjects are still persistently characterized as diseased or disordered and in need of "restorative" or conversion therapy by various publics constituted through overlapping authorities of religion and public health.[39] Health as a discourse is now especially the province of medical and psychological professionals, who have a spotty track record (at best) when it comes to issues of gender justice and sexual freedom. Even as the *DSM* has been emended to remove homosexuality as a pathology, the ambiguous definition and implementation of the gender identity disorder diagnosis function to target and police gender-aberrant youth and trans people.[40] Furthermore,

---

37. See Angela Davis, "Racism, Birth Control, and Reproductive Rights," in idem, *Women, Race, and Class* (New York: Random House, 1981), 202–21, 268–70.

38. See Stone, *Practicing Safer Texts*, 9. Indeed, queer populations must deal with such circularly judgmental arguments that HIV/AIDS is the "cure" for homosexuality (yet another reason to be cautious and critical about the adaptation of "health" modes for biblical interpretation).

39. See, e.g., Tanya Erzen, *Straight to Jesus: Sexual and Christian Conversions in the Ex-Gay Movement* (Berkeley and Los Angeles: University of California Press, 2006).

40. For a recent reflection on how trans youth are targeted (or gender-aberrant youth are, through psychological, medical, social, and religious norms about trans), see Butler, "Undiagnosing Gender," in *Undoing Gender*, 75–101, 253–55. For various trans stances about the utility *and* the constraints of the GID diagnosis, see Susan Stryker and Stephen Whittle, eds., *The Transgender Studies Reader* (New York: Routledge, 2006).

on a macro-level, "health" in these fields has been significantly influenced by the rise in the authoritative application of statistics in describing and prescribing ostensibly normal conditions.[41] In medicine, psychology, and now (sadly) most of our mass-communications cultures, any departure from a rather constrained range of "acceptable" variation can be classed as not normal, and thus an unhealthy threat to the individual and the community.[42] Furthermore, these kinds of "threats" are posed on biblical terms as issues of communal identity, purity, and unity. Indeed, M. Jacqui Alexander's pathbreaking, transdisciplinary work has carefully delineated how biblical condemnations about same-sex desires travel globally and transnationally and are cited to bolster claims about such desires' destructive influence on "national health."[43] Given the way in which HIV infection and transmission have increasingly become an issue of global health, it seems especially pressing to critically and suspiciously prepare queer coalitional engagements of such biblical argumentation for a range of publics.[44] This is no less the case than in the context of the United States, where biblical argumentation still most reliably recurs in public contexts when parties are deliberating about the virtue, legality, utility, and/or desirability of various LGBTIQ modes of existence, alliance, participation, filiation, or citizenship.[45] Unfortunately, in these instances biblical citations rarely function as arguments in the affirmative, unless one counts the affirmation of queer judgment, marginalization, or destruction.

---

41. For reflections on the rise of statistical norms and how they operate as evaluative norms, see Michael Warner, *The Trouble With Normal: Sex, Politics, and the Ethics of Queer Life* (Cambridge: Harvard University Press, 1999), 52–61.

42. One remarkable instance of the physical management of populations on the basis of the purported virtue of fitting within a statistical norm is the high incidence of surgery on infants in potentially intersexed conditions. See Suzanne J. Kessler, *Lessons from the Intersexed* (New Brunswick, N.J.: Rutgers University Press, 1998).

43. See M. Jacqui Alexander, *Pedagogies of Crossing: Meditations on Feminism, Sexual Politics, Memory, and the Sacred* (Durham, N.C.: Duke University Press, 2005), 21–65, 181–254.

44. See, e.g., the more recent (though not necessarily queer) efforts of Musa W. Dube: Musa W. Dube and Musimbi R. A. Kanyoro, eds., *Grant Me Justice! HIV/AIDS and Gender Readings of the Bible* (Maryknoll, N.Y.: Orbis, 2004); Musa W. Dube, ed., *HIV/AIDS and the Curriculum: Methods of Integrating HIV/AIDS in Theological Programmes* (Geneva: WCC Publications, 2003); Musa W. Dube, *The HIV and AIDS Bible: Selected Essays* (Scranton, Pa.: University of Scranton Press, 2006).

45. For a helpful and provocative study of specifically religious, mostly Christian, and often biblical influences on the American discourse of legal and sexual norms, see Janet R. Jakobsen and Ann Pellegrini, *Love the Sin: Sexual Regulation and the Limits of Religious Tolerance* (New York: New York University Press, 2003).

These dynamics suggest that scholars must proceed with caution when adopting a concept like "public health" as a paradigm for specifically identifying and counteracting the oppressive effects of biblical interpretation. Those few scholars who have begun this work are correct that such issues deserve urgent attention and that biblical scholars can no longer ignore such effects if we seek to be an ethically accountable group of educators. Yet, given the background and dominant practices of those who appeal to the health of a public, a nation, or a society (mostly outside of graduate biblical studies), I suggest that we must also remain cautious and critical when adapting such a metaphor. Indeed, we cannot underestimate the ability of forces to adapt and reestablish themselves in different forms, even when it seems that we argue "on the right side." As Jasbir Puar and others have shown, the "acceptance" of nonnormative sexualities can also function as an imperial marker of cultural advancement and nationalized health ("homonationalism"), bolstering claims of superiority over and justifying abusive practices toward a range of groups identified as the racialized, religiously, and sexually differentiated other.[46] Such a phenomenon signals that the institutionalization of an agenda, like communal affirmation of homosexuality or the health of the public, can actually be turned to reinforce those impulses the agenda was originally meant to counteract (now in different form). This, of course, does not mean that one should never pursue something like safety and social justice for all; rather, it indicates how such an effort requires continuous critical reflection and vigilant attention to its persistent and shifting effects.

In such contexts, relying solely on historiographic skills would seem to leave graduate biblical educators woefully ill equipped for the constantly evolving challenges of our time. An ascendant and imperially gendered normativity can expand and express its power through a range of dynamics in terms of racialized scapegoating, heterosexist democratization, and homonationalist justifications which, on the surface, might only appear to be contradictory. This underscores, then, the utility of increasing biblical scholars' familiarity with current developments in queer studies, as they have aided this particular analysis to recognize and counter such ethically problematic dynamics, with or without the explicit use of biblical argumentation.

---

46. See Jasbir K. Puar, *Terrorist Assemblages: Homonationalism in Queer Times* (Durham, N.C.: Duke University Press, 2007). For reflections on the way U.S. military interrogators and the government of the Netherlands uses depictions of same-sex affection in various abuses of power, see Butler, "Sexual Politics, Torture, and Secular Time" and "Photography, War, Outrage."

4. Toward a Desirable Subject

The historicization of sexuality that occurred as lesbian and gay studies and, then, queer studies developed has done little to stem the appeal of such citational practices as arguments for a number of publics.[47] This ongoing contextual challenge suggests specific strategies that graduate biblical studies should adopt if it seeks to be continuously critical and accountable. First, biblical studies must be brought into more regular contact, conversation, and even contestation with the variegated insights and approaches of queer studies. To produce the next generation of LGBTIQ scholars (or at least those able to address the concerns of these communities), graduate programs of study should delineate and develop queer forms of biblical studies. Second, such efforts at developing facility in queer studies and biblical methodologies cannot remain exclusively focused on the history of erotic or sexual norms, regulations, and activities. Since homophobic and heteronormative arguments rely upon considerably more than just historical ideas when they employ biblical authority in their claims, a biblical scholar concerned with the ethical, political, and social impact of her work must become adept at engaging the rhetoricity of these texts and their various interpretations.[48] To become such a desirable subject, we must expand the resources available in graduate biblical education and initiate programs of study, research, and advising that foster wide ranging and critically eclectic readings of a transdisciplinary variety. There are already some institutional resources available to biblical scholars in graduate schools and seminaries in the United States. Seminaries such as the Pacific School of Religion and Chicago Theological Seminary support a Center for Lesbian and Gay Studies in Religion and Ministry and the LGBTIQ Religious Studies Center.[49] The divinity schools at Harvard and Vanderbilt offer a religion,

---

47. See, e.g., Foucault's three volumes of *The History of Sexuality*, which, in turn, influenced works such as David M. Halperin, *One Hundred Years of Homosexuality: And Other Essays on Greek Love* (New York: Routledge, 1990); and David M. Halperin, John J. Winkler, and Froma I. Zeitlin, eds., *Before Sexuality: The Construction of Erotic Experience in the Ancient Greek World* (Princeton: Princeton University Press, 1990).

48. On the vacillating importance and uses of authority as it relates to historicity in the employment of biblical arguments by and within publics ecclesial and otherwise, see Mary Ann Tolbert, "A New Teaching With Authority: A Re-evaluation of the Authority of the Bible," in Segovia and Tolbert, *Teaching the Bible*, 168–89.

49. In addition, the Institute for Judaism and Sexual Orientation at Hebrew Union College-Jewish Institute of Religion is developing considerable programming on curriculum, liturgy, community, and educational training, while Hartford Seminary's Hartford Institute for Religious Research gathers information and research about homosexuality and religion.

gender, and culture doctoral program and a certificate program in religion, gender, and sexuality, respectively.[50] In each of these contexts, though, the education of biblical scholars-in-training is often peripheral to the centers' and programs' already considerable missions. Graduate students in biblical studies must individually pursue connections to feminist, queer, gender, or sexuality studies, since every graduate institution assumes that these sets of commitments entail separate programs of study. Indeed, in every case except the Harvard doctoral program, students cannot pursue a primary course of study in gender and/or sexuality as it relates to graduate work in religion and theology. In many educational contexts, creating a center for particular topics or (sub)disciplines might operate not as a legitimizing endorsement of its importance, but an effective strategy for containing critical questions or foundational challenges to the institution's established structure. Creating areas of study in such marginalized positions demonstrates a concern with preventing the "contamination" of the traditional fields of study, typically seen as the *real* work of seminaries and graduate programs. The existence of these programs and centers, then, might just be an indication of how entrenched the norms for graduate biblical education are. The issues raised by feminist, postcolonial, or queer studies are not able to more significantly transform and refine graduate biblical education, since these areas are so rarely integrated into the education.

One reason why queer studies has entered into the accepted discourse of so few institutions is likely the still often marginalized role of feminist voices and approaches in graduate biblical education. The progress made in queer or critical sexuality studies in religion has tended only to occur where schools have already taken such voices seriously and created (or allowed) venues for the expansion of feminist, gender, or women's studies in graduate religious studies. This signals how far biblical studies must still go in most academic contexts; we as scholars are simply not letting queer and feminist studies help us do the important work of forming relevant and responsive subjects.

Furthermore, in those few contexts where biblical studies and queer or critical sexuality studies are interacting, the place of biblical scholars in this working relationship is often limited and, in some ways, repeating the normalized training we received. If we are fortunate, programs and centers come to biblical scholars to serve as experts to answer "what *does* the Bible say about homosexuality?" and offer the occasional course that illuminates the contours of the ecclesial and political questions about (homo)sexuality. Certainly, these

---

50. Vanderbilt's Carpenter program offers a certificate to graduate students on masters and doctoral levels, just as Duke Divinity School offers a certificate in Gender, Theology, and Ministry.

trends reinforce the biblical scholar's constitution as the only legitimate expert on such topics. In some ways, this is most welcome and we prove ourselves useful when we attempt to shed some light on this rarely illuminated corner of misunderstood and malinterpreted texts. Yet, in other ways, it potentially limits the import of biblical scholarship and gives an inflated sense of our actual influence. As scholars like Berlinerblau have been prone to lament of late, when the public and, particularly, the media turn for information about biblical literature and interpretation, they seek a representative sampling of religious leaders over the Society of Biblical Literature and its thousands of Ph.D.s.[51]

Though biblical scholars have been educated and socialized as the expert repositories of academic knowledge about this literature, most people do not view us this way and fewer still are inclined to listen to us. This could change, if we learned to identify, assess, engage, and counteract the relevant public and private biblically styled argumentation. The increased place of queer studies in graduate biblical education should help in this regard. Instead of asking master's students to turn to us for their one and only course on "homosexuality and the Bible," we as biblical scholars could grapple with queer theories to better learn how to interrogate what is included and thus validated as appropriate coursework, exam topics, outside disciplines, or complementary concentrations for graduate studies.[52] Indeed, any time scholars might seek to engage in critical meta-reflections on approach, paradigm, or curriculum (as in a volume of this kind), a comfort and facility with both queer positioning and critique would aid in the assessment and transformation of these programmatic elements from their operations in processes of legitimization and exclusion.

This returns my argument to the description of the subject of graduate biblical education as one who already embodies an odd desire: to become a biblical scholar. Socially and pedagogically, I frequently notice and then attempt to compensate or explain away this queer positioning. When feeling judged or distrusted, I attempt to reassure others that I am somehow "normal." When introductory students become uncomfortable (as they do)

---

51. See, e.g., Jacques Berlinerblau, "'The Old Is Dying and the New Cannot Be Born!' Biblical Studies: A Sack of Potatoes" (paper presented at the SBL International Meeting, Edinburgh, Scotland, 3 July 2006); and "'Poor Bird, Not Knowing Which Way to Fly': Biblical Scholarship's Marginality, Secular Humanism, and the Laudable Occident," *BibInt* 10 (2002): 267–304.

52. A queer analytic could still aid in interrogating the history of graduate biblical studies and how certain disciplines have been allowed to "belong," which specialized topics "count," or which concentrations are worthy of being "complementary" to advanced studies in biblical education.

at basic and now-long-standing historical-critical positions and arguments, I hurry to reassure them that the Synoptic problem or the Documentary Hypothesis are norms that are "not fully mine (alone)." In moments like these, we might sense (perhaps accurately) our own vulnerability. But, if the insights of Butler are to affect my or our formation as educators, this precarious kind of existence should be acknowledged as humanly unavoidable. Rather than skirting the topics of scholarly power, propriety, and normativity, then, biblical scholars could embrace our peculiar positionality and engage more deeply and trans-disciplinarily with queer studies. To do so, however, does not mean "giving up" on either the historical or the biblical domains as we develop greater facility in feminist, postcolonial, or queer studies (among others). In order to recognize and contest how biblical arguments are used in dominating and destructive ways, we must be able to address such arguments on as many grounds as possible. To ignore biblical claims so as to avoid reinforcing their authority, as some have suggested,[53] seems to unnecessarily cede a still viable, if not endlessly fruitful potential sphere for generating counterhegemonic strategies. Furthermore, if graduate biblical education is at all interested in communal and ecclesial relevance or other forms of contemporary accountability, it cannot ignore the ongoing, effective use of biblical arguments in public political contexts such as the United States, where the "defense" of marriage against a spectrally same-sex "threat" can still fulfill considerable social, cultural, and political aims. Showing that the Bible (and especially the Gospels and Paul's letters) could hardly be described as a series of promarriage texts is not explanation enough for the continuing function of biblical argumentation in these contexts.[54] Rather, it might be more valuable to recall the key role moral panics play at times of heightened communal uncertainty (like "national crises"). Such panics produce internally threatening scapegoats who must be isolated, expelled, and/or eliminated while, just as importantly, installing an increasingly regressive regime to manage entire populations now unified, pure, and safeguarded.[55] Such repetitive dynamics of policing and power help to highlight how and why biblical arguments (start again to) have particular impacts in the twenty-first century, even as it also alerts us to attend to the rhetorical pairing of externalizing threat with

---

53. See, e.g., the observations in Jakobsen and Pellegrini, *Love the Sin*, 88–89.

54. For recent reflections on "marriage" in the Second Testament and early Christianities as it relates to appeals to "biblical" visions of heteronormative, Christian marriage, see Dale B. Martin, "Familiar Idolatry and the Christian Case against Marriage," in idem, *Sex and the Single Savior*, 103–24, 224–28.

55. See, e.g., Gayle Rubin, "Thinking Sex: Notes for a Radical Theory of the Politics of Sexuality," in *Pleasure and Danger: Exploring Female Sexuality* (ed. Carole S. Vance; London: Pandora, 1989), 267–319, esp. 267–71, 294–97.

internalized control in biblical arguments of the first century. These forms of argumentation and social management would have been harder for a biblical scholar to identify without the advances of queer studies and its predecessors, like Gayle Rubin. The manifest resources queer studies could provide to an analysis of the impact of biblical arguments in current contexts demonstrates the rhetorical utility of biblical scholars learning to read widely and outside of "our" discipline. Such a transdisciplinary practice could be adopted and adapted in graduate programs in forms similar to Kwok Pui-lan's proposed strategy of "parallel processing."[56] Parallel processing involves reading and researching within frameworks wider than biblical studies so as to lend new perspectives to our subjects *and* to provide depth and texture to the application of new approaches beginning to be utilized in the guild (including postcolonial and queer approaches). Too often, our versions of queer scholarship like Butler's, Foucault's, and sometimes Eve Kosofsky Sedgwick's come through disciplinary interlocutors like Stephen Moore, Ken Stone, Bernadette Brooten, and Dale Martin. Yet, the approaches these biblical scholars present have their own specific characteristics, circumstances, and limitations and cannot always offer an adequate introduction to the resources one might encounter by reading extra-biblical queer work oneself. The agenda of queer biblical scholars should be to push past Moore or Stone to Butler, Foucault, and Sedgwick, but also beyond these figures to work not yet prioritized in biblical studies. Queer approaches in graduate biblical studies would more easily expand and adapt to engage the concerns of the twenty-first century by knowing the work of those who suggest different interventions or have critical and creative insights about the more prominently referenced intellects. This can be achieved both by going back to Rubin, Jeffrey Weeks, and Teresa de Lauretis and moving further to recent challenges by Judith Halberstam, Roderick Ferguson, or Jasbir Puar (among others).

A vigorous and creative form of parallel processing in coursework, exams, research, and writing would also enable us to see a range of connections between argumentative practices from seemingly disparate or disconnected subfields. Returning to the example of moral panics, the targeting and management of (supposedly) sexually aberrant or nonnormatively erotic subjects often also coincides with or runs parallel to other schema of panic, where women, Jews, and/or other racialized "others" were and are scapegoated as modes of social control. To recognize this means that queer studies must remain reflexively and self-critically accountable to insights from feminist,

---

56. See Kwok, "Jesus/the Native," 75–81. For other forms of "doubling" required for biblical doctoral studies, see Schüssler Fiorenza, "Rethinking the Educational Practices," 67, 69, 72–73.

race-critical, and postcolonial studies.[57] Queer scholars must become comfortable with continuous crossings of boundaries and, if biblical scholarship is to remain or become relevant, it too must learn from such transdisciplinary trajectories. These interconnections also indicate that the normative subject of queer approaches, in and outside of biblical studies, cannot be just another version of an elite pale malestream.[58]

Such insights indicate the utility of reading eclectically and researching widely while pursuing an increasingly intersectional, or multiaxial form of analysis. If scholars were to learn to engage in various forms of "parallel processing," these dynamics of domination, differentiation, and destruction become easier to recognize and resist, making biblical studies more adept at being critically accountable (to the field and as a field) to those against whom such arguments are deployed. A most desirable kind of graduate biblical education should constantly stretch and contest the norms of our field by not remaining disciplined solely within it. Queer approaches, in particular, aid in attending to how disciplinary procedures and viewpoints become normative and legitimate.

If we are to transform graduate biblical studies as safer practices of textual intercourse, then scholars must develop a simultaneous set of skills, able to contest and disrupt norms even as we are being educated in them. The challenges of queer studies (and other transdisciplinary efforts) can clarify and qualify the conditions and constraints of those "healthy" desires stoked and shaped in graduate biblical education. Strategic practices like the ones highlighted here should aid in accounting for and assessing the desires in and about graduate studies, quite possibly leading to what Gayatri Chakravorty Spivak would call an "uncoercive rearrangement of desires."[59] In this moment, it is a desire and an aim as yet unfulfilled but still quite possible.

---

57. For the interconnections between queer and race-critical studies in a "queer of color critique," see, e.g., José Esteban Muñoz, *Disidentifications: Queer of Color and the Performance of Politics* (Minneapolis: University of Minnesota Press, 1999); Roderick A. Ferguson, *Aberrations in Black: Toward a Queer of Color Critique* (Minneapolis: University of Minnesota Press, 2004); and E. Patrick Johnson and Mae G. Henderson, eds., *Black Queer Studies: A Critical Anthology* (Durham, N.C.: Duke University Press, 2005). For postcolonially queer challenges (that also often attend to gender *and* sexuality), see Gopinath, *Impossible Desires*; and Puar, *Terrorist Assemblages*.

58. This point is particularly driven home by the overlapping essays on the relevance of state heterosexualization, white gay capital, and neoimperial service economies to contemporary queer (and feminist, postcolonial, and race-critical) critiques in Alexander, *Pedagogies of Crossing*.

59. Gayatri Chakravorty Spivak, "Terror: A Speech after 9-11," *boundary 2* 31 (2004): 81–111, esp. 81 and 93, in contrast to 96–97, and 101.

To a Black Student in First-Year Hebrew

Nyasha Junior

Introduction

I believe that plans for the transformation of graduate biblical education should include the recruitment, retention, and launching of the successful careers of racial and ethnic minority students. In my experience, efforts to recruit minority students concentrate on encouraging students to apply to doctoral programs in biblical studies, but often these efforts do not provide students with an understanding of the hazards involved in entering this field.

My grandmother used to say, "Dancers don't have pretty feet." That is, everything has a price. In this essay I seek to inform prospective recruits of the potential difficulties in entering and successfully exiting a doctoral program in biblical studies. This essay details the things that I would say to a black undergraduate student in first-year Hebrew who intends to pursue a career in biblical studies. It highlights what I wish that someone had told me at that stage, and it provides a more thoughtful version of the usual advice that I give to students at Society of Biblical Literature (SBL) receptions.

My remarks are based on my experiences and observations as a recent graduate of the doctoral program in Old Testament at Princeton Theological Seminary and as a tenure-track assistant professor in the Department of Religious Studies at the University of Dayton. Instead of providing general advice with an aside to minority students, I am directing my comments specifically toward racial/ethnic minority students. I am writing to a black student because I am black and the students who solicit my advice are usually black. I am writing to a first-year Hebrew student because the student who has enrolled in Hebrew has taken a preliminary step toward entering the field. Nevertheless, most of my comments are relevant to nonblack, nonminority, or first-year Greek students as well.

Some readers may object to my tough-love approach. They may contend that black students need to be encouraged and that we need more black faculty in all fields. I would respond by saying that if a student is discouraged by one article, then she should not enter the field. I hope that the future of graduate biblical education includes more racial and ethnic minority students, but I want those students to get in and out of graduate school and to be around for the long run.

My parents instilled in me the principle: "Each one teach one." Usually, this principle applies to the importance of sharing the knowledge that you have acquired, especially with those who have not enjoyed similar opportunities. In this case, I have modified the principle: "Each one alert the others." My primary aim is to recruit students. This is my chosen profession. I love what I do, and I would like to see other blacks entering the field. Nevertheless, my route "ain't been no crystal stair," and I would be remiss if I did not seek to warn others who are considering this path. I will provide seven key points of advice for a hypothetical black student who seeks to enter biblical studies. These include:

- ► Learn more about the academy.
- ► Explore the field of biblical studies.
- ► Research doctoral programs.
- ► Seek advice from faculty.
- ► Seek advice from students.
- ► Plan your exit.
- ► Examine your motivations.

Learn More about the Academy

You have experienced higher education as a student, but now you need to find out about the lives of faculty. From your perspective, professors teach a few classes and hold office hours once or twice a week. Otherwise, they exist in a state of suspended animation until the next class meeting. You need to learn how the other half lives. Educate yourself about faculty research, teaching, and service requirements. Learn the lingo. Become familiar with terms such as adjunct, tenure-track, ABD, CC, SLAC, and 4-4. Start reading higher-education journals such as the *Chronicle of Higher Education* and *Diverse Issues in Higher Education*. Read reputable websites and blogs devoted to academic affairs. For example, check out *Inside Higher Ed* and Tomorrow's Professor. Look at the Council of Graduate Schools website and its Ph.D. Completion Project. Also, see the American Association of University Professors website and its annual salary survey (see the suggested reading section below for a list of resources). Higher education is an industry: if you plan to seek employment in this industry, you need to learn more about it, just as if you were seeking employment in the automotive or health care industries. You can no longer think of it as "school."

Explore the Field of Biblical Studies

You may have a limited view of biblical studies based on one or two Bible courses and your interaction with faculty at your current institution. Now is the time to learn about the wider field and to gain a sense of the diversity of the field. Subscribe to the *Review of Biblical Literature* newsletter and start perusing peer-reviewed biblical studies journals such as the *Journal of Biblical Literature, Biblical Interpretation,* and *Catholic Biblical Quarterly.* Scan the table of contents to see what catches your eye and read the abstracts of articles that interest you.

Attend the Regional SBL Meeting in your area and the SBL Annual Meeting. Go to as many sessions as you can. If finances do not permit your attendance at a meeting, borrow a copy of the SBL abstracts and program book. Note the range of things that people do. You will not find everything interesting, but you can determine if you are getting excited about joining some of these conversations. Ask yourself, "Is this my tribe?"

You may think of biblical studies, religion, theology, and other fields as blending together. You should be aware that biblical studies is a separate field. It is text-based and divided into two main segments: Old Testament/Hebrew Bible (OT/HB) and New Testament/Christian origins (NT/CO). Scholars with degrees in related fields such as Near Eastern languages and civilizations or Judaic studies may work alongside of biblical scholars and even teach Bible courses, but those fields are not typically understood as biblical studies.

Before you commit to biblical studies check out our colleagues on the other side of the aisle in the American Academy of Religion (AAR). See the AAR program book and flip through the *Journal of the American Academy of Religion* to determine if you are still interested in the SBL side. Note that some biblical scholars conduct multidisciplinary research that crosses AAR-SBL lines. Nevertheless, often these scholars developed or pursued these interests after the successful completion of their doctoral studies and in some cases after receiving tenure. For example, New Testament scholar Vincent Wimbush directs the Institute for Signifying Scriptures at the Claremont Graduate University. He conducts and facilitates multidisciplinary research on the importance and role of scripture within reading communities, but his 1983 Harvard University dissertation was titled "Ὡς μή: Paul's Use of an Expression in the Context of Understandings of 'World' in Early Christianity (1 Cor 7:29–35)." In other words, it may take years before you can engage in the kind of exciting work that more established scholars can. If you are certain that you are interested in combining interests and investigating topics like film and Bible, ethics and Bible, or hip hop and Bible, you may wish to consider applying to programs in those areas rather than to biblical studies programs.

Research Doctoral Programs

If you are still interested in pursuing doctoral biblical studies, as a first step, you must decide if you are leaning toward OT/HB or NT/CO. Then, start to compile a short list of programs that you want to consider. You are not looking simply for brand name schools. Ask your professors for the names of top-tier programs that have a good placement record. Your professors will differ on the ranking of those programs, but the same few programs are usually on everyone's list. If you have particular requirements or restrictions, you may need to add additional programs to the list.

Investigate the programs on your initial list. Programs differ greatly in terms of admissions requirements, financial support, program requirements, and faculty specialization. Study the websites for these programs. Look at the CVs of the biblical studies faculty to determine where they received their doctoral degrees. Consider adding some of these programs to your list. Make a grid with key elements for each program and determine which programs interest you most.

One central question to ask is if you are a good "fit." In part, this means that your interests fit with what the program offers and specifically with the interests of some of its faculty. For example, if you are interested in postmodernism and postcolonial hermeneutics, you will not fit well with a program that focuses on archaeology and ancient Israelite history and religion. You may be a good candidate, but you have to be a great candidate for a particular program. The admissions committee wants to know that you have done your due diligence and that you are interested in what its program offers.

Seek Advice from Faculty

You need some good advice, and you are probably not getting it right now. In my experience, black students who express interest in pursuing doctoral studies receive encouragement from all quarters. Professors who have taught you, teaching assistants who have graded your work, and classmates who know of your outstanding academic performance beam enthusiastically when you mention that you are thinking of pursuing doctoral studies. You do not need this pat on the head. In fact, you should be wary of this.

At a cocktail party a couple of years ago, I mentioned a particular black M.Div. student who was interested in applying to doctoral programs in biblical studies. Those who had taught him and interacted with him agreed that he was a mediocre and overconfident student who would have difficulty in gaining admission to a program, especially given his lack of language training. Despite this consensus, one senior scholar explained that he would never discourage a racial/ethnic minority student under any circumstances regardless of his assessment of the student's potential. He feared being labeled as a racist if he offered anything other than encouragement.

I was fortunate to receive discouragement from my first Hebrew professor. When I told him that I wanted to pursue a Ph.D. in Hebrew Bible, he asked, "Are you independently wealthy?" When I replied in the negative, he said, "Then, I don't recommend it." He wanted to end the conversation there, but I pressed him to tell me what he would tell someone who was determined to do it anyway. Eventually, he told me about the challenges of successfully completing a doctoral program and the difficulties of landing a tenure-track job. Another professor who taught Old Testament did not encourage or discourage. Instead, he began to list the things that I needed in order to be a competitive applicant, including language requirements, GPA expectations, and GRE scores. He told me if I did not gain admission to and receive full funding from a top-tier program, then I should pack up my BDB and find something else to do. I was sobered but determined.

To obtain good advice, find the faculty member who you know is willing to kill the dream. You are thinking of this person right now because she is the one person whose advice you do not want. Find a professor who will tell you the cold hard truth. Ideally, that person should be a biblical scholar, but it is more important to find someone that you trust to tell you the truth. Share your current transcript and GRE scores (if available). Talk about your current interests and plans to apply to programs. If you are applying soon, ask "What are my chances of gaining admission to programs?" or "How would you rate my current academic preparedness?" Ideally, if you are a few years away from applying, ask "What can I do to be a competitive applicant?" Of course, one can overcome the odds, but most folks in academia have a pretty good idea of what will cut it and what will not. At the NFL Combine, a potential player who runs the 40-yard dash in 6.0 will not secure a running back position. Sure, there are exceptions, but you should be realistic about your application.

Seek Advice from Students

Faculty members have a wealth of experience, but often, they have forgotten or repressed their memories of graduate school. Talk to those with their boots on the ground. If you do not have access to graduate students in biblical studies at your current institution, make sure that you attend the SBL Regional and Annual Meetings. At the Annual Meeting, attend the student orientation and the women's student orientation (if you are a woman). Also, attend receptions for racial/ethnic minorities and sessions that focus on racial/ethnic minority hermeneutics. Even if you are not interested in that session, you will have an opportunity to talk to a number of racial/ethnic minority faculty and students in one place. Introduce yourself and explain your interests and plans. If possible, use a snowball approach and ask someone with whom you have a good conversation to introduce to you to other faculty and/or students. Do not limit yourself to seeking advice from racial/ethnic minority faculty and students. I have found that most people are more than happy to offer their advice.

Find students who are one, two, and three steps ahead of you. The steps will vary depending on whether you are a masters student, an undergraduate, or an undergraduate who will pursue a masters before applying to doctoral programs. For example, if you are a first-year M.Div. student, find an M.Div. senior who is applying to or has recently been accepted to a doctoral biblical studies program; find a doctoral student in coursework; and find a doctoral student who is taking exams. Of course, it will be useful to talk to any student in one of the programs to which you plan to apply, but you should make sure that you cover your bases with these three types of students.

Using this scenario, ask the student who is one step ahead of you what he has learned about the application process. To which programs did he apply and why? Which language courses and Bible courses has he taken? What advice would he offer about the application process? Ask the student who is two steps ahead what she learned about the admissions game and getting started. To which programs did she apply and to which programs did she gain admission? Why did she choose her current program? Which courses is she taking now? How has she handled the transition to doctoral student? For the student who is three steps ahead of you, ask about his coursework experiences. Which exams is he taking? Did he have a choice of exams? How does he feel about his decision to enter this program? How long will it take to complete the program?

If you develop a good rapport with some students, ask them about some of the personal costs of graduate school. Graduate school is tough in any field, but anecdotally, biblical studies is more difficult partly because language requirements tend to increase time to completion. You do not need to ask personal questions. Instead, ask about what she has seen among colleagues. Any typical cohort of students may experience divorce, staggering debt, chronic depression, eating disorders, or substance abuse. The toll on family members may be even greater. One professor advised me that one of the keys to successful graduate studies is having a family that thrives on neglect.

Talk to as many students as you can. Recognize that even students in the same program have different experiences of that program. For instance, a male professor may meet male graduate students at his home office and offer them a beer while they discuss the NBA playoffs and possible proposal topics. That same professor may meet female graduate students in the school cafeteria and talk only about work-related matters. One dissertation advisor may provide advisees with a mentoring relationship that includes job-hunting advice and invitations to Sunday dinner, while another advisor may know nothing more personal about her advisees than their email addresses. Also, single students may feel comradeship by working together in late-night study groups, while married students in the same program may experience isolation by working alone at home after putting their kids to bed.

Black students who talk to me are often in their third year of the M.Div. before they begin to consider applying to doctoral programs. This is rather late in the game. If you follow my recommended steps, you can determine if and how you should proceed. As well, often black students tell me of their desire to enter biblical studies due to encouragement that they have received from faculty. Here is some advice: a star college quarterback is not necessarily a star NFL quarterback. The pro game has a different pace with different challenges and demands. Likewise, a great undergraduate/masters student is not necessarily a good candidate for doctoral biblical studies. You may have earned an A on a final Hebrew exam or on an exegesis paper. You are probably out-performing your current classmates and may have received some attention and affirmation from your professors. Get over it. A high GPA and a "great job" and smiley face on your paper do not necessarily indicate that you are ready for doctoral biblical studies. You will have to elevate your current A-game significantly.

Graduate school is not a warm, welcoming, and affirming experience. You are not a beautiful and unique snowflake. I have not experienced any overt racial or gender discrimination in classroom settings; instead, most students that I know would agree that professors are equal opportunity torturers. One of my former professors makes *American Idol*'s Simon Cowell look like Mister Rogers. No one will ask you to journal your feelings about a text. Your colleagues and professors will critique your writing and ideas in public. One professor said of a colleague's paper, "It was like modern art—interesting but ultimately unintelligible." As such, you must develop a thick skin.

Faculty will brag about the star student who graduated in record time, published an award-winning dissertation, and wrote a best-selling novel in her free time after putting her triplets to bed. That will not be you. Instead, listen when students tell you about the phantom of the program. Almost every program has one. He is a ninth-, twelfth-, or fifteenth-year student who is seen on campus almost as often as an ivory-billed woodpecker. You want to hear the horror stories about exam failure, proposal rejection, loss of financial aid, the death of an advisor, and fighting among dissertation committee members. Of course, some of the details have been exaggerated, but you need to be scared out of your mind before you sign up for this.

Plan Your Exit

Many couples focus so much on the details of the wedding that they neglect to think through key issues that will face the marriage that follows. Similarly, many students focus on gaining admission to a graduate program without thinking about the career that follows. Most biblical studies jobs are posted online in the SBL Career Center. Read the postings to get a sense of the job market in biblical studies. Think about the type of institution where you would like to work. Recognize that you may not land at a place similar to your doctoral institution. For example, I received my Ph.D. from a Presbyterian seminary, but I teach at a Catholic university. Do you want to teach at a small, church-affiliated college in the Bible Belt or at a seminary that has and welcomes openly gay and lesbian students? Do you want to teach at a large state school or at a historically black college or university? Are you willing to sign a statement of faith or to abide by a morals clause? Are you prepared to live in a town without an airport?

After earning your doctoral degree, you may have difficulties in landing a job, especially a tenure-track position. Those difficulties are compounded if you choose to limit your search to particular types of schools or to specific geographic locations. Are you prepared to move multiple times if you do not secure a tenure-track position initially or if you do not find a desirable tenure-track position? Will your spouse/partner be able to find a job nearby? If single, will you find suitable partners on the local dating scene? If you have children, how will this process affect them? If you do not have children and intend to do so, how will this affect your plans to start a family? I do not know anyone who has a happy home life, a great publishing record, and stellar teaching evaluations. I have only a couple of colleagues who have two of the three.

If you secure a position, you may teach outside of areas in which you were trained. Often, junior faculty members teach introductory or general education courses regardless of specialty. I teach three courses each semester. I teach two sections of Introduction to Religion, a required first-year general education course. I also teach one undergraduate or masters-level course in Hebrew Bible. I do not teach biblical languages, and since almost none of my students have studied Hebrew or Greek, my Hebrew Bible classes are taught in translation. My department does not offer doctoral courses in biblical studies.

Are you willing to teach Old or New Testament or Bible survey courses after spending years learning the languages and methodologies used in your specialization? Are you willing to teach courses such as World Religions or Death and Dying? As a black faculty member, how will you respond if asked to teach liberation theology, Civil Rights history, or Afro-American religion? Some search committees and colleagues may assume that you can and desire to teach African-American hermeneutics and that you will become a mentor to black students. In a job interview one administrator asked me, "How will you help our African American students who need support in ministerial formation?" I responded, "I thought that this was a Hebrew Bible position." I did not get the job.

EXAMINE YOUR MOTIVATIONS

Think about why you want to do this. Are you interested in being Dr. So-and-So? Do want to become a public intellectual who appears on National Public Radio or Tavis Smiley? Do you want to wear a suit and bowtie and talk to a captive audience twice a week in wood-paneled lecture halls? Do you want a cameo film appearance like Cornel West in *The Matrix Reloaded* and *The Matrix Revolutions*? Are you trying to outdo your sister the cardiologist or your brother-in-law the investment banker? Are you trying to avoid getting a "real" job? Are you working out your daddy issues? Figure out what motivates you now and determine if entering biblical studies is the best way to get what it is that you really want.

Often, black students who express interest in biblical studies tell me of their desire to bridge the church-academy divide. They took one course by an exceptional biblical scholar and armed with a little knowledge, they desire to bring scholarly biblical tools to the folks in the pew. They tell me of their commitment to remaining involved in the local church during their doctoral programs and to supporting their church educational efforts. I am not, however, convinced that these motivations are enough to sustain a student through a multi-year doctoral program. Maybe your Sunday school classes were a formative part of your development. Perhaps you enjoy teaching Bible study. Do you love biblical studies enough to reconstruct hypothetical Proto-Semitic forms, vocalize Ugaritic, and recite Syriac paradigms on demand? You can study Bible without entering biblical studies as a profession. Are you certain that this path will lead you to where you want to go? During coursework, my colleagues outside of biblical studies would tease when they saw me reading Hebrew from my *BHS*. They would say, "Girl, the Bible has already been translated! I have a Bible in English right here. Why are you wasting time with that?!" Is that you? Ask yourself, "Do I want to engage in academic biblical scholarship?"

REFLECTIONS

Despite the horrors of graduate school, the highly competitive job market, and my hectic rookie year as a faculty member, I am glad that I entered and successfully exited graduate school. I love my teaching and research as a biblical scholar. I realized how fortunate I am when I talked to my grandfather soon after I moved to Dayton, Ohio. I have family in nearby Cincinnati. My grandfather was planning to visit them and expressed an interest in coming to Dayton. I told him that I taught on Tuesdays and Thursdays and would be free for long weekends. He looked down at his feet for a few seconds and bashfully asked, "Do you think that they will put you on full-time at some point?" I laughed and hugged him as I explained that I did, indeed, have a full-time job. To many of my family members who engage in hourly work, it is important to work as many hours as possible and to get as much overtime as you can. To my grandfather, teaching twice a week could not possibly be a full-time job. I am fortunate to do what I love and to get paid for it. It would be nice to have some company along the way.

Suggested Resources

American Academy of Religion: http://www.aarweb.org/.
American Academy of University Professors: http://www.aaup.org/aaup/.
Fund for Theological Education: http://www.fteleaders.org/.
Review of Biblical Literature: http://www.bookreviews.org.
Society of Biblical Literature: http://www.sbl-site.org/.
Inside Higher Ed: http://www.insidehighered.com/.
Tomorrow's Professor Blog: http://amps-tools.mit.edu/tomprofblog/.
Council of Graduate Schools: http://www.cgsnet.org/.
Avalos, Hector. *The End of Biblical Studies*. Amherst, N.Y.: Prometheus, 2007.
Bailey, R. C. "Academic Biblical Interpretation among African Americans in the United States." Pages 696–711 in *African Americans and the Bible: Sacred Texts and Social Textures*. Edited by Vincent L. Wimbush. New York: Continuum, 2001.
Brown, Michael J. *What They Don't Tell You: A Survivor's Guide to Biblical Studies*. Louisville: Westminster John Knox, 2000.
Harris, Trudier. "Mind Work: How a Ph.D. Affects Black Women." *The Chronicle of Higher Education* 49.31 (11 April 2003): B14. Online: http://chronicle.com/free/v49/i31/31b01401.htm.
hooks, bell, and Cornel West. *Breaking Bread: Insurgent Black Intellectual Life*. Boston: South End, 1991.
Hunt, Mary E. *A Guide for Women in Religion: Making Your Way from A to Z*. New York: Palgrave McMillan, 2004.
Toth, Emily. *Ms. Mentor's New and Ever More Impeccable Advice for Men and Women in Academia*. Philadelphia: University of Pennsylvania Press, 2008.
Wilson, Shari. "Love In (and Out of) Academe." *Inside Higher Ed* (28 November 2005). Online: http://insidehighered.com/views/2005/11/28/wilson.

Intoxicating Teaching as Transformational Pedagogy

Wil Gafney

Introduction

Engaged pedagogy does not seek simply to empower students. Any classroom that employs a holistic model of learning will also be a place where teachers grow, and are empowered by the process.[1]

The transformation of individuals, communities and institutions is one of the primary goals of feminist pedagogy and, thus, my own teaching in particular. In the essay that follows, I will articulate one black feminist pedagogy for Hebrew biblical studies in a seminary context. This essay reflects my teaching practices as I envision and intend them; there may be some dissonance in the ways in which they are experienced.

My Contexts

My teaching context is one of the theological seminaries of the Evangelical Lutheran Church in America (ELCA), but I am an Episcopal priest who also belongs to a Reconstructionist (Jewish) minyan. As a non-Lutheran and lacking white and male privileges, I am on the margins of the seminary faculty and our larger teaching-learning community. At the same time, I hold hierarchical academic and class privileges. Based on the identities of my fellow faculty members and my students, one might think that I do not teach in a black context. However, I am black, descended from enslaved persons in the Americas, and I carry my blackness with me into the classroom. There, my ancestral

---

1. bell hooks, *Teaching to Transgress: Education as the Practice of Freedom* (New York: Routledge, 1994), 21.

and cultural contexts intersect with the cultural and ancestral contexts of my students, namely, the contexts of the dominant culture, African American, African immigrant, Afro-Caribbean, Asian American and European immigrant cultures.

The aspect of my cultural context that most significantly shapes my teaching is my religious formation in the black church. African American Christianity shares with the wider black church a deep devotion to the biblical text; this devotion is frequently expressed as literalism or in claims of inerrancy. I am mindful of these claims, having been partially formed by them and in response do quite a bit of close work with the text; this demonstrates my love of and respect for the text even while I unravel some of its claims and foundations, for deconstruction is never the goal. My aim is to draw student-learners more deeply into the text and its contexts than is easily facilitated by surface readings. To do this, I engage the text as a primary conversation partner, at the center of the shared teaching-learning space and position secondary scholarship in a secondary posture distinct from the text which holds so much authority for the communities represented in the room. This treatment of the text facilitates conversations that include literalist, feminist, womanist, and queer readings in the same space.[2] The biblical text is the starting place in my pedagogy because of the value(s) ascribed to it by students, scholars, religious communities and its continuing role in the wider public discourse.

Teaching Paradigm

"I will lead you and I will bring you to the house of my mother—how she teaches me! I will have you drink from the spiced wine, essence of my pomegranates." (Song 8:2)[3]

"How-she-teaches-me!"[4] *Telammdeni*! This single word in the Songs of Songs is evocative of the feminist pedagogy in biblical studies in a theological context that I will explore in this essay. Specifically, the Song reference provides a paradigm for exploring feminist pedagogy and practitioners, its content and context.

The teacher and her disciple in the Song are on the margins in the canon. The Song is exceptional in its sensual language and dominant women's voices.

---

2. One aspect of my teaching is critical analysis of language, my own and that of others. This means that I do not use normatively language that insists on a male god, i.e., "theology" to the exclusion of other constructions and portrayals, i.e., "theaology."
3. All translations are mine unless otherwise indicated.
4. I translate the one Hebrew word with four conjoined English words.

These exceptional characteristics may have led to the Song's exile to the margins of the scriptures, particularly in lectionary cycles and contributed to the Jewish and Christian practice of reading the Song normatively as an allegory. In those readings the Song is (and only) about the love between God and Israel or the love between Christ and the church and not about the love sexually expressed between two human persons. These allegorical readings answer an unarticulated question: How could a text about women, wine and song be scripture? And what does such a text reveal about transformational feminist pedagogy?

The teacher and her disciple in the Song are women. As a woman who teaches, I am drawn to this image here and elsewhere.[5] As a feminist scholar, I look for more than gender when assessing a text for feminist or womanist implications. Obviously, not all women's teaching is feminist, and feminine gender is not a prerequisite for transformative teaching. Both the pedagogue and the learner referred to in Song 8:2 are women. Like these characters, I myself am a woman, but this alone does not qualify my teaching as "feminist." What, then, does make Song 8:2 paradigmatic for my feminist pedagogy? The form of the verb inspires me.

The Song is a series of poems full of wordplay and love-play replete with images that delight the senses and inspire the imagination: wine and perfume, flowers and trees, gazelles, goats and a garden, fabric and thread, crimson and purple. The descriptions build upon one another lavishly seemingly unconcerned about the coherence of the final picture. The beauty of the lovers is extolled through a series of similes that when juxtaposed do not resemble any living human being—desirable or otherwise.

My reading is likewise poetic and (neo-) midrashic, building upon the words and the images they create in the spirit of rabbinic exegesis, beginning with the letters, their jots and tittles. The verb, *l-m-d*, means "learn" in the *qal* conjugation and "teach" in the *piel*. It is *piel* in its form in Song 8:2.

The *piel* stem can indicate intensive, declarative, denominative, or causative actions and can be thought of as bringing about the state of being articulated in the verbal root, in this case learning.[6] I am choosing the results-oriented aspect of the *piel* stem here to read that the woman is not *merely* teaching but *truly* teaching.

---

5. See also Jer 9:19–20, where women teach women funerary songs for what I argue is a prophetic performance in *Daughters of Miriam: Women Prophets in Ancient Israel* (Minneapolis: Fortress, 2008), 19–123, 159–60.

6. Bruce K. Waltke and Michael Patrick O'Connor, *An Introduction to Biblical Hebrew Syntax* (Winona Lake, Ind.: Eisenbrauns, 1990), 396–417. Here Waltke acknowledges the overlap with the *hiphil*, which is beyond the scope of this treatment.

The *qal* conjugation is the most simple form of the verb in terms of spelling (vowel changes), prefixes, and suffixes and is also simple in meaning, expressing simple, active (versus passive) action. Of note in this reading, the *qal* serves as the foundational paradigm for verb conjugation in Biblical Hebrew. It is a type of foundation stone on which the entire verb structure is built. This is in keeping with the way the verbs are understood, taught and learned in Hebrew; the system is called a *binyan*, a building.

In this playful, poetic reading, ordinary but significant—foundational—teaching is designated by the *qal* stem, indicating simplicity and lightness. *Piel* teaching is transformational, building on that foundation, bringing about the desired result articulated by the root, learning, so that "How-she-teaches-me!" can be understood as "Truly-she-teaches-me!" In this case, "truly" does not mean that there is some mystic truth only available to feminists but evokes the type of consciousness raising frequently present in feminist learning environments.

The image of the verb paradigms as a building will be paradigmatic for feminist teaching, in my reading. That is, holding a faculty appointment in biblical studies, designing courses, writing syllabi, and instructing students is foundational teaching or *qal* teaching. Feminist pedagogy is an entirely different level of teaching, frequently building on and expanding canonical configurations of knowledge, with transformation of the student, teacher, learning community and constructions of knowledge as goals. Sometimes feminist teaching and learning begins with demolition or ground-clearing before constructing a new paradigm. Other times feminist teaching and learning recycles and reuses the building blocks of former constructions of knowledge.

Depending on which translation one reads, the woman's teaching may be replaced with birth-giving, (see NRSV "one who bore me" and NJPS "her who taught me") due to divergent manuscript traditions and the different weight accorded them by translation committees. Ironically, exercising one's reproductive prerogatives in the academy can also lead to a female pedagogue being redefined as "mother" versus "teacher." However, the teaching-woman in the Song is described as both "mother" *and* "teacher" in the text.[7] In this essay the mother-teacher is the feminist pedagogue and the daughter-disciple is the student (see Jer 9:19–20 for another example of this model).

---

7. The use of the parent/child metaphor to indicate a subject matter expert and/or professional practitioner in relationship to an apprentice is a common one in the Hebrew Bible. See my discussion of father/son, as in the "sons/children" or, better, "disciples" of the prophets, in *Daughters of Miriam*, 4, 38–41, 75–117, 119–23.

This teaching in the Song takes place in the larger context of blackness. In the continental context, biblical Israel connects Africa and Asia. In the narrative context, the daughter/disciple is black, as black as the hair of Kedari goats, with a sunburn, complicating and enhancing her blackness (Song 1:5–6). In the wider literary and canonical contexts, this teaching takes place in the formative space that produced a variety of ancestral and contemporary Judaisms and Christianities.

This intensive teaching takes place in the woman's own space, her house. There is no other authority figure in her house—neither patriarch nor kyriarch.[8] She is sovereign in her own space. The woman's teaching space is situated in a larger androcentric context—the Hebrew Scriptures. Her feminist teaching space survives and thrives in androcentrism, and some would argue patriarchy. I should note here that I am not the first scholar to read this woman's teaching as situated in a theological context. The Zohar, the primary mystical text of rabbinic Judaism, understands the teaching space to be the Holy of Holies (*Chelek Beit amud* 257b). The rabbinic commentary on the Song of Songs understands the space to be Sinai (*Midrash Rabbah Shir Hashirim* 8:2).

The content of the teaching in this paradigm is spiced wine and essence of pomegranate; together they are delicious, nutritious, and ultimately transformational, representing two types of knowledge construction in my reading. Spiced wine is fermented, requiring time to produce. "Spiced wine knowledge" is ancestral, traditional knowledge, passed down for generations like family recipes. The intoxicating effect of fermentation suggests the intoxicating effect of transformational learning. Essence of pomegranate is fresh squeezed juice. "Pomegranate knowledge" is contemporary, recent and perhaps even radical (pomegranate juice is full of free radicals touted for a variety of beneficial effects in popular culture). These two elixirs, encompassing old and new knowledge production, form a hendiadys, a metaphor for all knowledge production and construction from ancient to innovative. The two elixirs are combined into one delicious, nutritious and intoxicating cocktail. Returning to my earlier metaphor, the two types of construction, foundation and elaboration, produce a new structure.

The final, or perhaps keystone, aspect of this teaching is its transformational nature. The internalization of the teaching—consumption of spiced wine and pomegranate juice—is ultimately transformative. The consumption, internalization of nutrients, leads to a number of transformational processes: the human organism is nourished, strengthened and fueled for spiritual,

---

8. Elisabeth Schüssler Fiorenza, "Feminist/Women Priests—An Oxymoron?" *New Women, New Church* 18.3 (1995): 10–13.

intellectual and physical activity. Building components are also transformed in the construction process. There is a necessary transformation that takes a construction project from completion to use: infrastructure, connectivity and décor to name a few. Good feminist pedagogy is truly transformational teaching, enabling students to connect the knowledge they are constructing to the larger word, building on the legacy of the teachers and learners who proceeded them even when they dismantle their/our structures and celebrating their empowerment and agency with all the passion of the lovers in the Song.

I identify strongly with this African woman who lives, loves, and teaches passionately in the Song. She teaches only one woman-disciple in the Song, but ultimately instructs generations of students in ancient, traditional knowledge and innovative constructions of knowledge from a marginal place within the sacred literature of Judaism and Christianity. In the Song, the daughter-disciple is a radical militant feminist. She speaks for herself and of her own desires, particularly her sexual desires, which she pursues in the face of physical violence. Her text, spoken in her voice and the voices of her women friends—together their speaking parts out-number male voices in the Song—has transformed the way readers and hearers think about women, men, gender, sex, sexuality, relationality, scripture and God in the biblical and contemporary worlds. The lessons learned and taught have led to some women and men speaking, acting, writing, teaching and preaching in new and different ways leading to transformational opportunities in congregations and the theological academy.

A Transformational Feminist Pedagogy: Spiced Wine and Pomegranate Essence

I will use examples from some of my classes to demonstrate what I hope are transformational teaching practices, framed by the teaching paradigm I have elicited from the Song.[9] Before students enter the classroom we will share for any subject, they are assigned, "Writing on Water: The Ineffable Name of God." In Bos's essay students confront the anti-Semitic and anti-Judaistic underpinnings and implications of Christian and Gentilic scholarship that seeks to articulate a spelling and pronunciation of the name of God.[10] Bos argues convincingly that "the full vocalization of the Tetragrammaton par-

---

9. The examples are drawn from M.Div. and M.A.R. curriculum courses: Introduction to Biblical Hebrew; Introduction to the Scriptures of Israel; Exodus in African and African American Exegesis; and Heroines, Harlots and Handmaids: The Women of the Hebrew Scriptures.

10. Johannah van Wijk-Bos, "Writing on Water: The Ineffable Name of God," in *Jews,*

takes of the 'teaching of contempt' that is an aspect of the hatred of the Jews that made the Shoah possible," by exploring the overlap between the chronology and location of the dominant school of historical biblical criticism and the theologies and social constructions that contributed to the Shoah.[11] Those of us who self-identify as Christian "After Auschwitz" can never allow ourselves to forget that the Shoah, the Holocaust, was perpetrated in Christian lands by baptized hands.[12] One manifestation of this self-understanding as a Christian teaching-learning community is that we wrestle with the ways in which many authors we read name God.[13] As a Christian teaching Hebrew Bible in a Christian context, I intentionally engage in a post-Shoah pedagogy informed by Bos and Irving Greenberg, who makes the point more forcefully: "no statement, theological or otherwise should be made that would not be credible in the presence of the burning children."[14]

We start in this difficult place to eradicate the notion that biblical studies (or any other academic discourse) is neutral, benign, or even historically virtuous. Specifically, we reflect on the timing of the emergence of historically critical biblical scholarship, at the end of the nineteenth and beginning of the twentieth centuries. We consider the location of the emergence of critical biblical scholarship, Europe, particularly in France and Germany. And we take seriously the concomitant rise of theologically fueled anti-Semitic and anti-Judaistic ideologies that swept Europe at that time. Since I teach in a Lutheran context, we celebrate Lutheran resistance to fascist theologies and exegesis as we confront Martin Luther's own anti-Semitism—now rejected by the church that bears his name—and its legacy in contemporary biblical studies and theology that has spread beyond Europe and a single reformational ecclesiology. We also consider the role of biblical studies in the Trans-Atlantic slave trade, colonization, and discrimination against women and sexual minorities.

My next practice in the classroom is to simultaneously demystify the biblical text as a text and to mystify the biblical text as scripture. In this process, the fundamental learning objectives are to explore the notion of *text* in, through, beyond and apart from written or printed material while explicating

---

Christians and the Theology of the Hebrew Scriptures (ed. Alice O. Bellis and Joel S. Kaminsky; SBLSymS 8; Atlanta: Society of Biblical Literature, 2000).

11. Ibid., 49.

12. Johannah van Wijk-Bos, *Making Wise the Simple: The Torah in Christian Faith and Practice* (Grand Rapids: Eerdmans, 2005), xviii.

13. For example, see Frank Frick, *A Journey through the Hebrew Scriptures* (Belmont, Calif.: Thompson Wadsworth), 2003.

14. Irving Greenberg, "Judaism, Christianity, and Partnership after the Twentieth Century," in *Christianity in Jewish Terms* (ed. Tikvah Frymer-Kensky et al.; Boulder, Colo.: Westview, 2000), 27.

the processes necessary to sanctify a text as scripture. Given that the classroom in my teaching practice is ostensibly a Christian theological space—occasionally shared with Jews—we think through such categories as revelation, transmission, preservation and canonization of that which has become (or been declared) *scripture*, focusing on human participation in those processes. In introductory classes, I teach first and second-year students together; the first-year students are taking their initial theology course at the same time. It is important for them to think through the assumptions they hold about the Bible while being given a framework to do so safely. The second-year students have had a year to think about theological meaning-making processes and usually a year of New Testament. While much of my initial teaching is familiar to them, they are surprised by canonical fluidity, as this is not how they were introduced to the Greek New Testament. This mystification/demystification process is also essential in upper-level classes because of the variety of introductions to the study of scripture that students have experienced, and as a refresher for those students who may have left complicated notions of text behind when they left introductory biblical studies classrooms behind one or two years ago.

We demystify *the Bible* as a singular, religious, and cultural icon. There are Jewish Bibles, the order of the books vary with Chronicles either opening or closing the final section, and yet neither of these canons are canonical in Samaritan Judaism which only recognizes the Torah as scripture. There are Christian Bibles, there are Protestant Bibles, there are Catholic Bibles and Orthodox Bibles that all vary in content and length and also in authority of source material—Hebrew Bible, Greek Septuagint, Latin Vulgate, Aramaic Peshitta. The transformation sought in this step is the troubling of the notion that there is a common understanding of the terms *scripture* and *Bible* and the recognition that an individual's understanding is not shared by others in the world, in the religion, in the denomination, in the seminary, or even in the classroom.

The current exercise I employ to achieve this aim, in part, is to send students to the library to copy and bring to class the tables of contents from a variety of Bibles: any New Revised Standard Version (NRSV), Jewish Publication Society Tanakh (NJPS), 1611 King James Version (KJV) reprint or facsimile, the Douay-Rheims Bible (DRB), Jerusalem Bible (JB), and Leningrad Codex (LC/MT) facsimile. It is essential for the students to get their hands on these varying collections of scripture to see biblical books that they did not know existed presented without apology or explanation as scripture along with texts that are familiar to them. In the ensuing discussions students begin to describe the biblical canon with which they are familiar as their own without assuming it is shared by their classmates or instructor. I emphasize that the sixty-six-book canon accepted by the ELCA and most other Protestant communions is the most narrow collection of Christian scripture. The majority of Christians (represented by the Roman Catholic and Anglican communions) recognize a seventy-three-book canon, including the long versions of Daniel and Esther.

Having introduced students to the notion that the scriptures are not (and the Bible is not) a single document, text, icon or idea, I invite them to mystify their own relationship to the text. There is in Christianity an appropriative relationship to the biblical text, particularly with regard to the scriptures of Israel, which tempts some Christian readers to think that they either fully know or own the Israelite sacred corpus.[15] ("Scriptures of Israel" is my preferred term because it includes all of the Hebrew, Greek, and Aramaic biblical texts shaped by ancient Israelites in a variety of canonical formations: Masoretic Text, Septuagint, Dead Sea Scrolls, Targumim, etc.) The process of mystification includes articulating how distant are contemporary readers socially, culturally, religiously and geographically from biblical cultures and religions—again, variety and pluralism in the text are illuminated.

I conclude the canon discussion and exercise by inviting the students to borrow a paradigm from classical Christian theology, Incarnation, to frame our study of the scriptures of Israel. I remind them that Yeshua l'Natzeret, Jesus of Nazareth, is described in incarnational theology as being both human and divine: in the gospel, Yeshua is described as the Word. The scriptures are also the Word; they are also human and divine. And, I suggest that each of us will have to come to terms with what that means for us in this class and on an on-going basis, emphasizing that I am also a learner in each course.

Transforming the Biblical Classroom in a Theological Educational Context

I use the geographical and temporal contexts of the biblical text to demonstrate the distance of all contemporary readers from the biblical text itself. In this effort, I employ the disciplinary tools of the biblical guild: historical criticism, archaeology, social/cultural anthropology and, literary and liturgical analysis to illuminate the differences between biblical religions and the living traditions that have evolved from them. The traditions are related, but they are not the same as their ancestral forms.

---

15. Johanna W. H. van Wijk-Bos's caution that "after Auschwitz, it cannot be simply business as usual ... for a Christian approach to the Hebrew Bible" (*Making Wise the Simple*, 10) is a formative one for my teaching.

To this end, we use source theory to discuss the cultural production of the biblical text and contemplate the processes that contribute to the sacralization of text. We use the archaeological record to assess external evidence for biblical claims; this is particularly effective when reading the account of the conquest of Canaan in the book of Joshua, which conflicts with the majority of available archaeological evidence. Frank Frick's presentation of these data is quite useful.[16] We analyze completing and conflicting biblical claims, such as Judges versus Joshua on the arrival of the Israelites in Canaan or Elhanan and David both killing Goliath in separate narratives, to illustrate that conformity of narrative is not privileged in the Israelite scriptures. We use the literature of the ancient Near East to situate Israel in its broader cultural context. We compare and contrast creation and flood stories and legal corpora to gauge interrelatedness and cultural distinctiveness. And, I choose to offer a discipline of prayer and devotion at the beginning of each class; I regularly do so using a *siddur*, prayerbook, from a Jewish tradition. Not only does this time offer a formative spiritual practice, but it also provides a glimpse of the deployment of biblical texts and tropes—and those that have evolved from them—in a religious practice that is not native to our community.

Many of the teaching practices that I articulate above are in classrooms that are not inherently feminist and in many cases have been used in misogynist teaching practices. It is my contention that the tools of scholarship, even though they are produced in antifeminist contexts, are not inherently antifeminist. This is a "spiced wine/pomegranate essence" issue. Malestream discourses can be used to contribute to or even craft feminist knowledge when they are decentered as absolute Truth or value- and culture-free paradigms. In addition they must be integrated into knowledge-production systems that have previously been excluded or marginalized.

One example is my practice of looking beyond the ancient Near East or trajectory of Western scholarship for interpretive tools and practices with which to engage the biblical text. I use a variety of contemporary cultural contexts to read the text, including the philology of African Semitic languages, Asian theologies and religious practices, contemporary and recent American history, film, literature and popular culture.

On the first day of class in Biblical Hebrew, Introduction to the Old Testament, or an elective in a single book such as Exodus, I use maps of Africa and the Sinai Peninsula to underscore the Afro-Asian continental context of the people who spoke this language and produced this literature. We also deconstruct and reject the term "Middle East" and use "West Asian" and "Afro-Asian" normatively. Edwina Wright's article, "The Relationship between

---

16. Frick, *Journey through the Hebrew Scriptures*, 253–55.

Hebrew and African Languages" helps students to see the land, literature, and people in their own geographic and cultural contexts apart from the European and North American contexts through which they previously encountered the biblical text.[17] We reinforce this understanding through slide shows detailing the modern African nations in which Semitic languages are spoken—Mali and Niger (Berber), Kenya, Somalia, Sudan, Ethiopia and Northern Tanzania (the Kushitic linguistic family), Chad, Niger and Nigeria (the Chadic linguistic family), and near the Lake Turkana region of Northern Ethiopia (Omotic).[18]

When introducing Genesis, I use American history and suggest that the beginning of Israel's scriptures was the fall of its successor nation, Judah to the Babylonians in 586 B.C.E., including the destruction of the temple by Nebuchadnezzar, an event that was experienced as theologically incomprehensible. I suggest that Nebuchadnezzar's assault was as unimaginable as—not the events that we remember on September 11, for the towers had been struck previously—but rather as unimaginable as the Japanese assault on Pearl Harbor and as incomprehensible as Japan's ultimate surrender to her own citizens.

When introducing the complex offering system in Leviticus, I remind the students of the geographical context of biblical Israel: the two continents whose nexus form the landmass on which Israel and Canaan are located are Africa and Asia. I posit that the type of care given to deities in the ancient Near East, including ancient Israel, is contiguous with the care given to deities in contemporary Eastern religions. Many of our students have visited a Hindu temple as part of the Prologue to Theological Education at this seminary. I teach that the care and feeding of the Hindu deities has its origin in the same continental culture that gave rise to the offerings in Leviticus.

I maintain that the physicality of the Hindu deities across the ages and the physicality of the deities of the peoples who surrounded Israel have some corollary in the icons with which the God of Israel is associated: bulls, cherubim, the asherah—a sacred tree rooted in the earth, carved to resemble the goddess of the same name. Like icons in Orthodox churches and sancta in many churches, these images are sanctified through invocational prayer. In Hindu terms, they are *enlivened*. Once the spirit of the deity inhabits the object, God is permanently resident in that place. This differs in contemporary Christianity in which God can be invited to reside in a sanctuary that can later be decommissioned and the building used for another purpose. In the broad

---

17. Wright's article is in *The African American Jubilee Edition of the Holy Bible* (ed. Cain Hope Felder; New York: American Bible Society, 1995).

18. I use slides from the Biblical Archaeology Society and philology from Roger S. Woodard, ed., *The Cambridge Encyclopedia of the World's Ancient Languages* (Cambridge: Cambridge University Press, 2004).

ancient and continuing Eastern practice, the habitation of the deity is permanent. I emphasize why the people of a local deity who comes to dwell with them would never be willing to give up that sanctuary or its land.

Also stemming from ancient Near Eastern practice is the feeding of the deity as part of its care. The noncorporeal state of the God of Israel did not prevent consumption. In part, because smoke was not viewed as being substantial, the Israelite God's offerings were immolated to produce a sweet, calming smell (Gen 8:21; Exod 29:18; Lev 26:31; Num 15:3; Deut 4:28). There are numerous texts about the delightful smell of burnt offerings giving God pleasure or the sweet smell of incense that Moses uses to calm God while killing in a rage, as in Num 16:20–50.

These approaches, comparative linguistic studies of African languages, invoking 9/11 and the attacks on Pearl Harbor to frame the production of Genesis, and using Hinduism to explain ritual practices in Leviticus demonstrate the integrative aspect of feminist pedagogy that is not restricted to the classical canons of historical critical biblical studies as configured in the West. A final aspect of the integrative and interdisciplinary work we do collectively in the feminist classroom in a Christian seminary requires using non-Christian religious scholarship normatively to interpret the biblical text. I introduce the students to rabbinic scholarship at every phase of their education and use it as a primary interpretive resource. For example, in my course on Suffering in Job and the Holocaust, we study the genesis and evolution of Jewish critical biblical scholarship, focusing on the scholarship of Rabbi Akiva, Saadia Gaon, Moses Maimonides, and Levi ben Gerson (Gersonides).[19]

Textual analysis in the classroom space that I facilitate takes the biblical text very seriously as a meaning-making icon. I offer a three-step interpretive framework that I describe as "simple, but not easy." (1) What does the text say? This question involves original language-work and conscious acceptance of a particular canon and text as a starting place. (2) What did the text mean in its own context? This is a very difficult step because it simply cannot be done with certainty. This interpretive step provides a concrete space for us as a community of interpreters to articulate and explore our own assumptions about the text and its context. This process also forces us to explain the sources that we privilege, that is, traditional interpretations, theology, comparative religions, biblical languages, archaeology, and so on. (3) What does the text say in our context? We learn together that contemporary meanings assigned to the biblical text do not have to—and frequently do not—replicate ancient meaning or authorial intent—if such a thing could even be identified with certainty. We

---

19. Stephen Vicchio's two volumes, *Job in the Ancient World* and *Job in the Medieval World* (Eugene, Ore.: Wipf & Stock, 2006), are very helpful in this regard.

explore and own our meaning-making systems, accepting their inconsistencies and limitations, while asserting their validity and claiming the biblical text as scripture.

These practices and questions are essential to guide critical thinking in the theological learning community, particularly with regard to the biblical text that many of my students are not prepared to engage in such a fashion. bell hooks' observation that our society is "so fundamentally anti-intellectual" that "critical thinking is not encouraged" is particularly apt in the theological classroom and the congregations which supply seminary classrooms with students.[20] Yet, at the same time, "[t]he classroom, with all its limitations, remains a location of possibility."[21]

We move from that which is presumed to be familiar—although it is my regular finding that my students are unfamiliar with the Hebrew Bible in any detail—we move to ways of thinking about scripture that are new, challenging and occasionally disturbing. I invite my students into conversation with a number of scholars intentionally moving from scholars with whom I expect my students to agree substantially to those whose voices I expect from experience to provoke resistance. Here I will use my teaching on Exodus to illustrate my Africana—a postcolonial, black feminist—approach to teaching Bible in a seminary context.

Beginning with traditional voices in black liberation theology (James Cone, Deotis Roberts, etc.), my students explore the identification of enslaved Africans with the ancient Israelites and the affirmation of the liberating God. We then note Delores Williams's powerful womanist critique of black liberationist approaches to Exodus, "If one reads the Bible identifying with the non-Hebrews who are male and female slave ('the oppressed of the oppressed'), one quickly discerns a nonliberative thread running through the Bible.... There is no clear indication that God is against [the] perpetual enslavement [of non-Jewish people]."[22] I compare Williams's reading with Robert Allen Warrior, who makes this point most forcefully: "Do Native Americans and other indigenous peoples dare trust the same god [of Israel] in their struggle for justice?"[23]

---

20. hooks, *Teaching to Transgress*, 202.
21. Ibid., 207.
22. "Womanist God-Talk and Black Liberation Theology," in her *Sisters in the Wilderness* (Maryknoll, N.Y.: Orbis, 1993), 145–46.
23. "A Native American Perspective: Canaanites, Cowboys and Indians," in *Voices from the Margin: Interpreting the Bible in the Third World* (ed. R. S. Sugirtharajah; Maryknoll, N.Y.: Orbis, 1995), 284.

We also read Musa Dube to explore Israel's progression from oppressed to oppressor. As a postcolonial reader, Dube explores the connections between land and power in the Israelite exodus and in the colonization of Africa, and the biblical warrant for colonization: "For unless the biblical values authorized coming into foreign lands and geographically dispossessing foreign people, such an expansionist program would have been ethically inconceivable for its Western readers."[24] My students explore the dissonance between reading as a diasporized African in America—cut off from one's ancestral land—and reading as a colonized African, dispossessed from one's own land. Musa Dube also demonstrates the importance of gender in postcolonial work through the rubric of "God, gold, glory and gender."[25] The implications of postcolonial feminist reading for Western feminism include the acknowledgement that "both women and men of certain nations participate together in oppressing women and men of distant countries."[26] This complicates feminist analysis, because dominant culture women, who may experience gender-based marginalization, are themselves implicated in the marginalization of colonized women and men.

Next we explore gender in its complexity with regard to the Exodus narrative, using Mona West's "Outsiders, Aliens, and Boundary Crossers: A Queer Reading of the Hebrew Exodus." West explicates a queer reading of Exodus in which the dominant homophobic culture seeks to "deal shrewdly" with LGBT folk in order to annihilate them through "physical violence, hate crimes, and denied access to goods and services."[27] In the same volume, Irene Monroe explores the "endangered black male" hermeneutic applied to Exodus by the Nation of Islam and others, observing that, "Combining the icon of racial suffering and racial liberation into the sole image of the black heterosexual male creates a gendered and sexual construction of black racial victimhood."[28] This in turn gives rise to the theology in some African American Christian and Muslim communities that the black male is "an endangered member in his community who must be saved in order to liberate his entire people," further marginalizing women and sexual minorities in the process of liberation.[29]

---

24. Musa W. Dube Shomanah, *Postcolonial Feminist Interpretation of the Bible* (St. Louis: Chalice, 2000), 16.
25. Ibid., 56ff.
26. Ibid., 20.
27. Mona West, "Outsiders, Aliens, and Boundary Crossers: A Queer Reading of the Hebrew Exodus," in *Take Back the Word: A Queer Reading of the Bible* (ed. Robert Goss and Mona West; Cleveland: Pilgrim, 2000), 73.
28. Irene Monroe, "When and Where I Enter the Whole Race Enters with Me: Que(e)rying Exodus," in Goss and West, *Take Back the Word*, 85.
29. Ibid.

An additional practice of my pedagogy includes focusing on cultural productions of biblical (and quasi-biblical) narratives. I require students to read Octavia Butler's short story "Bloodchild" and Orson Scott Card's novel *Pastwatch: The Redemption of Christopher Columbus* and to watch the *StarTrek: Insurrection* movie. In "Bloodchild," Butler tells the story of earthers who land on an inhabited planet, and unlike the dominant culture science fiction narratives, become marginalized and have to trade their bodies—incubating the larvae of the indigenous population in the bodies of human males—in order to survive. Their "Canaan" is not the Promised Land. In *Pastwatch*, Christopher Columbus's notion of Christianity is expanded—so that he will not see indigenous people as potential slaves—by visitors from the future, including a black woman in the guise of the Holy Spirit, whom he immediately identified as Satan—based on her blackness—but later married. Here the Promised Land of the Americas is also an inhabited Canaan, and the new "Israelites" learn how to get along with their neighbors, forming a new religion, a Christianity in which nonviolence governed empires that were not bent on expansion. And in *StarTrek: Insurrection*, a highly desirable habitation (constructed as a quasi–Promised Land), is almost stolen out from under its inhabitants by the moral authority in the universe (on behalf of another people) until some members of the dominant culture rebel against their leaders and side with the vulnerable. In the end, it is revealed that the would-be conquerors are the kinfolk of the would-be conquered.

I would like to revisit one aspect of my teaching that I mentioned briefly in the description of the Exodus elective: queer biblical interpretation. Feminist pedagogy in biblical studies requires a theological setting that requires "affirm[ing] the full personhood and divine image of all humanity and combat[ing] oppressions—racism, sexism, heterosexism, classism, elitism, imperialism—on multiple fronts in response to the presence and activity of God in the cosmos" as articulated in the scriptures and expressed in the theologies drawn from them.[30] All of my classes include the works by dominant culture and marginalized scholars holding racial, ethnic, gender and sexual minority status.

Virtually all of my classes end by spiraling—not circling, because we never return to the same place—we spiral back to the first lecture goals of the class and shaping questions which we pondered throughout the semester. Revisiting those questions enables us to mark and bear witness to our own individual and communal transformation.

---

30. Wil Gafney, "Hearing the Word—Translation Matters: A Fem/Womanist Exploration of Translation Theory and Practice for Proclamation in Worship," in *Text and Community: Essays in Memory of Bruce M. Metzger* (Sheffield: Sheffield Phoenix Press, 2006).

Here is a quote from an alumna expressing her understanding of her learning and its impact on the community she pastors: "Thanks to God for you that because of your courses, I have had a record number of parishioners attend our midweek Lenten Evening Prayer and Bible Study. I have chosen texts that I gleaned from your courses, *Heroines, Harlots, etc.* and *Prophets on the Margin*.... Most people had never read anything from the book of Judges and were amazed to discover how women have been abused and ignored from way back then until now. Others have raised questions about why these type[s] of stories are in the Canon at all. Still others have become inspired to want to probe deeper into the chosen texts." What is most significant for me reading her note is the permission feminist pedagogy has extended through this pastor for communicants to question the text even as they study it as scripture.

As I continue to struggle with the hierarchy invited by the teaching profession I have begun describing myself as a "teaching-learner," and my students as "learning-teachers." I believe that the Song passage also supports this interpretation. The very song of the daughter/disciple is a form of pedagogy. She who learns from her mother/teacher now instructs all who read and hear her Song. Surely, among the students-turned-teachers is her teacher-become-student.

I began the "Teaching Paradigm" section of this essay with an exegesis of an intensive Hebrew verb that describes a woman's teaching. Let me end with an exegesis of that verb in a different text. In Jer 2:33, the prophet condemns an unnamed woman (possibly Jerusalem) for teaching "wicked women" her ways. Transformational pedagogies are not always well-received by the guardians of the guild and its traditions. In verses 23–24, the castigated teacher is charged with pursuing gods other than the God of the Hebrew Scriptures and with having unrestrained passion, expressed in pornographic terms. Feminist women who question, challenge and/or reject the God of Israelite scripture are vulnerable to the verbal and physical abuses heaped on the woman whose teaching is rejected as heterodox. The teaching of both of these audacious women, the teaching-learner and the learning-teacher—and others who I have not addressed—coexist in the complicated set of texts that comprise the Scriptures of Israel.

Beyond Socialization and Attrition: Border Pedagogy in Biblical Studies

Roberto Mata

Introduction

In the last decade, the number of racial and ethnic minority students (REM) entering the field of biblical and theological studies has increased significantly. According to the Association for Theological Schools in the U.S. and Canada, the total number of REM enrolled in seminaries and divinity schools during the academic year 2008–2009 surpassed 50 percent.[1] In comparison to the academic year 2002–2003, where only 30 percent of REM accounted for student enrollment, this represents a sharp increase.[2] This growth in student diversity is due in part to major demographic shifts in the U.S.,[3] to recruitment efforts by graduate schools, and to the advocacy work of REM student organizations.[4] However, in order to ensure the democra-

---

1. Association of Theological Schools, "Annual Tables 2008–2009"; online: http://www.ats.edu/Resources/Publications/Documents/AnnualDataTables/2008-09AnnualDataTables.pdf.

2. In terms of enrollment by ethnic groups the ATS Fact Book 2002–2003 reported: white 69.1%, black 11.6%, Asian 7.1%, Hispanic 3.5%, Native American 0.4%. Although in the academic year 2008–2009 white students remained the largest group, collectively REM have now slightly surpassed those numbers. See the ATS "Fact Book 2002–2003" online at http://www.ats.edu/Resources/Publications/Documents/FactBook/2002-03.pdf.

3. In the case of Hispanics, the U.S. Census Bureau reports that this population surpasses 45 million, 15.1% of the total 301.1 million, and remains the fastest-growing ethnic group in the nation; see the U.S. Census Bureau report at http://www.census.gov/popest/national/asrh/NC-EST2009/NC-EST2009-03.xls.

4. At Harvard Divinity School, for instance, student organizations such as Nuestra Voz (the Latino/a student group) continuously encouraged the administration to actively recruit both REM faculty and students. Fortunately, in recent years, the school has started to hire REM faculty and to recruit REM students through their Diversity and Explorations program.

tization of biblical studies, it is imperative to also address the pedagogical needs of REM.[5]

According to Elisabeth Schüssler Fiorenza, the type of knowledge taught and the type of pedagogy used to communicate this knowledge has not changed over the same period.[6] This raises two critical questions: (1) What are the traditional educational models in biblical studies, and how do they impact the performance and success of REM?[7] (2) What alternative pedagogical models and practices can enable REM to not only enter the field but also to transform it into a radically democratic space of equals?[8] In this paper I argue that "banking models" of education enable and sustain forms of academic socialization that can lead REM to embrace hegemonic notions of the idealized biblical scholar, while potentially leading those who interrogate it into academic attrition. In order to address this quandary, I suggest that REM may undertake a border-crossing journey that entails critical awakening, journeying, crossing, negotiating, and transforming. In this manner, REM become border-crossers who map, cross, and reconfigure the hegemonic borders of biblical studies.

STRUCTURE

Divided into seven sections, the first section of this paper covers questions of social location, experiences and realities that have inspired this work and informed my theoretical framework. The second section presents a brief discussion of traditional educational models in biblical studies. In the third section, the discussion moves onto the critical task of mapping Eurocentric forms of academic socialization and its deployment at the institutional and departmental levels. Moreover, the fourth section links socialization with student isolation and the subsequent threat of attrition.[9] While section five

---

5. Frances E. Contreras and Patricia Gándara, "Navegando el Camino/Navigating the Roadway: The Latina/o PhD Pipeline: A Case of Historical and Contemporary Underrepresentation," in *The Latina/o Pathway to the PhD: Abriendo Caminos* (ed. Jeannette Castellanos; Virginia: Stylus, 2006), 98–99.

6. Elisabeth Schüssler Fiorenza, "Rethinking the Educational Practices of Biblical Doctoral Students," *TThRel* 6 (2003): 67.

7. Elisabeth Schüssler Fiorenza, *Democratizing Biblical Studies: Toward an Emancipatory Educational Space* (Louisville: Westminster John Knox, 2009), 127–28.

8. Ibid., 127.

9. As a result of such socialization, REM students are unable to bridge the spaces and negotiate forms of knowing in the academy and in their respective cultural and religious communities. Unable to reconcile the series of contradictions between their complex religious and academic commitments, they may eventually have to decide whether to uncriti-

summarizes an important discussion on alternative pedagogical models in biblical studies, particularly those of Fernando Segovia and Tina Pippin, section six delineates the theoretical foundations of border pedagogy as framed in the works of Paulo Freire, Henry A. Giroux, bell hooks, and Elisabeth Ellsworth. From this foundation, section seven defines and discusses at length the five elements of the border-crossing journey; namely, awakening, journeying, crossing, negotiating, and transforming. In general, my social location informs each and every aspect of this paper.

SOCIAL LOCATION

My background as a Hispanic, Pentecostal immigrant at a prestigious university has shaped and inspired my approach to this paper. While pursuing a B.A. in biblical studies, I realized that Hispanic scholars were but a small minority in the study and production of biblical literature, partly because graduate schools did not actively recruited Hispanics.[10] Consequently, the resources available for divinity schools seminaries are translated from English and are often irrelevant to the Hispanic immigrant context.[11] In order to address the need, I enrolled at Harvard Divinity School. There I realized other REM faced similar struggles. In addition, I understood that borders are not simply "a dividing line"[12] or a way to demarcate "safe and unsafe" spaces,[13] but also places where power is asserted, negotiated, and resisted.

Thus, in several departments, only those REM who embrace the hegemonic ideal of the "true" biblical scholar seem to have a place at the table of dialogue, while those who interrogate power, race, class, and gender are often silenced. Such was my case when a teaching assistant dismissed my postcolonial critique of his argument as untenable during a class discussion. When I cited REM scholars with similar views, he said: "their work is not real scholarship." Considering this situation, I dedicate this paper to those REM who are struggling to enter the field, to those *atravesados* who are negotiating to

---

cally embrace the idealized notion of the biblical scholar, resist it and attempt to transform it, or become bitterly disillusioned and abandon the field altogether.

10. Edwin I. Hernandez and Kenneth Davies, *Reconstructing the Sacred Tower: Challenge and Promise of Latino/a Theological Education* (Scranton, Pa.: University of Scranton Press, 2003), 47.

11. Samuel Solivan, *The Spirit, Pathos, and Liberation: Toward an Hispanic Pentecostal Theology* (Sheffield: Sheffield Academic Press, 1998), 95.

12. Gloria Anzaldua, *Borderlands /La Frontera: The New Mestiza* (San Francisco: Spinters/Aunt Lute, 1987), 25.

13. Ibid.

remain in it,[14] and to those who have silently left their programs. My hope is this paper will help formulate questions, voice our concerns, and offer constructive alternatives to hegemonic pedagogical models in biblical studies.

TRADITIONAL PEDAGOGIES IN BIBLICAL STUDIES

The "banking model of education" has traditionally influenced biblical studies classrooms.[15] According to Paulo Freire, such a model sees learning as the acquisition, retention, and repetition of facts.[16] In addition, it creates and reinforces the "teacher-student contradiction," which presupposes that teachers know everything while students know nothing.[17] In this manner, the banking model enforces a hierarchy where students, as empty receptacles, are below the teacher—who is perceived as the source and regulator of knowledge.[18] Apart from the banking model, Schüssler Fiorenza also discusses two other models; namely, the "master-disciple" and "consumer" models of education.[19] In her view, the "master-disciple" is a top-down model that encourages students to adopt the perspectives or interpretive frameworks of the teacher.[20] As such, it still maintains the hierarchical teacher-student contradiction discussed by Freire.

Moreover, Schüssler Fiorenza describes the "consumer" model as having two interrelated approaches; namely, a "smorgasbord" and a "therapeutic" approach.[21] While in the former students select what they think is useful and teachers act as experts and salespersons, in the latter, students select courses or workshops in terms of whether or not these make them "feel good," or whether these satisfy their needs.[22] Despite their variations, these educational models reinforce hegemonic educational practices and Eurocentric forms of socialization.[23]

---

14. For Anzaldua, the atravesados are "the squint-eyed, the perverse, the queer, the troublesome, the mongrel, the mulato, the half-breed, and the half-dead, in short, those who cross over, pass over, or go through the confines of the normal" (ibid., 4).
15. Paulo Freire, *Pedagogy of the Oppressed* (New York: Continuum, 2000), 91.
16. Ibid, 71–86.
17. Ibid, 91.
18. Ibid.
19. Schüssler Fiorenza, *Democratizing Biblical Studies*, 130–38.
20. Ibid, 133.
21. Ibid.
22. Ibid.
23. Because Tina Pippin's reflections are founded on critical pedagogy, the strengths and limitations of which she has acknowledged, I do not include her work among the educational models described above.

In addition, there is a third model, which I shall baptize the "rat race" model of graduate education. In this model, students adopt a competitive salesperson and celebrity mentality in order to ensure admission, permanence, and completion of their graduate programs.[24] As salespersons, students must continually compete with each other to sell their projects to faculty, particularly if they are applying to doctoral programs or are in the prospectus stage. In order to do so, of course, they must negate genuine concerns and tailor their work to fit the faculty's theoretical frameworks. Similar to celebrities, they must spend lots of time thinking about how they are perceived or rated by faculty and peers.[25] Through advice disguised as best practices, pedagogues reinforce such a model as they encourage students to ensure that every course paper, independently of course subject, becomes a dissertation chapter, or at the very least part of comprehensive exams bibliography, and to see the dissertation as one's first book.[26]

In the end, the rat race model is counterproductive for students. While paying attention to how one is perceived by faculty and peers is important, graduate students, unlike Hollywood stars and salespersons have neither the time nor the emotional energy to invest in selling projects or to continuously check their ratings. In addition, another danger is that students can go through their programs of study without critically reflecting on how the institutional norms, pedagogies, and overall ethos of the academy impinges on their education and enables socialization.

SOCIALIZATION

Socialization refers to "the process through which students gain the knowledge, skills, and values necessary for successful entry into a professional career requiring an advanced level of specialized knowledge and skills."[27] The logic arising from this definition and traditional understandings in general is that socialization is not only positive but also necessary in order to enable students

---

24. Such a model thrives on the fear of failure and is first inaugurated at orientation when students are told by the faculty: "Do you see the students sitting to your left and right? Some of them will not complete this program. Only those who go out of their way to get our input and excel will make it."

25. Hence, their task is continuously to demonstrate to their faculty and peers that they merited a place in such program or school and that in fact the school was not mistaken in granting them admission.

26. Gregory Colon Semenza, *Graduate Study for the Twenty-First Century: How to Build an Academic Career in the Humanities* (New York: MacMillan, 2005), 155.

27. John Weidman and Elisabeth Stein, "Socialization of Doctoral Students to Academic Norms," *Journal of Research and Higher Education* 44 (2003): 3.

to effectively transition from their role as doctoral students to their professional role as scholars. Yet, as Schüssler Fiorenza points out, the field of biblical studies has traditionally promoted a scientific-positivist and value-free ethos, which devalues student voices.[28] In this manner, REM are pressured to set aside their questions and to ascribe to a Eurocentric understanding of what a "good education" is and what a "true biblical scholar" should be.[29] This socialization is promoted at four levels: classroom, department, interactions with faculty and students, and professional guilds, such as the Society for Biblical Literature. In general, banking pedagogies, hegemonic paradigms, as well as teachers and peers reinforce hegemonic forms of socialization.

For a time I doubted REM could be socialized to the extent of denying their own voice and uncritically embracing the portrait of the idealized Eurocentric scholar. Yet, I ignored that class played a significant role in determining the extent of one's socialization. While REM from challenging socio-economic backgrounds are just as susceptible to socialization, most of the students who ascribed and defended their socialization came from an upper middle-class background.[30] Thus, even REM international students from privileged backgrounds aligned along Eurocentric paradigms in class discussions or informal interactions. On one particular occasion, a Hispanic colleague from a privileged background hesitated to accept an invitation to attend a lecture titled "Postcolonialism and The New Testament." In a rather exasperated tone she said: "I am not sure; I get uncomfortable with political issues. I think we should just study the New Testament for its own sake and put our bias aside."[31] Thus, the pervasiveness of socialization transcends race and class and constitutes but one end of the spectrum. Yet, those REM who

---

28. Schüssler Fiorenza, "Rethinking the Educational Practices," 67.

29. To the extent that uncritical students adhere to the "portrait of the true scholar," they receive affirmation and acceptance in their departments, classroom, and formal interactions with faculty and students. This affirmation may in turn increase their chances of successfully navigating through the program, for studies have shown that expressed faculty interest in students' ideas and research topics made students feel valued.

30. On the other hand, I have been surprised to find support among white students from lower middle class backgrounds during class discussions. I am not speaking here about the white liberal student who uncritically speaks for REM but of those white students who have themselves wrestled against marginalization and socioeconomic disenfranchisement to stay afloat.

31. On another occasion, during a conversation over the recent influx of Hispanics and REM to biblical studies, a male Hispanic student in the masters program ranted that Hispanics needed to stop "making a fuss" about our "so-called marginalization" and "exclusion" in the academy, for our rise in numbers showed that institutional racism was a lie. "It is clear," he said, "that only the most qualified get admitted, regardless of race, gender or sexual orientation."

interrogate socialization become gradually and inconspicuously susceptible to attrition.

ATTRITION

Socialization can potentially lead critical REM to become increasingly isolated in their classrooms, the guilds, and in their formal and informal interactions with peers and faculty. Such isolation is detrimental to REM's academic performance and is one of the main factors in academic attrition.[32] Attrition refers to the process and dynamics that lead students to drop out of a doctoral program before completing their degrees.[33] This includes the students who are still in the process of completing their dissertations, otherwise known as "ABDs."[34] The process of attrition begins with confusion about program requirements, lack of communication with program administrators, and miscommunication with faculty and peers.[35] Eventually, these factors turn into frustration, lack of integration, and ultimately isolation.[36] Other factors that can lead REM to isolation and subsequent attrition are racial, class, and gender discrimination, which has a strong impact on satisfaction level and commitment to degree completion.[37]

To these, one may add the overwhelming display of "white privilege" in biblical studies classrooms. Such privilege may be defined as "a right, advantage, or immunity granted to or enjoyed by white persons beyond the common advantage of all others; an exemption in many particular cases from certain burdens and liabilities."[38] REM often find that most of the faculty are white and that the curriculum often reflects the dominant group's cultural, social, and political view. Furthermore, as bell hooks points out, in these academic settings white people often "act as though our presence is less a function of our skills, aptitude, genius, and more the outcome of philanthropic charity. Thinking this way, they see our presence as functioning primarily as a testa-

---

32. Barbara E. Lovitts, *Leaving the Ivory Tower: The Causes and Consequences of Departure from Doctoral Study* (Lanham, Md.: Rowman & Littlefield, 2001), 177.
33. Azad Ali and Frederick Kohun, "Dealing with Isolation Feelings in IS Doctoral Programs," *International Journal of Doctoral Studies* 1 (2006): 2.
34. Ibid.
35. Ibid.
36. Lovitts, *Leaving the Ivory Tower*, 177.
37. Evelyn M. Ellis, "The Impact of Race and Gender on Graduate School Socialization, Satisfaction with Doctoral Study, and Commitment to Degree Completion," *Western Journal of Black Studies* 25 (2001): 37.
38. Joseph R. Barndt, *Understanding and Dismantling Racism: The Twenty-First Century Challenge to White America* (Minneapolis: Fortress, 2007), 96.

ment to their largesse; it tells the world they are not racist."[39] But perhaps more latent is the tendency of white students to speak for REM and other marginalized groups. While some want to help REM, they are reluctant to consider how their privilege contributes to the latter's silencing and isolation.

When attrition materializes, it reverberates among all REM across departments, making the borders of biblical studies all the more tangible. About a year ago, a REM student was having difficulty with some of the academic requirements that are considered an essential part of a "true" scholar's training. Reluctant to conform to the pressure he perceived in interactions with others in the department, he was gradually isolated and became increasingly frustrated with the program. One afternoon, near the end of the spring semester and his second year, he approached my desk and said, "I just came to say goodbye; I cannot work with this academic system so I am leaving the program. I will stay in touch." We shook hands for one last time and then he vanished through the library stacks, never to return. Unable to cope with the socialization practices of the institution, he succumbed to academic attrition.

As a third-year Hispanic doctoral student, my friend's departure not only made real the threat of attrition, but it also left an open question; namely, who will be next? In conversations and interactions with REM—be they Hispanic, African-American, African, or Asian—the question often comes up: What if I cannot cope with program requirements? Hence, while REM write papers, engage in conversations, and attend classes, the fear of attrition looms in the background like Damocles' sword. Therefore, it is important that academic institutions not only recruit REM more aggressively, but that they also change their institutional practices and pedagogies.[40] Otherwise, such pedagogical practices and their consequences, as attrition shows, can become "quality control" systems that purge out those who "don't make the cut."[41] Furthermore, student attrition reinforces prejudices against REM in certain elite intuitions; namely, that REM leave programs because they are lazy, unqualified, and lack genuine interest in the field.[42] In turn, this view allows the educational institution to continue "business as usual" and avoid raising questions concerning the efficacy of their student support systems, curriculum, pedagogical models, and, of course, hegemonic socialization practices. Thus, everyone assumes the

---

39. bell hooks, *Teaching Community: A Pedagogy of Hope* (New York: Continuum, 2003), 33.

40. Contreras and Gándara, "Navegando el Camino," 98–99.

41. See Lovitts, *Leaving The Ivory Tower*, 92.

42. Barbara E. Lovitts and Cary Nelson, "Hidden Crisis in Graduate Education: Attrition from PhD Programs," *American Association of University Professors* 10 (2000): 78.

problem is with the student and not with the institution.[43] Although recent studies have provided insights for academic institutions along the lines of recruitment and retention,[44] REM are still left to their own devices when dealing with the issues of socialization and attrition.[45]

ALTERNATIVE EDUCATIONAL MODELS

Apart from the pedagogical proposal delineated by Schüssler Fiorenza in *Democratizing Biblical Studies*, Fernando Segovia and Tina Pippin have also presented constructive alternatives.[46] In his work, *Decolonizing Biblical Studies: A View from the Margins*, Segovia presents a twofold pedagogical proposal. First, it takes to heart "diversity in texts, diversity in readings, and diversity in readers."[47] Second, it views "the reality of empire, or imperialism and colonialism, as an omnipresent, inescapable, and overwhelming reality in the world."[48] In this manner, Segovia attempts to incorporate diversity as well as the reality of the imperial/colonial dimensions into the discipline at "the level of texts, readings of texts, and readers of texts."[49]

Although Pippin does not necessarily elaborate a pedagogical proposal, she demonstrates how critical pedagogy can be applied in the context of the religious studies classroom.[50] In this project, she envisions two liberatory spheres: "the classroom as an open, democratic space and the connection of participants in a ... religious studies course with cultural worker's in the community."[51] In several ways, this paper is indebted to the work of these fellow border-crossers. Like Pippin, I do not entirely elaborate a proposal here, but rather seek to elucidate the ways in which border pedagogy can address two specific and concrete issues facing REM in biblical studies, namely, socialization and attrition.

---

43. Ibid.
44. Hernandez and Davis, *Reconstructing the Sacred Tower*, 93.
45. Ibid.
46. Schüssler Fiorenza, *Democratizing Biblical Studies*, 16.
47. Segovia, *Decolonizing Biblical Studies*, 92.
48. Ibid, 93.
49. Ibid.
50. Tina Pippin, "Border Pedagogy: Activism in a Wymyn and Religion Classroom," *CSSR Bulletin* 24 (1995): 7; see also her "Liberatory Pedagogies in the Religious Studies Classroom," *TThRel* 1 (1998): 177–82.
51. Pippin, "Liberatory Pedagogies," 182.

Border Pedagogy

Due to the challenges that hegemonic paradigms and their "banking pedagogies" pose, REM must "creatively invent ways to cross borders."[52] To this end, this paper proposes a form of border pedagogy as a creative method to map, decenter, and transform the borders of biblical studies in the interest of REM. In terms of its theoretical foundations, border pedagogy is rooted in critical pedagogy; it links the practice of education to a radical struggle for a more democratic society and sees the notion of difference as part of this transformative struggle.[53] Furthermore, it rests on Freire's understanding of dialogue as "the encounter between people, mediated by the world, in order to name the world."[54] From this it follows that no one can name the world for others.[55] Drawing on postmodern discourse, border pedagogy also seeks to find ways in "which those master narratives based on white, patriarchal, and class-specific versions of the world can be critically challenged and effectively transformed."[56] Building on Gloria Anzaldua's imagery and understanding of borders,[57] Henry A. Giroux expands the category of border to signal "a recognition of those epistemological, political, cultural, and social margins that structure the language of history, power, and difference."[58] In general, border pedagogy understands education as a process of liberation, which is an essential part of border-crossing.

From these foundations, border pedagogy can be understood as entailing the following six components: (1) it points to forms of transgressing those borders that have been created under social, political, and economic oppression;[59] (2) it calls for the creation of pedagogical conditions and practices that may enable students to become border-crossers in order to understand otherness on its own terms; (3) it seeks to create a classroom of borderlands in which diversity in students, epistemologies, and meanings can flourish, a class-

---

52. bell hooks, *Teaching to Transgress: Education as the Practice of Freedom* (New York: Routledge, 1994), 184.
53. Henry A. Giroux, *Border Crossings: Cultural Workers and the Politics of Education* (New York: Routledge, 2005), 20.
54. Freire, *Pedagogy of the Oppressed*, 88.
55. Ibid.
56. Henry A. Giroux, *Pedagogy and the Politics of Hope: Theory, Culture, and Schooling* (Boulder, Colo.: Westview, 1997), 147.
57. The use of border and borderlands as categories is not merely incidental but invokes powerful imageries of struggle, social and geographical dislocation, hope, and transformation that are so much a part of the experience of Latinos/as and other REM.
58. Giroux, *Border Crossings*, 20.
59. Ibid.

room practice in which difference is celebrated even as it is interrogated and refashioned;[60] (4) it exposes the "socially and historically constructed strengths and limitations" of the borders we inherit and within which we operate in order to reconfigure them in the interest of the oppressed;[61] (5) it insists that no one can name the world for others; thus, it dispenses of the teacher-student contradiction that predominates in banking models of education;[62] and (6) it also incorporates into the curriculum epistemologies forged in the peripheries of dominant culture so that educational practices and student experiences "need no longer be mapped or referenced solely on the basis of the dominant models of Western culture."[63]

Building on the theoretical and practical work of Gloria Anzaldua, Henry Giroux, Paulo Freire, and bell hooks, among others, this paper suggests that border pedagogy enables REM to map, decenter, and transform hegemonic pedagogies that sustain socialization and attrition in biblical studies. Specifically, border pedagogy requires that both faculty and students learn to undertake a social, cultural, and political border-crossing journey that entails the following stages: critical awakening, journeying, crossing, negotiating, and transforming. In this manner, REM and others become border-crossers who seek the transformation and democratization of biblical studies.

CRITICAL AWAKENING

In contrast to the banking pedagogies of biblical studies, which are conducive to both socialization and attrition, border pedagogy demands that border-crossers or *mojados* (wetbacks) engage in a process of critical awakening before undertaking the border-crossing journey.[64] Such critical awakening is in fact a process of conscientization through which border-crossers learn to map the social, cultural and political borders of their oppression.[65] Without this critical awakening, REM are unable to become border-crossers.[66] Hence,

---

60. Ibid, 21.
61. Ibid, 20.
62. Freire, *Pedagogy of the Oppressed*, 70.
63. Giroux, *Pedagogy and the Politics of Hope*, 147.
64. Mojado is a pejorative term to designate those who cross the U.S.–Mexico border illegally.
65. Freire uses the term as the learning to read social, political, and economic contradictions and to take action against them; see *Pedagogy of The Oppressed*, 36.
66. As point of departure, this paper situates its basic framework under the umbrella of the Fourth Emancipatory paradigm in biblical studies. As delineated by Schüssler Fiorenza, the Fourth Emancipatory paradigm acknowledges its own social locatedness, influences, and interests; thereby, it challenges the Eurocentric, positivist neutrality espoused by

border pedagogy encourages REM to first map the Eurocentric character of the borders that undergird socialization and attrition in biblical studies. How does this work?

As REM enter the field, they soon realize that neither the content nor framework of study speaks to their experiences. Such uneasiness or experience of not belonging, of being alien and unwelcome triggers what Gloria Anzaldua refers to as *la facultad*—that is, "the capacity to see in surface phenomena the meaning of deeper realities, to see the deep structure below the surface."[67] This "irrational" and acute sensing leads REM to further interrogate why it seems as if they are not a part of the process in shaping the field and the knowledge it produces.

In addition, critical awakening bids us to map how hegemonic paradigms and pedagogies create and reinforce two portraits in biblical studies; namely, the portrait of the "true scholar" and the portrait of the "wretched scholar."[68] Mapping the portrait of the "true scholar" and its oppressive underpinnings entails tracing the colonial heritage of the scientific-positivist ethos of the field, as well as the socialization practices that enforce it. Akin to this reality, Fernando Segovia suggests a thorough analysis of the link between biblical interpretation and Western hegemony and colonialism, particularly in the nineteenth and early twentieth centuries, when, as he points out, "both the formation of the discipline and the process of expansionism found themselves at their respective peaks."[69] Through critical awakening REM map the portrait of the objective, neutral, and value-free scholar. Such a portrait creates what Albert Memmi refers to as a "portrait of wretchedness,"[70] which demonizes the "other" as ignorant, lazy, racially inferior, primitive and irrational.[71] Subsequently, it is used to justify the socio-economic, political and psychological exploitation of the oppressed.[72]

---

hegemonic paradigms and their pedagogies in biblical studies; see Elisabeth Schüssler Fiorenza, *Rhetoric and Ethic: The Politics of Biblical Studies* (Minneapolis: Fortress, 1999), 42.

67. Anzaldua adds that *La Facultad* is also "an instant sensing, a quick perception arrived at without conscious reasoning. It is an acute awareness mediated by the part of the psyche that does not speak, that communicates in images and symbols which are the faces of feelings" (*Borderlands/La Frontera*, 38).

68. Furthermore, through critical awakening we see that the same institutional structures that grant REM acceptance can turn into some sort of quality control systems that reaffirm those who accept socialization.

69. Segovia, *Decolonizing Biblical Studies*, 176.

70. Albert Memmi, *The Colonizer and The Colonized* (Boston: Beacon, 1991), 82.

71. Ibid.

72. Similarly, in biblical studies, this portrait of wretchedness depicts noncompliant

Furthermore, critical awakening calls attention to the ways in which Eurocentric paradigms and pedagogies perpetuate power and privilege. Just as the portrait of the "true scholar" is reinforced by socialization, the portrait of the "wretched scholar" is then reinforced by attrition. As previously suggested, universities and seminaries across the nation invoke attrition to argue that REM dropped out of graduate programs because they were not qualified in the first place. This reinforces the stereotypes of REM as lazy, incompetent, and academically challenged students. Finally, critical awakening calls attention to the ways in which traditional curriculum design, instructional practice, and forms of academic assessment sustain white privilege in the biblical studies classroom. Specifically, it pays attention to the ways in which dominant groups deploy notions of difference in order to establish, reproduce, and legitimate their privilege over other groups.[73] Once these borders or limit-situations are delineated, border-crossers must engage in a journey to transform them.[74]

JOURNEYING

In journeying, border pedagogy demands that teachers and students commit to a course of liberating action, work with each other, and interrogate their own motivations for journeying. While it is now common to argue that knowledge and power are related, border pedagogy shifts "the emphasis of the knowledge/power relationship away from the limited emphasis on the mapping of domination to the politically strategic issue of engaging the ways in which knowledge can be remapped."[75] Such remapping entails the very transformation of these borders. However, before this takes place, one must first map them, and then commit to liberating action by journeying with others. Freire makes this explicit noting that: "When a word is deprived of its dimension of action.... It becomes an empty word, one which cannot denounce the world, for denunciation is impossible without a commitment to transformation, and there is no transformation without action."[76] In other words it is not enough for prospective border-crossers to simply denounce the dangers

---

REM, those who question socialization, as lazy, incompetent, problematic, and irrational or as not doing "real and serious" scholarship.

73. Carlos Tejeda and Kris D. Rodriguez, "Fighting the Backlash: Decolonizing Perspectives and Pedagogies in Neocolonial Times," in *Latino Education: An Agenda for Community Action Research* (ed. Pedro Pedraza and Melissa Rivera; Mahwah, N.J.: Lawrence Erlbaum Associates, 2005), 286.
74. Freire, *Pedagogy of the Oppressed*, 72.
75. Giroux, *Pedagogy and the Politics of Hope*, 147.
76. Freire, *Pedagogy of the Oppressed*, 85.

posed by socialization and attrition; we must also seek constructive alternatives. While these days it is trendy to "speak for the oppressed,"[77] journeying demands that border-crossers learn to speak "with" but never "for" others.

Committing to liberating action in a concrete sense also entails learning to work with others. Because the border-crossing journey of REM in biblical studies is filled with perils, threats, and uncertainties, it is never undertaken alone. Rather, one travels with prospective border-crossers or *mojados* from diverse ethnic, economic and socio-political backgrounds. Therefore, we must learn to speak in ways that transcend our differences. Throughout my graduate studies I have traveled along with Asian, African-American, African, White, and Hispanic students. At various intervals of the journey, we have comforted, encouraged, and given advice to each other, thereby developing a sense of community. Often Asian and Hispanic students in the masters program approach me to inquire about the doctoral program. Although they could easily inquire about it at the admissions office, they are looking for a different type of knowledge. They want to know which faculty will support a research project from what Chela Sandoval refers to as an "oppositional consciousness" perspective.[78] Furthermore, they want to know whether faculty members are fellow border-crossers or simply *la migra* (the border patrol or gate keepers) in disguise.[79]

Because in journeying, prospective border-crossers must learn to work with one another, they must also interrogate their own motivations for doing so. As Elizabeth Ellsworth warns, uncritical pedagogues may in fact be "implicated in the very structures they are trying to change."[80] Thus, border-crossers must embrace a dialogical perspective and dispense with any arrogance, paternalism, and white privilege, for as Freire asks:

> How can I dialogue if I always project ignorance onto others and never perceive my own? How can I dialogue if I regard myself as a case apart from others—mere "its" in whom I cannot recognize other "I"s? How can I dialogue if I consider myself a member of the in-group of 'pure men,' the owners

---

77. Elizabeth Ellsworth, "Why Doesn't This Feel Empowering? Working through the Repressive Myths of Critical Pedagogy," in *Feminisms and Critical Pedagogy* (ed. Carmen Luke and Jennifer Gore; New York: Routledge, 1992), 101.

78. Chela Sandoval, *Oppositional Consciousness in the Postmodern World: United States Third World Feminism, Semiotics, and The Methodology of The Oppressed* (Michigan: University Microfilms International, 1993), 215.

79. They want to identify individuals who can orient them without enforcing the silencing that comes with socialization.

80. Ellsworth, "Why Doesn't This Feel Empowering," 101.

of truth and knowledge, for whom all non-members are 'these people,' or 'the great unwashed'?[81]

Because dialogue is rooted in humility, it cannot be an act of arrogance.[82] In journeying, border-crossers must view and treat each other as equals. In addition, our actions must contribute towards building a relationship of mutual trust. As Freire points out, "trust is contingent on the evidence which one party provides the others of his true, concrete intentions; it cannot exist if that party's words do not coincide with its actions. To say one thing and do another—to take one's own word lightly—cannot inspire trust."[83] Thus, the dialogical border-crosser must have faith in others' "power to make and to remake, to create and to re-create the world, faith in their vocation to be more fully human (which is not the privilege of an elite, but the birthright of all)."[84] Only after border-crossers—students and educators alike—have interrogated their own motivations for journeying will they be able to cross the borders of biblical studies.

CROSSING

REM become border-crossers or *mojados* (wetbacks) as they disavow the student-teacher contradiction, activate peripheral epistemologies, and reclaim their right to speak and name the world with others. In this crossing, REM and others transgress hegemonic borders of meaning, maps of knowledge, social relations and values. Thus, they destabilize, the continuum of domination created by Eurocentric paradigms and banking pedagogies.[85] Yet, critics have often wondered how teachers are to orient students to become autonomous border-crossers who speak for themselves without directing or deploying some sort of authority.[86] In the dialogical nature of border pedagogy "the teacher-of-the-students and the students-of-the-teacher cease to exist."[87] Instead, they both emerge as border-crossers who name the world together. In this manner, border pedagogy prevents teachers from constructing for themselves privileged positions as both the sources and regulators of what can and should be known.[88] Because no one can name the world for

---

81. Freire, *Pedagogy of the Oppressed*, 90.
82. Ibid, 85.
83. Ibid, 90.
84. Ibid.
85. Giroux, *Pedagogy and the Politics of Hope*, 147.
86. Ellsworth, "Why Doesn't This Feel Empowering,"100.
87. Freire, *Pedagogy of the Oppressed*, 85.
88. Ellsworth, "Why Doesn't This Feel Empowering," 115.

others, crossing enables *mojados* to reclaim their right to name the world and to speak for themselves.

In this manner, crossing becomes an act of noncompliance with Eurocentric paradigms and pedagogies of biblical studies. As such, it will seem threatening to *la migra* (border patrol).[89] But this is to be expected since, as bell hooks points out, "the liberatory voice will necessarily confront, disturb, demand that listeners even alter ways of hearing and being."[90] For a long time, perhaps too long, it has been REM and Anzaldua's *atravesados* in biblical studies who have had to adjust and alter not only their ways of learning and speaking, but also of being.[91] As previously noted, Eurocentric pedagogies have defined and objectified REM through portraits of wretchedness.[92] We come to biblical studies with a desire to contribute to the field but soon find our opinions devalued and cast aside. Such an experience of disillusionment is best captured by Frantz Fanon when he notes: "I came into the world imbued with the will to find a meaning in things, my spirit filled with the desire to attain to the source of the world, and then I found that I was an object in the midst of other objects."[93]

Consequently, even the most idealist of REM will at some point or another face the fact that our questions and concerns have been ignored by what William Myers terms, "the subtle politics of omission," through which Eurocentric approaches "lock the history of interpretation in the past and evade contemporary issues such as racism and intercultural dialogue."[94] Thus, border pedagogy takes seriously student voice and the struggle for self-reconfiguration. With Jean-Pierre Ruiz it refuses to brand student voice as naïve and irrelevant, "for such dismissals replicate the destructive patterns of

---

89. Those who not only enforce the Eurocentric paradigms and banking pedagogies but who also see the shaping of biblical studies as their exclusive right.

90. bell hooks, *Talking Back: Thinking Feminist, Thinking Black* (Boston: South End, 1989), 16.

91. Anzaldua, *Borderlands/La Frontera*, 38.

92. When I speak of the REM's voice and experience, I am aware that these cannot be constructed in essentialist terms, and that is precisely my point. Eurocentric portraits of wretchedness have framed and casted the "voice" and "experience" of the REM in such a way that they are unable to name the world for themselves. Such portraits of wretchedness must be eradicated not so much for REM to find their authentic voice and experiences, since the West has shaped a lot of what we know, but so that they can have the freedom to construct it in liberating terms.

93. Frantz Fanon, *Black Skins/White Masks* (New York: Grove, 1996), 109.

94. Williams H. Myers, "The Hermeneutical Dilemma of the African American Biblical Student," in *Stony the Road We Trod: African American Biblical Interpretation* (ed. Cain Hope Felder; Minneapolis: Fortress, 1991), 41.

academic elitism and classism that support the status quo."[95] However, with Elizabeth Ellsworth it understands that, if not interrogated, the struggle for student voice can become part of what she deems a repressive myth, in which teachers fail to see how they are implicated in the educational systems they are trying to change and both voice and experience are casted in essentialist terms.[96] After critically interrogating student voice, however, one must still allow student's experiences and knowledge to inform the curriculum and daily class discussions, for as Giroux reminds us, this is what gives meaning to students' lives and what they use to critique hegemonic culture.[97]

NEGOTIATING

After crossing, border pedagogy requires that *mojados* learn to negotiate their survival in the borderlands to which they have arrived.[98] From journeying up until crossing, border-crossers relied on *la facultad*, other *mojados*, and their *intellectual coyotes*—those scholars who are committed to the transformation of the field and are adept at finding ever new and creative ways to cross the borders of biblical studies without getting caught by *la migra*. In the stage of negotiating, however, border-crossers must also learn to use what Audre Lorde refers to as the master's tools.[99] They must be, as Fernando Segovia puts it, gentle as doves and wily as snakes, and this entails certain compromises. Although the crossing has taken place, border-crossers must understand that *la migra* still conducts intellectual deportations. Such *deportaciones* can easily silence border-crossers by branding them as "unscholarly" or as overly political. Hence, in order to negotiate our permanence and survival in the field we must also move about the power center with a *mica chueca,* which should also enable us to work with the established norms, paradigms, and pedagogies even as we work to reconfigure the them in the interest of REM.[100]

Due to the dialogical nature of border pedagogy and departing from any trash and burn approach, it is necessary that border-crossers become adept with the various validated paradigms and methodologies of scholarship in biblical studies. They must also move with ease through the established

---

95. Jean-Pierre Ruiz, "Tell the Next Generation: Racial and Ethnic Minority Scholars and the Future of Biblical Studies," *JAAR* 69 (2001): 665.
96. Ellsworth, "Why Doesn't This Feel Empowering,"100.
97. Giroux, *Pedagogy and the Politics of Hope,* 157.
98. In this negotiating, one must learn how to sing song of the L*rd while in a foreign land, so to speak.
99. Audre Lorde, *Sister Outsider* (New York: Crossing, 1984), 112.
100. A *mica chueca* (literally a twisted green card) is really a fake green card that illegal immigrants purchase in order to be able to work and thus survive in the U.S. borderlands.

paradigms of biblical studies and deal with a diversity of texts, readers, and readings, as Fernando Segovia proposes.[101] Although aware of the socialization these represent, border-crossers must also become versed with the European languages of research, such as French and German, in order to keep up with the expectations of the field and develop competency.[102] Without this negotiating, our next generations of scholars, as Jean-Pierre Ruiz warns, could be easily dismissed as poorly trained.[103]

Furthermore, it is important that border-crossers establish bridges as they move between center and periphery, between academy and society, between biblical studies in the academy and biblical studies at their respective congregations. In addition, this continuous negotiation should prevent REM from becoming "schizophrenic," in a figurative sense, when Eurocentric paradigms dismiss "their faith-based questions, religious experiences, and fundamental convictions and therefore do not have the possibility to work through them critically in dialogue with hegemonic discourses in the field."[104] Hence, through the deployment of their various border-crossing skills—which include their bilingual and bicultural skills and the use of the *mica chueca*—the border-crosser becomes a "transformative, connected, and integrated intellectual who is able to communicate with a variegated public with the goal of personal, social, and religious transformation for justice and well-being."[105]

TRANSFORMING

The objective of the border-crossing journey is to transform the borders that demarcate, legitimate, and enable hegemonic pedagogies. In order to accomplish this, however, border-crossers must decenter hegemonic epistemologies and activate peripheral ways of knowing. However, as Trinh Minh-ha asks, "What kind of educational project could redefine 'knowing' so that it no longer describes the activities of those in power who started to speak, to speak alone, and for everyone else, on behalf of everyone else?"[106] Border pedagogy offers a potential solution to this quandary as it encourages borders-crossers to draw upon what they know about the world, both collectively and individually, to challenge the Eurocentric ethos of biblical studies.[107] Certainly, this redefining

---

101. Segovia, *Decolonizing Biblical Studies*, 92.
102. Indeed, a border-crosser becomes multilingual and is also able to understand the significance behind certain types of silence.
103. Ruiz, "Tell the Next Generation," 664.
104. Schüssler Fiorenza, "Rethinking the Educational Practices," 67
105. Schüssler Fiorenza, *Rhetoric and Ethic*, 42.
106. Trinh T. Minh-ha, "Introduction," *Discourse* 8 (1987): 7.
107. Giroux, *Pedagogy and the Politics of Hope*, 147.

of "knowing" cannot be casted in essentialist terms, for Western epistemologies have long dominated the educational scene. Consequently, it would be difficult to ascertain what REM's "authentic" and "true" ways of knowing are.[108] Yet, one must also recognize that the marginalized have, throughout history, developed alternative ways of knowing, continually adapting and recreating them in the interest of the oppressed.[109] In dialogue with established epistemologies, this knowledge from the margins can enable border-crossers to redefine and reconfigure the field without having to construct it rigorously along Eurocentric points of reference.[110]

Through this knowledge, border-crossers who struggle to understand themselves along the social, political, and cultural borders established by the elite can now open up spaces for multiple realities, histories, and ways of imagining and recreating the world. As Freire reminds us, "Knowledge emerges only through invention and re-invention, through the restless, impatient, continuing, hopeful inquiry through which human beings purge the World, with the World, and with each other."[111] In naming the world, in this recreating and re-inventing, border-crossers transform it. Most importantly, it is through this naming, according to Freire, that border-crossers also find significance as human beings.[112] Because in the borderlands, these alternative and multiple ways of knowing are constantly shifting, they are not only contradictory at times, but, as Elisabeth Ellsworth points out, partial and irreducible as well.[113] Therefore, it is in these restless forms of knowing that the border-crosser learns to think and speak as an "I" among other "I"s, constantly undertaking the border-crossing journey to enact the democratization of biblical studies.[114]

CONCLUSION

In this paper I addressed two fundamental questions raised in Schüssler Fiorenza's *Democratizing Biblical Studies*. First, what are the traditional edu-

---

108. Similarly, it is also difficult to assume that what border-crossers know about the world has not been framed or influenced by the West in one way or another.
109. Particularly in colonial settings and relations of domination.
110. Giroux, *Pedagogy and the Politics of Hope*, 147.
111. Freire, *Pedagogy of the Oppressed*, 75.
112. Ibid, 88.
113. Ellsworth, "Why Doesn't This Feel Empowering," 112.
114. Due to socialization and the overall influences of the Eurocentric master narrative, one's own voice may at first sound foreign and we may even doubt ourselves. Through time and through the continuous critical awakening, journeying, crossing, negotiating, and transforming, we will learn to trust our voice as subjects and agents in the transformation of the field.

cational models in biblical studies and how do they impact the performance and success of REM? Second, what alternative pedagogical models and practices can enable REM to not only enter the field but also to transform it into a radically democratic space of equals? In an effort to provide a constructive alternative, I have argued that, on the one hand, "banking models" of education in biblical studies enable and sustain forms of academic socialization that can lead REM to embrace Eurocentric notions of the biblical scholar; on the other hand, such models can potentially lead those REM who resist it into isolation and subsequent academic attrition. As a result, elite institutions will argue that the problem is with failing REM and not with the school, thereby enabling them to ignore questions regarding hegemonic socialization practices, efficacy of their student-support systems, and curriculum. In order to address this quandary, I suggest REM may undertake a border-crossing journey that entails: critical awakening, journeying, crossing, negotiating, and transforming. In this manner, REM work to transform the field into that radical and democratic space of equals that Elisabeth Schüssler Fiorenza and other border-crossers have long envisioned.

4. Transforming the Curriculum

Redesigning the Biblical Studies Curriculum: Toward a "Radical-Democratic" Teaching Model

Susanne Scholz

The academic field of biblical studies faces serious challenges during the early years of the twenty-first century. It must compete with flashy, noisy, and attention-seeking modes of engaging the world; and that is just the beginning. A visit to any technology store presents a variety of computers, printers, televisions, ipods, cell phones, and cameras of any size and price that is simply overwhelming to the senses. But an equally challenging fact is that very few people have ever heard of the existence of biblical studies and many are quite comfortable to defend literal biblical meaning, as if scholars had not long disproven, dismantled, or deconstructed it. For instance, the tensions within the Anglican Communion over the ordination of GLBT people in U.S.-American and Canadian congregations have again proven the ongoing popularity of literalist biblicism[1] despite abundant research on the topic in biblical studies.[2]

---

1. For an example of the popular insistence on the Bible's literalist meaning, see www.gafcon.org, the website of an Anglican group that has formed within the Anglican Church in opposition to GLBT people's ordination in Episcopalian churches in the United States and Canada. In a statement at the end of a meeting in Jerusalem in June 2008 ("GAFCON Final Statement"), the group asserts: "The Bible is to be translated, read, preached, taught and obeyed in its plain and canonical sense, respectful of the church's historic and consensual reading." For reports in the press, see, e.g., Robert Pigott, "Rival Meeting Deepens Anglican Rift," *BBC* (22 June 2008); online: http://news.bbc.co.uk/2/hi/middle_east/7468065.stm; Laurie Goodstein, "Rival Conferences for Anglican Church," *New York Times* (June 20, 2008); online: http://www.nytimes.com/2008/06/20/world/20anglicancnd.html?_r=1.

2. See, e.g., John Boswell, *Christianity, Social Tolerance and Homosexuality: Gay People in Western Europe from the Beginning of the Christian Era to the Fourteenth Century* (Chicago: University of Chicago Press, 1980); Bernadette Brooten, *Love between Women: Early Christian Responses to Female Homoeroticism* (Chicago: University of Chicago Press, 1998); Robert E. Goss and Mona West, eds., *Take Back the Word: A Queer Reading of the Bible* (Cleveland: Pilgrim, 2000); Deryn Guest, ed., *The Queer Bible Commentary* (London: SCM, 2006); Theodore W. Jennings Jr., *Jacob's Wound: Homoerotic Narrative in the Lit-*

Yet the challenges do not only come from the outside but also from within the field; one in particular pertains to the curricular design of teaching biblical studies. Current curricula illustrate that the field has remained aloof from a world not only distracted by the newest technological gadgets and often intellectually caught in literalist biblicism but also endangered by nuclear destruction, environmental pollution, military devastation, poverty, hunger, illness, disease, and economic, racial, ethnic, and gender violence. There is a curricular apathy toward these challenges that does not foster pedagogical innovation, intellectual curiosity, and sociopolitical, religious, and cultural change. In contrast, Elisabeth Schüssler Fiorenza calls for "a radical democratic emancipatory form" of teaching biblical studies today.[3]

This essay asserts that the curricular structure of biblical studies, as taught at *all* levels of academic learning, is firmly stuck in a nineteenth-century Christian-Protestant vision, as initially articulated by Friedrich Schleiermacher. Because of its orientation toward past accomplishments, biblical curricular design at all levels has adapted little to continual sociocultural and epistemological-political developments. Recently, Schüssler Fiorenza suggested that "some creative thinking and educational transformation [has been] happening at the Masters of Divinity and College levels" but that no such pedagogical creativity seems to occur at the doctoral level.[4] Schüssler Fiorenza's assessment about undergraduate and master level teaching is perhaps too optimistic. At these levels, too, the curriculum remains largely frozen in the "philological-historical or exegetical-doctrinal disciplinary paradigm"[5] developed during the nineteenth-century as part of the "new model for the production of knowledge and higher education ... of German scientific research."[6]

The reticence toward curricular change in biblical studies does not surprise when one recognizes the interrelationship of graduate and undergraduate teaching and learning, the hiring practices in the field, and the credentialing

---

erature of Ancient Israel (London: Continuum, 2005); Dale B. Martin, *Sex and the Single Savior: Gender and Sexuality in Biblical Interpretation* (Louisville: Westminster John Knox, 2006); Ken Stone, *Practicing Safer Texts: Food, Sex and Bible in Queer Perspective* (London: T&T Clark, 2005), Ken Stone, ed., *Queer Commentary and the Hebrew Bible* (Cleveland: Pilgrim, 2001).

3. Elisabeth Schüssler Fiorenza, "Rethinking the Educational Practices of Biblical Doctoral Studies," *TThRel* 6 (2003): 69, 72–73. See also the revised version of this article in idem, *The Power of the Word: Scripture and the Rhetoric of Empire* (Minneapolis: Fortress, 2007), 239–66.

4. Schüssler Fiorenza, "Rethinking the Educational Practices," 68. See also idem, *Power of the Word*, 241, 261.

5. Ibid.

6. Ibid., 70.

requirements of aspiring Bible professors. All of these areas are connected, and so curricular changes need to be made at all teaching levels. For instance, if curricular changes were to be made only at the doctoral level, it would take decades to implement them in the undergraduate and master-level curriculum. Until then, newly minted Ph.D.s applying to teaching positions would be ill-prepared for the expected teaching assignments and most likely not be offered positions, perhaps drop out in frustration, or enter only graduate programs that promised adequate training for future job openings. Even if young professors, trained at innovative graduate programs, landed positions at master-level and undergraduate institutions, rank issues would make it difficult for them to create lasting curricular modifications. If, on the other hand, curricular changes were made only at the undergraduate level, these changes would probably be regarded as less legitimate and scholarly than if they came from graduate institutions due to existing hierarchies between graduate and undergraduate institutions. The implementation of curricular change is difficult because issues of authority, power, and hierarchies burden the process. Only when the scholarly conversation on curricular design reaches the entire field will creative thinking and educational transformation become sustainable, desirable, and executable at all levels.

Based on this insight, the following analysis takes a closer look at the undergraduate curriculum in biblical studies to suggest that improved interaction among graduate, master-level and undergraduate curricular needs, expectations, and opportunities benefit all of them if they want to successfully confront the curricular challenge. The article looks at three different areas of undergraduate teaching to illustrate its close connections to the graduate curricular design in biblical studies. The article begins by describing the nineteenth-century curricular model of theological studies, as developed by Friedrich Schleiermacher. It then examines two teaching instruments to demonstrate the ongoing popularity of this curriculum both in undergraduate and graduate education. Among the teaching instruments are course descriptions at several U.S.-American undergraduate institutions and undergraduate Bible textbooks of major textbook publishers. The article then discusses ideas about an alternative curriculum based on a "radical-democratic" model of biblical studies education[7] that develops in students intellectual-religious maturity, historical-cultural understanding, and literary-ethical engagement of the

---

7. For an elaboration on these and other pedagogical models, see Schüssler Fiorenza, "Rethinking Educational Practices," 69. See also her other publications that include further explanations on the models: *But She Said: The Practices of Feminist Biblical Interpretation* (Boston: Beacon, 1992); *Wisdom Ways: Introducing Feminist Biblical Interpretation* (Maryknoll, N.Y.: Orbis, 2001).

world. The briefly outlined alternative implies modified curricular goals, strategies, and techniques both for graduate and undergraduate teaching. Overall, then, the article argues for a comprehensive curricular redesign at all levels of graduate, master-level, and undergraduate teaching of biblical studies.

1. Friedrich Schleiermacher's Curricular Vision of Biblical Studies

Rarely did a curriculum reform enjoy as much success as the one envisioned by Friedrich Schleiermacher in his *Brief Outline on the Study of Theology*, published in 1811.[8] The vision that theological education should cover the trilogy of historical, theological-philosophical, and practical investigation still shapes many biblical studies programs. The genius of this curriculum, persuading generations of theology professors, was its distinction between the quest for knowledge of God and the academic task of theological education, namely the training of future clergy. To Schleiermacher, theological education should be conceptualized as a purely academic pursuit. Its foundational method is historical criticism.[9] Schleiermacher believed that theology had to be founded on this method since otherwise it would not be part of the scientific enterprise as defined, promoted, and established by the universities of his time.

This conviction also applied to biblical studies since it viewed historical criticism as the key to scientific-modern knowledge. Academic Bible study was considered historical work because only "the historically situated scientific method"[10] creates the kind of knowledge that furthers the understanding of the church. Historical investigation is essential to Schleiermacher's curricular vision because "[h]istorical criticism is the all-pervasive and indispensable organ for the work of historical theology, as it is for the entire field of historical studies."[11] Only when the Christian religion is related to past developments, Schleiermacher maintained, would scholars be able to address the Church's future. He explained: "The present simply cannot be regarded as the kernel

---

8. Friedrich Schleiermacher, *Brief Outline on the Study of Theology* (trans. of the 1811 and 1830 editions, with essays and notes, by Terrence N. Tice; Lewiston, N.Y.: Mellen, 1990); Friedrich Schleiermacher, *Kurze Darstellung des Theologischen Studiums zum Behuf einleitender Vorlesungen: Kritische Ausgabe herausgegeben von Heinrich Scholz* (Darmstadt: Wissenschaftliche Buchgesellschaft, 1993).

9. Robert W. Ferris, "The Role of Theology in Theological Education," in *With an Eye on the Future: Development and Mission in the Twenty-First Century—Essays in Honor of Ted W. Ward* (ed. D. H. Elmer and L. McKinney; Monrovia: MARC, 1996), 101–11. Available online at www.applyweb.com/apply/ciu/review_article.pdf.

10. Ibid.

11. §102 of Schleiermacher, *Brief Outline*, 57; idem, *Kurze Darstellung*, 43.

of the future that is to correspond more nearly to the full conception of the Church, or to any other notion, unless one recognizes how it has developed out of the past."[12] Or put more succinctly: "The present, however, can only be understood as a result of the past."[13]

Schleiermacher was primarily interested in Christianity and the New Testament. To him, the New Testament is the "first" discipline of "historical theology" because "[knowledge of primitive Christianity] rests entirely upon the correct understanding of these writings."[14] It was difficult for him to integrate the Hebrew Bible into this Christian framework, an anti-Jewish bias characteristic of much of Christian thought that also affected his curricular vision. He addressed the New Testament more frequently than the Hebrew Bible because, in his view, the Old Testament had little to contribute to Christian doctrine. He wrote: "That the Jewish codex does not contain any normative statements of faith regarding distinctively Christian doctrines will doubtless be recognized almost universally."[15] Still, he also believed that the Old Testament should receive the same exegetical treatment as the New Testament, and in one brief sentence he affirmed that the Old Testament, too, should be examined with historical methodologies: "The same applies to the ordering of the books of the Old Testament in our Bible."[16]

Not only, then, did he define biblical studies as a historical discipline, he also regulated the exegetical process. He directed scholars to begin with the biblical text, to create an exegetical apparatus based on philological standards, and to work with the original languages—all of which was not yet regularly done at the time. Schleiermacher dismissed commentary literature as academically inadequate when it "lack[s] philological spirit and art," "remain[s] within the bounds of general edification" and "only produce[s] confusion by its pseudo-religious tendency."[17] His unwavering commitment to developing an academically rigorous and methodologically sound biblical studies curriculum, grounded in historical analysis, has shaped the teaching of the Bible at universities, divinity schools and seminaries, and colleges worldwide since.[18]

---

12. §26 of Schleiermacher, *Brief Outline*, 16; idem, *Kurze Darstellung*, 11.
13. §82 of Schleiermacher, *Brief Outline*, 47; idem, *Kurze Darstellung*, 35.
14. §88 of Schleiermacher, *Brief Outline*, 50; idem, *Kurze Darstellung*, 38.
15. §115 of Schleiermacher, *Brief Outline*, 63; idem, *Kurze Darstellung*, 47. Yet he also wanted to continue early church practice that united "the Old Testament with the New Testament to one whole book."
16. Ibid.
17. §148 of Schleiermacher, *Brief Outline*, 77; idem, *Kurze Darstellung*, 58.
18. Shanta Premawardhana, "Preparing Religious Leaders for Our Time," *TThRel* 9 (2006): 71.

It should also be mentioned that this curricular vision encountered repeated attempts of scholarly critique. In 1899, W. R. Harper questioned some of Schleiermacher's assumptions, followed by critiques from William Adams Brown and Mark A. May in 1934, H. Richard Niebuhr in 1956, and Edward Farley in 1983.[19] In 1992 and 1993, David H. Kelsey noted that the curriculum at theological schools is a cause for the "fragmentation of theological education."[20] Kelsey reminds his readers that the division into biblical, historical, systematic-theological, and practical fields emerged in the late eighteenth-century pietist and the nineteenth-century "Berlin" model. He also notes that this model has become so pervasive that it shapes the theological curriculum at theological schools almost anywhere.

Most importantly, Kelsey worries that due to its modern scientific assumptions Schleiermacher's curricular vision rejects the original task of educating clergy, which he defines as the preparation of future clergy toward a better understanding of God. The existing curriculum alienates students from their professional tasks because it introduces them to the latest scholarly discourse and lacks a systematic focus on spiritual-theological issues. Accordingly, the agenda of academic disciplines in (Protestant) theology is "more deeply shaped by interests currently central to the relevant guild"[21] than most mission statements of seminaries would indicate. As a consequence, curricular tensions characterize theological education that is torn between research interests on the one hand and professional training on the other hand. Kelsey explains:

> [D]isciplines tend to develop an agenda of their own as sets of practices with interests rooted in the social location of these practices (e.g. universities). They tend, in short, to take on a life of their own, having the power to order and govern the courses comprising a course of study. In this context, commitment to specialization and its central disciplines may lead to a commitment to preserving one's own area ... thereby preserving the cur-

---

19. Edward Farley, *Theologia: The Fragmentation and Unity of Theological Education* (Philadelphia: Fortress, 1983); Richard H. Niebuhr, Daniel Day Williams, and James M. Gustafson, *The Purpose of the Church and Its Ministry: Reflections on the Aims of Theological Education* (New York: Harper & Brothers, 1956); William Adams Brown et al., *The Education of American Ministers* (4 vols.; New York: Institute of Social and Religious Research, 1934); William Rainey Harper, "Shall the Theological Curriculum Be Modified and How?" *American Journal of Theology* 3 (1899): 45–66.

20. David H. Kelsey, *To Understand God Truly: What's Theological about a Theological School* (Louisville: Westminster John Knox, 1992), 232–34; idem, *Between Athens and Berlin: The Theological Education Debate* (Grand Rapids: Eerdmans, 1993).

21. Kelsey, *To Understand God Truly*, 234.

ricular fragmentation.... For that reason, in the present state of inquiry in theological schooling it may be difficult for theological schools to embrace the disciplines without threat to the theological integrity of their theological task.[22]

To Kelsey, the theological curriculum threatens the integrity of theological education because it invites disciplinary fragmentation. Some educators, such as Pheme Perkins, want to ease this tension and suggest combining historical criticism with a theological vision.[23] This is a compromise, an "add-on" approach with its own set of problems, but it is part of a "tradition" that searches for alternatives to the Schleiermacher curriculum.

Another such voice comes from Catholic educator Lawrence E. Boadt in a discussion on the purpose of biblical studies at Catholic universities and seminaries. Boadt, too, hopes for a biblical studies curriculum that moves beyond the narrow confines of historical criticism. He suggests including what he calls a "post-critical interpretation" that values the "existence and active role [of the Bible] in the believing community from which it arose and for and to which it speaks."[24] Boadt distinguishes between a strict academic and a faith-oriented study of the Bible when he writes: "University scholarship may limit its task to the examination of how this relationship works itself out in the actual composition of the biblical texts and its history of interpretation, but seminary biblical studies must also communicate to its students how to translate this into the lives of a believing community."[25] This proposal is theologically conservative—after all, Boadt favors a religious and liturgical approach to the Bible. Still, it is important to recognize that Boadt's assessment questions the universal validity of Schleiermacher's model. Like other theological educators, he envisions a curriculum that goes beyond the historical paradigm. Still, he and the other critics have not been able to advance a comprehensive reform of the dominant curriculum in biblical studies.

The curricular situation is different for undergraduate (and graduate) institutions that adhere to Christian-fundamentalist, evangelical-conservative positions. They promote a biblical studies curriculum divorced from the theo-pedagogical and academic-scientific developments according to Schleiermacher's vision. Embracing the Bible as the literal or "infallible Word of

---

22. Ibid.
23. Pheme Perkins, "Revisioning the Teaching of Scripture," *Current Issues in Catholic Higher Education* 7 (1987): 29–32.
24. Lawrence E. Boadt, "Biblical Studies in University and Seminary Theology," in *Theological Education in the Catholic Tradition: Contemporary Challenges* (ed. Patrick W. Carey and Earl C. Muller; New York: Crossroad, 1997), 262.
25. Ibid., 263.

God,"[26] doctrinal positions shape their biblical curriculum. An example is Grace College in Winona Lake, Indiana, "an evangelical Christian community of higher education which applies biblical studies values in strengthening character, sharpening competence, and preparing for service."[27] Its "covenant of faith" states:

> We believe in THE HOLY SCRIPTURES: accepting fully the writings of the Old and New Testaments as the very Word of God, verbally inspired in all parts and therefore wholly without error as originally given of God, altogether sufficient in themselves as our only infallible rule of faith and practice (Matt. 5:18; John 10:35, 16:13, 17:17, 2 Tim. 3:16, 2 Peter 1:21).[28]

When the Bible is publicly proclaimed as the inerrant word of God in the context of higher education, it is studied abundantly, but the Schleiermacher curriculum is discarded because it asserts the separation of faith and academic theological work. Theologically conservative schools want to claim academic rigor in their undergraduate biblical studies curriculum but, more often than not, their faith convictions get in the way.[29] By contrast, academically "mainstream" seminaries and colleges stand in the tradition of Schleiermacher's curricular vision that shapes their Bible courses today. They exemplify the close connections between undergraduate and graduate biblical studies, and provide little room for curricular innovation and educational transformation.

2. The Hebrew Bible at U.S.-American Liberal Arts Colleges

Many course descriptions at several liberal arts colleges in the United States give evidence of a biblical studies curriculum that advances the "philological-historical or exegetical-doctrinal disciplinary paradigm"[30] and emphasizes content description and historical-literal presentation of biblical literature. The following discussion illustrates the prevalence of this paradigm as it appears in the online course descriptions of several undergraduate academic catalogs.[31] The selected colleges share several traits but also exhibit some

---

26. See, e.g., the website of Trinity Christian College, a four-year liberal arts college southwest of Chicago: http://www.trnty.edu/About-Us/mission.html.
27. See http://www.grace.edu/about/gracehistory.
28. See www.grace.edu/about/mission/covenant.pdf.
29. A list of colleges with a similar outlook can be found at the "National Christian College Athletic Association," available online at www.thenccaa.org.
30. Schüssler Fiorenza, "Rethinking the Educational Practices," 68.
31. The discussion is also enhanced by personal correspondence with several professors who teach at the selected colleges.

differences. All of them are located in the United States; they are four-year, private, liberal arts colleges, and all of them have name recognition in the United States. A few are denominationally (Christian) affiliated, several are women's colleges, and one is a historically black college. They are the College of the Holy Cross, Kalamazoo College, Wellesley College, Pomona College, Barnard College, Agnes Scott College, and Morehouse College. This is a relatively small number of institutions, but cursory study of the curriculum at other schools indicates the overall validity of the following observations. For the sake of disciplinary coherence the focus is on the Hebrew Bible.

It is important to remember that, before going further, the observations made in this article do not claim absolute universality. They describe curricular tendencies and trends, and they *suggest* the validity of the charge that the dominant approach in undergraduate classrooms emphasizes content description and historical-literal presentation of biblical literature. Since a comprehensive study of the undergraduate biblical studies curriculum does not currently exist and because it is always difficult to undertake such a review due to the shifting dynamics in any teaching environment, this article invites readers to add their professional experiences with undergraduate teaching in biblical studies when they consider the validity of the following observations.

A relatively consistent pattern emerges from the various Hebrew Bible course descriptions. Historical analysis shapes the pedagogical agenda although other methodological and hermeneutical developments are sometimes included. For instance, the Department of Religious Studies at the College of the Holy Cross in Worcester, Massachusetts, a Catholic liberal arts college, offers a "bread and butter course"[32] on the Hebrew Bible entitled "Religious Studies 126—Introduction to the Old Testament." The course places the Bible "in the social and cultural worlds that produced the texts, examines the biblical texts themselves, and investigates assumptions and methods employed by pre-modern, modern (post-Enlightenment), and postmodern interpreters of the Bible."[33] Another course listed in Holy Cross's catalog is "Women and/in the Bible" which examines "the function of patriarchy in the biblical texts, in the ancient world that produced the texts, and in the interpretations of the Scriptures throughout history."[34] According to Alice Laffey, professor of Old Testament at Holy Cross, the specifics of the course changed since it was first offered in the early 1980s. Yet other markers remained the same. The descrip-

---

32. I acknowledge gratefully Dr. Alice Laffey, who took the time to correspond with me about the department's curriculum and who used this phrase in an email message on 28 June 2008.
33. See http://www.holycross.edu/academics/religiousstudies/courses.
34. Ibid.

tion still refers to the "Bible" because originally the course covered both the Old and New Testaments.

Other courses not listed in the online catalog but taught in recent years include "Old Testament and Contemporary Prophets" as well as seminars and tutorials on the prophetic literature, the Psalms, and Hebrew language. Since, according to Laffey, Holy Cross students do not usually register for advanced courses in Old Testament, the department does not often offer them. She explains that "most of [our undergraduate] students ... are not interested in an advanced course in Old Testament."[35] In contrast, the departmental online catalog lists five intermediate and advanced New Testament and a New Testament introduction course although none of the courses promotes a Roman Catholic or other denominational faith perspective.[36] In general, then, this curriculum stands in the Schleiermacher tradition, favoring historical analysis and emphasizing the New Testament.

Similar tendencies appear at Kalamazoo College in Kalamazoo, Michigan, originally founded as a Baptist college in 1833. The online catalog lists an introduction course to the Old Testament which is described as the "study of ancient Israel's sacred literature in its historical and religious development."[37] Again, historical analysis shapes the outlook although the lack of details leaves room for developing the course into various directions. In 2008, the catalog also listed another course, entitled "Studies in Old Testament," which consisted of a "detailed examination of some aspects of the Old Testament, for example the Wisdom literature: Job, Proverbs, Ecclesiastes etc, and their relationship to the wisdom heritage of the ancient Near East and to the sacred traditions of Israel." According to the available information at Kalamazoo College, then, students encounter the academic study of the Hebrew Bible primarily as a historical project.

Likewise, the curriculum of Wellesley College in Wellesley, Massachusetts, presents Hebrew Bible courses as historical study although literary approaches also make it into several course descriptions. For instance, the course entitled "REL 104 Study of the Hebrew Bible/Old Testament" is a "critical introduction to the Hebrew Bible/Old Testament, studying its role in the history and culture of ancient Israel and its relationship to ancient Near Eastern cultures," but it also focuses "on the fundamental techniques of literary, historical, and source criticism in modern scholarship, with emphasis on the Bible's literary structure and compositional evolution."[38] Another course, "REL 243 Women

---

35. In an email message to me on 28 June 2008.
36. Dr. Laffey made this point in an email message on 28 June 2008.
37. See http://www.kzoo.edu/programs/?id=28&type=2.
38. See http://www.wellesley.edu/Religion/courseofferings/courseofferings.html.

in the Biblical World," locates biblical studies in the historical paradigm. The blurb specifies the content: "The roles and images of women in the Bible, and in early Jewish and Christian literature, examined in the context of the ancient societies in which these documents emerged. Special attention to the relationships among archaeological, legal, and literary sources in reconstructing the status of women in these societies."[39]

Other Bible courses follow this pattern, such as a seminar on "The Sacrifice of the Beloved Child in the Bible and Its Interpretation," which examines both the historical and cultural significance of Genesis 22, or a topical course on "Jerusalem: The Holy City,"[40] which also includes cross-religious references to Judaism, Christianity, and Islam. The course catalog in biblical studies for 2007–2008 lists three Old Testament and five New Testament courses. The trend is clear: undergraduate Hebrew Bible courses focus on historical methodology and so reinforce the paradigm that emerged in the nineteenth century. Sometimes courses also include approaches such as literary criticism and, especially on the introductory level, they emphasize content description.

Yet several undergraduate religion departments stretch their biblical studies curriculum into more innovative hermeneutical directions. Among them is the department of religious studies at Pomona College in Claremont, California. Its academic catalog includes courses that explore biblical literature with decidedly cultural and postmodern methodologies. For instance, a course entitled "The Biblical Heritage" acknowledges the Bible as "important for the formation and ongoing structure of U.S. American culture" and then promises to "explore the [biblical] texts through careful reading and critical analysis, using a variety of interpretive strategies, including historical, literary, and ideological critical analyses."[41] Other courses give a nod to the historical context of the Bible, such as a course on "Life, Love and Suffering in Biblical Wisdom and the Modern Word" or a course, firmly grounded in historical methodology, entitled "New Testament and Christian Origins." Yet courses on film ("Celluloid Bible: Hollywood, the Bible, and Ideology") and queer theory ("Queer Theory and the Bible") examine the Bible's intersection with culture. In these courses, cultural-theoretical concerns prevail, as the following course description exemplifies:

> 184. Queer Theory and the Bible. This course will look at how the Bible can be read productively through queer theory. We will examine biblical

---

39. See http://www.wellesley.edu/Religion/professors/Geller/geller.html.
40. See http://www.wellesley.edu/Religion/courseofferings/courseofferings.html.
41. For all courses mentioned here, visit http://www.pomona.edu/academics/departments/religious-studies/courses/all-courses.aspx.

passages that are central to prohibitions on homosexuality, and the larger discourses of heteronormativity (constructed around gender, sexuality, class, national identity, state formations, kinship, children etc.) in which homophobic readings of the Bible emerge. We will also look at the ways in which these discourses and the identities they shore up can be "queered," as well as at biblical texts that can be read as queer friendly. This process of queering will allow and require us to approach the biblical text in new ways.

Not even referencing the historical paradigm, this course focuses on queer theory as a lens for examining biblical texts and the history of interpretation. It is grounded in cutting-edge biblical scholarship that engages biblical literature as integral part of past and present discourse, as a hermeneutically relevant resource for contemporary readers in today's world.

Similar curricular innovation is part of the religious studies department of Barnard College in New York City. Next to traditional courses, such as "Rel 3501 Hebrew Bible: Introduction to the Literature of Ancient Israel against the Background of the Ancient Near East," other courses advance newer hermeneutical developments. An example is the following course:

> 4730 Exodus & Politics: Religious Narrative as a Source of Revolution: Examination of the study of the Israelite exodus from Egypt, as it has influenced modern forms of political and social revolution, w/emphasis on political philosopher Michael Walzer. Examination of the variety of context this story has been used in: construction of early American identity, African-American religious experience, Latin American liberation theology, Palestinian nationalism, and religious feminism.[42]

The course investigates the book of Exodus through its history of interpretation and relates the academic study of the Bible to society, politics, culture, and religion. Perhaps these are the kind of courses Schüssler Fiorenza had in mind when she thought of creativity and innovation at the undergraduate level. Yet they appear to be rare in a biblical studies curriculum that accentuates historical methodology.

Sometimes the undergraduate curriculum also perpetuates another dynamic that has haunted Christian theology for the millennia. Although the data are limited here, it may serve as a cautionary note on the inherent difficulties of teaching Bible to broad audiences, as is the case at the undergraduate level. The problem is that sometimes the undergraduate curriculum contains a total of one Hebrew Bible course. As a result, in-depth courses are rare, and generic courses emerge. Such a situation seems to have evolved at

---

42. See http://www.barnard.edu/catalog.pdf.

the religious studies department at Agnes Scott College in Decatur, Georgia, which lists only a single Hebrew Bible course entitled "100 Hebrew Bible." The blurb states: "Religious history and society of the people of ancient Israel as contained in their sacred Scriptures with a link to contemporary Jewish practice and interpretation."[43] Grounded in historical analysis, the course covers two broad areas, Israelite history and contemporary Judaism, and so the course connects the study of the Hebrew Bible with Judaism. But locating the Hebrew Bible as part of Judaism only is problematic because it marginalizes the Old Testament as an integral part of the Christian canon. It assumes that the Old Testament is secondary to Christian theology. The second-century Christian theologian Marcion is among the most renowned proponents of this anti-Jewish attitude toward the Old Testament, a position that the Early Church rejected.[44]

The Agnes Scott catalog lists an introductory course on the New Testament that aggravates the problem. In parallel design to the Hebrew Bible course, the New Testament blurb promises to examine the New Testament literature "with links to contemporary Christian practice and interpretation."[45] The course thus reinforces the notion that the Hebrew Bible belongs only to Judaism and the New Testament is more important to Christians than the Hebrew Bible. It would be advantageous theologically and pedagogically to include Jewish and Christian practices and interpretations in a single Hebrew Bible course to avoid misunderstandings about the Hebrew Bible's significance to Christianity.

Similarly, Kenyon College in Gambier, Ohio, mentions in its online course catalog only one Hebrew Bible course entitled "RLST 310 Hebrew Scriptures/Old Testament." The description states:

---

43. Agnes Scott's Academic Catalog of 2007–2009 lists only one Hebrew Bible course, but other courses include the study of Judaism and Christianity. Among them are: New Testament; Jesus in History and Culture; Introduction to Christianity; Judaism, Christianity, and Islam; Sacred Texts of the World's Religions; Jewish Faith and Practice; Roman Catholic Faith and Practice, Protestant Faith and Practice, Gender in U.S. Religion, Feminist and Womanist Ethics and Spirituality. See http://www.agnesscott.edu/academics/catalog.

44. See, e.g., Padraic O'Hare, *The Enduring Covenant: The Education of Christians and the End of Antisemitism* (Valley Forge, Pa.: Trinity Press International, 1997); Craig A. Evans and Donald A. Hagner, eds., *Anti-Semitism and Early Christianity: Issues of Polemic and Faith* (Minneapolis: Fortress, 1993); Charlotte Klein, *Anti-Judaism in Christian Theology* (trans. Edward Quinn; Philadelphia: Fortress, 1978).

45. The complete course blurb states: "101 Literature of the New Testament and its origins and development in the early Jesus movement and early Christianity, with links to contemporary Christian practice and interpretation."

This course will serve as an introduction to the Hebrew Scriptures (Old Testament), as they reflect the myths, history, and institutions of ancient Israel. Topics to be explored will include biblical narratives and poetry, law codes, prayers and ritual, the prophetic critique of religion and society, and wisdom literature. Students will be given an opportunity to read a selection of short fiction and poetry that have been inspired by biblical literature.[46]

This course places the study of the Hebrew Bible firmly within the historical paradigm although it also promises to trace the Hebrew Bible in literature. The historical outlook evades the curricular problem of the Agnes Scott curriculum, but it, too, does not move beyond the nineteenth-century model.

Other colleges pursue yet a different route and develop a comprehensive "mini-seminary" curriculum. This is the case at the department of philosophy and religion at Morehouse College in Atlanta, Georgia, where an Old Testament introduction course is followed by the New Testament equivalent and several specialized Bible courses, such as "235 The Eighth Century Prophets" and "230 Understanding the Bible," followed by courses on church history, systematic theology, and psychology of religion.[47]

In short, then, these undergraduate departments conceptualize Hebrew Bible courses primarily as history courses that illuminate ancient Near Eastern and Israelite history. Sometimes they also include literary approaches, and only a few courses investigate the Hebrew Bible with contemporary hermeneutics and methodologies. Overall, then, the undergraduate curriculum remains closely tied to the Protestant vision of Schleiermacher which conceptualized biblical studies as a historical enterprise.

Admittedly, only a few examples substantiate the points made above, but another indicator supports the accuracy of the observations. This one comes from undergraduate textbooks that illustrate that the undergraduate curriculum mimics the graduate curriculum of Schleiermacher's vision. The books are published in edition after edition because there are many Bible courses that require them. Accordingly, they preserve a curriculum that fosters historical-literalist description of biblical texts. The next section examines popular textbooks in Hebrew Bible to demonstrate the prevalence of this curricular pattern.

---

46. See http://www.kenyon.edu/x11447.xml. Two additional courses in biblical studies appear in the online catalog; one introduces the New Testament ("RLST 225 New Testament") and another investigates the phenomenon of prophecy in biblical and contemporary literatures and sociopolitical movements ("RLST 382 Prophecy").

47. The course blurb explains: "210 Introduction to the Old Testament: Survey of the literature of the Old Testament, bringing to bear upon it the fruits of modern historical and archaeological research." See http://www.morehouse.edu/academics/phil/courses.html.

3. Undergraduate Textbooks on the Hebrew Bible

Anyone who teaches at the undergraduate level receives textbooks that arrive in the office mailbox without request. Publishers send them because they know that professors are continuously looking for new books to be used in future semesters. Many of these books outline the biblical story line in accessible prose aided by graphs, photos, and art pictures. As a whole, the books simplify complex historical, linguistic, and scholarly discussions, and they summarize seemingly straight-forward Israelite history, events, and characters. Usually, they omit details on postmodern hermeneutical advances or the difficulties of historical reconstruction. Discussions on multiple meanings, newer exegetical methods, and the significance of social location are largely absent, as is information on the use of the Bible in contemporary U.S.-American society such as the Ten Commandments or the creationist controversy. Content overviews, historical dates, and shortened historical analyses predominate.

A good example is Stephen L. Harris's *Understanding the Bible*, a book that describes the Christian canon in 533 pages.[48] The book follows the canonical order of the Bible and surveys biblical content and historiographical discussions. Devoting a single page to "[t]he Bible read from different social perspectives,"[49] Harris mentions hermeneutical issues. He acknowledges that "[i]n recent years, scholars have become increasingly aware that the meaning of any book—including the Bible—is to a large extent dependent on the reader's individual experience and viewpoint."[50]

Harris's statement is not entirely accurate since debates on social location are not often defined by "individual" experiences or viewpoints but are instead a matter of collective historical, cultural, and political investigation. Furthermore, the ensuing short description on African American, Native American, and feminist hermeneutics is too brief to give readers a sense of the research as it has developed since the 1970s. For instance, Harris states that "[a]s feminist critics have pointed out, women of all nationalities may read the Bible from a perspective different from that of most men."[51] This short comment shortchanges feminist accomplishments and makes feminist goals seem naive. Feminist interpretations are not grounded in essentializing notions that emphasize differences between women and men, but they investigate the rela-

---

48. Stephen L. Harris, *Understanding the Bible* (7th ed.; Boston: McGraw Hill, 2006).
49. Ibid., 33.
50. Ibid.
51. Ibid.

tionship between the Bible and androcentrism and increasingly also between gender and other social categories.[52]

A specific reference to Pauline gender politics does not remedy Harris's cryptic discussion of feminist biblical scholarship. In a literalist statement on Pauline and post-Pauline passages, Harris writes:

> Paul's flat refusal to permit a woman to teach in his churches (1 Cor. 14:34–35) or the Pastor's insistence that the first woman must be blamed for humanity's downward spiral into sin and death (1 Tim. 2:13–14) may spark feelings of incredulity or resentment unknown to the men listening to the same passages. But, as feminist scholars have also observed, the same apostle who allegedly forbade women to address the congregation also recognized the role of women prophets (1 Cor. 11:5) and women as church officeholders, as well as 'fellow workers' in the Christian fold (Rom. 16:1–5). At his most insightful, Paul endorses a vision of radical equality—legal, ethnic, social, and sexual.... (Gal. 3:28).[53]

In this brief statement on women's places in the early Christian movements, Harris refers to popular New Testament passages as if this short description summarized the complex results of feminist research. Content description of selected verses becomes a substitute for a thorough representation of the pertinent scholarly positions. This nod at contemporary hermeneutical accomplishments confirms the overall impression that Harris promotes a curriculum mostly based on the historical-literalist paradigm. Many similar textbooks also engage the literalist-descriptive strategy evident in Harris's book, advancing the Schleiermacher paradigm.[54]

---

52. For information on these developments in Hebrew Bible, see Susanne Scholz, *Introducing the Women's Hebrew Bible* (London: T&T Clark, 2007), esp. 100–121.

53. Harris, *Understanding the Bible*, 33.

54. Barry L. Bandstra, *Reading the Old Testament: An Introduction to the Hebrew Bible* (Belmont, Calif.: Wadsworth/Thomson Learning, 2004); Bernhard W. Anderson with Steven Bishop and Judith H. Newman, *Understanding the Old Testament* (5th ed.; Upper Saddle River, N.J.: Prentice Hall, 2007); Corrine L. Carvalho, *Encountering Ancient Voices: A Guide to Reading the Old Testament* (Winona, Minn.: Saint Mary's Press, 2006); Christian E. Hauer and William A. Young, *Introduction to the Bible* (Upper Saddle River, N.J.: Prentice Hall, 2005); Adam L. Porter, *Introducing the Bible: An Active Learning Approach* (Upper Saddle River, N.J.: Prentice Hall, 2005); John J. Collins, *Introduction to the Hebrew Bible* (Minneapolis: Augsburg Fortress, 2004); Stephen Harris and Robert Platzner, *The Old Testament: An Introduction to the Hebrew Bible* (New York: McGraw-Hill, 2002); Henry Jackson Flanders, Robert W. Crapps, and David A. Smith, *People of the Covenant: An Introduction to the Hebrew Bible* (New York: Oxford University Press, 1996); Frank S. Frick, *A

Another textbook that is solidly grounded in historical analysis tries to accomplish more. Written by J. Bradley Chance and Milton P. Horne,[55] *Rereading the Bible: An Introduction to the Biblical Story* is not limited to canonical content description interspersed with historical research because, as the authors state, "it is virtually impossible to survey the sixty-six books of the Bible in a typical fifteen-week semester" and "inevitably, professors must be selective."[56] Thus, Chance and Horne make "no pretence to cover everything." They organize the materials according to the scholarly conviction that "the Bible came to be as a result of interpretive readings of earlier texts and traditions." The pedagogical goal is that students learn "how the Bible came to be."[57] Thus, Chance and Horne start with the latest "rereading" contained in the Hebrew Bible canon, the postexilic books of Ezra and Nehemiah. The hermeneutical decision puts the postexilic books into a prominent and unusual position. In contrast to other textbooks, here Ezra and Nehemiah appear in the initial chapters of the book. In addition, post-exilic Jewish topics organize the entire presentation of the Hebrew Bible, among them "the Temple, the Torah, and an ideology of self-exclusion endorsed by many Jewish people of this era."[58]

Yet even this innovative approach is limited to traditional conventions of the biblical studies curriculum. Emphasizing historical origins and authorial meaning, it excludes the rich post-canonical history of interpretation. It also does not include discussions on the rhetorical functions of biblical texts in past and present contexts, or an examination of the ideological meanings in variously located sociopolitical and religious discourse. Although the book tries to break with a linear description of biblical content mixed with historical critical information, it too does not go beyond the nineteenth-century paradigm. Chance and Horne aim for a "radical-democratic" curricular model, but ultimately they do not succeed. They limit themselves to historical methodology and content description.

These and other books, then, demonstrate the pervasiveness of the traditional nineteenth-century seminary curriculum. Similar to Hebrew Bible courses, they emphasize historical-literalist analysis. Kelsey observes that theological teaching, research, and writing reinforce each other. They are

---

Journey through the Hebrew Scriptures (Fort Worth: Harcourt Brace College Publishers, 1995).

55. J. Bradley Chance and Milton P. Horne, *Rereading the Bible: An Introduction to the Biblical Story* (Upper Saddle River, N.J.: Prentice Hall, 2000).
56. Ibid., xviii.
57. Ibid., xx.
58. Ibid.

discipline-preserving activities that make change difficult to attain whether on the undergraduate or graduate level. Both course descriptions and textbooks illustrate the validity of this observation.

4. A "Radical-Democratic" Model for Teaching Biblical Studies

Elisabeth Schüssler Fiorenza contends that research and teaching of biblical studies need to "articulate a radical democratic religious imaginary that sustains wo/men, in transnational struggles against the injustice and devastations of global empire and for the survival and well-being of all."[59] This rhetorical-emancipatory model is based on "an ethical-political turn"[60] that "investigates and reconstructs the discursive arguments of a text, its socioreligious location, and its diverse interpretations in order to underscore the text's possible oppressive as well as liberative/performative actions, values, and possibilities in every-changing historical-cultural situations."[61] This is the abstract agenda of a radical-democratic curriculum in biblical studies. It teaches how to understand a text's discursive arguments, examines the various socioreligious and political contexts within which these arguments are made and read, and recognizes the oppressive and liberative textual histories and potentials within multiple reading contexts.

Schüssler Fiorenza's proposal is clear. A biblical studies curriculum cannot be limited to content description and historical-literal presentation. Schleiermacher's vision, modified or not, is insufficient in an era in which human and ecological needs are perhaps greater than ever. Is it then preferable and more effective to nurture students' faith, as evangelical departments of theology and religion tend to do? Schleiermacher rejected vehemently this option during a time in which historiography counted as superior intellectual work. Yet his priority does not match contemporary needs which are increasingly characterized by "multicultural versus fundamentalist" sensibilities.[62] Our times are different from the nineteenth-century European enthusiasm for historically defined truth, valid anywhere and for anyone.

Taking these ideas into account, I developed an anthology entitled *Biblical Studies Alternatively*, which contains scholarly resources for teaching Bible

---

59. Elisabeth Schüssler Fiorenza, *The Power of the Word: Scripture and the Rhetoric of Empire* (Minneapolis: Fortress, 2007), 27.
60. Ibid., 253.
61. Ibid., 253–54.
62. See, e.g., the informative discussion on this dynamic by Jeffrey W. Robbins, "Terror and the Postmodern Condition: Toward a Radical Political Theology," in *Religion and Violence in a Secular World: Toward a New Political Theology* (ed. Clayton Crocket; Charlottesville: University of Virginia Press, 2006), 187–205.

courses grounded in the "radical-democratic" teaching model.[63] More specifically, the materials help in correlating the study of the Bible to gender, race/ethnicity, and class. They are a resource for interpreting biblical literature as a site of theo-ethical and sociopolitical struggle in the past and the present, "as a site of struggle over authority, values, and meaning" with "public character and political responsibility."[64] Some articles in the volume do not reject the historical-literalist model. Yet all of them provide perspectives and resources to enhance a radical-democratic approach. The anthology promotes multiplicity of meanings, reader centeredness, and sociopolitical explorations in biblical literature and interpretation.

Suffice it to say that the book aims to bring biblical literature "back" into the intellectual debates on today's social, political, cultural, and religious issues, and to release the Bible from its academically isolated, undervalued, and privatized space.[65] As one of my students said: "In this Bible course we have talked about *everything*: money, sexuality, race, religion, politics—is this still a course on the Bible?" I told the students that, yes, this is a course on the Bible, and I also asked them why they would not expect to learn about all of these issues in a biblical studies course. What followed was a good discussion on the inclination of many Western readers to historicize, sentimentalize, and privatize the Bible and its academic study.

An example shall demonstrate how the resources in *Biblical Studies Alternatively* foster a "radical-democratic" approach that develops in students' intellectual-religious maturity, historical-cultural understanding, and literary-ethical engagement. The book includes several articles that investigate the issue of class in relation to particular biblical texts. Debates on classism are not a popular topic in U.S.-American society and undergraduate students whom I taught during the past ten years are rarely asked to think critically about poverty and wealth. The mostly white undergraduate students whom I taught in the past decade take for granted that they belong to the numinous "middle class," and they tend to be firm believers in the ideology of the "American Dream." It takes several handouts and meetings to explore why most U.S.-Americans believe that they belong to the middle class, whether they are poor, independently wealthy, or enjoy a paycheck each month. Students also learn that contemporary U.S.-American society allows for less class mobility than contemporary European societies.

---

63. Susanne Scholz, ed., *Biblical Studies Alternatively: An Introductory Reader* (Upper Saddle River, N.J.: Prentice Hall, 2003).
64. Schüssler Fiorenza, *Power of the Word*, 254.
65. For an analysis of this problem, see Hector Avalos, *The End of Biblical Studies* (Amherst, N.Y.: Prometheus, 2007).

The work benefits from data on the overwhelming number of poor people in today's world which challenges students to think about their ethical responsibilities toward economic inequity.⁶⁶ Students are usually appalled about the level of inequality in the United States, but they find it difficult to let go of politically conservative ideas about social welfare, charity, and the acquisition of wealth. They believe in the merits of a capitalist economy: "If you work hard, you will make it." They also often reject expanding foreign aid to poor nations because, in their opinion, too much money flows already into impoverished countries. Additional handouts quickly dispel these notions.⁶⁷

Once the contemporary context is at least superficially scanned, the work continues with biblical texts and interpretations on wealth, poverty, and economic justice. For instance, we read Jon L. Berquist's "Dangerous Waters of Justice and Righteousness: Amos 5:18-27," which examines the famous prophetic passage in Amos that Christians and Jews like to mention in debates on socioeconomic injustice.⁶⁸ Berquist presents three interpretative traditions that focus particularly on verse 24. In the early twentieth-century, interpreters emphasized the aspect of punishment in the prophetic announcement. The Revised Standard Version (RSV) illustrates this viewpoint in its use of the noun "judgment" in verse 24 for the Hebrew term *mišpat*. Accordingly, God pronounces "judgment" upon the people for their failings and condemns them to punishment. Amos is seen as a prophet of doom whose prophecy gives the people one last opportunity for change.

Later in the twentieth century, another interpretative tradition becomes prevalent that highlights the poem's positive ethical dimensions. It rejects the idea that God performs punitive justice, and instead stresses that people have to commit themselves to the doing of justice. Ethics solves the problem of religious ritual, and thus, for instance, Martin Luther King Jr. quoted verse 24 to instill hope for social change. This reading is optimistic about people's ability to function as agents for social justice. It assumes that we can change

---

66. Jeffrey Selingo and Jeffrey Brainard, "The Rich-Poor Gap Widens for Colleges and Students," *Chronicle of Higher Education* (7 April 2006): A1, A13; Jo Blanden, Paul Gregg, and Stephen Machin, "Intergenerational Mobility in Europe and North America: A Report Supported by the Sutton Trust," *Centre for Economic Performance* (April 2005); online: http://cep.lse.ac.uk/about/news/IntergenerationalMobility.pdf; Bob Herbert, "The Mobility Myth," *New York Times* (6 June 2005): 19; see also websites such as: http://www.undp.org/poverty; www.globalissues.org/TradeRelated/Poverty.asp?p=1; and www.policy-almanac.org/social_welfare/poverty.shtml.

67. See, e.g., "Relief Agency Criticizes Rich Lands," *New York Times* (6 December 2004): A12.

68. Jon L. Berquist, "Dangerous Waters of Justice and Righteousness," in Scholz, *Biblical Studies Alternatively*, 327–41.

society for the better if we understand that working toward social change is doing God's work. In contrast to the earlier interpretative tradition, then, the prophet is not seen as a bringer of doom. The second tradition affirms the human ability to create justice on earth and views humans as the potential doers of God's will.

Berquist describes yet another interpretative tradition that stresses the significance of "the waters" in verse 24. Here the poem does not address a problem with ritual or worship practice, a position that sometimes has led to anti-Jewish interpretations in Christian commentaries. Rather, the poem wrestles with the problem of unequal distribution of wealth and power, and offers a unique solution by proposing radical and fundamental social change. It calls for the total destruction of society because anything less would compromise divine justice and righteousness. Without such comprehensive and all-destructive change, the inconsistency between religious practice and societal justice would result in blasphemy.

This third interpretation requires an in-depth look at the terminology, especially the meaning of "the waters" in verse 24. Berquist explains that "the waters" should not be imagined as soothing and refreshing liquids, but instead as having dangerous and all-destructive qualities. They are forceful like Noah's flood that destroyed everything in its way. "The waters" contain the raw force of a tsunami that wipes out everything and everybody in its path. They are harbingers for divine justice and righteousness, eliminating unjust social conditions and ushering in a new beginning. The poem suggests that justice and righteousness, to be worthy of divine affiliation, arrive only after the annihilation of known society.

According to this interpretative tradition, then, God is seen as destroying all people to restore justice and righteousness in society. Like religious fundamentalists of any persuasion, Amos emerges as a prophet who calls for complete, uncompromised, and total change. Neither divine purging nor human intervention suffice to implement divine order or to eradicate socioeconomic injustice. It requires "the destruction of known society with the fulfillment of divine intention."[69] Thus, the poem is "extremely countercultural."

Students in my classes find the third interpretative tradition that characterizes Amos as a religious fundamentalist completely unacceptable. They associate fundamentalism with people flying planes into buildings, and thus favor socioeconomic moderation and compromise. They do not support a position that solves the problem of poverty by calling for the total destruction of unjust society. It is difficult for them to view social injustice as such a grave problem to merit such extreme action. When students learn that other

---

69. Ibid., 340.

biblical passages (e.g., the book of Proverbs) address issues of wealth and poverty, yet are differently interpreted than the Amos poem, students are usually astonished about the plurality of biblical and interpretative viewpoints. They also begin to grasp the complexities of reading the Hebrew Bible with socioeconomic issues in mind. Exam after exam shows their growing intellectual-religious maturity, historical-cultural understanding, and literary-ethical engagement. It is a rewarding process, and, if space allowed it, additional examples could illustrate that this approach creates important pedagogical and intellectual learning in the undergraduate teaching of biblical studies.

In short, a "radical-democratic" approach—according to this specific example—examines the structures of globalized inequalities and injustices in the social, political, economic, and religious realms of human societies and relates them to the reading of biblical texts such as Amos 5:24. Understood as "a site of struggle over authority, values, and meaning,"[70] such a biblical studies curriculum defines the academic study of the Bible as helping students understand the contributions of biblical interpretations to past and present political, societal, and economic Bible readings. It educates students toward an active participation in society and religion, freeing "them from all forms of kyriarchal inequality and oppression."[71]

IN CONCLUSION

This article described the biblical studies curriculum as articulated by nineteenth-century theologian, Friedrich Schleiermacher. It investigated the ongoing contemporary dominance of this curriculum and illustrated the benefits of an alternative approach, one that envisions the teaching of biblical studies according to the "radical democratic" model as defined by Elisabeth Schüssler Fiorenza. This model is not often practiced in biblical studies, and the article demonstrated that many undergraduate Bible courses and textbooks mimic a graduate curriculum that is committed to Schleiermacher's influential design of biblical studies as a historical-literalist enterprise.

This, then, is the pedagogical challenge from within the field of biblical studies: to move from curricular apathy to a "radical-democratic" practice that educates students toward an understanding of the complexities and challenges in our world and towards an increase of "knowledge, values and skills that will prepare them for active and effective participation in society."[72] It is

---

70. Schüssler Fiorenza, *Power of the Word*, 254.
71. Ibid.
72. Carol M. Barker, *Liberal Arts Education for a Global Society* (2000): available at http://carnegie.org/fileadmin/Media/Publications/PDF/libarts.pdf.

not an easy task for various reasons, not the least of which is the fact that the nineteenth-century model of theological education is well and alive.[73] Furthermore, many contemporary Western people are "allergic" to Christian fundamentalism and prefer to eliminate *all* religious study from higher education. In turn, Christian fundamentalists try to combat the secular disregard for religion. They fear a critical examination of the Bible because, in their view, it led to religion's demise in the first place. For sure, the Christian Right in the United States works hard to reclaim the Bible—alas, in a religiously and sociopolitically conservative fashion. The result is a tug of war in which neither side wants to use rational arguments. The pedagogical aim of a radical-democratic curriculum runs into resistance from many sides.

Still, it is time to develop a biblical studies curriculum on all levels of higher education that teaches biblical studies as an academic field of inquiry, needed for a comprehensive understanding of culture, politics, and religion. Can the biblical studies curriculum be reshaped to account for the social, political, religious, and intellectual struggles in our world today? It is good to remember that Schleiermacher did not get discouraged when he saw little of the theological education he had in mind. Of course, in 1811, he was in a powerful academic position—really at the heart of the academic enterprise in Berlin, and able to implement changes as he saw fit. Many of us are not located in places of academic power, and nowadays it often seems as if change arrived there last anyway. But a move toward the radical-democratic teaching model is possible wherever we teach, and a sustained conversation on the biblical studies curriculum at all levels ensures that we develop a viable future for the field. This is, perhaps, more urgent now than in the nineteenth century because, as William M. Plater states, "the entire system of American postsecondary education is undergoing a profound transformation."[74] Yet these university-wide developments are beyond the topic of this paper.

---

73. Another difficulty relates to the changing socioeconomic dynamics in U.S.-American universities as institutions of higher learning; see Marc Bousquet, *How the University Works: Higher Education and the Low-Wage Nation* (New York: New York University Press, 2008).

74. William M. Plater, "The Twenty-First-Century Professoriate," *Academe Online* (July–August 2008); online: www.aaup.org/AAUP/pubsres/Academe/2008/JA/Feat/plat.htm.

Biblical Studies for Ministry: Critical and Faithful Interpretation of Scripture in an Either/Or World

Cynthia Briggs Kittredge

Introduction

In ten years of teaching in an Episcopal theological seminary, I have adapted the most valuable tools and critical methods for studying the Bible that I acquired in my doctoral education in order to meet the needs of those being trained as leaders in Christian communities who interpret, preach and teach Scripture in the churches.[1] As essential as those tools are to my pedagogy, the seminary context of ministerial formation has raised significant questions left unaddressed in my doctoral training and has demanded a very different set of skills. In the course of developing with my colleagues a biblical studies curriculum for teaching ministers in a theological school, I discovered that hermeneutical freedom and pedagogical innovation prospered in a way that it could not or did not in the setting of the academy, either in university graduate studies or in the majority of scholarly discussions at annual meetings of the Society of Biblical Literature. Theoretical questions that preoccupied SBL groups for years were being solved on the ground daily in classrooms and pulpits.

This essay reflects on the particular challenges of teaching biblical studies for ministry in a denominational seminary. I will describe the shift in perspective that the transition from graduate biblical studies to ministerial biblical studies required and the curriculum designed to integrate the historical and the hermeneutical with the practical arts of ministry, teaching and preaching. The experience of teaching in this context suggests areas for greater attention in programs of graduate biblical education to prepare those who will teach

---

1. Seminary of the Southwest, Austin, Texas, 1999 to the present.

future leaders in communities of faith. As teachers and preachers of the Bible, these leaders will convene communities in which the Bible transforms people and institutions.

Discussion about teaching the Bible in a theological seminary takes place in the midst of considerable strife about the perceived conflicts between the church and the academy. In polemical style the tensions between their values are posed as oppositions. This debate is carried out on a wider scale in global political struggles about power and wealth, empire and democracy, and sectarianism and pluralism. In the narrower world of biblical studies, the extremes are articulated as "the Bible as cultural product" and "the Bible as scripture" or between "historical critical interpretation" and "theological interpretation." Feminist and liberationist critiques of the Bible are usually placed on the critical/cultural/historical side of the polarity. In a world that grows ever more divided and violent over these issues, one of the most important skills for biblical scholars and for pastors, preachers, and teachers is to be able to give a sympathetic account of the different positions and to be able to name and describe areas of hermeneutical or theological difference in order to carry on constructive conversations.

Doctoral biblical studies and ministerial biblical education have distinct but overlapping purposes. Although some theorists dramatically oppose "religious studies" and "theological studies," there are important common values. Doctoral studies prepare scholars and professors to teach and to do scholarship in a variety of educational, public, and professional settings among which are theological seminaries. A seminary prepares preachers and teachers of the Bible for communities of faith for whom the Bible is scripture, a source of tradition and teaching, and a force to shape its imagination and language. In one way then, teaching ministers is one of the things that a doctorally-trained biblical scholar might do. In addition, the aims of the two fields overlap in important ways. Both the professor of biblical studies and the Christian preacher are responsible to wider publics on whom their expert scholarship and authoritative proclamation has an impact. Both the ideals of learning the liberal arts in a university and the ideal of learned Christian ministry intend to form thoughtful, imaginative leaders who will use their education in concert with their faith or their ideals for the well-being of human society. Important critiques of the values of the university have been made from a Christian theological perspective, and their observations have merit. However, I stress here how their goals converge. Both graduate biblical studies and ministerial biblical education seek to teach ways to conduct these conversations responsibly and skillfully in order to make it possible to negotiate the conflict.

ETHOS AND AIMS OF GRADUATE BIBLICAL STUDIES

The ethos of biblical studies at the university divinity school where I did both my ministerial training and my doctoral study was historical-critical: its aim was to describe as accurately and objectively as possible the social and historical context of the biblical authors in order to ascertain the meaning of the text in its own time.[2] For students in the Master of Divinity program the primary tool of evaluation was the exegesis paper. Written on a short passage of text, the paper was to conclude with a one sentence statement paraphrasing the meaning of the text. Students were to read the Bible like any other text and employ the same statutes of narrative analysis and historical investigation as they would other contemporary or ancient literature. The focus of analysis were the human words in human history of people who sought to understand the purposes and character of God. Parallel Canaanite stories shed light on the narratives of the Hebrew Bible, and Greco-Roman genres and categories clarified the style and aims of the Gospels. From this perspective, the New Testament formed a diverse collection of distinctive understandings of Jesus and the Canon represented a selection of a wider body of early Christian literature. Disciplined study of the wide range of noncanonical literature advanced the understanding of the landscape of early Christianity and its canonical writings. Though the distinction between what the text meant and what the text means was maintained as a useful tool for analysis, the division of labor between exegete and theologian was a fact of life, whether intentional or not. Krister Stendahl's "Ten Commandments of Preaching" set out a rigorous program of "biblical preaching" that prohibited homogenizing Gospel portraits of Jesus or making facile "relevance." In short, the dominant ethos of the early to mid 1980's was shaped by faculty trained in the historical-critical perspective.

Historical criticism has been widely and justifiably criticized for its limitations. However, the attacks on pure historical criticism as antiquarian, ethically nearsighted, and dismissive of faith do not fairly characterize the way such methods were exercised and embodied by the faculty at Harvard Divinity School. On the contrary, when practiced by skilled teachers, many of whom were also priests, pastors, and preachers committed to church communities beyond the academy, these historical methods had ethical intentions: namely, to take seriously the experience of historical people, to aid in understanding the divisions between Judaism and Christianity, the debates around orthodoxy and heresy, and although it was not put this way, to read the biblical texts with integrity and faithfulness. Many ministerial students found this

---

2. Harvard Divinity School, 1981–1984, 1986–1988, 1989–1996.

way of studying the Bible, though very different from their backgrounds in biblical reading, to be intellectually challenging, thrilling and intriguing, and productive of fascinating questions for theology. There was an optimism and confidence that, while this method brought results that were in tension with church doctrine or piety, somehow these differences would get worked out, and that the Bible and those who identified with it would survive the challenges posed. These questions were loosely acknowledged, but left to those with more interest in them to answer.

The area of primary historical focus was the early first century. Most important was the author's meaning in the text itself and in the prehistory and sources of the text. Little attention was given to the interpretation of the texts by the early Church Fathers or those who collected the works at the time of canonization. As a result biblical studies was separated from church history and the history of interpretation. Scholarship on the Christian Old Testament was carried out in the Department of Near Eastern Languages and Civilizations. The theologians did their work without direct engagement with biblical studies, and biblical scholars were reluctant to enter into the territory of theological construction. Faculty did not engage their scholarship with questions of current politics; to do so would have been seen to interfere with scholarly objectivity.

For the most part, the doctoral programs in biblical studies bracketed pastoral and theological questions. An exception was the feminist hermeneutical model, introduced explicitly into the curriculum when Elisabeth Schüssler Fiorenza joined the faculty. The model of "remembrance, suspicion, reconstruction, evaluation, and proclamation" helped to integrate the pastoral and the theological in a way that historical methods did not. The model not only allowed for but required theological evaluation and critique as part of studying the Bible. The critical dimension that in the earlier era of historical criticism was applied to some of the claims about authorship, history, and unity of the text, was extended by the feminist hermeneutical model to the cultural perspective of the biblical text. The feminist lens allowed one to recognize and name the androcentric perspective of the text and to describe and grapple with the effect of these texts in shaping households and churches in Western culture. The perspective recognized and addressed questions brought to the Bible by those who had not historically been in the majority of biblical interpreters. When it was employed by some of us among the doctoral students, usually in concert with historical criticism, it significantly reshaped the academic discussion of various exegetical issues and had significant implications for ministerial practice.

The dominant historical-critical ethos of graduate biblical studies at Harvard Divinity School had aims that were not in themselves hostile to other ways of reading the Bible, especially by historic communities of faith. But that ethos meant that a great deal was neglected—the history of interpretation by Christian communities, the current ways of reading the Bible in contemporary congregations, liturgical and artistic readings of the Bible, and most nonrational and nonlinear modes of thinking. Our training was occupied with producing a dissertation to demonstrate competence in our area of specialization; only voluntary peripheral programs and projects addressed issues of pedagogy. Practical questions such as who we would be teaching and how we would teach them were left for us to figure out on our own. That different skills and strengths might be required for the varied ethos of the university, the denominationally based college, or the theological seminary was not directly addressed.

BIBLICAL INTERPRETATION FOR CHRISTIAN MINISTERS

When I began teaching students preparing for ordained ministry at Seminary of the Southwest, the ethos of the denominational seminary required a shift of perspective. Replicating the model of graduate biblical studies would not suit the educational needs and vocational goals of our students. My colleagues, who shared a similar doctoral education and who were also pastors and preachers, collaborated to revise the historical-critical model in which we had been trained.[3] For those being formed to interpret scripture for faith communities, the goal could not be the reconstruction of biblical history for its own sake, but to assist in the interpretation of the text. A one-sentence summary of "what the text meant" would not suffice for leaders who would be convincingly proclaiming this text as gospel. Daily worship in the community constantly raised questions about the use and interpretation of scripture in the daily office, the Eucharistic lectionary, and in preaching. Historical study of the formation of this canonical literature would have to make a meaningful contribution among the evident multiple ways of reading and using scripture in the Christian community.[4]

Limited time for instruction, competing expectations and demands on students, and high stakes for interpreting the Bible are complications of our

---

3. Seminary of the Southwest, Austin, Texas: Michael H. Floyd, Raymond W. Pickett, and R. Steven Bishop have taught during the period from 1999 to the present.

4. For helpful perspectives on the theological interpretation of scripture, see Ellen F. Davis and Richard B. Hays, eds., *The Art of Reading Scripture* (Grand Rapids: Eerdmans, 2003). For a recent treatment of practical theology as an integrating discipline in theological education, see Dorothy C. Bass and Craig Dykstra, eds., *For Life Abundant: Practical Theology, Theological Education, and Christian Ministry* (Grand Rapids: Eerdmans, 2008).

situation that have influenced how we teach the Bible for ministry. Like most mainline theological schools in North America, the seminary where I teach is accountable to many constituencies. Teaching the most up-to-date literature in biblical studies is only one among many expectations. Local churches, dioceses, and church adjudicatories pressure seminaries for practically oriented pastors, with leadership skills drawn from professional literature in business, congregational studies, church growth, and evangelism. Church officials may share some of the general cultural suspicion about the antagonism of scholarship to faith. Congregations and examining boards expect students to hold views of biblical authority consonant with their traditions and ordination vows, be able to preach forcefully and with conviction, make the Bible come alive, and to teach the Bible as the canon of the church. All of these pressures complicate the teaching of biblical studies.[5]

Students come to biblical studies with various backgrounds, some from fundamentalist traditions, others from little or no familiarity with biblical narratives, language, or sensibility. Teachers are confronted with the challenge of immersing postmodern students in the literature of the Bible and introducing methods of critical interpretation. They represent a range of academic ability from those who have recent professional degrees in law and medicine to those who have not been in school for many years. Theological students in seminaries bring many gifts for ministry but do not always possess the linear, verbal, "left brain" skills rewarded by schools and required by doctoral programs in biblical studies.

The current political and cultural theological environment affects our students' biblical education—most particularly the "Jesus wars" played out in the media, the fundamentalist-liberal polemics in the church and popular press, and most urgently and with the apparently highest stakes, the disputes around the role of gays and lesbians in church leadership. These controversies are closely intertwined with questions of biblical authority, critical theological evaluation of the Bible and tradition and its symbolic universe. These controversies effect denominational examinations and sometimes employment and placement. The polarized environment is a fraught one for biblical studies. Traditionalists portray the conflict as a battle about revelation, the essentials of the faith and eternal salvation. Our students must either take sides in

---

5. For analysis and reflection on the challenges of changing contexts for theological education, see Malcolm L. Warford, ed., *Practical Wisdom: On Theological Teaching and Learning* (New York: Lang, 2005). See also Charles R. Foster, Lisa E. Dahill, Lawrence A. Goleman, and Barbara Wang Tolentino, eds., *Educating Clergy: Teaching Practices and Pastoral Imagination* (The Carnegie Foundation for the Advancement of Teaching; San Francisco: Jossey-Bass, 2006).

this way of phrasing the debate or be able to articulate an alternative way of describing the issues.

To address the need for pastors to negotiate this complex climate for biblical interpretation, our Bible faculty developed a series of three required courses that places historical study of the biblical text into a larger interpretive process. Biblical interpretation is focused around two ministerial practices, teaching and preaching. The goal of teaching and preaching the Bible is critical and faithful appropriation of scripture in a particular, historical Christian community. Attention to pedagogy is implicit throughout and explicit in the final required course. The emphases on the importance of particular contexts for interpretation, attention to issues of power in interpretation, and interest in the character of the community formed to interpret owe a great deal to the perspectives of feminist and liberation theology, but the model draws eclectically from a range of biblical scholarship. Practicing the model shows many of the oppositions set by the academy or in the culture wars to present false choices. Its goal is to empower teachers and preachers to be both critical of tradition and self-critical, to proclaim and make vivid the visions of scripture, and to engage communities of biblical interpretation with the world beyond the church.

PEDAGOGY AND PROCESS

The three courses mentioned above were designed and taught by teams of two or three of us from among our small faculty of three biblical studies professors. Developing, revising, and teaching these courses in different configurations has required our cooperation, effort, and trust. This collaborative approach has had advantages for us as teachers and as learners and for our students. The energy generated from teaching together and interacting with each others' hermeneutical perspectives and expertise has been professionally formative. From the beginning students witness a diversity of temperaments, ways of reading, and styles of teaching. They see us asking each other questions, admitting when we do not know the answers, and teaching and learning more together than we could separately. Our interaction in all the sections and topics of the courses undercuts the strict separation of the disciplines of New Testament and Old Testament.

HISTORY AND HERMENEUTICS: THE HERMENEUTICAL CIRCLE

To incorporate the values of historical study of the Bible into a theological setting, our biblical studies courses put historical study into a larger process. The two-semester introductory Bible course presents history and hermeneutics together while it covers Second Temple Judaism, the Deuteronomistic History, the Pentateuch, and Christian origins. History and hermeneutics are treated not as independent, sequential steps in which "history" is determined and interpretation follows, but as mutually interdependent steps in an ongoing hermeneutical circle. Students begin by completing Norman Gottwald's "Self-Inventory on Biblical Hermeneutics."[6] Our name for the model is "the hermeneutical circle," and the expressions "world of the text," "world behind the text," and "world in front of the text" convey interlocking steps of the circle. The world of the text includes observation of the text itself, description, and formal analysis. The world behind the text includes historical reconstruction, exploration of the sources and prehistory of the text. The world in front of the text includes the centuries of interpretation through which we read the text in the present, as well as our own cultural-philosophical temperamental lenses and perspectives. From the outset, the course stresses that each of these movements is dependent upon the others; our cultural biases affect our historical reconstructions which therefore are provisional, open to correction and modification. Readings of the text for ministry, preaching and teaching will always explore each of the three "worlds" in the hermeneutical circle in order for the scriptural text to have meaning in the present.

We stress the importance of each related step in the process. The text alone is not self-interpreting but requires a community of readers. To stay in the world behind the text risks losing both the text and its power to speak. Staying in the world in front of the text with one's own associations, preoccupations, and expectations of "relevance" is to avoid the challenge of the text's cultural and historical otherness, as well as its possibility to speak as God's word. Exploring the world in front of the text will take into account modern canons of evidence and reason and critiques of the Bible, feminist analyses of the gender constructions in the text, and interpretations of the text in Christian doctrine in different periods. In our courses, the world in front of the text is distinguished from the other moments, but not excluded.

Adequate interpretation must take account of all three elements in the circle. This scheme gives students a way to sort out the variety of methods and arguments about interpretation that they encounter in scholarly literature and in their communities. For example, a partition theory for Philippians is a source theory, a "world behind the text" argument, based on observation of the stylistic features of the letter (world of the text) and conforming to con-

---

6. Norman Gottwald, "Framing Biblical Interpretation at New York Theological Seminary: A Student Self-Inventory on Biblical Hermeneutics," in *Reading from This Place: Social Location and Biblical Interpretation in the United States* (ed. Fernando Segovia and Mary Ann Tolbert; 2 vols.; Minneapolis: Fortress, 1995), 1:251–61.

temporary views of how a unified letter would look (world in front of the text). Arguments about the historical Jesus are "behind the text" arguments that are sometimes contrasted with a Gospel portrayal of Jesus.

By keeping historical reconstruction in the circle, we are able to demonstrate and insist on the value of historical study, the way it helps to clarify what the text "meant" in a different historical setting, de-familiarizes the material, distinguishes the diverse portraits of Jesus and stands in some tension with the orthodox interpreters and creators of the canon. At the same time the circular nature of the process makes us aware that the way we write history is shaped by perspectives and interests of the present.

SECOND TEMPLE JUDAISM: TEACHING THE TESTAMENTS TOGETHER

The most important period for the reconstruction of the immediate "world behind the text" is the period from the restoration under Ezra to the late Second Temple period, the time when scripture emerged as the focus for Jewish piety and the matrix of both the Jewish Bible and the Christian New Testament. To understand the changing forms of religious life throughout this period and the shifts in interpretation of temple and Torah, we must see how these forms changed in response to different forms of political organization under sequential empires: Persian, Greek, and Roman. The variety of Jewish texts from the Second Temple period creates a concrete picture of the range of piety and visions of God's justice in sectarian Jewish life at the time of Jesus. These diverse approaches to the question of law observance, Jewish identity, the Temple, prayer, and sacrifice in this period were sorted out differently as orthodox Christianity and rabbinic Judaism began their slow, intense, conflicted process of mutual self-definition after the destruction of the temple in 70 C.E.

A unit on the Deuteronomistic History completes the first introductory semester course. Through the Deuteronomistic History we introduce questions of historiography, the purposes for which one tells the people's history, the modern theories about sources and perspective of the Deuteronomistic historians on Israel's history of conquest, judgeship, monarchy, and exile. A study of the Pentateuch begins the second semester. The Pentateuch preserves a conversation about God, history, leadership, and worship that despite its final editing leaves many of these questions open ended. By the time we reach the unit on Christian origins and introduction to the New Testament literature, the ideas of scripture, law, and story are categories the students have begun to internalize and know how to use. The Gospels read the story of Jesus and Jewish practice from a post-70 C.E. perspective, updating and revising the story in light of contemporary events and issues.

The historical framework is the structure into which students place whatever biblical texts they study and in which they ask what the text in Genesis, Judges, or Matthew might have "meant," what it was reflecting on, in the time it was written. We emphasize that Israel, the writers of scripture, were restlessly asking how God was involved in current political circumstances and what God was demanding of faithful people in that situation. Organizing the courses so the Old Testament and New Testament are studied together rather than sequentially and putting the canonical order into a historical framework, undercuts the commonly held supercessionist notions of the relationship between the Testaments and holds up the Old Testament texts as lively sources for Christian theological reflection. The historical framework allows the students to develop another narrative concerning the relationship of Jesus to the law, the Gospel writers to Jewish story and practice, and Christianity to Judaism, than the highly anti-Jewish account that is well-known and much repeated in churches, preaching, and Sunday school curricula. Questions about the way the biblical text portrays gender, race, violence, and justice arise inevitably as students read the texts and reflect on their own location and perspectives that they have tried to identify in the hermeneutics inventory.

As we study history, questions of hermeneutics are raised at every point. History itself is understood to be an imaginative construct, based on literary and material evidence, but inevitably shaped by features of the world in front of the text, the lenses of those telling the story. The question of the historical Jesus is treated as a valid and important question, but its "results" provisional. Within the hermeneutical circle, one picture of the historical Jesus is not the criterion for interpretation of a text. Rather, the reconstructions of Jesus are themselves subject to analysis and theological critique.[7] This methodological self-criticism is a much stronger feature of our seminary teaching than it was in my graduate biblical education.

INTERPRETATION FOR PREACHING AND TEACHING

Using the hermeneutical circle, students are expected to be able to evaluate arguments and their implications of others and be aware of the choices they are making. The purpose of the careful, sometimes laborious, exercise of the interpretive process is to be able to say something meaningful about what the biblical text "means" in the present. To press this point, the two other required courses emphasize the practices of ministry—preaching and teaching.

---

7. Elisabeth Schüssler Fiorenza, *Jesus: Miriam's Child, Sophia's Prophet: Critical Issues in Feminist Christology* (New York: Continuum, 1994).

Several questions raised here encourage students to bring the text from its past into the world of the present: Who are you? What are you going to do with this scripture in the community of faith? What are you going to say is true about it? How is it good news? The result of interpretation here is not an exegesis paper (although exegesis itself is required) but a sermon, a lesson plan, or presentation for a public setting. Just as the biblical writers did in their times, preachers engage the word of God with their communities in a particular historical and political context. Thus scripture is conceptualized as "an open-ended prototype rather than the Bible as an archetype that has to be repeated in every generation."[8] By preaching a sermon, interpreting a text for preaching in the presence of peers, we begin to build a community of interpretation in which individual readings of a text are subjected to testing among others in a community. Although the content of the interpretation for preaching course varies, as in the first year, we always teach the Old and New Testaments in the same course, referring back to the historical framework. Readings of the Pentateuch or the prophetic books in the New Testament are part of the world in front of the Old Testament text. Readings of the Old Testament text in its own time and diverse interpretations in the first century are distinguished from Paul or a Gospel writer's reading of the same text. The historical approach problematizes typical ways of viewing the Old Testament/New Testament relationship, often encouraged by the lectionary: law/gospel, prediction/fulfillment, harsh/lenient, problem/solution, or inadequate/complete.

The final required course, Biblical Interpretation for Teaching, focuses around the task of teaching the Bible in a community of faith. The biblical texts may be New Testament epistolary literature, prophetic literature, wisdom writings or psalms. The course puts into dialogue the text, the historical communities "behind the texts," and the contemporary community reading the text. Students discuss the rationale for teaching the range of authors in the canon and the implications of teaching literature outside the canon. They analyze the variety of understanding of biblical authority in their parish cultures and the wider church and clarify and articulate their own. Reading a variety of articles on critical pedagogy, they conceptualize what creating a community of teachers and learners requires and what model of leadership to employ. Meaning(s) emerge from reflection and study in the faith community, and call for response, repentance, and action. In teaching presentations they practice engaging the whole person in learning using multiple media and points of access. Their own seminary learning is a subject for methodological reflection.

---

8. Elisabeth Schüssler Fiorenza, *The Power of the Word: Scripture and the Rhetoric of Empire* (Minneapolis: Fortress, 2007), 265.

Students wrestle with these questions with their peers: How should I treat biblical authorship in their teaching? What are the minefields around those questions, and what are the spiritual, social, and theological implications for people in my care? How might these differences be negotiated in a parish community? What language will I use for this process of interpretation: Word of God, the activity of the Holy Spirit, revelation? What outcome will teaching this biblical text have? How will it matter? In the community of the class, students reflect on how they conceive of and exercise their authority as teachers of the Bible.[9]

PASTORS AND SCRIPTURE IN PUBLIC LIFE

While teaching and preaching are mainly inner-community activities, the biblical studies courses attend to the ways in which the biblical interpretation of pastors and preachers is accountable to a wider public. Media presentations of the Jesus wars—as evidenced by the annual Easter issue of *Time* or *Newsweek*—are subject to analysis and evaluation based on what students have studied in the introductory course. Students' teaching presentations relate the prophet or epistle being taught with current cultural issues and debates. Some elective courses require the preparation of a public presentation at an ecumenical event—in which Christian readings of a text or texts are put into dialogue with those of other faiths or at a public meeting. In these ways, students get practice imagining those for whom the Bible is not authoritative and learn to be in discussion with them.

ART AND PROCLAMATION

Feminist and liberation theologians have been explicit about the role of the imagination in interpretation, teaching, and preaching.[10] In Schüssler Fiorenza's model, one important step is "the hermeneutics of creative imagination."[11] Imagination is broader than intellect or rationality; it is a spiritual and theological faculty. Although imagination was, as far as I recall, never recommended as a desirable characteristic of biblical interpretation ("Fantasy!" "Eisegesis!")

---

9. For a discussion of pedagogy closely akin to the values of this course, see Rebecca S. Chopp, "A Rhetorical Paradigm for Pedagogy," in *Teaching the Bible: The Discourses and Politics of Biblical Pedagogy* (ed. Fernando Segovia and Mary Ann Tolbert; Maryknoll, N.Y.: Orbis, 1998), 299–309.
10. Chopp speaks of imagination as a pedagogical value in "Rhetorical Paradigm for Pedagogy," 307.
11. Elisabeth Schüssler Fiorenza, *Wisdom Ways: Introducing Feminist Biblical Interpretation* (Maryknoll, N.Y.: Orbis, 2001), 179–83.

and never taught as part of a method, I have found that engaging the imagination of ministerial students in their biblical preaching and teaching is one of the most valuable aspects of our teaching. As in the hermeneutical circle, the imagination is employed in concert with the intellect. For example, studying Jewish apocalyptic texts and reading anthropological and sociological studies of "apocalyptic" prepare for imaginative engagement with Mark 13. Many courses have assignments that interpret scripture using media other than the word processor—dance, movement, paint, and music. In these modes of expression, our diverse students easily surpass their faculty, who are trained to excel in a narrow range of argument and analysis. Aspects of the interpretation of texts in the arts are drawn upon as a rich part of the world in front of the text. Incorporating art and imagination into biblical studies has the effect of valuing the varied gifts of all students and not just rewarding the ones confident of their scholarly skills. It pushes many to grow into areas of inexperience or fear. In my experience, the expansion into the area of artistic interpretation is the farthest stretch from graduate biblical training which was so rigorously restricted to historical, anthropological methods and rules. But this emphasis on the art of biblical interpretation has made sense of ministerial training in a way that pure academic, rational methods/approaches do not.

By teaching the interrelated steps of a complex interpretive process, the biblical studies courses put emphasis on the "outcome" of interpretation, which is its proclamation. At the same time, they help students to analyze controversies and disagreements over interpretation. Historical study is essential, but is not allowed to become an unquestioned objective fact against which to hold the biblical text. Criticism of toxic, hurtful readings of the text, and the recognition of the limitations of its perspectives is an essential necessary piece of the interpretive process. Neither is criticism an end in itself, but rather it is a step toward rearticulation, proclamation, and construction. By teaching the broad spiral of biblical interpretation, we attempt to equip students to enter into and intervene positively in the current highly conflicted, sometimes violent arguments in churches and in culture over biblical authority. Learning to state the problem, its issues and assumptions and to enumerate the stakes is a step toward diffusing the destructive outcome and moving toward common goals.

The skill of distinguishing and naming differences is very different than the polemical rhetoric that characterizes many of these controversies. Such rhetoric poses dichotomous choices, such as either acknowledging the authority of the Bible or using historical, literary, anthropological methods to understand it. In this view, reading the Bible as scripture is opposed to reading historically or critically. Practice with the hermeneutical circle, especially in communities teaching the Bible, can show such choices to be false ones. Those who have read it, studied it, preached and taught it, played with it, and asked hard questions of it can speak of the authority of scripture in an authentic way. Confronting the limitations of the perspectives of the biblical writers in their vision of societal organization, sexuality, gender, leadership, and marriage leads to a strong affirmation of the vision of inclusion and mutuality held by larger scriptural witness. Christian leaders, preachers and teachers of the community's sacred texts can negotiate these questions with confidence both within their communities and in the wider, pluralistic context.

Experiencing the challenges, frustrations, and successes of teaching biblical interpretation in a denominational seminary raises questions about how graduate biblical studies might prepare one for teaching in such a setting. It has highlighted for me the tremendous value of the humanistic and liberal learning of the university, the freedom of thinking, the fearlessness of applying tools of reason to sacred ideas and institutions, and the confidence in human good will and cooperation. The dominant method of historical criticism is an essential tool for understanding the Bible. At the same time those who will be leaders of faith communities and themselves give influential readings of scripture through teaching and preaching must be able to take into account the wider world of communities of memory, faith, and ritual and the history of their reading of scripture.

The emphasis on the role of pastoral leaders as teachers of scripture in our seminary curriculum suggests that attention to and practice in pedagogy in graduate biblical studies is more crucial than I knew it to be in my doctoral program. If they are trained to be self-reflective about their own methods and observant of the values and ethos of their teaching context, graduate students will be able to creatively shape their teaching to address the particular challenges of the community where they teach. They will be prepared to draw on a wide range of traditional, artistic, theological readings of scripture in the history of interpretation and be able to analyze and compare them with historical-critical readings. Focus on the many dimensions of pedagogy would equip those who teach in seminaries to deploy the insights and methods of the range of academic approaches to the Bible in order to form pastoral leaders as preachers and teachers of scripture in their communities.

Placing Meaning-Making at the Center of New Testament Studies

Hal Taussig with Brigitte Kahl

At the end of the long and rich afternoon in Washington, D.C., wherein a number of us had made relatively brief presentations on our respective Ph.D. programs in Bible, Hebrew Bible, and/or New Testament, I found myself in front of a gentle and erudite gentleman, surprised and perhaps a bit frustrated by what I had said in my presentation. In the presentation I had explained—ever so briefly—how our New Testament studies program at Union Theological Seminary in New York was committed to the integration of theological inquiry and New Testament studies.[1] This gentleman, whom I had never met before but who represented a leading biblical studies program of an important evangelical institution, blurted out how his institution had finally accepted the validity of historical-critical methods. Just in time, he added with a gracious smile, to hear that an institution at the center of the establishment of the paradigm of historical-critical studies of the Bible—namely, Union—now placed theological inquiry near the heart of New Testament studies and saw historical-critical work as an occasional hindrance to authentic theological inquiry.

There was, I sensed, a melancholy note in his observation. It is not clear to me that it would be possible to find much common ground between an evangelical version of doctoral-level biblical studies and Union's New Testament program, simply by virtue of both having a commitment to theological inquiry. On the other hand, I do think that conversation about theological inquiry and New Testament studies between liberal and evangelical traditions

---

1. This essay is written only in relationship to doctoral studies in New Testament at Union. Union has an exemplary doctoral program in Hebrew Bible/Old Testament under the leadership of Professor David Carr. But that program in Hebrew Bible/Old Testament has distinctly different emphases than the New Testament program addressed here.

and programs could lend clarity, depth, and honesty to the larger set of interactions between these two traditions.

This essay seeks to make the case that a complex and disciplined reclaiming of theological inquiry within the discipline of New Testament offers a set of new departures for the field itself and for the field's relationship to a broader set of relationships to different societies, different religious traditions, and pivotal educational and religious institutions. This essay uses the Union program in New Testament studies as an example to advance this argument.

THEOLOGICAL INQUIRY, MEANING-MAKING, AND NEW TESTAMENT STUDIES

In this essay the terms *theological inquiry* and *meaning-making* are understood as nearly synonymous. That is, it is meaning-making discourse on New Testament/early "Christian" literature that characterizes what I mean by *theological inquiry*. I generally prefer the term *meaning-making* but keep its approximate equivalent, *theological inquiry*, at the center of this essay in order to emphasize the meaning-making modality and potential of theological rhetoric. The term *interpretation* is also seen as a close synonym to both meaning-making and theological inquiry.

This proximate relationship between theological inquiry, interpretation, and meaning-making of early Christian literature is grounded in the simultaneity of ambitious attempts within that literature to make meaning in relationship to a range of important lived issues in the ancient world and the literature's own explicit use of theological language. Put more simply, the New Testament takes on big human issues of its day and uses explicit theological categories to do so. It uses discourse about "God" and "Jesus" to address a wide range of human experiences in the Hellenistic Mediterranean. In our day, making New Testament theological inquiry and meaning-making more or less synonymous is also almost inevitable, given the heavy dependence of the whole of Christian tradition and practice on New Testament categories and ambitions.

Our reclaiming of theological inquiry within New Testament studies seeks to make meaning in the midst of the spectrum of twenty-first century life. That is, this embrace of meaning-making in dialogue with New Testament texts is not at all an antiquarian endeavor. Although, as seen throughout this essay, the ways first and second century writers and hearers made meaning for their time is important for making meaning of those same texts today, such analysis of early Christian meaning does not determine the meanings made of the text today. The Union program assumes a plurality of meaning of New Testament texts in the twenty-first century and requires investigation of early Christian meanings as a part of the complex process of contemporary theological inquiry.

Both the legacy and setting of Union enhances such an emphasis on theologizing within the context of today's society. Although it is true that much of New Testament studies prior to the 1990s shied away from addressing social issues of the day, Union itself is perhaps the most well-known seminary in the world for its activist scholarship and teaching throughout the past 150 years. Union's current program emphasizes what it means to study theology in a world city. The intensity and diversity of life in New York City is now much more than background, as the seminary constantly reaches out into a wide variety of city settings in its scholarship, teaching, and curriculum. This encourages both teaching and scholarship at Union to make sense proactively of a complex and threatened world. Of course, the range of scholarship beyond Union's walls is an important asset, but the intensity and cutting edges of life experiences and social issues serves as an even more dramatic resource for Union's program.

Studying New Testament at Union today has a primary focus on how to make meaning in twenty-first century life. Knowing history, analyzing literature, negotiating methodologies, and learning ancient languages are subsidiary to serving the contemporary public's search for meaning in relationship to the New Testament and other early "Christian" writings. At both the masters and doctoral levels the program seeks to train public intellectuals that address significant issues in the lives of people today through disciplined study of the New Testament.

From the perspective of this essay and the Union program, interacting with New Testament textualities is itself theological inquiry. A vast majority of North Americans use early Christian texts in one way or other to make sense of their lives. New Testament studies needs then to service this larger public discourse, in which early Christian texts play important roles in making meaning. Reducing New Testament studies to highly technical literary and historical studies makes it irrelevant and misses its primary function, that of interacting with the ongoing life of the New Testament in today's societies. Placing all the technical skills associated with New Testament studies in the past 150 years in the service of making sense of contemporary life reclaims a broader role for this field in society.

Communities from a wide range of cultures make meaning with the New Testament. Our work at Union owns New Testament scholarship's active relationship to these cultures' meaning-making. It is important, however, also to make clear that this proposal does not imply that all necessary meaning lies in the New Testament or that the whole New Testament is "naturally" meaningful. Indeed, it is certain from this essay's perspective that some meanings made with New Testament texts today need to be challenged. However, the character of that challenge needs to shift from an objectivist put-down of meaning-making itself to active engagement in the issues where meaning is sought through New Testament texts.

This call to New Testament interpretation for meaning stands in counterpoint to the place of New Testament studies in the Western world in the past century in three ways. First, it is in some contrast to the larger picture in which New Testament scholars have been seen as the handmaidens of ethicists and systematic theologians. It contradicts those who would make theological inquiry the exclusive prerogatives of systematic or advocacy-based vocabularies. (By no means is this an assertion that New Testament theological inquiry is superior to other theological modalities. Nor does this assertion question the validity of other theological fields and starting points. It is simply a reassertion of the place of New Testament studies as a field where meaning-making occurs as a primary activity.) The Union program at both the master's and doctoral levels does not see itself simply as providing technical skills about ancient literature that other fields can use in order to make sense of the world for our time. While in no way shortcutting these crucial technical skills, neither the beginning master's student in the "Introduction to New Testament" nor the Ph.D. candidate in comprehensive exams can avoid the requirement to interpret the New Testament for the contemporary world. The twentieth-century model of a major book on New Testament historical or literary issues with less than a page conclusion about its meaning in the contemporary world is not permitted in the work of either professors or students.

Second, the Union program recognizes that New Testament scripturalizing is already a major component of contemporary meaning-making, no matter what academic theological discourse asserts. The stuff of theology in North America consists to a large extent in assumptions about and language of the New Testament. In the public arena, the theological academy, and the churches, New Testament categories are very present in Christian (and often non-Christian) reflection on meaning for today's world. In contrast to certain tendencies over the past century, the Union program does not downplay the significance of the New Testament for contemporary consciousness. It does not give the Bible away to public pundits, other theological fields, or pious enactments. Rather this program requires master's students at every juncture to produce art works, write sermons, and engage twenty-first century social movements. It attracts Ph.D. students who have central and passionate engagements with poverty, feminism, queer studies, African American studies, Minjung theology, Chicano/Chicana cultures, and spirituality.

The third contrast to nineteenth- and twentieth-century precedents is this program's structural focus on the dramatic value of New Testament studies for public discourse about meaning. For instance, both senior professors have substantial and on-going engagement with the seminary's Poverty Initiative, a program that seeks to tie theological studies to the struggle against poverty. This means that Union students in New Testament enter into direct contact with poor people, while they meet their New Testament requirements. As is the case in many parts of Union's program, studying New Testament cannot occur without each student thinking seriously about her or his own social location relative to the major social issues of our day. Although all points of view are respected, commitment to social engagement while studying New Testament is an explicit value. (It is also true that these requirements of meaning-making skills make preparation for a Union New Testament Ph.D. one of the longest in the larger theological academy. It is our experience that requiring students to learn how to interpret ancient texts for contemporary meaning while also mandating their command of all the traditional technical, linguistic, and historical tasks in the field generally makes for a longer doctoral studies program than in some other fields or some other institutions.)

Assumptions of a Meaning-Making Centered Program

Making-meaning of early Christian texts for the twenty-first century is not a naïve enterprise. Union's work in this regard makes some assumptions about this process that focus and delimit the meanings made. These assumptions are not random and involve technical skills in the field. In the end, the consensus involved in these assumptions allows a certain more concentrated conversation within the program.

The first assumption concerns the study of texts. This assumption is that New Testament texts are simultaneously central and evasive. Although Union's program focuses on the interpretation of texts for the twenty-first century, what a text is and means is subject to great flux. The program is centered on the study of texts, and students at all levels spend the majority of their time in focusing on the interpretation of early Christian texts. It is, of course, important to remember that the notion of text is slippery. Being too certain of the ancient meaning or even the exact content of an early Christian text can betray the meaning-making possible in the twenty-first century. Early Christian texts are quite volatile and therefore often unreliable when treated as straightforward data. Factors such as textual lacunae, manuscript traditions, levels of redaction, the ambiguity of canon-making processes, and ancient cultural frames of reference make it difficult to posit exact and certain meaning.

The second assumption is that the term "New Testament" for twenty-first century meaning-making is arbitrary, over invested, and presumptuous; and that proper appropriation of it demands the inclusion of the wide variety of other early "Christian" documents beyond the New Testament. Even though—

as noted above—the necessity of theologizing as New Testament scholars rests on the resonance and content of the New Testament in North American society, the very term "New Testament studies" to describe a seminary program or a field has severe limitations. Its use in this essay is at best proximate and ironic, as indicated by occasionally putting the phrase in quotes. In addition, to the pretense and ambiguity of the term "New Testament," this phrase carries with it another specific difficulty in making meaning of the culturally resonant New Testament. This difficulty has to do with the complex ways that New Testament texts in antiquity were intertwined with extracanonical, Jewish, and other literature. The Union program takes on these connections, especially by including the interpretation of extra-canonical early Christian texts, in both their ancient and twenty-first century contexts.

The same problem of overinvestment and presumption applies to the term "Christian." It is not a term inherently dominant in the first four centuries, and only rarely mentioned in the New Testament. Assuming that these texts in question wanted to be thought of as "Christian" hinders their possible meanings. When these ancient texts are over-identified with Christendom or Christianity, their meaning for their own time and today is obscured. Since contemporary consciousness increasingly has to face the limits of that labeled "Christian," Union's program assumes that meaning-making with these texts is evoked more powerfully if they are not exclusively appropriated as "Christian" meaning. This essay's use of the term "early Christian" must then also be seen as proximate and problematic.

The fourth assumption concerns the legacy of Christian theologizing with New Testament texts. We assume a sharp double-edge in relating to church and academic prerogatives to the interpretation of the New Testament. As noted above, the dense and millennia-long investment in the New Testament for making sense of the world makes it nearly impossible to ignore such theological legacies of the past and the churches' on-going practice of such meaning-making. Students at Union are, however, also encouraged to see the fallibility and danger of New Testament for meaning-making, given the long historical trajectories of New Testament meaning-making that resulted in oppression, denial, violence, and manipulation of power. To participate in theological inquiry about the New Testament inevitably makes one complicit in the oppression, reductionism, and self-serving character of much of Christianity as well as it serves as a resource for future interpretation.

The fifth and final assumption acts as a counterpoint to the first four. These first four assumptions map out necessary limitations on the way New Testament and meaning-making for today are formulated. The fifth assumption owns the longer legacy of studying the New Testament as theological inquiry and meaning-making. It was indeed only in the modern era that studying the New Testament became a technical field that was separate from theological inquiry. Prior to the nineteenth century, all Christian theologians were assumed to be scholars of the New Testament and vice versa. So, this fifth assumption is that New Testament studies belong to the longer tradition of making meaning with these ancient textualities, and that such a tradition is an asset (within the caveats of the first four assumptions).

CHARACTERISTICS OF NEW TESTAMENT STUDIES: ATTENDING TO
CONTEMPORARY MEANING-MAKING

As noted above, our work at Union in reclaiming theological inquiry for New Testament studies necessitates an embrace of further complexity for the field. Although at first glance, such interest in theological inquiry could be perceived as either nostalgia or hegemony, New Testament at Union rejects any return to precritical, unilateral, or church-centered ways. Rather, this insistence on the centrality of meaning-making projects "New Testament studies" actively into the ambiguities and challenges of locating one's self in the particularities that make up all meaning-making. That is, the character of this "theological inquiry" within New Testament studies must always be localized within the particular dynamics of specific cultures, societies, and/or communities.

The small, collegial, and personal character of Union's New Testament studies makes it very flexible and able to focus on particular students' intellectual and social projects. Especially in the Ph.D. program, which rarely admits more than one student per year, students with already articulated interpretive approaches to specific contemporary social locations can custom-make their doctoral studies. This allows the program's emphasis on theologizing with the New Testament to root itself in the particularities of the student's social location and interpretive project, helping to avoid the pretense of objectivist and universalizing agendas. The other dimension of such responsiveness to the students' own interpretive projects is the intense collegiality of the New Testament faculty at Union. This program—partly because of its smallness—creates a community of conversation among professors and students in which each Ph.D. student is intensely involved with both senior New Testament faculty, who work closely together in the supervision of all students.

In contrast to precritical theological inquiry, this loyalty to the meaning-making dynamics of specific peoples necessitates a pluralistic approach to the field. All notions of centralized church or academic guild authority disappear when New Testament scholars understand themselves as primarily obligated to a specific people's search for meaning. Neither meta-language with ambitions of transcending culture nor microscopic technical expertise can do justice to specific peoples' use of the New Testament in their search for meaning relative to their particular circumstances.

In this regard, a focus on New Testament and meaning-making cannot abandon any of the critical tools of the field. Rather, these critical skills and methodologies are all the more necessary in order to understand how to engage early Christian texts in the process of making meaning with specific contemporary cultures. Similarly recognizing the complexity of interpreting within specific contexts requires a rigorously social perspective. In the necessarily postmodern epistemologies of meaning-making in the twenty-first century, notions of individual consciousness take up much less space. Social analysis is a central component to such theological inquiry.

This means that theological language itself cannot have prerogatives for meaning-making either. Rather, authentic interpretation of New Testament and early Christian texts must be at the service of the particular language worlds of the specific cultures. Such "service" of the particular language worlds in which meaning is made with New Testament texts includes critical analysis of those language worlds as well as the ancient language worlds of the early Christian era. The haunting legacy of hegemonic theological discourse reducing, marginalizing, and evacuating the specific meanings of particular cultures underlines the necessity of critiquing theological language. This rejection of privileging theological language, however, in the end contributes in a much more dramatic and disciplined way to interpreting New Testament texts in particular social and cultural settings, which may have different categories for making meaning than the theological categories of the academy, the New Testament itself, or the theological literati.

This emphasis on meaning-making within a rigorously social framework accepts entanglement with often colliding sets of inherited and innovative values. It does not assume that New Testament studies can be done as a surgical exercise on lifeless material. Rather, it acknowledges the contributions and damage inherent in the values New Testament scholars bring to their trade, and it asks scholars to be self-critical, culturally critical, and open to on-going development of their own values. At Union, most New Testament work is done consciously with appreciation for the following values:

1. **Multilateral mutuality,** applied broadly to a range of economic, gender, class, and race issues. It may be possible to call such multilateral mutuality "justice," although the epistemology of justice at Union is still a work in progress.

2. **The efficacy of materiality.** The specificity of expression through material culture is both inevitable and productive. Texts themselves must be understood materially, in ways that underscore and challenge their power. This value comes to special expression in the important emphasis within the

Union program of "critical reimagination" of ancient social realities through the use of material culture. Professor Brigitte Kahl's extensive use of images, architecture, and public art from the ancient world in the study of New Testament social contexts is complemented by my own intense teaching of the social meaning-making setting of early Christian meals.

3. **Empire-critical perspectives.** Although the ways one makes empire-critical meaning differ drastically according to culture, the early twenty-first century does not know cultures in which early Christian texts are meaningful without imperial dynamics playing a damaging role. Union's New Testament program has hosted three different international conferences on the Roman Empire and New Testament studies within the past four years. These four conferences brought more than forty international scholars to Union to think together about empire-critical studies in relationship to early Christian literature and social life. Over two hundred Union students participated in these conferences between 2004 and 2008. Empire-critical perspectives on the study of the New Testament at Union include intense examination of both the ways Roman imperial power was in dramatic tension with early Christians and the ways Euro-American imperial power affects meanings for twenty-first-century New Testament theologizing.

4. **Collectivity.** Making-meaning with early Christian texts can only happen when group, community, and societal dynamics are taken into account. The social dimension of early Christianity is a primary focus for study at Union. The need for social integrity today in New Testament studies through work for mutuality and justice and through rigorous collegiality among professors and students determines much of the character of the Union New Testament program.

I state these particular values of New Testament studies at Union not in order to enshrine them with privilege, but to come clean on the necessity of consciously developing, critiquing, and negotiating values while studying early Christian literature. These values must be constantly challenged and renegotiated. Their particular merit is not the point here as much as the necessity for New Testament studies to break free of its pretensions to either value-free analysis or divinely ordained values. This list of values simply serves here as a necessary embrace of the task of developing explicit social values for the field.

SITUATING NEW TESTAMENT STUDIES THAT PRACTICES AND TEACHES
MEANING-MAKING WITHIN THE LARGER FIELD

As has been noted earlier, Union New Testament studies' recent initiatives to practice and teach contemporary, socially charged, culture-specific, interpretation as a central component are susceptible to challenge. In fact, this viewpoint is almost certainly a minority within the larger field. It may then be helpful to compare briefly this particular emphasis to other major approaches to New Testament studies.

Literary-critical approaches. Meaning-oriented New Testament studies are close to literary critical approaches in that both place more value on the meaning made in the texts than in the history determined, doctrine articulated, or ethic advocated. Interpretation of early Christian texts cannot happen without literary critical study in that often literary analysis of these texts points to major dimensions of meaning within the texts. Yet, rarely do literary critical approaches within New Testament studies end up proposing interpretations for today's society. By and large, literary critical studies stop short of making meaning with early Christian literature for their readers. A hidden reserve is maintained, even though literary criticism itself focuses on textual meanings.

Historical-critical approaches. Similarly, it is impossible to make meaning today with early Christian texts without many of the tools of historical-critical approaches. At Union, rigorous development of historical-critical skills is required. On the other hand, the claims of historical-critical studies to yield objective facts about the ancient world or even the text in itself have been thoroughly debunked in the last four decades. Leaning on the pretense of objective facts from historical-critical studies cannot yield any basis for the kind of interpretation of early Christian texts advocated in this essay. Meaning-making in New Testament studies today necessarily must go beyond the "facts" of the ancient world or the text in itself. At Union, the necessity to interpret early Christian texts for the twenty-first century makes historical-critical studies' objectivist epistemology untenable.

Doctrinally determined approaches. Dogmatic church-based approaches are the most explicitly welcoming of meaning-making in the field today. There is no modern inhibition in these doctrine-based approaches, when it comes to asserting that early Christian texts—especially the New Testament—are profoundly meaningful for contemporary life. Two strong differences remain, however, between these approaches and the interpretation advocated in this essay. First, Union's interpretation of early Christian texts requires cultural specificity to the meaning made, while doctrinal interpretations of the New Testament today assume the same meaning of an ancient Christian text for all people. Secondly, doctrine-based approaches to the New Testament give interpretational authority to churches, while Union's meaning-making with these texts does not. Union's program takes interpretation for churches today very seriously. Indeed, my own on-going work for thirty years as a pastor makes this point explicit for all in the program at every level. Nevertheless, such rootedness in church life makes one keenly aware of the ways doctrinally determined approaches can overstep their own social location and intention.

Emancipatory approaches. Interpretational schools within liberation theology, postcolonialist, feminist and queer movements actively make meaning with New Testament texts. Like the interpretation of texts outlined in this essay, these approaches often come to articulation through disciplined dialogue with a particular culture. It is possible to fit Union's New Testament studies within this approach. However, some emancipatory approaches have developed meta-language systems that can cut short specific meaning-making with early Christian texts by specific cultures which may not fit the terms of the socio-political meta-languages used. Postcolonial studies have been particularly sensitive to the potential meaning-making possible in some cultures, whose hybrid meanings sometimes violate emancipatory meta-language.

Poststructuralist readings. Poststructuralist readings emphasize both the cultural specificity of interpretation and the imperative of making meaning with early Christian texts in twenty-first century settings in ways very similar to the Union program. In its subtle and complex analysis of society-and-culture-specific meaning-making, poststructuralist New Testament studies underline many dimensions of this essay. Ironically, however, these powerful articulations of the necessity of interpreting early Christian texts do not for the most part propose meanings themselves. Rather, these approaches so far have contented themselves with the study of others who make meaning of early Christian texts for the twenty-first century. For Union, the step into specific and invested personal interactions with one's own meaning-making in a particular social setting is a necessary step, not generally reflected in poststructuralism.

Union's New Testament emphasis on interpretation and meaning-making for today then depends on all of the other existing approaches in the field. It orders those approaches under the larger mandate for making meaning with early Christian texts today.

The Union Program in New Testament Studies

Union's program enacts this reclaiming of the interpretive prerogative of New Testament studies mostly through its classroom teaching. There are no major curricular shifts from most seminary, undergraduate, or graduate programs. The overall shift is nevertheless dramatic.

New Testament courses at Union always require meaning-making for the twenty-first century. While insisting on a wide range of literary, historical-critical, socially analytical, ancient language, and methodological skills, students are asked in every course to produce an interpretation of early Christian texts for a twenty-first century situation. Often, these interpretations occur in groups and/or with a wide variety of artistic productions. Union's location in New York City regularly resources such creative interpretation. Second-year M.Div. students are required to take a course in "The Arts of Reading: An Exegetical Practicum," taught by all Old and New Testament faculty and given simultaneously with the similarly required "Introduction to Worship and Preaching" course. This means that students find themselves in small seminar-sized classes working on specific texts at the intersection of contemporary meaning-making and exegesis.

As noted above, our New Testament studies have an extensive relationship with a broad Union program called "The Poverty Initiative." This seminary-wide program addresses in a variety of ways the call to end poverty in America. New Testament faculty have collaborated with The Poverty Initiative on over ten seminary programs, including a three-credit course called "Reading the Bible with the Poor."

Current Ph.D. students in New Testament do their work respectively within the guiding frames of reference of fighting poverty in the United States (Liz Theoharis), African American hermeneutics (Darryl Jones), twenty-first-century community and spirituality (Celene Lillie), the role of empire in African American experience (Angela Parker), and contemporary gender and psychoanalytic theory (Maia Kotrosits). These doctoral studies are not somehow exceptional, but typical of the program's emphasis on meaning-making for the twenty-first century.

It is, of course, obvious, that the mandate for meaning-making with the New Testament at Union is enhanced by the school being a nondenominational seminary. Such dramatic gestures toward interpretation for particular cultures could not be done nearly as easily at a secular graduate program, a denominational seminary, or an undergraduate program. Similarly, Union's long history of courageous engagement with social realities of American cultures provides important momentum for these new steps in New Testament studies.

Mapping the Field, Shaping the Discipline: Doctoral Education as Rhetorical Formation

Melanie Johnson-DeBaufre

My graduate and professional education has been a process of learning to speak, hear, and interpret a variety of languages in different locations. When I entered graduate school, I spoke "Church." In my doctoral program at Harvard Divinity School, I learned "Academy" and several Ancient and Historical-Critical languages. By the time I took my first job at Luther College in Decorah, Iowa, my Church was rusty; I was just beginning to use my Feminism and knew only a few words in Pedagogy. In the Midwest, I discovered that I spoke Church with an American Baptist accent and that Lutheran educators say things like: "the dialogue of faith and learning." Teaching Introduction to the Bible to section after section of semiunwilling undergraduates quickly toned down my Academic and made me fluent in Student-Centered Teaching, or "Quit Lecturing and Be Creative," as it is called in the vernacular. After five years, I moved to the Graduate and Theological School at Drew University in Madison, New Jersey, where I began learning Poststructuralist Theory, Methodist, and Theological Education. Like living in the city, the social and intellectual diversity of Drew's students and faculty has given me an experience of heteroglossia unlike any I have experienced so far.

Rather than being defined by a discrete set of methods or questions, the field of biblical studies is a rich and multilocational set of discourses ranging around a group of texts. It is also a complex and competitive debate, where our arguments and self-positioning vie with others' for pride of place both inside and outside the academy. Who gets to speak? By "gets," I mean gets the funding, gets the job, gets published. And to whom are biblical scholars speaking anyway? Are those audiences listening?

I have tortured these metaphors of language and location in order to evoke an image of the field of biblical studies as a diverse landscape, with a wide array of locations and rhetorical practices. How does (or should) doctoral education orient students to and/or in this landscape? Unlike a map, the landscape is not flat. There are contours of rank, visibility, and access. Questions immediately arise: who decides which places matter and which languages are scholarly or required? Who is at the center of the map? How do the various academic locations relate to other places where people speak and make knowledge about the Bible?

Although doctoral education is a primary engine for the (re)production of academic fields, it is surprising how relatively little has been written analyzing and envisioning the future of Ph.D. education in biblical studies.[1] It is my hope that this landmark volume on transforming biblical studies will also mark a turning point in the field on this issue. This essay reflects on how the practices of graduate biblical education are bound up with larger debates in the field, the academy, and the society. Indeed, the very realities and inequities that may be encountered in the profession today are as likely to be perpetuated by doctoral programs as they are mitigated by them. I propose that the assessment and revision of doctoral programs in biblical studies should not center on how to more successfully discipline students into the discipline, but on more effectively *authorizing* students to shape the future of the discipline and *socializing* them to reinvent biblical studies in its various places in the academy and society.

Many Languages

Biblical scholars know a lot of languages. Studying the biblical texts in their original languages and engaging non-English European scholarship are cornerstones of higher criticism and fundamental requirements in North American graduate programs in both testaments. Participating in the 2006 SBL panel on graduate biblical education in which seven different institutions outlined their current curriculum for the Ph.D. in biblical studies confirmed for me William Countryman's 2003 assertion that "much of the hard work that qualifies a person as a biblical scholar in the first place, above all, [is] the mastery of ancient languages and the specialized knowledge of other cultures, ancient times, and, for most of us, distant places."[2]

---

1. Although there a few brief Web publications, the only sustained treatment of the topic to my knowledge is Elisabeth Schüssler Fiorenza, "Rethinking the Educational Practices of Biblical Doctoral Studies," *TThRel* 6 (2003): 65–75.

2. L. William Countryman, *Interpreting the Truth: Changing the Paradigm of Biblical Studies* (Harrisburg, Pa.: Trinity Press International, 2003), 10. The institutions participating in the SBL panel were: Dallas and Fuller Theological Seminaries, Yale, Vanderbilt, and Duke Divinity Schools, and Union and Drew Theological Schools.

It is interesting, however, to juxtapose this picture of the qualifications of the multilingual biblical scholar, who is an expert on distant Mediterranean places, with a series of linguistic and spatial images used to characterize the state of the field in the wake of global social movements for change and the shifting epistemology of postmodernity. Invoking the imagery of the biblical stories of Babel and Pentecost, some scholars have portrayed the *multiplication of methods and perspectives* in the discipline since the 1960s as a shift from a parochial and unitary language to the global context of many languages. In 1995, Fernando Segovia described the field as "on the verge of becoming global for the first time." Drawing on an image of a revised Pentecost scene, Segovia spoke of the progressive methodological and sociocultural liberation of the discipline from a paradigm of historical criticism to one of cultural studies: "What I have in mind is a 'speaking in tongues,' to be sure, but of a very different kind. Thus, it is not that one and the same group now speaks in other tongues to the multitudes at large—in fact, a rather accurate description of the situation up until this point—but rather that the multitudes at large have begun to speak in other tongues, their own tongues."[3] Segovia views this metaphoric multiplication of languages as marking positive political, ethical, and epistemic change, that is, as a decolonization of the field, facilitating a reduction of modernist alienation, and a reorientation reflecting the postmodern turn in which "the reader [in his/her human diversity] becomes as important as the text."[4]

John Collins notes how the Babel story has also served to convey this positive evaluation of multiplicity of method and perspective:

> The tower has been taken as a symbol of the aspiration to total, comprehensive, unitary interpretation, and the confusion of languages has come to symbolize the celebration of diversity. In the context of biblical studies, historical criticism, or the dominant mode of biblical criticism for the last two centuries or so, has been cast as the tower, and the confusion of languages is taken as the joyful chatter of new approaches.[5]

---

3. Fernando F. Segovia, "'And They Began to Speak in Other Tongues': Competing Modes of Discourse in Contemporary Biblical Criticism," in *Social Location and Biblical Interpretation in the United States* (vol. 1 of *Reading from this Place*; ed. Fernando F. Segovia and Mary Ann Tolbert; Minneapolis: Fortress, 1995), 1–32, quotation on 4–5.

4. Ibid., 32.

5. John J. Collins, *The Bible after Babel: Historical Criticism in a Postmodern Age* (Grand Rapids: Eerdmans, 2005). See also the positive use of both Babel and Pentecost in Jean-Pierre Ruiz, "Tell the Next Generation: Racial and Ethnic Minority Scholars and the Future of Biblical Studies," *JAAR* 69 (2001): 649–71.

This, too, entails a revision of the interpretive tradition, insofar as the evaluation of the multiplicity of languages in the Babel story as positive and desirable marks a shift away from a traditional view of the confusion of languages as divine punishment for human pride or as a human problem needing etiological explanation.[6] The use of Pentecost and Babel, biblical stories which narrate a momentous shift in human communication, evokes a sense of the profound, even threatening, challenge that has been made to both a monolingual ideal and the singular voice of the Euro-American historical critical scholar located in the centers of power.

Undoubtedly this imagery of multiplying languages is part of the engagement of biblical scholarship with larger academic and social debates. When asked what issues will shape the future of the study of religion, respondents to the 1991 Hart study on the state of religious and theological studies in American higher education produced the following list: ethics, the Bible, pluralism, feminism, and mysticism/spirituality.[7] These topics have also garnered great attention and energy within the subfield of biblical scholarship, that is, issues of *diversity*, the nature of *knowledge*, and *relationality* (for example, between the scholar and the larger world, between research and advocacy, and the role of academia in shaping the interactions among diverse people and communities). Emphasizing themes of multiplicity, epistemology, and ethics, Elisabeth Schüssler Fiorenza identifies the larger social context in which a reconceptualization of biblical studies is taking place as the multiplication and internationalization of knowledge, the rise of fundamentalisms, and the increased diversity of students and in the American religious landscape.[8] In this context, debates about diversity and the production of knowledge are not unique to biblical studies, nor are they restricted to the study of religion or to academia. As Ray Hart notes, many of the respondents to the AAR study were quite aware "that trends and issues in the study of religion are determined extra-academically by forces in the national and world cultures and within the academy by trends that cut across all humanistic and social scientific fields."[9]

The perceived diversity—and resulting cacophony—of the field is also linked to demographic changes. "It is not a coincidence that the creative surge in biblical scholarship of the late 1960s, 70s, and 80s was paralleled by the growth within the discipline at large and specifically within doctoral pro-

---

6. Collins, *Bible after Babel*, 2. See, e.g., Jacques Derrida, "Des Tours de Babel," *Semeia* 54 (1991): 3–34.

7. Ray L. Hart, "Religious and Theological Studies in American Higher Education: A Pilot Study," *JAAR* 59 (1991): 715–827, esp. 762–71.

8. Schüssler Fiorenza, "Rethinking the Educational Practices," 65–75.

9. Hart, "Religious and Theological Studies," 762.

grams of women scholars, racial/ethnic minorities, and third world scholars."[10] In her landmark 1987 presidential address to the Society of Biblical Literature, Elisabeth Schüssler Fiorenza linked epistemological and ethical disciplinary changes to the significant insights and challenges from voices traditionally marginalized in the discipline. She called for a contextualization of the field characterized by a "disciplined reflection on the public dimensions and ethical implications of our scholarly work" that would constitute a de-centering of traditional historical critical inquiry.

> Such an approach opens up the rhetorical practices of biblical scholarship to the critical inquiry of all the disciplines of religious studies and theology. Questions raised by feminist scholars in religion, liberation theologians, theologians of the so-called Third World, and by others traditionally absent from the exegetical enterprise would not remain peripheral or nonexistent for biblical scholarship. Rather their insights and challenges could become central to the scholarly discourse of the discipline.[11]

Similarly employing the spatial imagery of the challenges to the center from the periphery, the 1991 publication of *Voices from the Margin* called for, and itself marked, an increase in the participation of diverse and international voices and perspectives in the shaping of the field of biblical studies.[12]

Viewed within this larger frame of social-political debates and demographics, our multilingual biblical scholar who studies hard to master ancient

---

10. Mary Ann Tolbert, "Graduate Biblical Studies: Ethos and Discipline," *SBL Forum* (2003); online: http://www.sbl-site.org/publications/article.aspx?articleId=195. This point has been made by too many scholars to name here. Nevertheless, the shift is probably best understood as the prominence of a few white women and minority men and women rather than a widespread demographic shift.

11. Elisabeth Schüssler Fiorenza, *Rhetoric and Ethic: The Politics of Biblical Studies* (Minneapolis: Fortress, 1999) 30. The original SBL address was published in *JBL* 107 (1988): 3–17.

12. R. S. Sugirtharajah, ed., *Voices from the Margin: Interpreting the Bible in the Third World* (London: SPCK; Maryknoll, N.Y.: Orbis, 1991). The notion of the discipline as a contested space is revisited in the excellent collection of essays in idem, ed., *Still at the Margins: Biblical Scholarship Fifteen Years after the Voices from the Margin* (New York: T&T Clark, 2008); and in the introductory essay by editors Brian K. Blount, Cain Hope Felder, Clarice Martin, and Emerson B. Powery in *True to Our Native Land: An African American New Testament Commentary* (Minneapolis: Fortress, 2007), 1–7. They assert that "[s]pace matters. Where we come from and who we are influence how we read the Bible and how we translate it theologically so that it becomes meaningful and effective in our lives. The alternative to this kind of understanding is that only *one* space matters, namely, the space occupied by those in positions of privilege and power, who claim that there is only one meaning in the Bible and that *they* have the tools to unearth it" (2).

languages and distant places may not be as cosmopolitan as s/he might at first appear. Indeed s/he risks appearing methodologically monolingual and potentially out of touch with the larger world if s/he emerges from the hard work of graduate school as primarily or most importantly a certified specialist in ancient languages, distant places, and one set of approaches (usually doctrinal, historical, social scientific, or a combination of them). Although new Ph.D.s from most programs are surely aware of the diversity of the discourses in the field and about the Bible, it is not clear how much that multiplicity is being integrated into the curriculum at a structural level.[13] Taking an additive approach to the multiplication of languages, approaches, and locations can reify rather than disrupt the univocality of the field and can subtly communicate an evaluation of "alternatives" as nonessential, identity-b(i)ased, or decorative. This exacerbates rather than addresses a concern raised by biblical scholars of all ideological-theological persuasions: the disconnectedness of biblical scholarship from various groups and realities—either from sociocultural groups beyond Euro-Americans, from nonexpert Christian readers, from other humanistic or social scientific disciplines, or from democratic and justice-oriented social movements.

Although the past twenty years have seen a great deal of scholarly discussion of the rapid multiplication of methods and voices in biblical studies, it is not clear to me that this multiplication has had any significant impact on the structures of doctoral education. While the 1980s and 90s saw a robust effort by well-placed individuals to transgress the borders of traditional historical and/or doctrinal biblical scholarship, it seems that some recent publications indicate a shoring up of the borders by accommodating and thus containing

---

13. Julie Thompson Klein summarizes a range of approaches to integrating diverse content into college curriculum: (1) the contributions approach, "inserting discrete cultural artifacts and information … using criteria similar to those used in selecting mainstream elements"; (2) the additive approach, adding new content on as an appendage without changing the primary structure of the curriculum; (3) the transformational approach, altering curricular goals and structure from an approach that shows the contributions of diverse perspectives to mainstream culture toward an approach that highlights how mainstream culture emerged from and is produced in a "complex synthesis and interaction of diverse cultures"; and (4) the social action approach, takes the transformative approach and adds "components requiring students to make decisions and take actions related to the concept, issues, or problems studies in a particular unit. They become reflective social critics and agents of change" (*Humanities, Culture, and Interdisciplinarity: The Changing American Academy* [Albany: State University of New York Press, 2005] 213). As I will discuss later, I believe it is important for faculty to evaluate how biblical studies *doctoral* curriculum integrates multiplicity. I also think that doctoral students would benefit from reflecting on this question in relation to their own programs as well as how they might teach introductory courses in the field.

the diversity within the prevailing models of biblical studies. Thus William Countryman affirms that "diversity makes a contribution to the richness of our studies,"[14] but echoing traditional views of Babel, identifies the resulting chaos and inability to communicate—among academics and with "nonacademics concerned with Scripture"—as a central problem for the field. His book takes a recuperative approach and seeks to "*recover* a more unified field of discourse, not to limit the possible conclusions of our work, but to *restore* our ability to talk about them,"[15] particularly with nonexpert Christian readers. While Segovia asserted in 1995 that the disciplinary shifts in the field after the mid-1970s constituted the "swift demise" and the "collapse from within" of the historical-critical paradigm,[16] recent titles such as *The Bible after Babel: Historical Criticism in a Postmodern Age* (2005) and *Still at the Margins: Biblical Scholarship Fifteen Years after the Voices from the Margin* (2008) suggest that news of its death may be premature.[17] John Collins concedes that "there are some valid concerns and significant insights in the welter of new approaches," but he is also confident in the continuing central and definitional

---

14. Countryman, *Interpreting the Truth*, 1. Chapter 1 begins: "In itself, the contemporary chaos in biblical studies is not bad" (7). Collins says that "Diversity of approaches is at best a mixed blessing, and sometimes threatens to become a curse" (*Bible after Babel*, 3).

15. Countryman, *Interpreting the Truth*, 1 (emphasis added). Given the subtitle of Countryman's book ("Changing the Paradigm of Biblical Studies"), one cannot help but notice the lack of engagement with the extensive work of Elisabeth Schüssler Fiorenza on "shifting the paradigm" in the field. See, as only one example of many, *Rhetoric and Ethic*, 31–56. In her article on graduate biblical education, Schüssler Fiorenza also calls attention to the problem of communication among diverse languages and voices, but primarily because it allows the historical-critical and biblical-doctrinal paradigms to remain central ("Rethinking the Educational Practices," 68). Segovia recognizes the difficult challenge of conversation among different tongues but looks *forward* to that complex work as the "exciting and fragile," "direct and inevitable result of any process of liberation and decolonization" ("And They Began to Speak," 32).

16. Segovia, "And They Began to Speak," 1, 14.

17. The tension between traditional criticisms and postmodern methodologies is itself overstated if one compares overall framework and interests. A. K. M. Adam's *Faithful Interpretation: Reading the Bible in a Postmodern World* (Minneapolis: Fortress, 2006), for example, advocates a strong postmodern approach to the text but seeks to address the same problems as Countryman, that is, the inability of historical criticism to provide "sustenance" (1) to everyday religious readers. This stands in some contrast to Schüssler Fiorenza's efforts to expand the conversation of and about biblical studies *beyond* the academy and the church into the largest arenas of democratic society and Segovia's interest in engaging the fullest possible range of readers in the work of social-political empowerment and change.

place of historical criticism in the field.[18] Scholars who were and are part of the effort to transform the field from an unquestioned monolingualism have expressed frustration. R. S. Sugirtharajah asks what "has changed since the publication of *Voices from the Margin* fifteen years ago? Not much, as far as the attitude of the mainstream is concerned."[19] In 2003, Mary Ann Tolbert voiced a concern I have heard in several quarters—that the momentary interruption of the field by "new voices with different accountabilities" is now being countered by the "leveling out, or even in some places the decline, in the number of female scholars and racial/ethnic minority scholars teaching in doctoral programs. As voices of difference recede, it seems, so does innovative and challenging scholarship."[20]

This sense of a lack of change should turn our attention back to the basic structures for reproducing the field in doctoral programs. Of course biblical scholars know several languages and utilize a variety of methodological tools, but, which ones? Learning ancient languages and traditional methods equips students to do recognized and even transgressive work in the field.[21] I wonder, however, whether we have yet taken seriously enough the fact that a routine and programmatic emphasis on Mediterranean and European languages and cultures has a significant impact on the type of questions being pursued

---

18. Collins, *Bible after Babel*, 3, referring to Stephen Moore's work: "I do not think it either desirable or likely that *God's Gym or God's Beauty Parlor* will become the twin towers of biblical interpretation in the coming century."

19. Sugirtharajah, *Still at the Margins*, 8.

20. Tolbert, "Graduate Biblical Education," 3. While there are signs of retrenchment, there are also signs of continuing creativity and challenge with efforts at collaboration among, for example, global feminists and minority scholars across the discipline. See Kathleen O'Brien Wicker, Althea Spencer Miller, and Musa W. Dube, eds., *Feminist New Testament Studies: Global and Future Perspectives* (New York: Palgrave Macmillan, 2005); and Randall C. Bailey, Tat-siong Benny Liew, and Fernando F. Segovia, eds., *They Were All Together in One Place? Toward Minority Biblical Criticism* (SemeiaSt 57; Atlanta: Society of Biblical Literature, 2009).

21. Indeed, it is as much how one uses the tools as which tools one uses. See, for example, Elisabeth Schüssler Fiorenza's highly influential work to reorient historical-theological biblical studies within a feminist framework in *In Memory of Her: A Feminist Theological Reconstruction of Christian Origins* (New York: Crossroad, 1983), and Bernadette Brooten's use of traditional tools such as textual criticism and epigraphy to restore figures like Junia to biblical translation and Jewish women leaders to historical narratives (Bernadette Brooten, "'Junia ... Outstanding among the Apostles' [Romans 16:7]," in *Women Priests: A Catholic Commentary on the Vatican Declaration* [ed. Leonard Swidler and Arlene Swidler; New York: Paulist, 1977], 141–44; and idem, *Women Leaders in the Ancient Synagogue: Inscriptional Evidence and Background Issues* [Brown Judaic Studies 36; Chico, Calif.: Scholars Press, 1982]).

by graduate students in biblical studies, the way that we conceptualize the nature of the field itself, and on its demographics.[22] Students not only travel but also create the well-worn paths that lead from mastering basic language skills to dissertations utilizing philological methods and questions.[23] Alternative methodological paths of inquiry have struggled to gain ground and are routinely rendered less traversable when they are viewed as less appropriately serious projects (if qualifying as biblical studies research at all).[24]

Deeply embedding ancient languages and historical-critical methods into required exams and coursework also does its part to methodically perpetuate the discipline's privileging of inquiry into origins: into ancient meanings and worlds.[25] These traditional basics also function epistemologically to produce a

---

22. While love of ancient languages may draw some people to the field, this emphasis can also work to the opposite effect. For example, Kwok Pui-lan discusses the alienation of minority scholars from the discipline through the unexamined ethnocentric privileging of classical languages and the presumption that the students who struggle with these languages have academic problems despite the reality of the lack of opportunity for many students to study classical languages before graduate work. See Kwok Pui-lan, "Jesus/the Native," in *Teaching the Bible: Discourses and Politics of Biblical Pedagogy* (ed. Fernando F. Segovia and Mary Ann Tolbert; Maryknoll, N.Y.: Orbis, 1998), 71. Older students may also be daunted by learning new languages in later years.

23. Even the structures of requirements have implications. For example, in New Testament studies, Greek is always required, but Syriac, Coptic, Geez, and Aramaic are optional, thus reinforcing the longstanding focus on first-century Christian texts and origins apart from the diverse second- to fifth-century early Christian contexts that canonized and interpreted them. For a discussion of the epistemological and ethical effects of privileging the New Testament in the field, see Elizabeth A. Castelli and Hal Taussig, "Drawing Large and Startling Figures: Reimagining Christian Origins by Painting Like Picasso," in *Reimagining Christian Origins: A Colloquium Honoring Burton L. Mack* (ed. Elizabeth A. Castelli and Hal Taussig; Valley Forge, Pa.: Trinity International Press, 1996), 3–22.

24. The Hart AAR report raised questions about how the processes of tenure and promotion can result in a pulling back from innovative, collaborative, or transgressive scholarship because younger faculty might "withdraw into traditional specializations in order to advance" ("Religious and Theological Studies," 791). See a discussion of hiring and minority scholars in Tat-Siong Benny Liew, "When Margins Become Common Ground," in Sugirtharajah, *Still at the Margins*, 44–45.

25. For example, if a student is interested in using literary criticism to explore the power of a narrative, must she do her analysis on the Hebrew text? Why? Does the story have no power for its readers in another language? Surely something was lost in translation; something always is. But something is created as well. Is that of interest to the biblical scholar or is that the purview of literary studies? Another student interested in a particular African community's interpretation of the Gospels should logically work with the language of the reading community of interest to her. To privilege the original Greek would narrow any results to ancient readers or to the time of the translation of the Bible into the second language. But if she persists with her interest in a particular community of readers, could

stable and unified biblical text. Students become comfortable using one critical edition of the text (and its apparatus, which helps to organize the multiplicity of the text) rather than working critically with the many translations, versions, visual representations, hypertexts, or renditions.[26] Translations in languages that have no value for reconstructing the ancient Greek or Hebrew text—such as Filipino or Swahili—are not considered critical texts for study except in how they translate their source texts.[27] This raises basic questions about the definition of the field as it relates to the larger theme of multiplicity: are the social, political, and theological lives of the multitude of biblical texts worth scholarly investigation, explanation, and critical appraisal within the field of biblical studies? Or is it only (really) the ancient texts and their meanings? For various reasons, few scholars today argue that the goal of biblical research is to discover some pristine original meaning, and yet we must ask why exegeting or explicating ancient texts constitutes a large part of the basic training in the discipline. These kinds of emphases passively exclude and occlude other choices. As Tat-Siong Benny Liew asks, "Why is fluency in biblical languages

---

her study have been produced in a sociology of religion or an African studies program? In both cases, the step away from ancient languages also marks stepping out of the discipline. If the research is somehow related to the Bible, is that enough to certify the student as a biblical scholar? The ease with which such basic examples lead to questions about the edges of the discipline illustrates how much the structures of doctoral training draw out the borderlines that define the field. While the work of Vincent Wimbush in developing the Institute for Signifying Scriptures at Claremont demonstrates the far-reaching potential of biblical studies to expand beyond itself, it also presents a thoroughgoing disruption of the basic structures that make it recognizable as a discipline in the first place.

26. In his early proposals for dealing with the "hermeneutical dilemma of the African American biblical student," William H. Meyers called for an approach to canon that emphasizes the multiplicity of different canons in different social-cultural contexts ("The Hermeneutical Dilemma of the African American Biblical Student," in *Stony the Road We Trod: African American Biblical Interpretation* [ed. Cain Hope Felder; Minneapolis: Fortress, 1991], 51). In this sense, the emphasis of the biblical scholar should be not on text in context, but on the rhetorical contextualization of texts-in-worlds.

27. Given the strong philological roots of biblical criticism, the field could make a substantial transdisciplinary contribution to wide-ranging discussions about the theory and politics of translation. See Alan Williams, "New Approaches to the Problem of Translation in the Study of Religion," in *Textual, Comparative, Sociological, and Cognitive Approaches* (vol. 2 of *New Approaches to the Study of Religion*; ed. Peter Antes, Armin W. Geertz, and Randi R. Warne; Berlin: de Gruyter, 2004), 13–44; and Elizabeth A. Castelli, "Les Belles Infidèles/Fidelity or Feminism? The Meanings of Feminist Biblical Translation," in *A Feminist Introduction* (vol. 1 of *Searching the Scriptures*; ed. Elisabeth Schüssler Fiorenza; New York: Crossroad, 1993), 189–204.

more important than fluency in some interdisciplinary theories that may after all have their own vocabularies and even grammars like a language?"[28]

Although the study of ancient and modern European languages and cultures appears natural, programmatically prioritizing them contributes to perpetuating the Eurocentric and colonialist legacies of biblical criticism itself. The map and timeline of biblical studies that we internalize through these practices are strongly linear, tracing a singular path from ancient Near East and Mediterranean texts and contexts, through the scholarship of modern Europe and Anglo North America to today. But this is not the shape of the world—in the past or today.[29] This kind of map thus marks but also perpetuates the divides between technical and lay readers and between those who are culturally central on the map versus those who are peripheral. In this sense, both methodological and social diversity can be structurally controlled or excluded. This has been noted repeatedly by ethnic minority scholars in the field. In *Stony the Road We Trod*, the 1991 landmark volume on African American interpretation, William H. Myers described his view of the dilemma of the African American student who encounters "lectures, assignments, and examinations ... that prepare the African American student to answer more Eurocentric-oriented questions and concerns." Disavowing a vast conspiracy, Meyers nonetheless suggests that these practices can have "rather pernicious consequences" by creating the sense that the Eurocentric approach is normative and "without cultural bias" while casting the African American approach as culturally biased.[30] Meyers does not call for a replacement of the prevailing methods with alternative ones, but rather for a diversification of methods and an expansion of the horizons of time and place in biblical studies—taking an

---

28. Liew, "When Margins Become Common Ground," 43.

29. The importance of recognizing the links between the global map, multiple voices, and methodological diversity is stressed repeatedly by minority and non-U.S. scholars. For example, Musa Dube notes that she knows only four women New Testament scholars in all of Africa. "In Asia and Latin America, the situation is not any better. Indeed, even among the North American minority groups, the number of trained feminist New Testament scholars is only a handful. This situation speaks for itself; the future of FNTS [Feminist New Testament Studies] must strive to train women from Two-Thirds World, since the locus of the Christian religion has shifted to these places, particularly Latin America and Africa. Further, globalization itself brings multicultural communities and students to Western metropolitan institutions and neighborhoods. In making this effort, however, Two-Thirds World women must not be muzzled, or modeled after parroting Rahabs" (Musa W. Dube, "Rahab Is Hanging Out a Red Ribbon: One African Woman's Perspective on the Future of Feminist New Testament Scholarship," in Wicker, Miller, and Dube, *Feminist New Testament Studies*, 185).

30. Meyers, "The Dilemma of the African American Student," 41–42.

interest in the way the Bible functions in different times and places and in those contexts diversely. This changes the mappable timeline: away from a linear line from antiquity to the present via Europe and toward a three dimensional universe of many languages and people who traverse time and space in complex networks of interaction and influence.[31]

Diversification in itself, however, will not transform the discipline.[32] Ensuring that tomorrow's biblical studies scholar-teachers are cosmopolitan and multilingual—both linguistically and methodologically—is only the first step. The next steps must be to ensure that we are critically aware that *all* discourses including our own are situated in wide-ranging social-political debates, and that we are able to adjudicate the role of biblical interpretation in these contexts.[33] I am not proposing summarily abandoning the ancient

---

31. Liew describes a similar shift in time and space produced by diversity ("When Margins Become Common Ground," 40–43).

32. Citing Arjun Appadurai, Liew notes that "diversity must move from demographic and curricular changes … to challenging and transforming how knowledge is produced and disseminated.… Cultural diversity must be distinguished from and sustained by a culture of diversity" (ibid., 41, 45). There are broad political and economic forces that shape the discipline's approach to diversity. In the context of globalization, diversity sells, and thus Mark D. Wood calls for scholars of religion to face their part in the production of workers for a global market economy: "corporations increasingly require both technologically skilled and culturally sensitive employees. Multicultural theory and practice, as an updated expression of liberal pluralism, has proven pivotal to corporate owners seeking to negotiate alliances and market products, as well as to managers responsible for administrating a subjectively heterogeneous international workforce" ("Religious Studies as Critical Organic Intellectual Practice," *JAAR* 69 [2001]: 129–62, here 134). For a historical view of the emergence of the field of comparative religion in relation to Christian globalization (a.k.a. missionizing), see Russell T. McCutcheon, *The Discipline of Religion: Structure, Meaning, Rhetoric* (New York: Routledge, 2003), 38–53.

33. In my experience, many scholars will get on board with the project of contextualizing the discourses of the discipline. Establishing the grounds for adjudicating among diverse interpretations or reconstructions is another matter. Although feminist and various minority scholars have argued for integrating into scholarship an ethical, political, and values-based approach to such adjudication, many scholars (and doctoral programs) locate evaluative authority solely in scholarly standards, critical distance, and the rigor of methods. For extensive discussion of the importance of critical evaluation and the ethics of interpretation, see much of the work of Schüssler Fiorenza (e.g., *Rhetoric and Ethic*); and Gary A. Phillips and Danna Nolan Fewell, *Bible and Ethics of Reading* (*Semeia* 77; Atlanta: Scholars Press, 1997). In 1984, Jonathan Z. Smith questioned the centrality of the dissertation in doctoral education, suggesting that such a focus reduced Ph.D. curriculum to a "need-to-know" basis. He proposes a combination of cognitive and evaluative acumen that emerges from the contextualization of one's own field: "Whatever else they learn, graduate students should be exposed to their disciplinary past in such a way as to learn the art

language requirements or the European-American historical critical tradition. Rather, an approach that takes seriously the effects of what we privilege demands that programs make transparent the purpose and politics of each requirement and routine,[34] locate the study of languages and methods within a larger theoretical framework that recognizes and evaluates the plurality of languages and locations of the Bible, and build in more extensive avenues for border-crossing student-tailored combinations of diverse language study and methodological emphases.

Although there is a striking repetitiveness across most biblical studies Ph.D. programs, this kind of reflection on basic requirements will not likely, indeed hopefully will not, lead to identical outcomes. For example, in the doctoral program at Drew, students take classes and write dissertations with what I think is the highest concentration in the country of faculty using a variety of feminist, liberationist, postmodern, and postcolonial methodologies. In our context, we face different questions than might be faced at other institutions. For example, we seek to find a way to approach comprehensive exams that takes seriously both our valuing of methodological multiplicity and the students' need[35] to be literate in the history of the discipline and a historical

---

of critical evaluation and to gain the ability to account for this past in terms of a broadly based historical consciousness.... And they should be taught ways of 'cost accounting' for the decisions of choice and interpretation that they make" ("Here and Now: Prospects for Graduate Education," in *New Humanities and Academic Disciplines: The Case of Jewish Studies* [ed. Jacob Neusner; Madison: University of Wisconsin Press, 1984], 33–45, here 36). In her 1987 SBL address, Schüssler Fiorenza also called attention to the shortcomings of doctoral education in terms of contextualization and evaluation: "Do we ask and teach our students to ask in a disciplined way how our scholarship is conditioned by its social location and how it serves political functions?" (*Rhetoric and Ethic*, 23).

34. The structural implications of some of the rituals of my own program are now obvious to me: I "learned" that Hellenism is more important for understanding early Christianity than Judaism; I "learned" that feminist and other liberationist methods were peripheral, unpleasant, and must be done on my own time; I "learned" that having children is not structurally compatible with being a serious scholar; and I "learned" that theological and political interests have a place in discussions but never in writing. But, I also learned to always attend to the social, political, and material aspects of religion and to see and disrupt these structural tendencies. I also received support from mentors to do so.

35. This is an intellectual need in that knowledge of the history of the discipline provides important perspective on the context and rhetoric of the field and an economic need in that the job market largely works within a traditional understanding of biblical studies. More often than not, candidates who can meet an institution's desire for scholars interested in facility with diverse methods and theories (such as contextual hermeneutics or postcolonial theory) must still be recognizable as a biblical scholar who has mastered the traditional discipline.

approach to the text. Since students are working with a range of approaches in coursework, we question whether comprehensive exams should be the place for testing for knowledge of the "basics" of historical-critical methodologies. Locating the students' deep encounter with the traditional discipline primarily in exams can do two things: (1) it can implicitly confirm the common assumption that historical-critical methods are the *sina qua non* of the field; and (2) it can essentialize and ossify historical inquiry by segregating it as a "foundational" set of methods and results rather than equipping our adventurous students to continually interrogate it and rearticulate it alongside, in conversation with, and as part of the other modes of inquiry that they likely came to Drew to study in the first place. Indeed, historical inquiry concerning biblical texts has and can provide one kind of distance on a text useful for sparking critical reflection on a whole host of social and theoretical issues and questions.[36] It is important, however, not to equate such distance with scholarly objectivity[37] or authority. The "Othering" of the biblical text can

---

36. See the roots of historical inquiry in Protestant efforts to gain critical distance from a doctrinal approach to the Bible (see Collins, *Bible after Babel*, 4–8). For a teaching example in the context of a seminary, see Harry O. Maier, "The Familiar Made Strange: An Orientation to Biblical Study in Vancouver," *TThRel* 10 (2007) 80–86. For examples from a range of institutions, see Mark Roncace and Patrick Gray, eds., *Teaching the Bible: Practical Strategies for Classroom Instruction* (SBLRBS 49; Atlanta: Society of Biblical Literature, 2005).

37. Regarding objectivity, Collins notes that a "historical focus has been a way of getting distance from a text, of respecting its otherness." It is also a place where different people can have meaningful conversations as "participants try to persuade each other by appeal to evidence and criteria that are in principle acceptable to the other participants" (*Bible after Babel*, 10–11). Thus it is not the scholar who has objectivity (or is without subjectivity); it is rather the rules of the conversation that attempt to balance subjectivities around a set of agreed-upon standards. As Elisabeth Schüssler Fiorenza notes, "diachronic reconstructions distance us in such a way from the original texts and their historical symbolic worlds that they relativize not only them but also us" (*Rhetoric and Ethic*, 27). Regarding authority, Collins points out that early historical criticism claimed *autonomy* from ecclesiastical authorities by drawing on Enlightenment standards of rationality, scientific discovery, and humanistic learning (*Bible after Babel*, 5). According to Russell T. McCutcheon, early *Religionswissenschaft* scholars sought similar autonomy from the hegemonic control of Protestant denominations over American higher education. The rhetoric used to secure this autonomy asserted the scholar's authority with terms such as "scientific, serious, critical, academic, historical, objective, neutral, non-denominational, etc., all of which relied on the ever increasing authority of the scientific worldview" (*Discipline of Religion*, 51). This is the social process by which cognitive criteria becomes privileged over ethical criteria, resulting in the notion that true, authoritative scholarship is (and must be) autonomous from social, political, and ethical concerns and evaluation (Schüssler Fiorenza, *Rhetoric and Ethic*, 195–96).

be productive or alienating depending on contexts and interests and thus it should be as open to rhetorical-contextual analysis and ethical-political evaluation as any other positioning of readers and texts.

My concern is that the basic structures of doctoral education—such as language requirements, coursework, comprehensive exams, and acceptable dissertation topics—not only presume but manufacture an understanding of biblical studies as having a single center and unifying common language. That is, the structures (re)produce the tensions that emerge in the encounter with diversity, rather than being challenged by them. The question is not how biblical studies can survive amidst contemporary realities of diversity and the proliferation of knowledge. Rather, we should ask how the conceptualization of biblical studies itself can and should be transformed, and what structural changes to doctoral education should then be implemented accordingly.

Many Locations

Discourses in and around the Bible are multilingual because they are multilocational. Our rhetoric is shaped by and in our contexts. It is important for graduate students to be aware of and reflect on this fact because the map of biblical studies is being disputed and redrawn today. I have already discussed how a widening global perspective and the diversification of the discipline present profound challenges to the old geography. However, there is other shifting ground that will shape the future of the field in ways that we are only beginning to see. What are the effects of the American Academy of Religion separating structurally from the Society of Biblical Literature? How do the decline of mainline U.S. Protestant Christianity, the mainstreaming of evangelical and nondenominational institutions and the growth of global Christianities change the professional and economic landscape of the field? Given the increase in the popularity of the study of religion in colleges and universities, how will new students—who enter graduate education with different training and interests in biblical studies than students of the past—shape the future of the field?

These are important questions because discourses of scholarly authority and identity are produced within this context of contested, diverse, and uneven territories. Who is being authorized to speak and where? Although there has been much discussion about how and whether a scholar's identity should shape his or her scholarship, I agree with José Ignacio Cabezón that it is as important to turn the question around and ask how our locations shape our identities:

Given the roles that the academy in general and our institutions in particular play in constructing the boundaries of acceptable/required work, and given as well the constitutive role that our work plays in the construction of our identities, what kind of persons are we being propelled to be? Are these the persons we want to be? Are these the persons that our students and our various 'communities of solidarity' *need* us to be?[38]

Scholarly discourse and identity is formed in the distinctive locations of the field—with their attendant constituencies, institutional constraints, and economic pressures. Thus authorizing students to shape the future of the discipline means helping them to see and analyze its many rhetorical-contextual formations as well as the political and ethical effects of their places in this variegated terrain.

For example, one of the more prominent discussions related to the multiple locations of the field today concerns the definition and coherence of the field of the study of religion, often characterized as a divide between religious studies and theological studies or between the goals and disciplines of the public university and those of the parochial seminary.[39] The distance between these two locations is mapped historically—from the roots of American higher education in Protestant Christianity, with the Bible as the centerpiece of an early humanities curriculum,[40] to the rise of the study of religion in public universities after the *School District of Abington v. Schempp* decision in 1963—and theoretically as the difference between social scientific and comparative approaches to the study of religion versus phenomenological and hermeneutical approaches. Given the historical role of the Bible in the curriculum of the major divinity schools, these discussions usually locate biblical studies in "theological studies" and suggest that in order to be more academic, biblical inquiry should be framed in social-scientific terms or absorbed into areas such as the comparative study of scriptures, classics or ancient history, or literature studies.[41]

---

38. José Ignacio Cabezón, "Identity and the Work of the Scholar of Religion," in *Identity and the Politics of Scholarship in the Study of Religion* (ed. José Ignacio Cabezón and Sheila Greeve Davaney; New York: Routledge, 2004), 43–60, here 56.

39. In 1989, Jonathan Z. Smith was invited by the AAR to reflect on the unity of the field. He noted that "the study of religion, especially at its more advanced levels, is unique among the human sciences in its bilocality, often denoted in our professional shorthand by the dualism seminary/university" ("Connections," *JAAR* 58 [1990]: 1–15, here 2–3).

40. Smith, "Bible and Religion," 87–93. See also idem, "Here and Now," 39–44; and Thompson, *Humanities, Culture, and Interdisciplinarity*, 11–33.

41. This absorption is political in two different ways. For some, it actively rejects the self-evidentiary value ascribed to the Bible by religious communities and thus is appro-

Although these discussions turn on theorizing the study of religion and the category religion itself, one of the stakes of the debate is clearly rhetorical and locational, that is, it negotiates the position of the scholar of religion in relationship to the object of study, within his or her institution, and to particular audiences.[42] Thus the perceived divide in the field is most tellingly characterized as one between the "*academic* study of religion and the *religious* study of religion"[43] and as concerning the question of the scholar's location as "insider" or "outsider" in relation to what he or she studies. Because the Bible and its meaning is often the self-evident object of study,[44] biblical scholarship appears and has been relentlessly Christian, "to a remarkably large degree, an affair of native exegesis."[45] In the context of a public university (or a secu-

---

priately relativizing. For others, it circumscribes the scholarly discourse about the Bible to comparison and social description (rather than interpretation) and thus reduces the role that might be played by scholars in shaping, disrupting, and adjudicating the powerful role that the Bible continues to play in community and public discourses across the globe.

42. This theme emerges repeatedly in the excellent collection of essays from the Congress 2000: The Future of the Study of Religion conference. See Slavica Jakelić and Lori Pearson, eds., *The Future of the Study of Religion* (Studies in the History of Religions 103; Leiden: Brill, 2004).

43. This shorthand phrase is ascribed to Donald Wiebe in Charlotte Allen, "Is Nothing Sacred? Casting Out the Gods from Religious Studies," *Lingua Franca* (November 1996): 30–40, here 32 (emphasis original). Wiebe continues: "we believe in the academic study of religion."

44. If the Bible is a self-evident object of study, then one approaches it with unexamined presuppositions, such as assuming that the Bible means, makes sense, and is worth studying. In his plea for secularists to learn about the Bible, Jacques Berlinerblau discusses the basic problem of self-evidence in biblical scholarship (*The Secular Bible: Why Nonbelievers Must Take Religion Seriously* [Cambridge: Cambridge University Press, 2005], 75–76). He points out that, while there can and must be common political work among scholars across theological and secular lines, ultimately secularists (that is, nonreligionists) will point to the problem of invoking the Bible in any contemporary debates because to them it is not self-evident that the Bible is valuable or relevant (83). While this is an important distinction, it also masks the fact that scholars who locate themselves more openly in conversation with religious communities also challenge the primacy, relevance, and authority of the Bible in public discourses. See, e.g., Mary Ann Tolbert, "A New Teaching with Authority: A Re-evaluation of the Authority of the Bible," in Segovia and Tolbert, *Teaching the Bible*, 168–89; and Elisabeth Schüssler Fiorenza, *The Power of the Word: Scripture and the Rhetoric of Empire* (Minneapolis: Fortress, 2007) 35–68.

45. Smith, "Bible and Religion," 88. For Smith, the "native exegesis" of biblical scholarship represents "the sort of accounts that, for other religious traditions constitute data for the student of religion." While both Berlinerblau (see the previous note) and Smith call important attention to the rhetorically situated nature of biblical scholarship and the value of exposing its presuppositions and interests, both tend to identify the "outsider" who does this work as an outsider to religion. However, as various feminist, minority, and Jewish

lar society), such positioning threatens the academic authority of the scholar in a context where the study of religion is understood as "the scholarly neutral and nonadvocative study of multiple religious traditions."[46] That issues of authority are part of what is at stake is apparent in the one type of Hart report institution in which there was unanimous rejection of theological studies. This was the one where the study of religion is the least secure and is at risk of being deemed illegitimate as a scholarly field or absorbed into other disciplines: the public university with a small religion department.[47]

The mapping of one binary (insider/outsider) to another (religious/academic) can perpetuate, rather than expose, the self-evident value of *unsituated* scholarship.[48] The bilocal shorthand of university v. seminary creates strong dichotomies between university and seminary, nonreligious and religious, and neutral academics and located advocates. But neither these categories nor the distinctions between them hold.[49] Is not the scholar who takes up com-

---

scholars have repeatedly shown, there are many ways of disrupting the presumption of self-evidence and achieving the social-historical contextualization of biblical studies.

46. Hart, "Religious and Theological Studies," 716.

47. Ibid., 731, 748. The Hart report actually identifies eleven different kinds of institutions where a scholar of religion might work: (1) public university with undergraduate religion department; (2) public university with undergraduate and graduate department of religion; (3) private liberal arts college related to a "mainline" Protestant church; (4) private university with a religion department for both graduates and undergraduates; (5) private liberal arts college related to the "evangelical" Protestant church; (6) private university with a Protestant seminary and an undergraduate and graduate department of religion; (7) historically black Protestant seminary; (8) free-standing seminary related to "mainline" Protestant church; (9) free-standing seminary related to the "evangelical" Protestant church; (10) Roman Catholic institution with a seminary and graduate and undersgraduate religion department; (11) a Jewish seminary (718).

48. In his discussion of the category "Bible," Smith ("Bible and Religion," 88) rightly points out that basic questions such as "which Bible?" or "whose Bible?" or "the Bible when?" expose the situated nature of self-evidential scholarly discourse. But these kinds of questions have frequently been posed by a range of religious, political, and social "outsiders" to the dominant discourse, whether academic or not, and whether religious or not. While "native exegesis" for Smith means *Christian* exegesis, a feminist postcolonial Christian scholar might expose the *Western* political locations of religious and academic discourses by asking "native to what?" or "which natives?" or "what makes someone native?" or "can the 'native' study the Bible?" (Kwok Pui-lan, "Jesus/the Native," 80–83).

49. Indeed the biblical scholars interviewed for the report often could not place themselves into these categories. This points to the inadequacy of the categories as well as to the ways in which philological and historical disciplines cut across the humanities and social sciences. See Hart, "Religious and Theological Studies," 737–38. Julie Thompson Klein describes similar binaries in debates over humanities curriculum: "Even in the face of data to the contrary, however, stark polarities persist in the popular and the academic

parative religion in order to de-center the privileging of Christianity taking a valuable, but nonetheless advocative, stance in relation to public conversations about religion in America and globally? Is the seminary professor an insider or an outsider (and who decides that) if she challenges students to hear and juxtapose diverse voices in the Bible or in the history of interpretation thus interrupting traditional notions of Christianity? Does the presumed neutral stance of a historian mean that his writing of the history of religion is somehow outside of societal discourses about religion?[50] If it is the proper role of universities to describe the social-linguistic phenomenon of religion and the role of seminaries to contribute to the production of meaning within religion, then are students deeply misguided when students in university and college religion classrooms want some discussion of meaning[51] and seminarians attest to the power of getting critical distance on their own religious traditions? Can scholars ever step outside of the social discourses that invent and contest authority, tradition, culture, meaning, and ethics?

These stark binaries between locations and among diversely located scholars can "quite easily turn out to be a mere parody or mimicry of the religious impulse toward purity apparent in many, if not all human societies."[52] Thus these debates about the study of religion are not unrelated to those over diversity, knowledge, and ethics discussed above insofar as they attempt to secure scholarly authority in American higher education by requiring a clear distinction between the *apolitical/nonreligious* scholar-as-observer and the *political/religious* scholar-as-advocate.[53] Some have noted that this debate

---

press. Scholarship is pitted against teaching, past against present, Europe against America, Western heritage against other cultures, and a preservationist campaign to restore tradition against a reformist campaign to forge a critical alternative. The actual practice of humanities education is far more variegated across the roughly 4,000 postsecondary institutions currently operating in the United States" (*Humanities, Culture, and Interdisciplinarity*, 205).

50. For a discussion of the ways in which recent historical Jesus scholarship—whether working from a theological position or not—participates in contemporary debates about Christian identity, see Melanie Johnson-DeBaufre, *Jesus among Her Children: Q, Eschatology, and the Construction of Christian Origins* (HTS 55; Cambridge: Harvard University Press, 2006) 27–42, 115–29.

51. A senior scholar in religion interviewed by the Hart report notes that "what attracts students to the study of religion is that they have questions about the meaning of their lives, want to know what it is to be human and humane, and intuit that religion deals with such things" ("Religious and Theological Studies," 727).

52. Elizabeth A. Castelli, "Problems, Questions, and Curiosities: A Response to Ivan Strenski," in Jakelić and Pearson, *Future of the Study of Religion*, 186.

53. In biblical studies, this can mean that claiming a political location (such as feminist), making a connection to a religious community, *or* making a methodological step away from history or social science can all make biblical scholars appear more "theo-

comes precisely at a time when the methods and demographics of all humanities disciplines have been challenged by diverse voices and the epistemological disruption of grand narratives and the unsituated universal scholar. Although the theoretical discussion is quite sophisticated, drawing such strong lines between the religious and the nonreligious, and the political and nonpolitical, appears as nostalgic as a doctrinal effort to recover lost clarity, coherence, and authority.[54] As various feminists and ethnic minorities have been arguing for decades, something much more complex, self-reflective, and tensive is needed to characterize the relationship of the scholar to his or her work. Instead of a model of scholarship based on "disinterested curiosity about important questions concerning the nature and forms of religion and religious life," Elizabeth Castelli makes a case for "intentional interestedness" which:

> recognizes that those of us who study religion bring histories and subjectivities to our work. It rejects the view that there are objective or neutral positions for scholars to occupy, pristine outposts safely above the fray of worlds we seek to interrogate and understand. It takes seriously the ethical demand that any engagement with other human beings (historical or contemporary) makes upon us. It requires that we not only ask questions, but that we engage in sustained conversation.... The most interesting and curiosity-satisfying future for the study of religion will be found not in the formulation of a set of questions ... [but] in a broad, inclusive, risk-taking, and border-blurring *conversation*—conversation in all of its dialogical messiness, conversation inflected by a willingness to place the self at risk.[55]

---

logical" or biased and thus less scholarly, intellectual, or legitimate in contexts where the study of religion or historical criticism predominates. Although the growth of the study of diverse religious traditions beyond the Bible has had a positive effect on the diversification of scholars working in the field of religion, given that "religious" is often still linked with "ethnic," defining fields as necessarily apolitical/nonreligious can also have a negative effect on the demographics of hiring in particular institutions.

54. "Under the conditions of modern religious pluralism it would be naïve to expect homogeneity, stability, and unity in academic discourse.... The renewed hope cherished by some scholars of religion being able to reinstate a unified paradigm and generally binding terminology is the academic counterpart to an authoritarian dogmatism which many critical scholars of religion would readily associate with old ecclesiasticalism or religious 'fundamentalism'" (Friedrich Wilhelm Graf, "The Stubborn Persistence of Religion: Some Post-Secular Reflections," in Jakelić and Pearson, *Future of the Study of Religion*, 28).

55. Castelli, "Problems, Questions, and Curiosities," 186, 188. The idea that entering such a border-blurring conversation entails self-risk exposes the self-disciplining potential of graduate education. Both in terms of position and finances, graduate students (and untenured faculty members) may not see themselves as having a self to risk or may see the risk as too great. This points to the crucial role of mentoring and networking in fostering and recognizing border-crossing, creativity, and risk-taking in one's intellectual work. A

This idea of a border-blurring conversation[56] disrupts an easy divide between the university and the seminary as well as a comfortable (or frustrating) gulf between academia and the various publics who are our objects of study as well as our audiences.[57]

Although different institutions have, and even need, different ways of talking about their work, it is more helpful and accurate to think of the field as a set of border-blurring conversations than as a range of locations in opposition to or in no relation to each other. There is something to be learned by routinely inviting students to think about how biblical studies is framed and even constrained in different contexts and what it means or should mean to do one's work in those locations. That is, students should reflect on what scholars in particular locations study and teach, why and how they study and teach it, and what difference it makes.[58] At Drew, the doctoral program area is called "Biblical Studies," not "Scripture Studies" or the "Literature and History of Antiquity." This makes (historical and practical) sense because the graduate faculty at Drew is also the teaching faculty of the Theological School, a seminary of the United Methodist Church. The canonical Bible is (or often becomes) an important part of the scholarly focus of the faculty partially

---

colleague working in Buddhism recently told me that the presence of feminist scholars in her graduate institution was invaluable to her not because they worked in her field (they did not) but because their presence granted a certain permission to ask feminist questions in her own work.

56. In his response to Wilhelm Graf in *Future of the Study of Religion*, Peter Berger offers a critique of radical constructivism, which he sees as producing an "endless series of narratives" and perspectival readings. He juxtaposes this image of the scholar as one who "pronounces" to the "foundational principle of the historian and of any practitioner of the human sciences: the act of carefully, methodically listening to what others, past and present, have to say" ("The Stubborn Persistence of Debates about Religion: A Response to Friedrich Wilhelm Graf," in Jakelić and Pearson, *Future of the Study of Religion*, 45). However, Castelli's image of a conversation—with its dialogical messiness—allows for an image of the scholar as both speaker and listener.

57. Graf notes that "It is not only religious communities which play an important role in shaping public life, but scholars of religion too … by not being willing to comment on normative conflicts, … [scholars] only encourage a dangerous totalization of religious issues. If scholars of religion are not capable of naming the criteria for differentiating between the religious and non-religious fields, how can we prevent religious language from being exploited ubiquitously for all possible intents and purposes?" ("Stubborn Persistence," 41–42).

58. The influence of location on the development of scholarship and teaching in biblical studies is well attested in the reflections of North American scholars who have lived and taught abroad; see, e.g., the reflections on biblical studies in an oral culture in Patrick J. Hartin, *Third World Challenges in the Teaching of Biblical Studies: Occasional Papers 25* (Claremont, Calif.: Institute for Antiquity and Christianity, 1992).

because it is also central to the majority of teaching being done in the seminary. My own writing on canonical texts, therefore, is one way my publishing connects with my classroom. My current research on spatial discourses in the Pauline literature, for example, is not only shaped by my research questions but also by learning from my students about the way that traditional notions of church are falling short and facing renovation in today's religious landscape.

Recognizing this canonical focus in the context of the theological school presses me, as a scholar, to resist it (or, as Jonathan Z. Smith has said, to ask rude questions about it). I do not do so because I think that Christian seminaries would be better *academic* institutions if they stopped teaching the Bible alone and started teaching it in the context of world scriptures or the vast array of ancient literatures. I do it because over-focus on anything produces myopia. And narrowness of vision has specific political-ethical consequences for both the scope of scholarship and how religious leaders view the world and their sense of vocation. Thus I teach noncanonical literature in my introductory course for seminarians and I incorporate readings that interrogate the Jewish and Christian scriptures as particular sacred texts for particular communities. In this sense, I believe (and thus advocate) that explicitly comparative study, be it among traditions or more closely within one, is an important part of theological education.[59]

---

59. Ivan Strenski suggests that religious studies is "quite properly a part of theological education." He affirms that theology "is at the very least the intellectual expression of the life of a religious community....It is the intellectual interpretation of the life of a religious community within the changing historical contexts in which it finds itself" ("The Proper Object of the Study of Religion: Why It Is Better to Know Some of the Questions Than All of the Answers," in Jakelić and Pearson, *Future of the Study of Religion*, 149). I do not disagree with this idea; however, I would like to see more reflection on what scholars of the study of religion think that they are doing in the classroom and in their publishing. While they may not be "doing theology" in an active way, they are certainly contributing to the intellectual life of persons who either are religious or who have views of religion. Timothy Fitzgerald takes a different approach to the problem of the inextricability of all scholarship from the category of religion. He argues that "even attempts by scholars with a non-theological agenda to refine the concept of religion and make it work as a non-theological analytical tool fail for meanings are not merely a question of definition but also of power. I suggest that this category is far too deeply embedded in a legitimation project of western societies.... Consequently, the way forward for those scholars working within religion departments who do not have a theological agenda, but who recognize the phenomena usually described as religion as being fundamentally located within the arena of culture and its symbolic systems, is to redescribe and represent their subject matter *as the study of institutionalized values in different societies and the relation of those values to power and its*

Given Drew's context, it is not surprising that Ph.D. students in biblical studies take more courses in the canon than they will in noncanonical or non-Christian literatures, and do not have many opportunities to study the Christian Bible from a comparative religions perspective. This institutional canonical focus would be highly problematic if left opaque and unchallenged. Therefore, students are required to traverse canonical boundaries by studying the literatures of antiquity more broadly, and are encouraged to transgress the overly historical focus of much scholarship on the biblical canon by studying diverse methodologies and perspectives in the field. In addition, an extra-disciplinary comprehensive exam required of all Drew doctoral students presses them to identify and examine deeply another approach to academic inquiry that helps them to see the canons of their own field and even the academy in a way that might have otherwise remained invisible. While some of the requirements and realities in Drew's doctoral program build on the institutionally predictable focus on canon, others seek to counter and disrupt such a focus. If faculty and students focus on self-reflection rather than self-justification then we all learn to see and interrogate the ways that our own institutions orient our work. With this approach, we practice contextualizing and relativizing the histories and priorities of the object of study *and* the study of that object, thus attempting to train the students in scholarly inquiry that is reflexive, border-crossing, and inventive in whatever corner of the conversation the scholar may find him or herself.[60]

Fostering regular rhetorical-contextual analysis (of self and field) is more productive than dividing up the field based on the identity of the scholar and/or his or her position in relation to the object of study, either as insider or outsider.[61] The former can promote identity politics and ghettoization or a new

---

legitimation" ("A Critique of Religion as a Cross-Cultural Category," *Method and Theory in the Study of Religion* 9 [1997]: 91–110, here 95).

60. This approach fits well with a rhetorical approach to teaching that "pays attention to the local and contingent dimensions of pedagogy: the histories of the students; the history of the discipline (or subdiscipline) and how that history shapes its current concerns; the history of the instructor's own training and subsequent intellectual development; the history of the department or institution in which religion is taught; and the contribution that the classroom experience may make to the development of that discipline by producing new knowledge and new experiences. Several of these historical data are highly contingent matters, over which the instructor has little control.... Attention to such local factors reflects the concern in rhetoric for paying attention to contexts and circumstances—the 'who, what, when, where, and why' of rhetorical discourse" (Richard B. Miller, Laurie L. Patton, and Stephen H. Webb, "Rhetoric, Pedagogy, and the Study of Religions," *JAAR* 52 [1984]: 819–50, here 845).

61. The Hart report notes that the distinction between religious studies and theologi-

parochialism.⁶² The latter can essentialize both the insider and the outsider and reify the university or college and the seminary as mutually exclusive and competing conversations rather than as different but also overlapping sites of engagement with a whole range of larger societal debates.

Given that curricular emphases may shift institutionally, it is important for the field to develop flexible scholarly standards that emphasize disciplinary literacy, rhetorical contextualization, and cross-border inquiry, and graduate curricular programs that promote scholarly practices of comparison, self-reflexivity, and creativity.⁶³ These generic standards and practices would look different in various contexts depending on the nexus of students, faculty, and conversation partners in that institution. Doctoral students are not at Drew because the seminary context allows them to be religious insiders in their doctoral studies. But some of them—although not all—*are* at Drew because they are interested in joining the conversation of biblical studies in a way that is cognizant of and, perhaps, able to communicate with/in religious communities. Given the significant presence and impact of religious discourses in contemporary global issues, it seems all the more pressing that some biblical scholars emerge from graduate work able to speak critical dialects of Church.

The solution is not for doctoral programs to take sides⁶⁴ or to ignore these debates about theory and location in favor of an insular disciplinary focus. Rather it should be a regular goal of programs to expose students to current

---

cal studies seems to come down to "the study of religious traditions without commitment (personal subscription) to what is studied, whereas ThS is the study of a tradition to which one *is* committed" ("Religious and Theological Studies," 737).

62. For this phrase and discussion of this problem, see Graf, "Stubborn Persistence," 35–37.

63. Jody Nyquist, former director of the "Re-envisioning the Ph.D." project of the Pew Charitable Trusts, has suggested that "doctoral training should convey a small but powerful set of core competencies: disciplinary knowledge; vocational knowledge; ethical conduct and professional responsibility; communicative ability; pedagogic skills, broadly construed; and an understanding of the value of diversity." Summarized in Joseph Heathcott, "Trained for Nothing," *Academe Online*; online: http://www.aaup.org/AAUP/pubsres/academe/2005/ND/Feat/heat.htm.

64. For a provocative and insightful effort to get beyond the kind of stark binaries discussed above, see Jeffrey J. Kripal, "Comparative Mystics," in idem, *The Serpent's Gift: Gnostic Reflections on the Study of Religion* (Chicago: University of Chicago Press, 2007), 90–120. Kripal figures the scholar of religion as mystic/heretic and argues that the insider/outsider tensions in the discipline are constitutive: "The study of religion occupies a liminal and problematic place in the modern university because, as a hermeneutic discipline suited to understanding and appreciating religious experience, it often looks (and sometimes really is) religious. But as a social-scientific practice suited to observing the political, social, economic, psychological, and sexual aspects of religious phenomena, the academic

theoretical debates and their locations and to make the politics of scholarship more transparent to students, inviting them to engage these debates critically for themselves. In short, our doctoral programs should not shy away from training students to map, analyze, and evaluate the discursive formations of the field in its variety of contemporary contexts and locations, and in light of its ethics and effects. If one can do this in one place, one can do it anywhere.

EDUCATION FOR TRANSFORMATION

Although the respondents to the Hart study had a variety of views of the definitions and divisions of "religious studies" and "theological studies," there was widespread agreement across the eleven types of institutions that scholars in the field of religion feel misunderstood by someone—by colleagues, administrators, students, the media, religious communities, or the public at large.[65] This suggests that while we tend to wrangle with our disciplinary and academic colleagues for scholarly authority and institutional recognition,[66] we are more often than not dealing with the effects of much larger realities such as the decline of support for the humanities in American higher education,[67] the decreased status or influence of the academic-scholar in public discourse,[68] the corporatization of education and publishing, and the rise of anti-intellectualism and/or fundamentalism in religious communities. Although the popularity and potential of the study of religion has increased since 9/11, there

---

study of religion will appear irreligious to pious believers. Remove either pole of this paradox and the discipline collapses" (112).

65. Hart, "Religious and Theological Studies," 751.

66. In the Hart study, it is clear that scholars in public university or college settings see theological studies as the hegemonic understanding of the field in which they are trying to carve out space for religious studies. Conversely, scholars in seminaries say that there is an entrenched asymmetry across the field that gives the higher intellectual/scholarly value to religious studies. Attesting perhaps to the different institutional pressures, seminary faculty are generally more hospitable to religious studies than university faculty are to theological studies (741).

67. See Warren G. Frisina, "Religious Studies: Strategies for Survival in the '90s," *CSSR Bulletin* 26.2 (1997): 29–38, here 29; Hart, "Religious and Theological Studies," 723; and Jack Miles, "Three Differences between an Academic and an Intellectual: What Happens to the Liberal Arts When They are Kicked off Campus?" *Cross Currents* (Fall 1999): 303–18.

68. William Arnal insightfully locates the vehement response to feminist and minority scholars who unmask (mainstream) scholarly objectivity as "reflective of the embattled identification of the professional intellectual with a bygone cultural hegemony" ("Making and Re-making the Jesus Sign: Contemporary Markings on the Body of Christ," in *Whose Historical Jesus?* [ed. William Arnal and Michel Desjardins; Waterloo, Ont.: Wilfrid Laurier University Press, 1997] 308–19, here 317).

is still a significant tussle in American society over the purpose and funding of education and the role and status of the scholar-teacher in society.[69]

There is much being done nowadays to prepare doctoral students for careers in teaching, especially to impart instrumental teaching skills in Ph.D. programs.[70] However, it is important to invite students to think about critical pedagogy, that is, why we teach and what we are trying to accomplish in a classroom. As a Harvard student and teaching fellow, for example, I followed a syllabus but was not usually required to analyze a syllabus or a textbook as a rhetorical-ideological instrument that constructs the learning experience based on often unarticulated presuppositions and interests. In my years at Harvard only one large assignment asked me to reflect on the instruments and practices that produce and re-produce knowledge in the classroom and the field—that is, a paper on "How Would You Teach NT Christology?" assigned, not surprisingly, in a course designed by Elisabeth Schüssler Fiorenza. Engaging these kinds of questions is important because while "teaching for transformation" may have some purchase among feminist

---

69. Although the discussion about the differences between religious studies and theology are often framed in terms of diverging scholarly theories and methods, the stakes of this debate are as much about competing theories of education. For example, Russell McCutcheon argues that in the dominant (theological and liberal humanist) discourse on U.S. campuses, "the study of religion as a component of a liberal arts curriculum is conceived—and thereby justified—as the means whereby students will become 'civilized,' insomuch as they will learn of their own culture's supposedly deepest values as well as learn to understand, appreciate, and tolerate the 'Other's' equally deeply held beliefs and values. The study of religion is thus sold to university administrators, and the general public as well, as a crucial aspect of nation-building" ("Critical Trends in the Study of Religion in the United States," in Antes, Geertz, and Warne, *Textual, Comparative, Sociological*, 319). Don Wiebe, another leading voice in this discussion, identifies religious liberals and liberal humanists as primary targets: "Religion instructors promote a kind of mellow, ecumenical religiosity that actually excludes a lot of religious groups that aren't liberal.… They accuse us of trying to undermine religion, but we recognize the social impact of fundamentalist Islam or fundamentalist Mormonism, and they don't. Liberalism becomes the religion, and none can go too far astray." The writer of the article, Charlotte Allen, continues: "Indeed, methodological atheists such as Wiebe share an agenda with religious conservatives who object to the use of tax dollars to promote liberal religious studies at state-funded universities" (Allen, "Is Nothing Sacred," 33). These references to nation-building and to funding of public universities point to the connections between these debates about the nature of religious studies and those about the purpose and politics of higher education in the U.S.

70. In contrast to being sufficiently trained to transmit specific content in an academic field, instrumental skills emphasize managing the classroom: organizing a syllabus, coordinating assignments and goals, effective assessment, and balancing types of learning (Miller, Patton, and Webb, "Rhetoric, Pedagogy, and the Study of Religions," 819).

and liberationist scholars, the academy at large is in the throes of a backlash against "biased" or "agenda-driven" teaching. Indeed the role of the teacher in the classroom is under intense scrutiny today, thus it is important for the future of the field that graduate students recognize and begin to evaluate the politics of pedagogy.

This work should include reflection on the politics of scholarship and publishing. As I have suggested above, the neutrality of the scholar-researcher is also under dispute today and thus debating about the role of the teacher in the classroom should not be separated from examining the role of the researcher and writer in academic and "popular" publishing. Just as I ask my doctoral students to think about their goals and interests in teaching, so I ask them with whom they are conversing in their research, what they want to accomplish, and why that is important. Indeed I am somewhat notorious for asking students the "so what question"; that is, why should anyone care about what you are teaching, writing, or saying? Whether by talent or accident, some students will end up *either* focusing most of their professional energies on either teaching or research. But both tasks are part of the work of education in a society. While teaching is education in an interpersonal and practical sense, scholarship is also education insofar as researching and writing produce knowledge, shape disciplinary traditions, and engage with a range of audiences. Despite the difficult job market, we still tend to talk about Ph.D. programs as certification processes for scholars thus limiting the scope of our students' contributions to the academy and fellow scholars. This misses the role of and need for educators in many arenas of society both secular and religious. In a 2005 *Academe Online* article, Joseph Heathcott describes the crisis in the academic job market as "a structural problem, produced by the introduction of scarcity through real, identifiable, and thus reversible policy decisions." He recommends that faculty pressure administrations to remedy the problems of a growing casual labor pool and the reduction in funding for positions. But he also notes that "A fundamental problem will remain: departments continue to run doctoral programs on an outdated guild model in which professors and matriculants tacitly agree that the only worthy outcome for the apprentice is to land a journeyman position in academia, eventually becoming a tenured master." He calls for a reorientation of graduate education around students developing a passion for their field, or a "sense of vocation," and embedding "doctoral training within a much broader range of professional possibilities" beyond the professoriate.[71]

I am less concerned to expand the number of tables at a job fair for biblical scholars, however, than to expand the way we understand the work and

---

71. Heathcott, "Trained for Nothing," 1–3.

locations of biblical scholars as educators in a society.[72] In 1995 the Association of American Colleges and Universities affirmed a connection between "liberal learning" and the public health: "It is time to reframe and renew our commitments as educators for a democracy 'still in the making.'" They highlight five interrelated educational commitments: promoting (1) an awareness of grounded selves in order to enter into (2) relational pluralism by (3) contextualized and historicized learning for (4) dialogue amongst multiplicities[73] in context and for the sake of (5) full participatory democracies.[74] What would it mean to conceptualize graduate biblical education as a certification process for entering a broad societal field of education interested in producing knowledge for critical discussion, fostering communication, and deepening critical thinking for democratic engagement in the many locations of a pluralistic society and diverse world?

Elisabeth Schüssler Fiorenza has long advocated for a complete reframing of biblical interpretation (including but not exclusive to the academic study of the Bible[75]) within a rhetorical-emancipatory paradigm, in short, an approach to biblical scholarship and teaching that emphasizes the social, historical, and rhetorical contextualization of the biblical text and its interpretation, and places political-emancipatory analysis, evaluation, and conscientization at the center of inquiry and pedagogy. Such an approach recognizes the relationship between a critical pedagogy and the democratization of societal discourses

---

72. In 1983, William St. John pointed out that by the time students are socialized into the profession, it is usually too late for them to consider/imagine careers other than teaching ("'A Look Around': Employment Opportunities for Ph.D.s in Religion," *Criterion* 22.1 [1983]: 2–76). It is also important to think about the isolating effect of the guild model on the connections of the scholar-teacher in an academic position with the educational work being done in other social locations such as community organizing, religious education, nonprofit organizations, and social movements, etc. See Andrea Smith, "Social-Justice Activism in the Academic Industrial Complex," in the roundtable discussion entitled "Got Life? Finding Balance and Making Boundaries in the Academy," *JFSR* 23 (2007): 140–45.

73. Note that the point is not to appreciate differences but to understand and engage them in the context of democracy.

74. Elizabeth K. Minnich, Scribe for the American Commitments National Panel, *Liberal Learning and the Arts of Connection for the New Academy* (*A Report Prepared for American Commitments*) (Washington, D.C.: Association of American Colleges and Universities, 1995), 27.

75. This is a difference from both Jonathan Z. Smith and William Countryman. Smith focuses strongly on the integrity and theoretical coherence of the community of academics and the public of the university classroom. Countryman focuses his reflections on changing the paradigm in biblical studies on communicating with and improving religious community. Schüssler Fiorenza's focus is on wo/men in various communities and on fostering more just democratic communities and societies.

and structures—not just secular ones, but religious structures and ideologies as well.[76]

In a 2001 article in the *Journal of the American Academy of Religion*, Mark D. Wood proposed that for religious studies scholars and teachers to make vital contributions to local and global campaigns for justice and human rights "the field must break with corporate-sponsored, liberal-pluralist versions of multiculturalism that abstract the study of religion and culture from struggles over power and reduce the ethical project of religious studies to learning how to appreciate different ways of being spiritual." He also criticizes methods that abstract the field and pedagogically occlude a recognition and engagement with the global socioeconomic realities in which "we, as intellectual workers,"[77] our students, and religious communities exist. Schüssler Fiorenza's work is inflected in feminist and ethical-theological terms and Wood's in Marxist materialist ones, but they both call for a conceptualization of scholarship and teaching as the examination of and deliberation about religion and culture as "sites of struggle" over power, identity, and meaning. The goal of such engagement is what Bruce Wilshire calls the "educating act"—facilitating "the interaction of lives already underway" in order to "enlarge the domain of what we can experience meaningfully ... [and through it] ... supplement and correct each other."[78]

This idea of the Ph.D. as certification for facilitating the "educating act" broadly construed allows for scholar-teachers to identify locations in which their particular strengths can be most effective, satisfying, and compensated. It is not necessary that all graduates become public intellectuals *or* deep-delving

---

76. Kathleen O'Brien Wicker notes that a critical feminist pedagogy includes an interrogation of the political agendas of education itself in colonization and colonialism ("Teaching Feminist Biblical Studies in a Postcolonial Context," in *A Feminist Introduction* [vol. 1 of *Searching the Scriptures*; ed. Elisabeth Schüssler Fiorenza; New York: Crossroad, 1997], 367–80).

77. Andrea Smith challenges academics to see their own participation in the capitalist system and its hierarchies. "The standardization of academic qualifications—a given amount of labor and time in academic apprenticeship is exchanged for a given amount of cultural capital, the degree—enables a differentiation in power ascribed to permanent positions in society and hence to the biological entities that inhabit these positions" ("Social-Justice Activism," 141). Frisina challenges scholars to recognize their privileged place in the economic order and to give an account of their contributions ("Strategies for Survival," 30).

78. Cited from Frisina, "Strategies for Survival," 31. Miller, Patton, and Webb call this encounter among particular people in a classroom an "event of learning.... At the very least this approach requires the class to transform itself from a collection of isolated individuals to an interactive community" ("Rhetoric, Pedagogy, and the Study of Religions," 822).

specialists.[79] But everyone can think about how their work contributes to the cultivation of educated leaders, intellectual publics, and self-reflexive producers of knowledge. In 1997, Warren Frisina called for humanists to "articulate precisely how and what we do contributes directly to the overall health and well being of the community."[80] I would agree and add, as a feminist, that graduate education should also challenge students to reflect seriously on what we mean by "health and well being" and for what communities?[81]

Clearly the understanding of education that I have invoked here does not entail the impartation of content, passive reception, or skills acquisition but rather privileges a rhetorical pedagogy over an instrumental or transmissional one. Miller, Patton, and Webb define the rhetorical paradigm of teaching in this way: "The chief goal of rhetorical teaching is neither to improve technique nor simply to make students more knowledgeable, but to empower individual voices and to provide a space for practicing skills and rhetorical inquiry about matters of personal and public importance."[82] But here is where I find one of the most difficult challenges in my own work as a teacher in a Ph.D. program. While I talk about such pedagogy with my doctoral students and try to model rhetorical teaching in my master's classroom, I have to work hard to transfer this pedagogical openness to the Ph.D. classroom. I am—and surely my students are—quite aware of power dynamics and economic-professional pressures in the Ph.D. classroom and thus I often encounter the tensions of conflicting and competing interests when working with doctoral students. Although the body of literature on composing the undergraduate classroom and renovating theological education abounds, reflection on the pedagogy of the Ph.D. classroom and curriculum is rela-

---

79. While setting the "intellectual" in contrast to the "academic" creates overdrawn types, nonetheless Jack Miles's discussion of the differences between "specialists" (whom he calls academics) and "generalists" (whom he calls intellectuals) in terms of their audience, understanding of their discipline, and writing style offers many fruitful challenges for the discussion about the role of the researcher and writer in public discourse ("Three Differences," 303–18).

80. Frisina, "Survival Strategies," 30. In my opinion, it is this question that can be submerged if we configure the study of religion in entirely social-scientific terms insofar as the scholar becomes primarily a describer rather than participating in the production of meaning. However, although a scholar like Peter Berger rejects a strong role for the scholar of religion in the "search for common ground in public discourse," he affirms a public role that "*as a citizen*, the scholar of religion has distinctive resources to contribute to tolerance and communication among groups" (Berger, "Stubborn Persistence," 46).

81. According to Jack Miles, intellectuals address the public agenda where academics address the agenda of the discipline ("Three Differences," 315).

82. Miller, Patton, and Webb, "Rhetoric, Pedagogy, and the Study of Religions," 820.

tively scarce.[83] If the goal is to expand student's knowledge of the discipline and collectively perform certain guild habits, do we even need a pedagogy in the Ph.D. classroom? Obviously, I think that we do. Insofar as doctoral education is both certification and *socialization*,[84] we may be making more of an impact on the future of the field through unexamined daily practices of teaching and mentoring than we do with any requirements, content, or state-of-the-field interrogations.[85]

I have no magic solution to this challenge but I can offer a few observations from my efforts to compose a Ph.D. classroom and to mentor students and shape the culture of graduate biblical education at Drew. The first is to practice *transparency*. By explaining the pedagogical goals of requirements and inviting students to reflect on what readings I have chosen, why, and what is consequently omitted, I try to energize the students to think not only about what is being learned, why, and with what effect, but also about how teaching participates in the production of knowledge.[86] In terms of mentoring, I model "seeing" the field in a way that demystifies it,[87] recognizes its rhetorical-political contexts, and analyzes its ethics and effects. Transparency also means being aware of and honest about my own authority and the way that current apprenticeship models can inculcate the "self-destructive habit of constant subtle deference."[88]

---

83. As Jonathan Z. Smith noted in 1984: "There seems to be a curious embarrassment with respect to the topic of graduate education. While many faculty are well-scarred veterans of long and elaborate discussions of general or departmental undergraduate curricula, most are rank amateurs when it comes to discussions of graduate education" ("Here and Now," 33). See also Schüssler Fiorenza, "Rethinking the Educational Practices," 67.

84. I have borrowed this combination of certification and socialization from Kwok Pui-lan, "Jesus/the Native," 69–85. See also the issue of the socialization of minority students in Ruiz, "Tell the Next Generation," 651–52.

85. In the Hart report, respondents complained that graduate programs do not model good teaching, let alone teach good teaching ("Religious and Theological Studies," 757).

86. This places process and praxis at the center of learning rather than specific knowledge. See Miller, Patton, and Webb, "Rhetoric, Pedagogy, and the Study of Religions," 845.

87. See Heathcott, "Trained for Nothing," 3. He continues: "The debates in higher education over the nature and purpose of graduate education should be part of the curriculum. Exposing graduate students to opinions, ideas and positions on doctoral education socializes them into the profession and their discipline.... Shielding graduate students from this information disempowers them and cheats us out of valuable future allies." In the Hart report, many individuals reported that they emerged from their graduate programs with no knowledge of the demands of and debates about general education in undergraduate institutions ("Religious and Theological Studies," 757).

88. Miles, "Three Differences," 308. He continues: "Humane learning has many uses in the general marketplace, but the baroque peculiarity of American doctoral education

In an attempt to decentralize some of the power in the classroom, I emphasize collaboration and deliberation rather than competitive debate. I also use methods of individual and class self-evaluation that emphasize student *responsibility* for both the classroom and their own learning. If something is not working for them, I expect them to say so and to put their analytical minds to identifying what and why, and to propose solutions. I also try to leave room in class sessions and the arc of a course for students to propose and pursue interests and questions different from mine or from the field.[89] Such practices attempt to ritualize crucial but often unnamed aspects of being a scholar-teacher, that is, being an autodidact,[90] being self-motivated, and being able to give and receive critique constructively. Although I do presuppose that doctoral students will need less prompting from me, I do not expect that they simply know that such habits are important aspects of scholarly life.

Finally, I am a firm believer in declaring doctoral classrooms and meetings to be self-deprecation-free zones. This is my own way of reducing the amount of self-negation and throat clearing that can emerge in the spotlight of constant scrutiny and evaluation. I find that women students are particularly expert in inviting an audience to dismiss them before they even begin speaking. The goal here is not to encourage self-delusions, but to establish enough self-confidence that critical feedback can be constructive and even motivating. My goal is elusive: learning that is both exacting and empowering. Fostering it is not a science but an art. It requires me to pay attention to my own comportment as much as to my students. It requires me to model professionalism and appropriate boundaries—to be a teacher, mentor, and colleague,[91] and

---

produces an animal hyper-adapted to the baroque peculiarity of the American academic habitat." I note also that this process of enculturation is complicated by race/ethnicity when minority students often have white mentors (male or female). See Kwok Pui-lan, "Jesus/the Native," 74.

89. Heathcott notes that, "[a]lthough our primary task is to model intellectual rigor and commitment, mentorship also includes the work that we do to nurture aspirations, accentuate native talents, impart skills, build confidence, and direct energies without crushing a set of goals that may be different from our own."

90. The Hart report notes the importance of promoting autodidactic habits given that 86 percent of faculty in liberal arts colleges teach outside their specialization (759–60), thus being able to engage unfamiliar areas of scholarship intelligently and responsibly is a valuable part of being an educator in these contexts.

91. Paying close attention to how professors model collegiality, collaboration, and transdisciplinary interactions can have far reaching effects in that search committees are usually looking less for specialists and more for colleagues. See William St. John, "A Look Around." In addition, the Hart report found that the most robust programs in religion were ones that had leading figures who could make connections to other fields outside religion and who could publicly articulate the place of the religion curriculum within the

not a master, mother, or friend. It requires me to think about how to resist the affirming allure of personal and institutional self-replication in order to make room for student pursuit of their own interests and goals in relation to their own histories and commitments.[92] It presses me to ponder how I can cultivate a depth of literacy in the discipline without privileging the preservation of the discipline or demanding loyalty to me or a tribe of scholars.[93]

Little public discussion takes place about transforming the culture of doctoral education. There is an extensive and diverse conversation about this topic, of course, but it is largely informal, anecdotal, therapeutic, or accusatory. The culture of graduate education is powerfully formative and thus could be transformative of both the discipline and the profession. For example, one aspect of my time at Harvard that made a very positive impact on my professional life was the collegiality and community, among professors and students, but even more so among graduate students. With the encouragement of certain faculty members and on our own initiative, we made a concerted effort to resist the competitive, monastic, and sometimes degrading practices and structures of academia. The web of connections that I have with these fellow-students-now-colleagues across the country provides a valuable place where I receive constructive and critical feedback on my work, and the platform from which I enter the field, develop collaborative projects, and imagine new program units of the SBL. I am not arguing for a sentimental love-fest over the friends we made in graduate school. I am suggesting that fostering intelligent, self-reflective, and collaborative community among graduate students is pos-

---

institution and enter into broad ranging public debates from the perspective of the study of religion ("Religious and Theological Studies," 727).

92. I do this because I am convinced that the high quality content of courses—even doctoral ones—do not always determine the relative success of the course; student engagement also plays a role. As Wilshire says, learning happens at the nexus of "lives already in progress." While the history of the discipline and of my own intellectual interests are valuable for the course, the student's histories and experiences are also vital resources for learning and crucial sites for their ownership of the material. As Miller, Patton, and Webb note, "In the classroom, faces matter. Voices are particular and local. Teaching asks us to engage the specific histories, traditions, ages, and concerns of our students. And we must do so, the rhetorical paradigm suggests, not as impersonal, rational authorities, but as persons with our own assumptions, uncertainties, arguments, levity, and commitments" ("Rhetoric, Pedagogy, and the Study of Religions," 821). The recognition that the teacher and student are both situated figures in the classroom also means that the "event of learning" is potentially for the teacher as much as the student. "A rhetorical approach envisions teaching as potentially transformative for everyone in the 'public' of the classroom—including the teacher/rhetor" (820).

93. Frisina, "Strategies for Survival," 33.

sibly the most far-reaching way to promote the health, self-awareness, and critical deliberations of the field.[94]

The project of transforming graduate biblical education requires serious reflection on the state of the field in light of the major issues of our time as well as on the way that our everyday habits orient and socialize us and our students in subtle ways. Indeed, it requires that we take seriously the interests and effects of our programs, and that prospective students think seriously about the ethos of the programs they are interested in pursuing. Elisabeth Schüssler Fiorenza defines ethos as "the shared intellectual space of freely accepted obligations and traditions as well as the praxial space of discourse and action."[95] The ethos of doctoral education is thus invented both in its theoretical framing and daily community culture. As I have discussed here, it seems to me that there should be sustained and repeated critical reflection in graduate school on the history,[96] rhetoric, locations, and audiences of biblical scholarship itself.[97] Thus the question "what does the Bible mean?" is always accompanied

---

94. This need for a supportive community/network of scholars is also raised by minority scholars. See, e.g., Ruiz, "Tell the Next Generation," 654. This issue needs much more discussion in the field. For example, Drew has drawn an African American, Latino, international, and second-career student body to its programs because of its diverse faculty and the methodological predominance of postmodern, liberationist, and contextual methodologies and interests. However, given the size of the program, the students come at a great cost to themselves in terms of loans and working nonacademic jobs while studying. We cannot compete financially with larger institutions that offer full tuition waivers and stipends. As the SBL continues its work on empowering minority scholars in the field, I hope that it will take a structural approach—consider identifying and supporting institutions and programs with a *demonstrated* commitment to a diverse faculty and diverse methodological frameworks. Transforming the face of the discipline requires more than the important work of helping individuals survive in the halls of powerful institutions whose faculties and methodologies are still predominantly homogeneous.

95. Schüssler Fiorenza, *Rhetoric and Ethic*, 22.

96. There is a significant need for critical histories of the field. Jonathan Z. Smith's work is helpful toward this goal (see especially *Drudgery Divine* [Chicago: University of Chicago Press, 1990]; and "Bible and Religion," *CSSR Bulletin* 29.4 [2000]: 87–93). But I agree with Ralph Broadbent's suggestion that "using the tools of ideological criticism (e.g. cultural, feminist, postcolonial criticism) there is an urgent need for a critical, unified account of 'mainstream' first world biblical scholarship which exposes more deeply its ideological roots and trajectories" ("Writing a Bestseller in Biblical Studies or All Washed Up on Dover Beach? *Voices from the Margin* and the Future of [British] Biblical Studies," in Sugirtharajah, *Still at the Margins*, 148).

97. Russell McCutcheon notes that "the rhetorics used to authorize our interests and taxonomies deserve just as much critical study as any other group's behaviors." Thus he concludes that "we scholars of religion should become our own data" (*Discipline of Religion*, 80).

by other questions—To whom? When? How? To what effect? Who cares? Are there other ways to see it? Graduate biblical education will be most vital when these kinds of questions are standard vocabulary for anyone who speaks Bible scholar.

The Work We Make Scriptures Do for Us: An Argument for Signifying (on) Scriptures as Intellectual Project

Vincent L. Wimbush

I propose to argue in this essay for the agenda and practices of a research institute that a new agenda and set of practices put forward by a particular research institute offers a compelling future for biblical studies. In order to make such an argument about a direction for the future, I think it important for me to provide my own unavoidably tendentious current perspective on the personal and intellectual experiences and challenges of the past that have led me to this point.

I have begun to understand my career of twenty-five years as teacher/scholar of religion with its focus on the Bible (not the other way around) in terms of an ongoing quest on the part of a member of an over-determined demographic group—one of the communities of the late "modern" "black" Atlantic "diaspora"—to try to understand the history of uses of and to position myself to "speak back to" an overexegeted/overdetermined social-cultural artifact and "classic" "white" "scriptures." Precisely because the two categories are complex and fraught and loaded and contested in characterization and signification, their imbrication in my career mark and characterize periods of my academic-intellectual work and preoccupation, orientation, and political-critical consciousness. These periods inform my interest in addressing the matter of the future of biblical studies.

The first period from the beginning of my career in the early nineteen eighties to the mid-nineties—had to do with my attempt at representation and reinscription of the fairly traditional orientation, sensibilities, skills and practices of western Enlightenment-inflected academic biblical scholarship. Teaching at a well-regarded graduate theological school in a small town of elite colleges in Southern California, I cultivated the skills of the historian (of late ancient Near Eastern religion and culture) and the philologist (of ancient Greek and Latin texts especially ancient Jewish and Christian texts called "scriptures"). And I accepted as the primary agenda, established by that slice of mainstream academic culture in which biblical studies participated, to occupy myself in a disciplined way with one set of texts among the "classics." So I dutifully pursued the historical "facts" or "truth(s)" in and behind the classic texts that were the Christian Bible.

Within this system in this period I even found my niche and established a reputation by working as a biblical scholar/historian of religion invested in the critical exegesis of texts having to do with the origins, historical development, and theorizing of early Christian asceticism and forms of world renunciation. I even assumed positions of leadership among colleagues interested in such study. I convened several conferences and colloquia and conceptualized and organized collaborative publication projects. For my orientation and work associated with this period, I received the usual academic "rewards": promotion and tenure; recognition by the academic guilds (in appointments to important posts); and several fellowships and foundation grants.

The interest in *askesis* is itself worth pondering. I think I thought at the time that focus on renunciatory practices as ideologies and regimes of resistance might somehow help me get back to a place of my initial but difficult to articulate interests. I had keen interest in finding out what was behind different views of and orientations to the world, in the logics and politics behind different interpretations and uses of traditions. From the very beginning of graduate studies, I was clearly channeling these questions and issues through the experiences I knew from the world I knew, but given the antiquarianist, theory-allergic, and anti-self-reflexive orientation of the program I was undergoing, I had little or no opportunity certainly, no encouragement, to pursue the questions and issues in relationship to that world. I was on my own to figure things out, to be in touch with my self and hear my own voice, to figure out my own interests and how to negotiate them and relate them to the field of studies I had entered.

The second period from roughly the mid-1990s to roughly the year 2002 had to do with the beginning of my departure (with attendant fears and anxieties) from the traditions and orientation of my "classical" training and an attempt to model an alternate intellectual orientation and set of interpretive practices that would lead toward a more unitary self. The intellectual departure coincided roughly with my move in 1991 to New York City to assume the position of full professor at Union Seminary (and adjunct affiliate at Columbia University). Although I had all along at least from the graduate school years experienced doubts and ancestors' hauntings about what I was doing as a professional, I was with the move to the mouth of Harlem and with the challenges and expectations and needs of that location, including those of students of many different backgrounds, forced to begin a (re)turn. With the change in location and my own social and intellectual and political maturation, I came to realize that I could hardly continue to be the unqualified classic texts standard-bearer in my teaching and research. I simply could no longer find my-self and its history, could not "hear" clearly enough the ancestors within the intellectual guild system and its practices that I had trained for and with my "card" had been charged and expected to represent. And I was deafened and frustrated even more by attempting to carry out such a charge as part of the mission and agenda of the traditional western protestant theological paradigm—notwithstanding Union's incessant cries about its "liberal-progressive" modeling of it. Both the theological house in which I lived (figuratively and literally) and the intellectual guild discourse in which I worked were traditional and conservative; their expectations of me were complex, wanting the new "other" that I in personal-physical terms represented, on the one hand, but not really in terms of translating that other in terms of independent professional-intellectual orientation or full-throated articulations and arguments.

Both systems, academic biblical studies and a representation of the Protestant theological school, came to strike me as more and more irrelevant to, if not problematic and somewhat unhealthy for, who and what I thought I was. No matter how I seemed to comport myself, I became more silent and withdrawn and thought myself quite peripheral to both domains as they appeared more and more to me to represent mostly unconfessed if not unknowing protectors of (discourses about) "white-ness." Here I mean that both systems or domains had as their default orientation the structure of whiteness and its correlate racialism and racism that of course, defines and pollutes the West and all of its traditional dominant institutions.

The ever-clearer recognition of the situation left me somewhat discouraged. I made myself aware of some of the assessments and types of responses black intellectuals and social critics and activists had given to the situation. I determined that that response on the part of some to reconstruct and advance myths and other discourses of afrocentrism, ethiopianism, contributionism and vindicationism[1] as part of a long tradition in the search to empower a displaced and humiliated people, was understandable but not effective or compelling. And the particularly poignant and long history of effort on the part of some to find a few "black" figures in the "white" scriptures seemed to me to be a desperate but ultimately unwise and self-defeating game.[2]

---

1. See Wilson Jeremiah Moses, *Afrotopia: The Roots of African American History* (New York: Cambridge Univeristy Press, 1998), 16 (and passim). Also, see his *Golden Age of Black Nationalism, 1850–1925* (New York: Oxford University Press, 1978).

2. Wilson, *Afrotopia*, 44–96 (and passim).

In my teaching of and research into the past that was the "ancient world" that was the matrix for the Bible I could not see or hear my-self. The experience had come to a point of being intolerable and unacceptable. So slowly, or so it seems now, and thoughtfully, or so it seemed then I began to change my teaching focus and intellectual research agenda. It changed from the reconstruction of the (still mainly unproblematized) ancient Greco-Roman world context and the pursuit of the correct content-meaning of the ancient texts which was really, frighteningly, obfuscating discourse about whiteness or a construal of a part of European studies to the meaning of seeking meaning in relationship to ancient iconic texts called "scriptures." I committed myself to the raising of what I came to consider the most basic question that should be raised prior to the question regarding the content-meaning of the iconic texts: I began to ask not so much what is the meaning (liberal or conservative or whatever) of this or that text but what is the *work* we make (texts turned into) scriptures do for us. This was not a question that the western theological school system (including its liberal-progressive protestant wing), an historical religious-ideological reflection and extension of dominant territorial cultures of the book, wanted someone like me to pursue. Such agenda involves fathoming of some hard questions and issues, questions and issues not about a past on which anything in defense of the dominant arrangements can be inscribed without clearly defined attribution and interest, but about what we all continue to do with the texts we call scriptures and with what effects.

I arrogated to myself the right to take a step back and begin elsewhere. I decided not (as so many white and black expected and assumed, as even one administrator who had known me for years had assumed) to focus on the "black" interpretation of this or that text, but instead to make African Americans' historical and ongoing experiences and expressions and practices *be* the experiences and expressions and practices I use "to think with" about the phenomenon of scriptures. I became convinced that the default socio-religious-cultural and academic thinking would continue (even if the explicit claim is not always made) to presume the scriptures to be "white," that is, the representations and projections of the dominant history and culture. So I then began to conceptualize and develop a multi-disciplinary and collaborative research project on African Americans and the Bible that somewhat modeled the different academic-intellectual orientation for which I had sighed. Over a period of two years, beginning in 1997, I set up what was the first ever of a series of structured but enormously creative and rewarding extensive colloquia among historians, literary critics, sociologists, anthropologists, visual art historians, musicologists, and religion scholars around the topic African Americans and the Bible. These experiences led to my convening with grant support from foundations a major international conference on the topic in New York City in 1999.[3]

The third period, from 2003 to the present, represents my willingness to depart even further from the antiquarianist-theological play with "classics" and take on more academic-intellectual and programmatic risk: I accepted the ongoing challenge to attempt a complex nuance or intellectual calibration, a balance of focus upon my own world and its history, its traditions and forms of expressions, with comparative work, with the traditions and expressions of many different peoples. This challenge reflects my assumption that the experiences of African Americans may be different in some respects from others but not altogether exceptional or unique, and that such experiences are to be studied not as exotica but as analytical windows onto broadly shared if not universal practices, expressions and experiences. So what I began doing in this period represents not abandonment of but intellectual-programmatic building upon and expansion of the focus on African Americans and the Bible. I began to make use of continuing research on African Americans and the Bible as wedge for theorizing about and building a critical studies research program around "scriptures" as historical-comparative phenomenon in society and culture.

With my acceptance of an appointment at the Claremont Graduate University in 2003 and the convening in February 2004 of another international conference ("Theorizing Scriptures"), the Institute for Signifying Scriptures (ISS) was established as a small center to facilitate the sort of multilayered, transdisciplinary research on "scriptures" that I had for many years sought to encourage and model.[4] This rather unique research institute (ISS) has as its agenda the forcing of certain simple and basic but disturbing questions and issues about the complex phenomenon of "scriptures"—what they are or what the English term signifies as phenomenon/a; how they are variously represented; how they are invented; the work we make them do for us; and the ramifications in power dynamics and relations they create and foster and delimit. Because I was convinced that as with medical research we can learn much (more and differently) from shifting the focus of research of a particular syndrome and this particular phenomenon from dominants or presumed "traditional" or "normal" subjects, I have made the commitment to place privileged but not exclusive focus upon historically dominated peoples.

---

3. This event led to the publication of Vincent L. Wimbush, ed., *African Americans and the Bible: Sacred Texts and Social Textures* (New York: Continuum, 2000).

4. This event led to the publication of Vincent L. Wimbush, ed., *Theorizing Scriptures: New Critical Orientations to a Cultural Phenomenon* (Signifying [on] Scriptures Book Series; New Brunswick, N.J.: Rutgers University Press, 2008).

It is this focus around which I have come to find my-self, including myself as teacher-scholar. I find it compelling because it is an opportunity for me to communicate with passion my ideas and arguments and because it is the motor for my continuing journey toward the modeling of *integrity*, in the original and most profound sense of this term, of the different investments, challenges, orientations, interests, politics and passions of a career and personal life journey.

Given this historical sketch of my personal and intellectual transformation, I think it important to reflect more deeply on what are some of the critical issues and challenges that lie behind it and some of the implications and ramifications that grow out of it.

What in ISS is proposed is a challenge regarding the need, rationale, impulse for change in the study of scriptures and in fact, insofar as it still for the most still turns around the study of texts—the study of religion, in general. It is a challenge regarding the orientation of such study, including its starting point or underlying presuppositions.

I am concerned in this essay about a future but that future very much and necessarily in terms of a particular orientation, actually reorientation, to the past. The "past" represents the fulcrum around which or matrix within which the modern European-American field of biblical studies (and of course the study of religion/theology in general) was begun. Of course, this past is also that which shapes us and the larger circles and structures tribes; worlds to which we belong.

Of course, the major point here is that this "past" is a culture-specific invention and protectorate. The "antiquity" and the ancient "texts" in play reflect the prejudices and interests of dominance. These prejudices and interests have to do with the dynamics that come out of the first contacts between the West and the rest, the world of the Other. Among the many dynamics and consequences of the first contact is the construction of the modern fields of comparative studies of peoples and religions. And one need not dig too deeply before one can find the construction of the modern field of biblical studies and its originary and ongoing participation in the western European-American ideological maintenance of exploitative arguments, power dynamics and arrangements, including the modern era invention and classification/hierarchialization of "races" and "religions." The legacy of modern biblical studies' participation in, major support for and sometimes otherwise deadly silence in the debates about the "chain of being" that provided ideological support for modern trafficking in black slavery is well established.

Various disciplines, historical/philological, ethnographic/ethnological, philosophical, and psychological, were developed and employed for the sake of "race-ing" the Other as a tool for containment and dominance. Historian and theorist of religion Charles Long has been most eloquent in pointing out how the West signified the Other through proto-academic-disciplinary discourses in collusion with other interests with powerful and perduring consequences:

> through conquest, trade, and colonialism, [the West] made contact with every part of the globe.... religion and cultures and peoples throughout the world were created anew through academic disciplinary orientations—they were signified.... names [were] given to realities and peoples...; this naming is at the same time an objectification through categories and concepts of those realities which appear as novel and "other" to the cultures of conquest. There is of course the element of power in this process of naming and objectification.... the power is obscured and the political, economic, and military situation that forms the context of the confrontation is masked by the intellectual desire for knowledge of the other. The actual situation of cultural contact is never brought to the fore within the context of intellectual formulations.[5]

Anthropologist Michael Taussig reminds us that the consequences of first contact are certainly powerful and poignant but like Kafka's ape "tickling at the heels" of those at the top of the great chain of being, they are complex, multi-directional and multi-leveled, and can be for dominants and dominated reverberating and disturbingly and hauntingly self-revealing:

> [in the transition] from First Contact time ... to Reverse Contact now-time ... the Western study of the Third and Fourth World Other gives way to the unsettling confrontation of the West with itself as portrayed in the eyes and handiwork of its Others. Such an encounter disorients the earlier occidental sympathies which kept the magical economy of mimesis and alterity in some sort of imperial balance.[6]

What I have in mind here, and what I think Long and Taussig suggest, is the importance of beginning critical historical analysis in our time with the (expansive) point of first contact between the West and the Rest in order to understand not only what the dominant West has wrought but how the dominated may "speak back to" the situation, or resist and even make for themselves a world. It may also be helpful to try to understand what is at stake here by thinking of the words typically placed on the side view mirror of

---

5. Charles H. Long, *Significations: Signs, Symbols, and Images in the Interpretation of Religion* (Philadephia: Fortress, 1986).
6. Michael Taussig, *Mimesis and Alterity: A Particular History of the Senses* (New York: Routledge, 1993), xv.

automobiles—"Objects in mirror are closer than they appear." The (human-made) "objects" in our modern world social-cultural mirror generally colored peoples are always, as Homi Bhabha reminds us, forced to lag behind.[7] Such "objects" are frighteningly closer than we think. Our thinking with/about them may get us closer to what and who we all are, closer to an understanding of how and why we do what we do.

Even as I privilege in criticism those people who are generally positioned behind and are reflected in the analytical mirror, I reject the notion that the focus of the analysis is *only* about them! The look in the mirror, back at those who are behind is, or should be, disturbing to the point of helping us see things differently—including the reality that cultural historical interpretive practices, including the discourse and practice we call biblical studies, are not and never really were ever about the ancient world, the ancient "classic," the canonical texts per se, but about something else that remains unnamed and unclaimed.

So beginning critical interpretation with the framework or structure of power arrangements that come out of first contact between the West and the Other is imperative in order not simply to learn even more about dominants, including their interests and strategies, even though this is a likely and appropriate and needed result. Of course, we are always conditioned and oriented to learn about dominants. That is partly what it means to be dominant! We may also learn something about the dominated—on their own terms, and this is for so many rather obvious reasons a very much needed result.

Most important in my view is the likely result that by genuinely (re-)focusing on non-dominants we shall likely learn some new things about, and gain some different perspectives on, some widely shared if not universal phenomena—phenomena that have to do with the structures and frameworks, the inventions and artifice-iality of society and culture that fundamentally condition and determine us but have for the sake of maintaining the status quo remained veiled to us. What is needed in order to unveil what one of Zora Neale Hurston's folk characters referred to as things with a "hidden meanin'"[8] is a "reflexive awareness"—a recognition of and appreciation for the mimetics and ludic practices that facilitate the engagement of societies and cultures as they are made up, especially the connection with the uses of center-symbols.[9]

---

7. Homi K. Bhabha, *Location of Culture* (New York: Routledge, 1994), 191–92, 237, 246–56.

8. Zora Neale Hurston, *Mules and Men* (New York: Harper Perennial, 1990 [1935]), 125.

9. Taussig, *Mimesis and Alterity*, 254–55.

ISS has as its agenda what I think of as compelling work having to do with one of those center-symbols—scriptures. Most pointedly, it aims to facilitate research, teaching, conversations and community programming about the "work we [human beings] make scriptures do for us." Its scope is global and trans-cultural; its methods and approaches are comparative and multi-disciplinary; and its orientation is activist and political as it seeks to help throw light on and address some significant psycho-social-cultural-political interests and challenges, especially as they pertain to religion and the experiences of the historically and persistent ex-centric and poor.

In connection with the ISS, "scriptures" is an elastic, tensive concept, a fraught abbreviation that points not to a particular object or text but to a complex social-cultural phenomenon and set of dynamics—that of finding "hidden meanings" and establishing (and dis-establishing) centers and maintaining (and dis-rupting) center-ing politics and effects. At the same time, the term calls attention to, and invites earnest and intellectually and politically honest wrestling with, the problematics and politics of scriptures in the narrower more literal sense having to do with writing and reading and textuality and with the material object that is the text. With its explicit commitment to take seriously the range of experiences and signifying practices of historically ex-centric, disenfranchised and poor peoples as special focus, and given the religiously-inflected nature of conflicts and crises around the world, the ISS situates itself as a center focused on compelling public-health interests and issues. Fathoming the signifying practices of historically marginalized peoples as a way of facilitating the recognition and reclamation of (a people's own as well as others') voice and agency of meaning-making practices is a most compelling public-health issue.

Insofar as the agenda of the ISS is focused on the "work" human beings make "scriptures" do for them, the major research and programmatic activities of the ISS revolve around critical more self-reflexive operations of social-cultural histories, ethnographies and ethnologies. This involves comparative research into how peoples—again, especially but not exclusively, poor and ex-centric peoples around the world in their different local contexts and situations and through their different practices and gestures construct and communicate their stories or otherwise engage in meaning-making. This means fathoming how peoples read/interpret, construct and communicate meanings about themselves and the world. As incredible as it seems, it has been only rather recently that many ethnographers, ethnologists, historians, social policy analysts, organizations, and policy-makers have come to recognize in serious terms that in spite of the fact that they are not seen and heard in relationship to the center stage of power the poor and marginal peoples do indeed create and communicate meaning and worlds. And their practices and gestures and worlds should be understood on their own terms so that we may learn from them and about them. Such learning should lead to our addressing their stressful situations and identifying our historical involvements in such situations.

Taken from the traditions of signifying as part of the politics of vernacularization among African and African diaspora and other peoples, the use of the concept of signifying practices as an analytical wedge in connection with ISS is intended to open windows onto the rich and layered textures of life and the social and political sensibilities and orientations on the part of peoples who historically have generally been positioned off-center-stage. Rather than make assumptions about what domains and concerns (e.g., "religion," "politics") are or should be of compelling interest to them, and how they should represent and communicate their interests (e.g., texts and textualization), and what outcomes or results they should pursue (e.g., resistance, revolution), the creative self-reflexive ethnographic and ethnological research focus of ISS seeks to identify and excavate through their gestures, forms of representations, practices and sounds their wide-ranging significations.

That some if not most of the significations of peoples may pertain to or be associated with "scriptures," as such has come to be (conventionally) understood, is to be expected for two reasons: the term is really a place-holder for the practices and gestures and ideas and associations and affiliations that have to do with finding ultimate orientation in the world. This quest can be at times so complex and textured that it is communicated obliquely, indirectly, in other words. So ISS research must be oriented to un-veiling the indirectness and hidden-ness of signifying practices.[10]

Signifying practices are not to be collapsed into or equated with texts (understood in the narrowest and belated sense of the term). These practices may encompass and involve engagements of texts; but they are really reflections of the textures (understood in one of the broadest meanings of the term) of culture. Engaging such practices represents a turn from the interests and preoccupations and politics of historical criticism (including, in biblical studies, any of its ever dizzying and razzle-dazzle discursive offshoots) into critical history. This sort of history, which aims to get at a people's practices and worldview, should put focus on what Pierre Nora termed a people's *lieux de memoire* ("sites of memory"). The latter represent "a ... kind of reawakening ... a history that ... rests upon what it mobilizes: an impalpable, barely expressible, self-imposed bond; what remains of our ineradicable, carnal

---

10. James C. Scott, *Domination and the Arts of Resistance: Hidden Transcripts* (New Haven: Yale University Press, 1990), especially chs. 6 and 7.

attachment to ... faded symbols."[11] The sites are engaged by peoples for the sake of living creatively and meaningfully and with the hope of continuously re-covering and re-membering what is thought to have been lost or what is thought to have been dimmed, veiled, masked in terms of knowledge or immediate or direct experience.

In an essay entitled "Site of Memory," Toni Morrison sums up what may be considered the argument/agenda for biblical studies insofar as such studies is understood to revolve around unearthing the complex texture of lives that are woven around memories. Begin, she argues, with images that facilitate the flow of memory. With focus on peoples of the African diaspora in North America, whose memories have been, to put it mildly, greatly damaged, this means beginning with images of ancestors or something in association with them:

> [They] are my access to me; they are my entrance into my own interior life. Which is why the images that float around them—the remains, so to speak, at the archaeological site—surface first ... the act of imagination is bound up with memory ... You know, they straightened out the Mississippi River in places, to make room for houses and livable acreage. Occasionally the river floods these places. "Flooding" is the word they use, but in fact it is not flooding; it is remembering. Remembering where it used to be. All water has a perfect memory and is forever trying to get back to where it was. Writers [= readers/interpreters] are like that: remembering where we were, what valley we ran through, what the banks were like, the light that was there and the route back to our original place. It is emotional memory—what the nerves and the skin remember as well as how it appeared. And a rush of imagination is our "flooding" ... like water, I remember where I was before I was "straightened out."[12]

What might it mean for us to begin to think of scriptures as a type of site—not merely a text or collection of such, but a complex phenomenon in relationship to which peoples attempt to access or recover their most fundamental and poignant memories? What might it mean for biblical studies to think of its agenda in terms not of capturing, boxing, wrestling with the site, but engaging people engaging such a site? And what might it mean for such interested and critical engagement of people to get close enough to see that

---

11. Pierre Nora, "Between Memory and History: *Les Lieux de Memoire*," in *History and Memory in African-American Culture* (ed. Genevieve Fabre and Robert O'Meally; New York: Oxford University Press, 1994), 300.

12. Toni Morrison, "The Site of Memory," in *Inventing the Truth: The Art and Craft of Memoir* (ed. William Zinsser; Boston: Houghton & Mifflin, 1995), 119–20.

what is at issue has to do with "re-memory," with efforts to open the flow of those memories that define and locate different peoples? What might it mean for us to engage not the text as rule (*kanon*), and see it as the object to be exegeted for the sake of getting at the "historical" "facts" within and behind the texts, but instead engage the text as human sociality and its striving and power dynamics and relations and making do and play? What might it mean for us to redirect our intensity of interpretive work toward locating, engaging and interpreting the un-ruly, complex, text-ed self, the self formed and defined and determined in relationship to texts?

And how then would our approaches and methods change? What approaches and forms of intellectual practice would inform the critical history of signifying scriptures? And how would such changes (re)define and (re)locate and (re)orient the scholar whose work involves pointing out how a culture signifies and signifies on scriptures? To whom would we then be responsible? To whom would we address ourselves? How might we identify ourselves?

Insofar as the research focus is to be placed on people and the dynamics of their formation the agenda would be complex and not about small things, such as letters and texts and the territories that claim them. Instead, it would be about the sometimes-painful efforts to become a people, to realize ultimate goals that are sighed for, to gain power. It would be about how people manipulate their own and others' imaginations and are manipulated by the same, about why and how they project beyond themselves "realities" that they make up, and about how they make ongoing creative attempts to "live subjunctively"[13] in relationship to that which is made up.

Such work and the project involving the fathoming of such work and its politics would then be fascinating, heavy, pertinent, compelling. Should we trouble ourselves with a future involving anything less than that?

---

13. Taussig, *Mimesis and Alterity*, 255.

Breadth and Depth: A Hope for Biblical Studies

Kent Harold Richards

As indicated in the introduction to this volume, the Society of Biblical Literature program unit Graduate Biblical Studies: Ethos and Discipline held sessions at the Annual and International Meetings for a number of years starting in 2003. The sessions provided an opportunity for a variety of colleagues, young and more senior, to discuss a wide range of issues. The papers in this volume are representative of the discussions in the program unit. Of course, not all of the papers and panels could be included in a single volume, but we are grateful for those individuals who have offered their work on a topic so vital to biblical studies.

These essays confirm that biblical studies will continue to grow in breadth and depth. Nothing is more important to an area of study or discipline than to understand the boundaries between the old and new as windows, not barricades. Too often new methods and provocative questions are understood only as challenges to the once-established ways of teaching and doing research. In fact, the new issues, as well as the engagement with long-standing subjects, that emerge from colleagues in this volume and elsewhere in the guild are a beacon of hope.

Sometimes the edges between tradition and innovation seem ragged. The questions and answers appear inconclusive. They are often not the questions and answers we want to hear because they provoke us to examine our own perspectives. However, these edges of discovery are the real openings that will enable us to go forward and refine our work over time. Were it not for these trajectories in our work, the field would not progress and show signs of energy.

Granted, some of the new questions and the answers that emerge will be little more than frivolous paths that eventually lead nowhere. On occasion, however, some of our long-standing results will eventually be seen to be little more than misleading, if not totally incorrect. We must find every mechanism possible to encourage new methods, to refine the old standard questions, and to seek ever more leverage so that the text may come to life for new readers.

Reading these essays and recalling the earlier oral form of these presentations stimulated four questions that I ask myself as well as every colleague in biblical studies.
- Have we stayed abreast of changes in the humanities?
- Have we carefully and consistently evaluated the needs of our research?
- Have we listened to what our students are saying and asking?
- Have we asked ourselves how our teaching and research will challenge the wider cultures in which we do our work?

These questions are one type of interrogatory we always need to bring to our work. They are not the particular, more specific questions we also need to raise, such as: Have we a better angle given our new methods to describe the relationship of Ezra and Nehemiah and the difference that would make for understanding their impact on the development of cult and culture in the Persian period? Such specific questions will remain important, but the broader questions are ones that we must keep before us even in the midst of the details.

Have we stayed abreast of changes in the humanities? It is clear that some of our colleagues have done better in this regard than others. We all need to remember that we work in a wider world of scholarship. Some of the biggest examples of positive change in the field have come about from outside, from borrowing other enriched humanities work. Just think what the impact has been from new disciplines such as anthropology and linguistics. It would be hard to imagine the current status of Hebrew poetic analysis apart from the contributions of linguistics. Likewise, we would all be poorer in the absence of work that examines performance theory and application when it comes to "scripting Jesus."

Have we carefully and consistently evaluated the needs of our research? One of my concerns as I read these essays, and many other less "transforming" pieces, is that we often get so habituated in our work that we accept as a given the results of the past. We need to understand the results of past scholarship but remind ourselves that the results of the most generative research was accomplished in a climate of innovation, resisting the old solutions. Very few scholars would challenge the notion that feminist and gender studies have advanced our understandings of the text. However, we have often not taken the time to carefully understand the relationships between the grammar of gender and the ideology of gender. The intersection of innovation and tradition make for a moving target that we need to keep in mind. Our research has many new demands on it, so we must apply every bit of leverage we can. Technology is one of those drivers that we must continue to examine critically or we will find ourselves using antiquated tools and hence produce antiquated results.

Have we listened to what our students are saying and asking? One of the most lasting effects of this program unit on my thinking, and I believe it is apparent in the reading of these essays, is the fact that many of the younger voices who are engaged in our work have not been set free by our teaching and research. Instead, they have felt bound, constrained by those of us who have been in the field for a long time. I will never forget the one doctoral student (not among any of the colleagues in this volume) who said to me, "I am about to leave this highly regarded doctoral program I have entered." In this case the young scholar's major advisor could give no helpful response to the question about taking a course in another department in the humanities. The newcomer thought she had seen some new possibilities that would help her better respond to an old dilemma in the biblical text. By bringing this example I do not intend to say that every doctoral student who comes with this type of question should automatically get a pass and be told, "Sure, go ahead and take the seminar." What I do mean to say is that we all too frequently are bound, unconsciously, by the old constraints and do not see the opportunity of a new set of constraints. Yes, there will always be constraints!

Have we asked ourselves how our teaching and research will challenge the wider cultures in which we do our work? I know that some colleagues say that it is our business to focus on the advancement of biblical studies, to keep our eyes on the text and not worry about wider issues of concern. This is a short-sighted view. We academics have never fully understood the impact we make on people's understanding of the biblical texts. That is unfortunate. I think many of the younger colleagues, and even some senior colleagues, are more aware of the need to keep an eye on the implications of our scholarship for all those interested in reading and reflecting on the Bible. The readers of this volume will make note that these scholars give us signs that they are aware of wider cultural influences. They are addressing the intersection of the ancient text and its cultural surroundings with the wider culture, texts, and iconography of their own time. The stimulus for that methodological move seems imbedded in what we study.

The essays in this volume give me hope that these four questions will not be neglected and hence broaden and deepen our perspectives.

Appendix

Rethinking the Educational Practices of Biblical Doctoral Studies

Elisabeth Schüssler Fiorenza

The Problem

The current crisis in critical scriptural-theological and religious-historical/literary biblical studies, I suggest, is rooted in a dramatic change not so much in disciplinary paradigms as in social location. Biblical as well as theological and religious studies face four problem areas that stand in tension with each other and need to be dynamically integrated.

The Aims of Education

In the past two decades knowledge—the intellectual capital of religious and academic institutions—has become globalized, or, as I would prefer, internationalized and democratized. This has two implications for biblical graduate education and religious leadership: on the one hand, knowledge is no longer the preserve of male clergy but has become accessible through the communication revolution to anyone who seeks it. International interreligious dialogue and collaboration has not only become a possibility but a necessity.

On the other hand, the flood of knowledge available requires that students learn how to develop intellectual skills of investigation, ethical criteria of evaluation, and hermeneutical frameworks. Not knowledge accumulation but critical evaluation of knowledge is called for. Hence, theological disciplines and religious studies no longer can prove their excellence simply by understanding themselves as depositories of scholarship rather than creators of knowledge. Today the computer is such a site of knowledge storage. It can provide in seconds knowledge of historical sources, literary parallels, philological data, or foreign language translations—knowledge that our predecessors in biblical studies spent years or a lifetime to find, record, and learn.

It has become increasingly important that students learn to discriminate between different kinds of knowledge, work collaboratively, recognize intellectual problems, and learn how to debate them with others who have different experiences, standpoints, and belief-systems. They need to learn how to interpret and critically evaluate not only the rhetoric of biblical texts but also that of biblical interpreters. A collaborative model of education is called for, a model that is greatly facilitated by the Internet. Students learn from each other in teamwork, write critical evaluation and integration papers, explore different hermeneutical perspectives, lead discussions, explore different ways of communication, and learn to understand the field and its subfields, such as, for instance, New Testament ethics, as rhetorical constructions depending on a scholar's social location and systematic framework rather than as an area of scientific data and theological givens. The intellectual acuity and excellence of inquiry required today is much harder to achieve, to teach, and to certify than the traditional curriculum of packaged knowledge, competitive standards of evaluation, and skills acquisition that relies on memorization, repetition, and imitation of the great masters.

As a result, academic excellence cannot be judged in light of past models of scholarship but must come under critical scrutiny. Moreover, the stress on skills acquisition, training, and practical know-how rather than theory buys into the mentality of what Stanley Aronowitz calls the "knowledge factory" that turns teachers and professors into technicians of social control. Because of the university's close ties to business, what was once the hidden curriculum—the subordination of higher education to the needs of capital—has become an open, frank policy of public and private institutions. Where at the turn of the century critic Thorstein Veblen had to adduce strenuous arguments that, far from engaging in disinterested "higher learning," American universities were constituted to serve corporations and other vested interests, today leaders of higher education "wear the badge of corporate servants proudly."[1]

The articulation of excellence in terms of technical skills, data accumulation, quantitative publishing, market-research type evaluations, and didactic as producing consumer satisfaction, rather than critical pedagogy, feeds into this market mentality. Furthermore, the stress on products rather than critical thinking still determines curricular offerings and examinations. For instance, departments have to offer "bread and butter courses" such as Paul, Synoptic, and so on, which are taught in terms of the banking model rather than in terms of critical knowledge and hermeneutical ability. Moreover, ordination boards still tend to test their candidates not on whether they can critically

---

1. Stanley Aronowitz, *The Knowledge Factory. Dismantling the Corporate University and Creating Higher Learning* (Boston: Beacon, 2000), 81.

interpret and hermeneutically work with a text or a complex of problems but rather on whether they are able to reproduce packaged scientific theories such as, for example, the Two Source theory.

Exposing Artificial Objectivity

The academy has not yet been successful in overcoming the artificial disciplinary dichotomy between religious and theological studies, a dichotomy that has been institutionalized in departments of allegedly value-neutral studies of religion, on the one hand, and religiously committed denominational theological schools, on the other. This split goes very deep, as the AAR Hart report indicates.[2]

This split, however, obfuscates the fact that both religious and theological studies are not value-detached disciplines but speak from a particular socio-religious location and position. To avoid this disciplinary split, one has to reconceptualize both religious academic studies and ministerial theological studies as situated knowledges and textualities. In the past, Christian divinity schools and denominational seminaries had the function to educate future ministers and priests. Such seminaries were denominational (Protestant, Catholic, or Jewish) and followed a required curriculum that led to ordination. Because of the restriction of theological studies to clergy education, religious studies has developed as a discipline that supposedly investigates biblical and other religions from a value-neutral phenomenological academic standpoint. However, hermeneutics, the sociology of knowledge, ideology critique, feminist, critical theory, and especially postcolonial studies have questioned this reifying conceptualization of religious studies.

Moreover, in the last decade or so the Western (Christian) study of other "alien" religions is slowly being transformed. The hegemony of the traditionally Protestant Christian curriculum has been broken, and religious or theological studies do more and more feel the need for interreligious and interdisciplinary inquiry. Scholars of other religions (Jews, Muslims, Buddhists, or Hindus) study Christianity and the Bible and articulate knowledge about their own religions and Scriptures that is different from that of colonial Western religious studies but more similar to a theological studies approach, although they usually do not call their work theology, because "theology" is a Christian typed term.

---

2. Ray L. Hart, "Religious and Theological Studies in American Higher Education: A Pilot Study," *JAAR* 59 (1991): 715–82.

Diana Eck's book, *A New Religious America: How a "Christian Country" Has Become the World's Most Religious Nation*,[3] elucidates that this dialogue between religions has a sociopolitical location. It does not only take place in the academy but also on the local level. Hence, future ministers and religious leaders need to be schooled in both ecumenical and interreligious Scripture knowledge and communication. Future biblical scholars or professionals need to acquire the ability of theological, religious, and ethical reasoning as well as a critical analysis of power relations in the interest of justice for all. The question is how doctoral studies can be so designed that it fosters and ascertains such intellectual capabilities. How can it be shifted from an objectivist study of religions and scriptural or traditional texts to a study of the power of religion in general and Scriptures in particular for fostering violence or justice and well-being?

Countering Fundamentalist Thinking

In the past twenty years, forms of fundamentalism and religious extremism that are explicitly political have emerged in all major religions and in all societies around the globe. Studies of such fundamentalisms have shown that the term can be applied cross-culturally and cross-religiously. They have argued that the common denominator of such fundamentalisms is the opposition to modernism and secularism, Enlightenment values and institutions, and the contempt for all outsiders or others within and outside their community.

In his book *Defenders of God: The Fundamentalist Revolt against the Modern Age*, Bruce Lawrence, for instance, has pointed to several characteristics that fundamentalist movements have in common: (1) they are comprised of secondary-level male elites; (2) they utilize a technical vocabulary or discourse; (3) they profess totalistic and unquestioning allegiance to sacred scriptures or religious authority; and (4) they privilege the authority of their own leaders and subordinate democratic values and processes to this authority. Since traditional institutions of higher education often subscribe to the same positivist, albeit more academic rather than religious, values and discourses, they are not able to articulate discourses and practices that would foster a different radical democratic mentality and religious leadership. Research is necessary into the procedures and elements that reproduce such fundamentalist thinking in biblical studies, and doctoral dissertations should include this aspect of inquiry.

---

3. Diana L. Eck, *A New Religious America: How a "Christian Country" Has Become the World's Most Religious Nation* (New York: HarperSanFrancisco, 2001).

Most importantly, much more attention needs to be paid to religious identity formation that is not exclusive and antidemocratic. Radical democratic rather than positivist or fundamentalist teaching-learning experiences, however, are generally not part and parcel of graduate education in general and doctoral education in particular. While much creative teaching is done on the undergraduate and M.Div. levels, doctoral education is still very Eurocentric,[4] insofar as it is mostly focused on the Germanic or British scientific research and "master-disciple" model of the graduate seminar. Moreover, the dominant ethos of graduate schools often does not appreciate the change in knowledge production and populations but operates out of an outdated model of top-down education.

Doctoral education compels students to become in a certain sense "schizophrenic," that is, having, for instance, to write a critical exegesis for a qualifying paper and to preach biblicist literalism in their church. They are not encouraged to bring into the critical learning process their own faith-based questions, religious experiences, and fundamental convictions and therefore do not have the possibility to work through them critically in dialogue with the hegemonic discourses of the field. Instead, they are told that they need to reproduce as accurately as possible the standard knowledge of the field and remove their own preconception or prejudices from inquiry rather than being enabled to work through them. Yet, such a positivist disciplinary stance overlooks that the field of biblical studies presently cultivates a great variety of methods, subfields, and theoretical perspectives. It also overlooks that theological and religious studies can be scientifically responsible today only if they become interdisciplinary and interreligious.

A Changing Student Population

In the last two decades the population of divinity schools and religion departments and therefore the character of theological education in the U.S. have radically changed. Nondenominational university divinity schools such as Harvard Divinity School have granted full citizenship to populations previously not included, such as Catholics, Evangelicals, or Jews, as well as begun to attract Buddhist, Confucian, and Muslim students. Populations from different sociocultural locations and traditions such as white wo/men, African American, Native American, Asian, Latina/os, gay, lesbian, and transgendered people, who have traditionally been excluded from theological discourse or

---

4. For the imbrication of Eurocentric American biblical scholarship with racism, see Shawn Kelly, *Racializing Jesus: Race, Ideology and the Formation of Modern Biblical Scholarship* (New York: Routledge, 2002).

from elite religious educational institutions, have been admitted but not really been granted full academic citizenship.

In addition, second-career students seek the rich intellectual inquiry offered by theological and religious studies. This change in populations requires a change in the kind of knowledge taught and the pedagogy used to communicate it. It requires a complete reconception of academic disciplinary culture that has been defined not only by false claims to value-neutrality but also by the exclusion of the Other. This change is usually more real in the student body than in the faculty, who understandably shows some resistance to such change, since it throws into question professional expertise and traditional academic standards of excellence. It is an extremely serious problem in terms of faculty hiring and promotion.

Furthermore, student participants from many different Christian denominations and different religious persuasions, cultural contexts, social locations, and international areas seek to be equipped for religious leadership both in religious communities (churches, mosques and synagogues, temples), the academy society, and culture (communications, law, medicine, and the arts) at large. Hence, it is not only impossible but also not advisable to devise a set curriculum in terms of traditional ecclesiastical or academic requirements and Eurocentric elite male modes of certification. Rather then spend faculty time on developing fixed curricula, I argue, graduate biblical education needs to focus on evolving educational democratic processes of communication for different religious and cultural communities that are intellectually challenging while at the same time enabling students to qualify for academic and professional leadership, irrespective of whether they want or do not want to be ordained or join the clergy.

Additionally, schools also have to provide the intellectual resources for those students who want to go on for doctoral work in the study of diverse religious/theological disciplines or to get a degree in religion for leadership in other professions, such as, for instance, medicine, business, law, social work, public health, politics, journalism, or education. Finally, the life experiences and the professional know-how of second-career students and life-long learners must be allowed to fructify their doctoral studies.

Towards New Educational Models

In light of this situation, we need to find educational models that insist not only on difference and diversity as *sine qua non* of academic excellence but also on collaboration rather than competition and that allow for the intellectual integration of such rich diversity. For instance, at our last faculty retreat I suggested that we replace the traditional departments with transdisciplinary research teams that focus on problem areas rather than on disciplines in order to destabilize exclusive disciplinary boundaries in doctoral education and research. Interdisciplinary faculty and students would be involved in exploring a research problem such as, for instance, "religion and violence," a problem that not only addresses questions of academic and religious communities but would be of interest to the public at large. Such a problem-oriented research focus would not replace instruction in the traditional disciplines but would organize their knowledge to different ends. It would utilize the tools of research made available by the disciplines but use them to produce transdisciplinary knowledge. It requires therefore not only interdisciplinary but transdisciplinary work, a reorientation of the disciplines and a retooling of faculty.

Considering the array of critical questions that face the discipline of biblical studies, it is surprising how little substantive work has been done on graduate education that could address these questions. This applies especially to doctoral education in biblical studies. While there is some creative thinking and educational transformation happening at the masters of divinity and college levels, this in my experience is not the case for scientific graduate education. The allegedly "scientific" resistance to such renovation can be illustrated with reference to our doctoral programs in Religion, Gender, and Culture. While the Th.D. program was somewhat grudgingly but speedily approved, it took several years before it was approved as a Ph.D. program.

While emancipatory approaches such as feminist[5] or postcolonial critical studies[6] have brought about some change in the curriculum and education of ministerial and undergraduate students, doctoral biblical education—as a quick Internet search of departments can show—is still mostly devoted to the philological-historical or exegetical-doctrinal disciplinary paradigm. Although the annual Society of Biblical Literature (SBL) meetings display a great variety of methodological approaches and intellectual voices that increasingly are no longer able to talk to each other, the central paradigm for doctoral studies seems still to be the historical-critical or the biblical-doctri-

---

5. The Cornwall Collective, *Your Daughters Shall Prophesy: Feminist Alternatives in Theological Education* (New York: Pilgrim, 1980), Katie G. Cannon et al., *God's Fierce Whimsy: Christian Feminism and Theological Education* (New York: Pilgrim, 1985). See especially also Rebecca S. Chopp, *Saving Work: Feminist Practices of Theological Education* (Louisville: Westminster John Knox, 1995).

6. See especially William H. Myers, "The Hermeneutical Dilemma of the African American Biblical Student," in *Stony The Road We Trod: African American Biblical Interpretation* (ed. Cain Hope Felder; Minneapolis: Fortress, 1991); and Fernando Segovia and Mary Ann Tolbert, eds., *Teaching the Bible: The Discourses and Politics of Biblical Pedagogy* (Maryknoll, N.Y.: Orbis, 1988).

nal paradigm. Prospective students are told that the central requirement is the acquisition of several languages and that the goal of their training is the control of factual and disciplinary knowledge that is tested in qualifying exams.

In short, it seems that the self-understanding of the discipline is still that of antiquarian "hard science" or confessional theology that stresses the necessary language skills for professional education and subscribes to the positivist scientist or theological paradigms with their banking and master models of education. Hence a broad-based study not only of the populations but also of the theoretical production of biblical studies is called for. However, as a check with SBL has indicated, such a critical study is not yet possible because we do not have sufficient quantitative research "data" on populations of doctoral programs, the experience of participating students and faculty, as well as critical analyses of dissertations or annual meetings.[7] In addition, I have found only a very few critical pedagogical studies that challenge the discipline to a comprehensive articulation of its ethos and identity in such a way that it could pioneer a radical democratic emancipatory form of pedagogy. As in other areas of positivist scientific studies, pedagogy seems not to be a concern of research at all.

My personal experience with this research project in the past months has been illuminating here. Whenever I mention my current project, colleagues tend to turn the conversation to another topic as though I have said something embarrassing or improper, which I indeed had because in the eyes of many pedagogy is not a real scientific topic. Friends have been more outspoken and bemoaned the fact that I was in danger of squandering my theoretical acumen and research time on a project that has not much professional capital. Feminist friends in turn have cautioned that with this project I feed into the gender stereotype that holds that education is women's domain whereas the production of scientific knowledge is that of men, which women in turn have to mediate through education.

Since I am fully aware of the genderization of disciplinary discourse, I have decided to focus on doctoral education, which traditionally has been the exclusive domain of men, rather than on biblical education in general. Moreover, several recent critical studies elaborating the cooptation of feminist knowledge by the academy and its disciplinary formations have convinced me that it is necessary to engender a critical investigation and debate on doctoral studies because they are the professional space where future scholars and religious leaders are socialized.

---

7. See, however, the very important study by Oda Wischmeyer, "Das Selbstverständnis der neutestamentlichen Wissenschaft in Deutschland," *ZNT* 10/5 (2002): 13–36, which gives a critical review of graduate biblical education in Germany.

Hence, I want to focus here on the theoretical issues raised by professionalization and turn attention to the genealogy of modern scientific biblical studies, since disciplinary genealogy shapes disciplinary identity. It has now been more than twenty years that a paradigm shift is underway in biblical studies that indicates a shift in disciplinary ethos so that one can speak of four paradigms: the scriptural-theological, the philological-historical, the hermeneutical-postmodern, and the rhetorical-emancipatory paradigms.[8] However these paradigms do not describe successive stages but are to be understood as dynamically interacting with and correcting each other. Consequently my understanding of paradigm research differs from the conceptualization of Kuhn who stresses the struggle of paradigms for hegemony and the power of exclusion and replacement. While I recognize the impact of such struggles for power and hegemony especially on the institutional level, I nevertheless want also to draw attention to the possibility of constructing paradigm research in terms of dynamic intellectual collaboration.

To that end I will discuss the four disciplinary paradigms as analytic instruments to assess the ethos and location of doctoral studies. I also have proposed four pedagogical models—the preacher-banking model, the master-apprentice model, the consumer-psychological model, and the radical democratic model—of theological education that correspond to the four theoretical paradigms of biblical studies.[9] In addition, I want to see whether and how the seven critical feminist hermeneutical strategies that I have developed to overcome the split between exegesis and application, between what the text meant and means, between history and hermeneutic/theology, also can become fruitful for shaping doctoral education. For, the once-reigning hermeneutical division of labor between the exegete who describes what the text meant and the pastor/theologian who articulates what the text means has been seriously challenged in the past two decades and been proven to be epistemologically inadequate.

Although it was Krister Stendahl who advocated this division of labor between biblical scholar and theologian/pastor in his famous article on biblical theology,[10] he did so not in order to immunize historical-critical scholarship from critical theological reflection but in order—as he puts it—to liberate the theological enterprise from what he perceived as "the imperialism of bibli-

---

8. Elisabeth Schüssler Fiorenza, *Rhetoric and Ethic: The Politics of Biblical Studies* (Minneapolis: Fortress, 1999).

9. See Elisabeth Schüssler Fiorenza, *But She Said: The Practices of Feminist Biblical Interpretation* (Boston: Beacon, 1992); idem, *Wisdom Ways: Introducing Feminist Biblical Interpretation* (Maryknoll, N.Y.: Orbis, 2001).

10. Krister Stendahl, "Biblical Theology, Contemporary," *IDB* 1:418–32.

cal scholars" in the field of theology.[11] However, twenty years later Stendahl saw the problem somewhat differently when he called for scholarly attention to the public health aspect of biblical interpretation. Reflecting on the fact that his own exegetical-theological thinking has circled around two New Testament issues—Jews and women—he points to the clearly detrimental and dangerous effects that the Bible and Christian tradition have had as a major problem for scriptural interpretation.[12]

This call for a public-ethical-political self-understanding of biblical studies has become even more pressing today after the Moral Majority in the 1970s and the Christian New Right in the 1980s and the resurgence of religious fundamentalism in all major religions in 1990s have made biblical injunctions an object of public debate.[13] In such a public health self-understanding of biblical studies graduate students will learn to analyze the power relations that are inscribed in past and present biblical texts and discourses. To that end it needs to become conscious of its genealogy of professionalization.

Professionalization of Biblical Studies

Central to the self-understanding of biblical studies, whether practiced in the academy, in public discourse, or in religiously affiliated institutions, is its insistence on the scientific character and/or historical or theological truth of its research. Whereas it seeks to establish scientific positivism in terms of quantitative methods, refinement of the technology of exegesis, archeological research, production of factual knowledge, antitheological rhetoric, and the deployment of social-scientific models that are derived from cultural anthropology or quantitative sociology for authorizing its scientific character, it advocates theological positivism when claiming that scientific exegesis hands

---

11. Krister Stendahl, *Meanings: The Bible as Document and as Guide* (Philadelphia: Fortress, 1984), 1.

12. Krister Stendahl, "Ancient Scripture in the Modern World," in *Scripture in the Jewish and Christian Traditions: Antiquity, Interpretation, Relevance* (ed. Frederick Greenspahn; Nashville: Abingdon, 1982), 201–14, esp. 204.

13. The literature is extensive. See, for instance, Walter H. Capps, *The New Religious Right: Piety, Patriotism and Politics* (Columbia: University of South Carolina Press, 1990); Lawrence Grossberg, *We Gotta Get Out of This Place: Popular Conservatism and Postmodern Culture* (New York: Routledge, 1992); Sara Diamond, *Spiritual Warfare: The Politics of the Christian Right* (Boston: South End, 1989); James Hunter, *Culture Wars: The Struggle to Define America* (New York: Basic Books, 1991); Michael Barkun, *Religion and the Racist Right: The Origins of the Christian Identity Movement* (Chapel Hill: University of North Carolina Press, 1994); David Rose, ed., *The Emergence of David Duke and the Politics of Race* (Chapel Hill: University of North Carolina Press, 1992).

down the word of God as revealed truth rather than explicates the words of "men." Both discourses insist on such positivist knowledge in order to maintain their public credibility.

The discipline continues to socialize future scholars into methodological positivism and future ministers/theologians into theological positivism. Biblical discourses are advocating either literalist biblicism or academic scientism. As long as this is the case, I argue, discourses and struggles for justice, radical equality, and the well-being of all will remain marginal to biblical scholarship. By identifying itself as a scientific positivist practice, biblical studies are shaped by the theoretical assumptions that have shaped and governed scientific discourse.

Students tend to enter biblical studies for the most part either because they highly value the Bible and its history or because as future ministers or professors they have regularly to preach or teach biblical texts. In any case, their intellectual frame of reference accords the Bible intrinsic canonical authority or significant cultural value as a classic. Critical biblical scholarship, in contrast, is dedicated to the critical study of biblical texts that are denied religious authority or contemporary significance.

To enroll for graduate biblical studies, then, means to undertake a double agenda of professionalization. This entails a change of discursive frameworks from a discourse of acceptance of the Bible as a cultural icon or from a discourse of obedience to it as the word of God to a critical academic discourse that assumes the authority of inquiry and scholarship as a site from which to challenge the cultural and doctrinal authority of the Bible.

Like white male students, wo/men and other outsiders who enter graduate programs have to undertake a double agenda of professionalization: they are to be socialized both into "scientific" theological thinking and into professional training at once. Like male students, wo/men female students must undergo a process of transformation from "lay" person in the religious and educational sense to a scholarly professional one. Such a transformation requires not only that students become familiar with the methods, literature, and technical procedures of biblical disciplines but also that they transform their intellectual theological frameworks.

Professionalization, then, means for all students first of all to become socialized into the ethos of biblical studies as a scientific academic discipline. Florence Howe has pointed to the crucial shift in the ethos of American higher education after the Civil War.[14] For almost 250 years college education in the U.S. was understood as a discipline for the training of elite white men

---

14. Florence Howe, *Myth of Coeducation: Selected Essays 1964–1983* (Bloomington: University of Indiana Press, 1984), 221–30.

in "religious and moral piety." After the Civil War, the new model for the production of knowledge and higher education became that of German scientific research. This transformation of the curriculum after the Civil War replaced religion with science as a rational philosophy that claimed to account for the entire universe. This change resulted in a galaxy of separate "disciplines" and "departments" that accredit persons for a particular kind of professional work. The unifying ethos of objective method, scientific value-neutrality, and disinterested research in the emerging scientific academy unseated the centrality of the Bible and religion.

Despite claims to professional objectivity, virtually every academic discipline operates on the unarticulated common sense assumption of academic discourse that equates elite male reality with human reality. Intellectual histories and other canonized cultural and academic texts have generally assumed that natural differences exist between all wo/men and elite men, and have defined wo/men and colonized men as rationally inferior, marginal, subsidiary, or derivative. Wo/men and other subaltern intellectuals who have shown leadership and claimed independence have been judged as unnatural, aggressive, and disruptive figures.

As Adrienne Rich has eloquently stated, "There is no discipline that does not obscure and devalue the history and experience of women as a group."[15] A similar statement could be made about working class wo/men people, people of color, or colonialized peoples. The recourse of "scientific" arguments to biological determinism and gender differences is still frequent today in scientific debates that seek to defend the kyriocentric framework of academic disciplines as "objective and scholarly."[16]

The Genealogy of Scientific Biblical Studies

It is well known that biblical studies emerged on the scene together with other disciplines in the humanities that sought to articulate their discourses as scientific practices in analogy to the natural sciences. The feminist theorist Sandra Harding has pointed to a three-stage process in the emergence of modern science shaping and determining scholarly discourses, their presuppositions, and intellectual frameworks.

---

15. Adrienne Rich, "Toward a Woman Centered University," in idem, *On Lies, Secrets and Silence: Selected Prose, 1966–1978* (New York: Norton, 1979), 134.

16. See the critical reflections on the Arizona project for curriculum integration by S. Hardy Aiken, K. Anderson, M. Dinnerstein, J. Nolte Lensinck, and P. MacCorquodale, eds., *Changing Our Minds: Feminist Transformations of Knowledge* (Albany: State University of New York Press, 1988), 134–63.

The first stage, according to Harding, consisted in the breakdown of feudal labor divisions and slave relations and the emergence of a new class of inventors of modern technology.[17] The second stage is exemplified in the New Science Movement of the seventeenth century that flourished in Puritan England and brought forth a new political self-consciousness with radical social goals. To quote Harding, "Science's progressiveness was perceived to lie not in method alone but in its mutually supportive relationship to progressive tendencies in the larger society."[18] Scientific knowledge was to serve the people and to be used for redistributing knowledge and wealth. It is this notion of science that needs to be recaptured by graduate biblical education.

The third stage of professionalization produced the notion of purely technical and value-neutral science. The progress that science represents is based entirely on scientific method. The emergence of this third stage in the development of science also spelled the end of the collaboration between science and social, political, or educational reform—a price paid for institutionalization and political protection. "Pure" science, according to Harding, goes hand in hand with value-neutrality, which captures what is real through impersonal, quantitative language, and method, understood as norms, rules, procedures, and scientific technologies. Historically and culturally specific values, emotions, and interests must be kept separate from depoliticized transcendental scientific practices. Abstract thinking, mathematical intelligibility, and mechanistic metaphors become the hallmarks of true science.

The discipline of biblical studies is located at this third scientific stage, which constructs a sharp dualism between science and theology or scientific discourse and ideology, in order to prove itself as scientific. Disciplinary discourses reinscribe such structuring dualisms as a series of methodological dichotomies and oppositions. Thus, as a scientific discourse, biblical studies participates in the discourses of domination that were produced by science.

For it is also at this third stage of the development of academic scientific disciplines that the discourses of domination—racism, heterosexism, colonialism, class privilege, ageism—were articulated as "scientific" discourses.[19] While previously discourses of colonization were developed on the grounds

---

17. Sandra Harding, *The Science Question in Feminism* (Ithaca, N.Y.: Cornell University Press, 1986), 218, with reference to Edgar Zilsel, "The Sociological Roots of Science," *American Journal of Sociology* 47 (1942): 544–62.

18. Harding, *Science Question*, 219.

19. See Ronald T. Takaki, "Aesclepius Was a White Man: Race and the Cult of True Womanhood," in *The Racial Economy of Science: Toward a Democratic Future* (ed. Sandra Harding; Indianapolis: Indiana University Press, 1993), 201–9; Nancy Leys Stepan and Sander L. Gilman, "Appropriating the Idioms of Science: The Rejection of Scientific Racism," in Harding, *The Racial Economy of Science*, 170–93; and Nancy Leys Stepan, "Race

of Christian theology, now science takes the place of religion and continues its work of hegemonic legitimization. The discourses of domination were formed as elite discourses that justified relations of ruling. Hence, "soft" academic disciplines such as history, sociology, and anthropology, in their formative stage, developed as discourses of domination in order to prove that they also belonged to the "hard" sciences. Thereby academic social-science disciplines supported European colonialism and capitalist industrial development.

For instance, the nineteenth-century professionalization of history fostered scientific practices advocating commitment to an objectivity above the critical scrutiny of such categories as class and gender, along with strict use of evidence, less rhetorical style, the development of archives, libraries, peer reviews, and professional education. Scientific historical discourses created an intellectual space inhabited by an "invisible and neutered I" that was considered as a "gender- and race-free" community of scholars.[20]

American sociology in its formative years exhibits the same symptoms as scientific historiography. It was influenced by European anthropological discourses that emerged with imperialism and understood colonized peoples as "primitives" who were considered to be more natural, sexual, untouched by civilization, and inferior because of their innate biological differences—for instance, their allegedly smaller brains. In the U.S., Indian Americans and African Americans were those who represented the "primitive" in sociological and anthropological scientific discourses. They were construed to be either violent or childlike or both. People who were Not-white and Not-male were praised as "noble savages" or feared as "bloodthirsty cannibals" on biological and cultural grounds. Asians, Africans, native peoples, and white women were viewed as childlike, a factor used to explain their supposedly inferior intelligence.[21]

To give an example from the area of biblical studies: in a recent article entitled "The Use of the New Testament in the American Slave Controversy: A Case History in the Hermeneutical Tension between Biblical Criticism and Christian Moral Debate," J. Albert Harrill has convincingly shown that the discourse on slavery has decisively shaped the development of historical-crit-

---

and Gender: The Role of Analogy in Science," in Harding, *The Racial Economy of Science*, 369–76.

20. Bonnie G. Smith, "Gender, Objectivity, and the Rise of Scientific History," in *Objectivity and Its Other* (ed. Wolgang Natter, Theodore R. Schatzki, and John Paul Jones III; New York: Guilford, 1995), 59.

21. Patricia Hill Collins, *Fighting Words: Black Women and the Search For Justice* (Minneapolis: University of Minnesota Press, 1998), 100–101.

ical biblical studies.[22] He argues that the abolitionist arguments during the American slave controversy pushed the field toward a critical hermeneutics and a more critical reading of the text in terms of an ethics of interpretation. The pro-slavery arguments, in contrast, "fostered a move to literalism emboldened by the findings of biblical criticism that the New Testament writers did not condemn slavery."[23] According to the plain literal sense of the biblical text, Jesus and Paul did not attack slavery but only its abuse. Hence, the pro-slavery argument required a positivist literal reading of the Bible that was done in the name of biblical science. In sum, in the nineteenth and beginning of the twentieth century, the scientific ethos of value-free scholarship that was presumed to be untainted by social relations and political interest has been institutionalized in the professions that assure the continuation of the dominant disciplinary ethos.[24]

This professionalization of the academic disciplines engendered theoretical dichotomies such as pure and impure, theoretical or applied science. Dualistic opposites such as rational and irrational, objective and subjective, hard and soft, male and female, Europeans and colonials, secular and religious were given material form not only in professional disciplines but also in their discursive practices. For instance, the methodologically dense, scientific, depersonalized, empirical-factual text of the research paper emerged as a new standardized academic genre. This genre replaced the more metaphorically porous, literary varied, understandable forms of writing that were accessible also to the nonscientific popular reader. The development of biblical studies as a scientific discipline adopted a similar scientific professional elite male ethos.[25]

The Disciplinary Formation of Biblical Studies

The Society of Biblical Literature (SBL) was founded in 1880,[26] around the same time that the American Philological Association (1869), the American

---

22. J. Albert Harrill, "The Use of the New Testament in the American Slave Controversy: A Case History in the Hermeneutical Tension between Biblical Criticism and Christian Moral Debate," *Religion and American Culture* 10/2 (2000): 149–86.

23. ibid., 174.

24. Stepan and Gilman, "Appropriating the Idioms of Science," 170–93, esp. 173. See also Londa Schiebinger, *The Mind Has No Sex? Wo/men in the Origins of Modern Science* (Oxford: Oxford University Press, 1981).

25. See Anne Witz, *Professions and Patriarchy* (New York: Routledge, 1992), for the medical profession. For the notion of professional authority, see the sociological study by Terrence J. Johnson, *Professions and Power* (London: MacMillan, 1972).

26. For the history of biblical studies, see the various published contributions of

Social Science Association (1869), the Archeological Institute of America (1879), the Modern Language Association (1883), and the American Historical Society (1884) were initiated. The feminist historian Bonnie G. Smith has argued that, for instance, the ethos of the American Historical Association cultivated a value-detached, "gender-neutral" community of scholars and developed an "objective" narrative in the course of professionalization as "a modern scientific profession."

Its ethos and practices demanded "the strict use of evidence, the taming of historical narrative to a less rhetorical style, the development of archives and professional libraries, the organization of university training in seminars and tutorials, and in the case of the United States, a commitment to democratic access to the profession based on ability." In addition, professionalizing historians attempted to eliminate all personal or subjective meaning from their work. Thus historians "created a space inhabited by an invisible 'I,' one without politics, without an ego or persona, and certainly ungendered."[27]

Like its brother profession the American Historical Society, the SBL was founded according to Saunders by Protestant "gentlemen"[28] who were for the most part "European trained in such universities as Berlin, Heidelberg, Halle, and Tübingen."[29] The professional scientific stance was complicated in biblical studies by the struggle of the discipline not only to prove its scientific "value-neutral" character within the Enlightenment university, which had only very recently more or less successfully thrown off the shackles of religion. It also was marked, for instance, by the struggle to free itself from the dogmatic fetters of the Protestant and Roman Catholic churches.[30] This conflict emerged between the advocates of scientific higher criticism and those interested in

---

Thomas Olbricht, e.g., "Alexander Campbell in the Context of American Biblical Studies," *Restoration Quarterly* 33 (1991): 13–28; idem, "Biblical Interpretation in North America in the Twentieth Century," in *Historical Handbook of Major Biblical Interpreters* (ed. Donald K. McKim; Downers Grove, Ill.: InterVarsity Press, 1998), 541–57; and idem, "Histories of North American Biblical Scholarship," *CurBS* 7 (1999): 237–56.

27. Smith, "Gender, Objectivity," 52.
28. *JBL* 9 (1890): vi.
29. See Jerry W. Brown, *The Rise of Biblical Criticism in America 1800–1870: The New England Scholars* (Middleton, Conn.: Wesleyan University Press, 1988), the above references to Thomas Olbricht's work, and Ernest W. Saunders, *Searching the Scriptures: A History of the Society of Biblical Literature 1880–1980* (Chico, Calif.: Scholars Press, 1982), 6.
30. For the history of Roman Catholic scholarship see Gerald P. Fogarty, S.J., *American Catholic Biblical Scholarship: A History from the Early Republic to Vatican II* (San Francisco: Harper & Row, 1989); for Jewish scholarship, see S. David Sperling, ed., *Students of the Covenant: A History of Jewish Biblical Scholarship in North America* (Atlanta: Scholars Press, 1992).

safeguarding the theological purity of the Bible in the heresy trials at the turn of the twentieth century.

The same rhetorical tension remains inscribed in professional biblical studies today. Emblazoned in the professional ethos of biblical criticism is the conflict of how to study the Bible. Should it be viewed as a collection of ancient texts or as a normative document of biblical religions? Is the critical study of the theological meaning and normativity of traditions and scriptures part of the research program of biblical studies, or must it be left to confessional theology? Is it part of the professional program of "higher criticism" to study the communities of discourse that have produced and sustained scriptural texts and readings in the past and still do so in the present? Finally, does competence in biblical criticism entail the ability to engage in a critical theoretical interdisciplinary meta-reflection on the work of biblical studies? Would this require that students of the Bible be trained not only in textual-historical-literary analysis but also in the ideological analysis of the social and political discursive positionings and social religious-political relations of the discipline and its practitioners?

The scientistic academic ethos of the discipline also governs its pedagogical and credentializing practices. It reproduces the professional "club culture" that has engendered modern detached and value-free science. In Saunders's judgment, after one hundred years the Society becomes (some would say has become) an antiquarian association more closely resembling an English gentleman's club than a laboratory. Do the Cabots speak only to the Lodges and the Lodges speak only to God? Some think so.[31]

If professionalization seeks to discipline its practitioners, because it has the "making of professionals" as its goal, doctoral education becomes central to maintaining such a positivist elite masculine ethos. Hence, one must problematize the discipline not only in theoretical terms but also with respect to its educational practices. Rather than reproducing, for example, in dissertation after dissertation on Paul or John, the scientist-positivist approach that restricts biblical studies to ascertaining the single true meaning of the text, research could focus both on the rhetorical function of biblical and other ancient texts in their past and present historical and literary contexts and on the ideological justifications presented by their ever more technically refined interpretations. In short, professional ethos determines disciplinary discourses by establishing what can be said and what is *a priori* ruled out of court.

---

31. Saunders, *Searching the Scriptures*, 101.

Toward a New Paradigm

To change the educational practices of the discipline, I argue, would mean to change its ethos and vice versa. This ethos is institutionalized in disciplinary paradigms. Thomas Kuhn's categories of "scientific paradigm" and "heuristic model" provide a theoretical framework for comprehending theoretical and practical shifts in the self-understanding of biblical studies.[32] A paradigm articulates a common ethos and constitutes a community of scholars formed by its institutions and systems of knowledge. However, a shift in scientific paradigm can take place only if and when the institutional conditions of knowledge production change. Moreover, in difference to Kuhn I would stress that paradigms are not necessarily exclusive of each other but can exist alongside each other and are best understood as working in corrective interaction with each other.

In addition, paradigms are not just theoretical but also institutional formations that develop both distinct methodological approaches and disciplinary languages and cultures. Practitioners are judged by professional criteria of excellence maintained by the reigning paradigm of biblical studies, and students are socialized into its disciplinary practices. Within the doctrinal paradigm, for instance, they learn to understand biblical authority in terms of kyriarchal obedience often without knowing that this paradigm also has understood biblical authority in terms of salvation. Or, within the historical and literary paradigms, students are socialized into accepting scientific "facticity" and disinterestedness as authoritative without ever reflecting on the kyriarchal tendencies of the scientific ethos to marginalize and objectify the "others" of elite white Western men.

Today the traditional scriptural-doctrinal and the modern scientific paradigms seem to be in the process of being decentered and replaced by a (post)modern hermeneutical or cultural paradigm. Whereas a decade ago the historical-positivist and literary-structuralist paradigms of interpretation still were in ascendancy, today postmodern epistemological and hermeneutical discussions abound that are critical of both the religious truth claim and the positivist scientific ethos of biblical studies. Their theoretical and practical force has destabilized the foundations of the field. Even the critical theory of the Frankfurt school and ideological criticism have arrived on the program of biblical congresses. Critical theory, semiotics, ideology critique, reader-response criticism, social-world studies, and poststructuralist literary analyses, among others, have engendered the recognition of the linguisticality of all

---

32. Thomas S. Kuhn, *The Structure of Scientific Revolutions* (Chicago: University of Chicago Press, 1962).

interpretation and historiography and generated postmodern elaborations of the undecidability of meaning and the pluralism of interpretive approaches.[33]

Such a (post)modern disciplinary paradigm does not assume that the text represents a given Divine revelation or a window to historical reality, nor does it operate with a correspondence theory of truth. It does not understand historical sources as data and evidence but sees them as perspectival discourses constructing a range of symbolic universes.[34] Since alternative symbolic universes engender competing definitions of the world, they cannot be reduced to one single, definitive meaning. Therefore competing interpretations are not simply either right or wrong,[35] but they constitute different ways of reading and constructing historical and religious meaning. Texts have a surplus of meaning that can never be fully mined.

Feminist and liberation theological interpretation have played a great part in the (post)modern hermeneutical transformation of academic biblical scholarship. Nevertheless, even a cursory glance at the literature can show that the hermeneutical contributions of critical feminist scholarship are rarely recognized, and much less acknowledged, by malestream biblical studies, except to be co-opted or redefined. While the postmodern hermeneutical paradigm has successfully destabilized the certitude of the scientific objectivist paradigm in biblical studies, it still asserts its own scientific value-neutral and a-theological character. Consequently, it tends to result in a playful proliferation of textual meanings and to reject any attempt to move from kyriocentric text to the socio-historical situation of struggle that either has generated the text or determines its function today.

Thus, this third hermeneutical-postmodern paradigm of biblical studies also cannot address the increasing insecurities of globalized inequality nor accept the constraints that the ethical imperative of emancipatory movements places on the relativizing proliferation of meaning. Therefore, a fourth rhetorical-political paradigm needs to be acknowledged, one that inaugurates not just a hermeneutic-scientific but an ethical-political turn.

This fourth paradigm understands biblical texts as rhetorical discourses that must be investigated as to their persuasive power and argumentative functions in particular historical and cultural situations. It rejects the Enlight-

---

33. Amos N. Wilder articulated this literary-aesthetic paradigm as rhetorical. See his SBL presidential address, "Scholars, Theologians, and Ancient Rhetoric," *JBL* 75 (1956): 1–11; and his book *Early Christian Rhetoric: The Language of the Gospel* (Cambridge: Harvard University Press, 1971).

34. See the discussion of scientific theory choice by Linda Alcoff, "Justifying Feminist Social Science," *Hypatia* 2 (1987): 10–27.

35. Maurice Mandelbaum, *The Anatomy of Historical Knowledge* (Baltimore: Johns Hopkins University Press, 1977), 150.

enment typecasting of rhetoric as stylistic ornament, technical skill, linguistic manipulation, or "mere words" and maintains not only "that rhetoric is epistemic but also that epistemology and ontology are themselves rhetorical."[36] At the heart of rhetoric is both the ethical and the political. In this paradigm biblical studies are not understood as doctrinal, scientific-positivist, or relativist but rather seen in rhetorical-ethical terms.

Such a critical rhetorical understanding of interpretation investigates and reconstructs the discursive arguments of a text, its socioreligious location, and its diverse interpretations in order to underscore the text's possible oppressive as well as liberative performative actions, values, and possibilities in ever-changing historical-cultural situations. This approach understands the Bible and biblical interpretation as a site of struggle[37] over authority, values, and meaning. Since the sociohistorical location of rhetoric is the public of the polis, the rhetorical-emancipatory paradigm shift seeks to situate biblical scholarship in such a way that its public character and political responsibility become an integral part of its contemporary readings and historical reconstructions. It insists on an ethical radical democratic imperative that compels biblical scholarship to contribute to the advent of a society and religion that are free from all forms of kyriarchal inequality and oppression.

For these reasons, doctoral education has to be concerned not just with exploring the conditions and possibilities of understanding and using kyriocentric biblical texts but also with the problem of how, in the interest of justice and well-being for all, one can critically assess and dismantle their power of persuasion. Critical biblical scholarship, I have argued here, must construct a theoretical model and epistemological framework that allows one to move toward the articulation of a critical pedagogy in graduate biblical education. Such a critical pedagogy aims for the self-understanding of the biblical scholar

---

36. Richard Harvey Brown, *Society as Text: Essays on Rhetoric, Reason, and Reality* (Chicago: University of Chicago Press, 1987), 85. See also, for example, John S. Nelson, Allan Megill, and Donald McCloskey, eds., *The Rhetoric of the Human Sciences: Language and Argument in Scholarship and Public Affairs* (Madison: University of Wisconsin Press, 1987); Hayden White, *Tropics of Discourse: Essays in Cultural Criticism* (Baltimore: Johns Hopkins University Press, 1978); John S. Nelson, "Political Theory as Political Rhetoric," in *What Should Political Theory Be Now?* (ed. John S. Nelson; Albany: State University of New York Press, 1983), 169–240.

37. John Louis Lucaites and Celeste Michelle Condit, "Introduction," in *Contemporary Rhetorical Theory: A Reader* (ed. John Louis Lucaites, Celeste Michelle Condit, and Sally Caudill; New York: Guilford, 1999), 11: "Disagreement is thus considered a rather 'natural' result of different social, political, and ethnic groups, with different resources. On this view, struggle, not consensus, is the defining characteristic of social life; accordingly, social discord is not a pathology to be cured but a condition to be productively managed."

as a public, transformative,[38] connected, or integrated intellectual who is able to communicate with a variegated public with the goal of personal, social, and religious transformation for justice and well-being for all.

---

38. For the expression "transformative intellectual," see "Teaching and the Role of the Transformative Intellectual," in Stanley Aronowitz and Henry A. Giroux, *Education Still under Siege* (2nd ed.; Westport, Conn.: Bergin & Garvey, 1993).

Contributors

Cynthia M. Baker (MTS Harvard; Ph.D. Duke) is Associate Professor of Religious Studies at Bates College. She is the author of *Rebuilding the House of Israel: Architectures of Gender in Jewish Antiquity* (Stanford University Press, 2002). Forthcoming articles in biblical studies include "Jewish Feminist Biblical Studies" and "Nationalist Narratives and Biblical Memory."

Athalya Brenner is currently Professor in Biblical Studies at the Department of Hebrew Culture Studies, Tel Aviv University, Israel, and Professor Emeritus of the Hebrew Bible/Old Testament Chair at the University of Amsterdam, The Netherlands. She holds an honorary Ph.D. from the University of Bonn, Germany.

Philip P. Chia currently serves as an Adjunct Associate Professor at the Dept. of Cultural and Religious Studies, Chung Chi Divinity School, The Chinese University of Hong Kong. He is also the Director of CABSA (Centre for Advanced Biblical Studies and Application), a nonprofit organisation serving the GCR with a mission of bridging between the Bible, the church, and the public. One of his recent Chinese publications is *The Open Text: On the Relation between Biblical Studies and Public Theology* (2009). He received his Ph.D. from the University of Sheffield, U.K., in Old Testament Studies (1988).

Thomas Fabisiak is a Ph.D. candidate in Comparative Literature and Religion in Emory University's Graduate Division of Religion. His research tends to focus on the history of transformations of apocalyptic discourse in modern literature, philosophy, and popular culture. He is preparing a dissertation on revolutionary reconfigurations of Jewish and Christian texts in works by the Young Hegelian philosopher and atheistic higher critic Bruno Bauer.

Wil Gafney is an Associate Professor of Hebrew and Old Testament at the Lutheran Theological Seminary in Philadelphia. She received her Ph.D. in Hebrew Bible from Duke University in 2006. Her book *Daughters of Miriam* was published by Fortress in 2008, and she is one of the general editors of the

Peoples' Bible (Fortress, 2009). Her interests include womanist and feminist biblical interpretation, prophetic literature, and ancient Near Eastern and rabbinic literature.

Gabriella Gelardini is Senior Research Associate at the University of Basel, Switzerland. Her publications include a study of the Book of Hebrews, *"Verhärtet eure Herzen nicht": Der Hebräer, eine Synagogenhomilie zu Tischa be-Aw* (Leiden: Brill, 2007). Her forthcoming book explores the role of ethnicity and religion in the New Testament in shaping a collective Christian identity.

Melanie Johnson-DeBaufre is Associate Professor of New Testament and Early Christianity at Drew Theological School in Madison, New Jersey. She has an M.Div. and Th.D. from Harvard Divinity School and a B.A. from Eastern College. She is the author of *Jesus among Her Children: Q, Eschatology, and the Construction of Christian Origins* (Harvard, 2006) and co-author with Jane Schaberg of *Mary Magdalene Understood* (Continuum, 2006). She is also the co-editor of *The Journal of Feminist Studies in Religion*. Melanie is currently working on a book that utilizes critical space theory, as well as feminist and postcolonial theory and practice, to think about the production of Christian identity in the Pauline tradition.

Nyasha Junior, Ph.D., is Assistant Professor of Hebrew Bible/Old Testament at Howard University School of Divinity. She earned a Bachelor of Science in Foreign Service degree (with honors) from Georgetown University and a Master of Public Affairs degree from Princeton University. She holds a Master of Divinity degree from Pacific School of Religion and a Ph.D. in Old Testament from Princeton Theological Seminary.

Cynthia Briggs Kittredge is Professor of New Testament and Academic Dean at Seminary of the Southwest. Kittredge is a contributor to the new *Oxford Annotated Bible* and the author of *Conversations with Scripture: The Gospel of John* and *Community and Authority: The Rhetoric of Obedience in the Pauline Tradition*. She co-edited *The Bible in the Public Square: Reading the Signs of the Times* and *Walk in the Ways of Wisdom: Essays in Honor of Elisabeth Schüssler Fiorenza*. She earned degrees from Williams College (B.A.) and Harvard Divinity School (M.Div., Th.M., and Th.D).

Archie C. C. Lee, Professor in the Cultural and Religious Studies Department at The Chinese University of Hong Kong, is the head of the Division of Religious Studies of the Graduate School and former Dean of Faculty of Arts. His recent publications include "When the Flood Narrative of Genesis Meets Its

Counterpart in China: Reception and Challenge in Cross-Textual Reading," "The Bible in China: Religion of God's Chinese Son," and "Engaging Lamentation and *The Lament for the South*: A Cross-Textual Reading." He is also on the editorial committee of *Cambridge Dictionary of Christianity* (2010) and *Global Bible Commentary* (2004).

Kyung Sook Lee is the Executive Vice-President for Academic Affairs at Ewha Womans University in Seoul, Korea, where she teaches Hebrew Bible in the department of Christian Studies. She is very much interested in the the critical reading of the Hebrew Bible and feminist theology. Her research and teaching are focused on the Deuteronomistic redaction of the historical books and the prophetic books. She has written several books, including *Women in the Old Testament* and *God, History and Women in the Old Testament*, in Korean, as well as many articles in English and German.

Joseph A. Marchal is an assistant professor of religious studies at Ball State University, where he teaches in biblical studies and critical theories of interpretation. His research and teaching are focused on the intersections of feminist, postcolonial, and queer perspectives and practices. His most recent book is *The Politics of Heaven: Women, Gender, and Empire in the Study of Paul* (Fortress, 2008); he is currently preparing a book project on queer approaches to Pauline epistles and interpretation.

Roberto Mata is a doctoral student of New Testament/Early Christianity at Harvard Divinity School. His main area of research is the social setting of the book of Revelation. Roberto's project includes using postcolonial theory to find a new language to approach various issues in Revelation and to explore the intersection of power, gender, and status. Other areas and topics of interests include martyrdom in early Christianity, race/ethnicity in antiquity, and critical pedagogy.

Monica Jyotsna Melanchthon graduated with a Ph.D. from the Lutheran School of Theology, Chicago, and teaches Old Testament Studies at the Gurukul Lutheran Theological College, India. she is the co-editor General of International Voices in Biblical Studies, an online series, and secretary to the Society of Asian Biblical Studies. She is the author of several articles that bring the Bible, gender, and caste into conversation and critique of one another.

Kent Harold Richards is Professor of Old Testament and former Executive Director of the Society of Biblical Literature. He is the co-author of *Interpreting Hebrew Poetry* (Augsburg Fortress, 1992) and co-editor of *Second Temple*

Studies 2: Temple Community in the Persian Period (Sheffield Academic Press, 1994) and *Old Testament Interpretation: Past, Present, and Future: Essays in Honor of Gene M. Tucker* (Abingdon, 1995).

Susanne Scholz is Associate Professor of Old Testament at Perkins School of Theology in Dallas, Texas. She earned a Ph.D. from Union Theological Seminary in New York. Among her publications are *Sacred Witness: Rape in the Hebrew Bible* (Fortress 2010), *Introducing the Women's Hebrew Bible* (T&T Clark 2007), *Rape Plots: A Feminist Cultural Study of Genesis 34* (Lang 2000), *Biblical Studies Alternatively: An Introductory Reader* (Prentice Hall 2003), and *Zwischenräume: Deutsche feministische Theologinnen im Ausland* (LIT 2000).

Elisabeth Schüssler Fiorenza, Krister Stendahl Professor, Harvard University, The Divinity School, is the author of, among other works, *Democratizing Biblical Studies: Toward an Emancipatory Educational Space* (Westminster John Knox, 2009), *The Power of the Word: Scripture and the Rhetoric of Empire* (Fortress, 2007), *Jesus and the Politics of Interpretation* (Continuum, 2000), and *Rhetoric and Ethic: The Politics of Biblical Studies* (Fortress, 1999). Schüssler Fiorenza is also co-founder and co-editor of the *Journal of Feminist Studies in Religion*.

Abraham Smith, professor of New Testament at Perkins School of Theology, Southern Methodist University, received his Ph.D. from Vanderbilt University (1989). With numerous publications that vary from 1 Thessalonians to Luke-Acts, the Gospel of Mark, African American biblical hermeneutics, and cultural studies, Smith is also an associate editor of *The New Interpreter's Study Bible* (2003) and co-editor of *Slavery in Text and Interpretation* (Semeia 83/84,).

Yak-hwee Tan received her Ph.D. in religion, with an emphasis in New Testament from Vanderbilt University, Nashville, Tennessee. She teaches in New Testament Studies at Taiwan Theological College and Seminary, Taipei, Taiwan. Currently, she is the co-chair for Johannine Literature, International Meeting Society for Biblical Literature. Her research interests are Johannine literature, biblical theology, feminist criticism, postcolonialism, and missions.

Hal Taussig, Ph.D., is Visiting Professor of New Testament at Union Theological Seminary in New York and Professor of Early Christianity at the Reconstructionist Rabbinical College. His latest books are *The Thunder: Perfect Mind* (2010) and *In the Beginning Was the Meal: Social Experimentation and Early Christian Identity* (2009). Brigitte Kahl, Th.D. and Dr.Sc.Theol., is Professor of New Testament at Union Theological Seminary in New York.

Elaine M. Wainwright is Professor of Theology and Head of the School of Theology at the University of Auckland, New Zealand, having held that post for eight years. She is a New Testament scholar specializing in the Gospel of Matthew and in hermeneutical and contextual issues in and challenges to biblical studies. Her most recent book is *Women Healing/Healing Women: The Genderization of Healing in Early Christianity* (Equinox, 2006).

Vincent L. Wimbush is Professor of Religion and Founding Director of the Institute for Signifying Scriptures, Claremont Graduate University, where his research interests are comparative phenomenology and cultural-critical study of scriptures. Recent publications include *Theorizing Scriptures: New Critical Orientations to a Cultural Phenomenon* (Rutgers University Press, 2008), *The Bible and African Americans: A Brief History* (Fortress, 2003), and *African Americans and the Bible: Sacred Texts and Social Textures* (Continuum, 2000).

www.ingramcontent.com/pod-product-compliance
Lightning Source LLC
Chambersburg PA
CBHW021351290426
44108CB00010B/196